The Zen Canon

The Zen Canon

Understanding the Classic Texts

EDITED BY STEVEN HEINE

AND

DALE S. WRIGHT

UNIVERSITY PRESS

2004

OXFORD
UNIVERSITY PRESS

Oxford   New York
Auckland   Bangkok   Buenos Aires   Cape Town   Chennai
Dar es Salaam   Delhi   Hong Kong   Istanbul   Karachi   Kolkata
Kuala Lumpur   Madrid   Melbourne   Mexico City   Mumbai   Nairobi
São Paulo   Shanghai   Taipei   Tokyo   Toronto

Copyright © 2004 by Oxford University Press, Inc.

Published by Oxford University Press, Inc.
198 Madison Avenue, New York, New York 10016

www.oup.com

Oxford is a registered trademark of Oxford University Press

Library of Congress Cataloging-in-Publication Data
The Zen canon: understanding the classic texts / edited by Steven Heine and Dale S. Wright.
p.   cm
Includes bibliographical references and index.
ISBN 0-19-515067-8; ISBN 0-19-515068-6 (pbk.)
    1. Zen literature—History and criticism.   2. Zen Buddhism—Sacred books—Introductions.
I. Heine, Steven.   II. Wright, Dale S.
BQ9264.2.Z45 2004
94.3'85—dc 12   2003049864

9 8 7 6 5 4 3 2 1

Printed in the United States of America
on acid-free paper

Acknowledgments

The editors, Steven Heine of Florida International University and Dale S. Wright of Occidental College, thank Cynthia Read and Oxford University Press for their interest in the project and Theo Calderara and Heather Hartman for their skillful work on the book. They are also grateful for the support provided by their respective institutions in the preparation of the manuscript. Special thanks go to several assistants who worked on the manuscript, including Sandy Avila, Wendy Lo, Judy Squires, and Patricia Valencia.

Contents

Abbreviations

HTC/XZJ	*Hsü tsang ching/Xu zangjing*, 150-volume reprint edition of ZZ (Taipei: Hsin-wen-feng, n.d.)
T	*Taishō shinshū daizōkyō* (Tokyo: Taishō issaikyō kankōkai, 1924–1932).
ZZ	*Dainippon zoku zōkyō* (Kyoto: Zōkyō shoin, 1904–1912)

Contributors

WENDI ADAMEK is assistant professor of Chinese Religion at Barnard College, Columbia University. She received her Ph.D. in Religious Studies from Stanford University in 1998. Her dissertation is based on her translation of the *Lidai fabao ji*, and her current research focus is seventh- through tenth-century Chinese Buddhist donor inscriptions.

JEFF BROUGHTON is professor in the Department of Religious Studies at California State University Long Beach. His specialty is Buddhist Studies (early Chan texts). He holds a Ph.D. from Columbia's Department of East Asian Languages and Cultures and is the author of *Bodhidharma Anthology: The Earliest Records of Zen* (1999). He is planning two more volumes, one a set of translations of Dunhuang Chan texts and the other a translation of the Chan works of Guifeng Zongmi.

T. GRIFFITH FOULK teaches Asian religions at Sarah Lawrence College. He was trained in both Rinzai and Soto Zen monasteries in Japan, has published extensively on the institutional and intellectual history of Chan/Zen Buddhism, and is currently co–editor-in-chief of the Soto Zen Translation Project based in Tokyo.

STEVEN HEINE is professor of Religious Studies and History and Director of the Institute for Asian Studies at Florida International University. Heine has published numerous books and articles dealing with the life and thought of Dōgen and the history and philosophy of Zen Buddhism, including *Dōgen and the Kōan Tradition: A Tale of Two Shō-bōgenzo Texts* (1994), *The Zen Poetry of Dōgen: Verses from the Mountain of Eternal Peace* (1997), *Shifting Shape, Shaping Text: Philosophy and Folklore in the Fox Kōan* (1999), *The Kōan: Texts and Contexts in Zen Buddhism* (coedited with Dale S. Wright, 2000), and *Opening a Mountain: Kōans of the Zen Masters* (2001).

Ishii Shūdō is professor in the Department of Buddhist Studies at Komazawa University in Tokyo. His publications include *Sōdai Zenshūshi no kenkyū* (1987), *Chūgoku Zenshū shi hanashi* (1988), and *Dōgen Zen no Seiritsu-shi-teki Kenkyū* (1991), as well as dozens of articles on the historical development of Ch'an/Zen literature.

Mario Poceski is assistant professor in the Department of Religion at the University of Florida. Poceski has a Ph.D. from the East Asian Languages and Cultures Department at the University of California Los Angeles. His primary research interest is the history of Buddhism during the Tang Dynasty. His publications include *Manifestation of the Tathagata: Buddhahood According to the Avatamsaka Sutra* (1993) and *Sun-Face Buddha: The Teachings of Ma-tsu and the Hung-chou School of Ch'an* (1993).

Morten Schlütter has a Ph.D. from Yale University and has taught at Victoria University of Wellington, University of Wisconsin-Madison, UCLA, and Yale University. His publications include "'Before the Empty Eon' versus 'A Dog Has No Buddha-nature': Kôan Use in the Ts'ao-tung Tradition and Ta-hui's Kōan Introspection Ch'an," in *The Kōan: Texts and Contexts in Zen Buddhism* (2000); "Silent Illumination, Kung-an Introspection, and the Competition for Lay Patronage in Sung Dynasty Ch'an," in *Buddhism in the Sung* (1999), and "A Study in the Genealogy of the Platform Sutra," *Studies in Central and East Asian Religions* 2 (1989): 53–115.

Albert Welter is associate professor of Religious Studies at the University of Winnipeg, Canada. He has completed a number of studies of Chan and Chinese Buddhism, and is currently working on a project supported by the Social Sciences and Humanities Research Council of Canada on the formation of Chan Identity in Chan transmission history texts. His publications include a book on Chinese Ch'an, *The Meaning of Myriad Good Deeds: A Study of Yung-ming Yen-shou and the Wan-shan t'ung-kuei chi* (1993), and several articles and reviews on East Asian Buddhism.

Dale S. Wright is David B. and Mary H. Gamble Professor of Religious Studies and Asian Studies at Occidental College. His area of specialization and research is Buddhist philosophy, particularly Hua-yen Buddhism and

Ch'an/Zen Buddhism. His publications include *Philosophical Meditations on Zen Buddhism* (1998) and *The Kōan: Texts and Contexts in Zen Buddhism* (coedited with Steven Heine, 2000), as well as numerous articles in *Philosophy East and West, Journal of the American Academy of Religion, History and Theory*, and elsewhere.

Transliteration and Terminology

The Kōan used the Wade-Giles system of transliterating Chinese, but the chapters in this volume have been written using either Wade-Giles (Broughton, Wright, Welter, Ishii, Heine) or Pinyin (Poceski, Adamek, Schlütter, Foulk). Although it seems unusual to include both systems rather than standardize all contributions to the volume, the editors felt that it was preferable to allow authors to work in the system with which they were most comfortable, in part because most readers will not have difficulty recognizing equivalents. A complete list of conversions is provided in order to check the usages. Also, note that several key terms in Zen literature and thought are translated in different ways in various articles to allow the authors the most flexibility in making their analysis and arguments.

Pinyin–Wade-Giles Conversion Table

Pinyin	Wade-Giles	Pinyin	Wade-Giles
a	a	ci	tz'ŭ
ai	ai	cong	ts'ung
an	an	cou	ts'ou
ang	ang	cu	ts'u
ao	ao	cuan	ts'uan
		cui	ts'ui
ba	pa	cun	ts'un
bai	pai	cuo	ts'o
ban	pan		
bang	pang	da	ta
bao	pao	dai	tai
bei	pei	dan	tan
ben	pên	dang	tang
beng	pêng	dao	tao
bi	pi	de	tê
bian	pien	dei	tei
biao	piao	deng	têng
bie	pieh	di	ti
bin	pin	dian	tien
bing	ping	diao	tiao
bo	po	die	tieh
bou	pou	ding	ting
bu	pu	diu	tiu
		dong	tung
ca	ts'a	dou	tou
cai	ts'ai	du	tu
can	ts'an	duan	tuan
cang	ts'ang	dui	tui
cao	ts'ao	dun	tun
ce	ts'ê	duo	to
ceng	ts'êng		
cha	ch'a	e	ê, o
chai	ch'ai	en	ên
chan	ch'an	eng	êng
chang	ch'ang	er	êrh
chao	ch'ao		
che	ch'ê	fa	fa
chen	ch'ên	fan	fan
cheng	ch'êng	fang	fang
chi	ch'ih	fei	fei
chong	ch'ung	fen	fen
chou	ch'ou	feng	feng
chu	ch'u	fo	fo
chua	ch'ua	fou	fou
chuai	ch'uai	fu	fu
chuan	ch'uan		
chuang	ch'uang	ga	ka
chui	ch'ui	gai	kai
chun	ch'un	gan	kan
chuo	ch'o	gang	kang
		gao	kao

Pinyin	Wade-Giles	Pinyin	Wade-Giles
ge	kê, ko	kan	k'an
gei	kei	kang	k'ang
gen	kên	kao	k'ao
geng	kêng	ke	k'ê, k'o
gong	kung	ken	k'ên
gou	kou	keng	k'êng
gu	ku	kong	k'ung
gua	kua	kou	k'ou
guai	kuai	ku	k'u
guan	kuan	kua	k'ua
guang	kuang	kuai	k'uai
giu	kuei	kuan	k'uan
gun	kun	kuang	k'uang
guo	kuo	kui	k'uei
		kun	k'un
ha	ha	kuo	k'uo
hai	hai		
han	han	la	la
hang	hang	lai	lai
hao	hao	lan	lan
he	ho	lang	lang
hei	hei	lao	lao
hen	hên	le	lê
heng	hêng	lei	lei
hong	hung	leng	lêng
hou	hou	li	li
hu	hu	lia	lia
hua	hua	lian	lien
huai	huai	liang	liang
huan	huan	liao	liao
huang	huang	lie	lieh
hui	hui	lin	lin
hun	hun	ling	ling
huo	huo	liu	liu
		long	lung
ji	chi	lou	lou
jia	chia	lu	lu
jian	chien	luan	luan
jiang	chiang	lun	lun
jiao	chiao	luo	lo
jie	chieh	lü	lü
jin	chin	lüan	lüan
jing	ching	lüe	lüeh
jiong	chiung	lun	lun, lü
jiu	chiu		
ju	chü	ma	ma
juan	chüan	mai	mai
jue	chüeh	man	man
jun	chün	mang	mang
		mao	mao
ka	k'a	me	mê
kai	k'ai		

(continued)

Pinyin	Wade-Giles	Pinyin	Wade-Giles
mei	mei	pi	p'i
men	mên	pian	p'ien
meng	mêng	piao	p'iao
mi	mi	pie	p'ieh
mian	mien	pin	p'in
miao	miao	ping	p'ing
mie	mieh	po	p'o
min	min	pou	p'ou
ming	ming	pu	p'u
miu	miu		
mo	mo	qi	ch'i
mou	mou	qia	ch'ia
mu	mu	qian	ch'ien
		qiang	ch'iang
na	na	qiao	ch'iao
nai	nai	qie	ch'ieh
nan	nan	qin	ch'in
nang	nang	qing	ch'ing
nao	nao	qiong	ch'iung
ne	ne	qiu	ch'iu
nei	nei	qu	ch'ü
nen	nên	quan	ch'üan
neng	nêng	que	ch'üeh
ni	ni	qun	ch'ün
nian	nien		
niang	niang	ran	jan
niao	niao	rang	jang
nie	nieh	rao	jao
nin	nin	re	jê
ning	ning	ren	jên
niu	niu	reng	jêng
nong	nung	ri	jih
nou	nou	rong	jung
nu	nu	rou	jou
nuan	nuan	ru	ju
nun	nun	ruan	juan
nuo	no	rui	jui
nü	nü	run	jun
nüe	nüeh	ruo	jo
		sa	sa
ou	ou	sai	sai
		san	san
pa	p'a	sang	sang
pai	p'ai	sao	sao
pan	p'an	se	sê
pang	p'ang	sen	sên
pao	p'ao	seng	sêng
pei	p'ei	sha	sha
pen	p'ên	shai	shai
peng	p'êng		

Pinyin	Wade-Giles	Pinyin	Wade-Giles
shan	shan	weng	wêng
shang	shang	wo	wo
shao	shao	wu	wu
she	shê		
shei	shei	xi	hsi
shen	shên	xia	hsia
sheng	shêng	xian	hsien
shi	shih	xiang	hsiang
shou	shou	xiao	hsiao
shu	shu	xie	hsieh
shua	shua	xin	hsin
shuai	shuai	xing	hsing
shuan	shuan	xiong	hsiung
shuang	shuang	xiu	hsiu
shui	shui	xu	hsü
shun	shun	xuan	hsüan
shuo	shuo	xue	hsüeh
si	ssǔ, szǔ	xun	hsün
song	sung		
sou	sou	ya	ya
su	su	yai	yai
suan	suan	yan	yen
sui	sui	yang	yang
sun	sun	yao	yao
suo	so	ye	yeh
		yi	i, yi
ta	t'a	yin	yin
tai	t'ai	ying	ying
tan	t'an	yong	yung
tang	t'ang	you	yu
tao	t'ao	yu	yü
te	t'ê	yuan	yüan
teng	t'êng	yue	yüeh
ti	t'i	yun	yün
tian	t'ien		
tiao	t'iao	za	tsa
tie	t'ieh	zai	tsai
ting	t'ing	zan	tsan
tong	t'ung	zang	tsang
tou	t'ou	zao	tsao
tu	t'u	ze	tsê
tuan	t'uan	zei	tsei
tui	t'ui	zen	tsên
tun	t'un	zeng	tsêng
tuo	t'o	zha	cha
		zhai	chai
wa	wa	zhan	chan
wai	wai	zhang	chang
wan	wan	zhao	chao
wang	wang	zhe	chê
wei	wei		
wen	wên		

(continued)

Pinyin–Wade-Giles Conversion Table (*continued*)

Pinyin	Wade-Giles	Pinyin	Wade-Giles
zhei	chei	zhui	chui
zhen	chên	zhun	chun
zheng	chêng	zhuo	cho
zhi	chih	zi	tzŭ
zhong	chung	zong	tsung
zhou	chou	zou	tsou
zhu	chu	zu	tsu
zhua	chua	zuan	tsuan
zhuai	chai	zui	tsui
zhuan	chuan	zun	tsun
zhuang	chuang	zuo	tso

The Zen Canon

Introduction: Canon and Canonicity in the History of the Zen Literary Tradition

Steven Heine and Dale S. Wright

This volume is a sequel or companion volume to *The Kōan: Texts and Contexts in Zen Buddhism.*[1] It examines a rich variety of texts in various genres that are crucial to an understanding of the history and thought of the Zen (C. Chan) Buddhist tradition in East Asia. These texts form a major part of the Zen canon, the acknowledged core of Zen Buddhist sacred literature.

One theme that reappears throughout this literature is the Zen tendency to reject the Buddhist canon, showing disdain for sacred literature of any kind. Zen is well known for the slogan claim, attributed to its founding patriarch, Bodhidharma, that it represents "a special transmission outside the teachings, that does not rely on words and letters." The image of Zen as rejecting all forms of ordinary language is reinforced by a wide variety of legendary anecdotes about Zen masters who teach in bizarre nonlinguistic ways, such as silence, "shouting and hitting," or other unusual behaviors. And when the masters do resort to language, they almost never use ordinary referential discourse. Instead they are thought to "point directly" to Zen awakening by paradoxical speech, non sequiturs, or single words seemingly out of context. Moreover, a few Zen texts recount sacrilegious acts against the sacred canon itself, outrageous acts in which the Buddhist sutras are burned or ripped to shreds. All of these examples demonstrate the extraordinary Zen Buddhist effort to evoke an "awakening" by transcending ordinary language through powerfully direct means.

In spite of these exemplary stories however, it is clear that Zen represents one of the high points in Chinese and Buddhist literary culture, producing by far the most voluminous and important canon of sacred texts in East Asia. Beginning in the late Tang dynasty and continuing for centuries in China, as well as in Kamakura through Tokugawa Japan, Zen writers have produced an unparalleled volume of texts in a wide variety of genres. These sacred texts define the tradition of Zen in such a way that understanding them is fundamental to any acquaintance with this form of Buddhism. The variety of these texts is also extraordinary. Zen genres include the "recorded sayings" of an individual Zen master's life and teachings, collections of "recorded sayings" texts organized into the larger genealogical framework of Zen history called "transmission of the lamp" records, kōan collections containing prose and verse commentaries by famous Zen masters on earlier prototypical Zen sayings or stories, and monastic codes covering the rules of conduct for the life of Zen monks. Other forms of Zen interpretive literature go beyond these fundamental genres, for example, capping verses on kōan cases that come to be compiled into Zen phrase books, or esoteric commentaries known in Japan as *kirigami*.

Literary imagination and creativity have long been basic to the Zen tradition, and provide one key to the historical success of Zen throughout East Asia. Zen came to prominence in China during the politically troubled era of the late Tang and Song dynasties as well as the tumultuous Kamakura era in Japan. These were periods of intense religious and philosophical competition, and although Zen emerged on occasion as the dominant force, in all periods it was forced to compete with other Buddhist rivals as well as with Confucian, Daoist, and Shinto alternatives. In each of these arenas, literature was the key to the vitality and dynamism of the Zen tradition, and the dimension of its cultural creativity that enabled it to face these historical challenges. Indeed, today nothing is more emblematic of the Zen tradition than its impressive canon of texts.

Canon and Canonicity

One of the main goals of this volume is to clarify and amplify the significance of canonicity in Zen Buddhism. Zen does not have a canon in the formal sense of the term, although many of its classic texts are included in the modern East Asian Buddhist canonical collections, the *Taishō shinshū daizōkyō* and its supplement, the *Hsü tsang ching* (J. *Zoku zōkyō*). On the other hand, Zen tradition recognizes a core of writings in the various genres as seminal resources for the expression of doctrine. As Harold Bloom shows in *The Western Canon*, the term canonicity does not necessarily refer to a fixed body of writings that exert a dogmatic sense of authority, but rather indicates the role of texts that express a compellingly creative and powerful message.[2] Robert Alter points out in *Canon and Creativity*, "A canon is above all a trans-historical textual community. Knowledge of the received texts and recourse to them constitute the community, but the texts do not have a single authoritative meaning, however many the established spokesmen for the canon at any give moment may claim that it is the case."[3] Alter goes on to show that although univocal meaning may be claimed, in the various traditions of canonical interpreters we find a tremendous diversity and range of viewpoints that are supported by the canon. A key issue is whether and to what extent interpreters consider the plurality of voices legitimate or in need of being silenced. For the most part, diversity has been a hallmark of the Buddhist tradition.

This volume represents a correction to the de facto canon that has been created by the limited approach of Western scholarship to Zen writings. Despite the remarkable richness of Zen literature, at this stage in Western studies there are still only a relative handful of texts that are well known or that have been seriously studied and translated. These include Bodhidharma's "Two Entrances," the *Platform Sutra* attributed to sixth patriarch Huineng, Dōgen's *Shōbōgenzō*, and several kōan collections including the *Pi-yen lu* (Biyanlu/Blue cliff record) and the *Wu-men kuan* (or *Wumenkuan*, Gateless gate), as well as several recorded sayings texts such as those of Zhaozhou, Linji, and Dongshan, among others. Some texts have been translated in multiple versions, such as the *Platform Sutra*, the records of Linji, the *Wu-men kuan* and the *Shōbōgenzō*, with varying degrees of reliability. Other texts only appear or are discussed thoroughly in a single translation or study, whereas additional ones are only translated or examined partially or indirectly. In general, the kōan records have received the most attention, while other genres that are crucial for understanding the function of kōan cases and other dimensions of Zen theory and practice, especially the transmission of the lamp records and the monastic codes, have received relatively little attention. This volume expands the range of Zen literature in the West by providing seminal studies of important canonical texts long recognized by the Zen tradition.

Chapter Summary

The Zen Canon makes available learned yet accessible scholarly studies of some of the most important classical Zen texts, especially those that have yet to receive the attention they deserve. The contributors focus on key examples of the many important but as yet lesser known and lesser studied examples of Zen literature; perhaps the only text dealt with here that has already been well studied is the *Wu-men kuan*, but the analysis provided here by Japanese scholar Ishii Shūdō goes into much more analytic detail than do previous works. All the chapters examine in varying degrees of detailed analysis and depth many of the following issues: pre-text or context of sources; most significant predecessor texts; origins of text or reflections on the question of authorship; location of the text in terms of time and place, as well as lineage; internal structure of the text; literary genre and style; most important concepts or narrative segment; innovations represented by this text; versions, redactions, variations; and uses of the text throughout the history of Zen.

This collection illuminates a variety of interesting and important issues including the origins of Zen texts and the relation between T'ang and Sung Zen Buddhism, the difference between the Southern school and alternative standpoints, the role of (Dunhuang) Tun-huang materials, the function of Ma-tsu style encounter dialogue Zen pedagogy, the relation between Zen and other political ideologies and religious styles and views, the impact of the cultural contexts of China and Japan, the relation of textuality to orality as well as religious practice, and the historical evolution of various Zen textual genres.

Chapter 1, "Tsung-mi's *Zen Prolegomenon*: Introduction to an Exemplary Zen Canon," by Jeff Broughton, analyzes the *Chanyuan chuchuanchi duxu* (Prolegomenon to the collection of expressions of the Zen source; abbreviated as *Zen Prolegomenon*) by Kuei-feng Tsung-mi (or Zongmi) (780–841). The *Zen Prolegomenon* is a descriptive and analytical guide to the teachings and praxes of the numerous Zen lineages of the day. In this chapter, Broughton discusses and examines Tsung-mi's life and the *Zen Prolegomenon*'s assertion that the "ideas" (*yi*) of eight Zen lineages can be classified into three "theses" (*zong*). In ascending order, the first Zen thesis is identical to the sutras and treatises of the Yogācāra school; the second is identical to the sutras and treatises of the Madhyāmika school; and the third is identical to a wide range of sutras and treatises, including the *Avataṁsaka Sutra, Tathāgatagarbha Sūtra, Awakening of Faith*, and so on. He further examines editions of the text from Ming-dynasty China and Korea, the latter being particularly valuable. The text also discusses a substantial fragment of a Dunhuang manuscript and the way the text has been extraordinarily important in Korean Son (Zen).

Chapter 2, "*Mazu yulu* and the Creation of the Chan Records of Sayings," by Mario Poceski, focuses on the *Mazu yulu*, one of the most influential texts of the Chan records of sayings genre. The text, which was compiled around 1085, purports to record the life and teachings of the monk Mazu Daoyi (709–788). The chapter aims to accomplish two objectives. First, on a general level it serves as a survey of the *Mazu yulu* and its place in Chan literature. As such, it provides information about the text's provenance, internal structure, literary style, doctrinal contents, historical importance, and the ways it was used by the Chan/Zen schools throughout East Asia. Second, by using Mazu's record as an example of the recorded sayings genre, the chapter also considers the broader issues of the creation of texts that belong to this genre and their use as historical sources about Chan during the Tang Dynasty (618–907). Poceski argues that the creation of the Chan records of sayings indicate that there is a need to take a fresh look at accepted views about the history of Chan during the later Tang period, and undertake future studies with a clearer understanding of the provenance of all extant textual sources.

"The *Lidai fabao ji* (Record of the Dharma-Jewel through the Ages)," by Wendi Adamek in the third chapter, deals with the *Lidai fabao* ji, a long-lost Chan Buddhist text, resurrected from among the manuscripts discovered in 1900 in the hidden library at the Mogao caves of Dunhuang. The manuscripts and fragments are not substantially different, which suggested that they may be relatively faithful to the original. The *Lidai fabao ji* thus provides a rare opportunity to shed light on the ways in which historical contingencies shape sectarian identity. In this chapter, Adamek argues that the *Lidai fabao ji* is prototypical of two important Chan genres; the first part is in a format analogous to the later *chuangdeng lu* (transmission of the lamp records), and the second part shares features with the Song dynasty *yulu* (discourse records). Through the *Lidai fabao ji* we may thus gain glimpses of an earlier stage of the hagiographical sensibilities that shaped Song-dynasty Chan's distinctive literary styles and its images of exemplary practice, which were in turn the styles and images adopted by Japanese monks who founded the Zen schools of the Kamakura period.

Then in chapter 4, "The Huang-po Literature," Dale S. Wright carries out a literary, philosophical, and historical analysis of the classic Huang-po texts. Wright reflects on the origins of the text set in the context of what is now known as ninth-century Chan Buddhism. He further explores the relation of the Huang-po texts to significant predecessor literature and the question of authorship and the evolution of the Zen genre of "recorded sayings." His literary analysis includes discussion of genre, rhetorical style, narrative sequence, authorial voice, intended audience, and intertextuality or the extent to which these texts quote or allude to other Chan literature. This is followed by analysis of textual content and an evaluation of the ways in which works attributed to Huang-po constitute innovation in the tradition of Chinese Buddhism.

In chapter 5, "Lineage and Context in the *Patriarch's Hall Collection* and the *Transmission of the Lamp*," Albert Welter discusses the development of transmission records dedicated to the activities of the famous masters and their role as one of the unique contributions of Chan to Chinese literature. These *chuangdeng lu* (transmission of the lamp records) documented the lineal relations among Chan masters and their association with temples and government representatives. They gave rise to multilineal branches and became codified as the "five houses" of classical Chan. Probing beneath the surface of each record's generally harmonious transmission claims, Welter finds that we can discover preferences for particular factions and diverging views of Chan orthodoxy. He discusses the *Patriarch's Hall Collection* (*Zutang ji*) and its response to the "new style" Chan attributed to Mazu Daoyi (709–788). He also examines the connection between the *Zutang ji* and Korean Buddhism, evidenced through the prominent position accorded Korean Sŏn masters in the text, and compares the *Zutang ji*'s presentation of Chan lineages with the locus classicus of Chan transmission texts, the *Jingde chuandeng lu* (The Jingde era record of the transmission of the lamp) compiled in 1004.

Chapter 6, Morten Schlütter's "The *Record of Hongzhi* and the Recorded Sayings Literature of Song-Dynasty Chan," delves into our access to an unusual amount of information pertaining to the life history of Hongzhi's recorded sayings and the unique opportunity to observe it closely. Relatively few larger recorded sayings are still extant from the Song era, and Hongzhi's is one of the longest extant collections from that time. Schlütter covers the history of Hongzhi's recorded sayings, from when individual smaller collections were published during his lifetime through the enshrinement of the larger collection in the canon and its eventual loss in China and increasing prominence in Japan. He further examines the new life that Hongzhi's recorded sayings are currently gaining through English translations, as well as their meaning and significance.

In chapter 7, "The *Wu-men kuan* (J. *Mumonkan*): The Formation, Propagation, and Characteristics of a Classic Zen Kōan Text," Ishii Shūdō analyzes the *Wu-men kuan* text, a kōan collection containing forty-eight cases. The *Wu-men kuan* text is one of the most widely read Zen texts and yet it is also often criticized from various sectarian perspectives. Ishii explores the *Tsung-men t'ung-yao chi* as a source for the *Wu-men kuan*'s contents, and asserts that the importance of this background text must no longer be disregarded. He looks at the formation process of the *Wu-men kuan* as well as why there has been so much attention and concern for this text throughout Japanese history, while it has not been read or studied to the same extent in China. Ishii further examines the special features of the *Wu-men kuan* in the context of Song Chan textual history.

Chapter 8, "The *Eihei kōroku*: The Record of Dōgen's Later Period at Eihei-ji Temple" by Steven Heine, examines the textual history and structure of the *Eihei kōroku*, one of the two main texts produced by Dōgen, the founder of Sōtō Zen in thirteenth-century Japan. It is the primary work that represents the later period of Dōgen's career and until recently has received far less attention than the other main Dōgen text, the *Shōbōgenzō*. Both the *Shōbōgenzō* and the *Eihei kōroku* consist mainly of collections of sermons delivered by Dōgen to his assembly of disciples, often based on interpretations of kōans or allusions to other kinds of Buddhist works. However, they reflect two very different styles of sermonizing, with the former, Japanese vernacular text representing an informal style and the latter, Chinese text representing a formal style. In addition to analyzing the structure and the function of the *Eihei kōroku* genres in their historical context, Heine discusses the two main editions of the text from 1598 (Monkaku edition, also know as the Sozan edition) and 1672 (Manzan edition), in addition to an abbreviated version of the text known as the *Eihei goroku*. He shows the various biographical and literary levels of significance that permeate the *Eihei kōroku*.

In the final chapter, rather than focusing on a single text, T. Griffith Foulk's "*Chanyuan qinggui* and Other 'Rules of Purity' in Chinese Buddhism" covers an entire class of Zen literature: the so-called *qinggui* (J. *shingi*) or "rules of purity." He shows that the *quinggui* genre is actually several genres, some having been written to regulate only one community and others clearly having been intended to serve as schedules for diverse Buddhist communities, including monasteries. Foulk traces the historical origins and development of the *quinggui* class of texts. Much of the material in the texts comes from Chinese translations of various rescensions of the Indian Buddhist *Vinaya* and associated commentaries. From Song China to modern Japan, moreover, later *quinggui* have borrowed from and adapted earlier ones. His goal is to make these intertextual relationships clear, while also elucidating the changing social and political contexts in which successive *quinggui* have been edited and implemented in China and Japan.

NOTES

1. Steven Heine and Dale S. Wright, eds., *The Kōan: Texts and Contexts in Zen Buddhism* (New York: Oxford University Press, 2000).

2. Harold Bloom, *The Western Canon: The Books and School of the Ages* (New York: Riverhead Books, 1995).

3. Robert Alter, *Canon and Canonicity: Modern Writing and the Authority of Scripture* (New Haven and London: Yale University Press, 2000), p. 5.

I

Tsung-mi's *Zen Prolegomenon:* Introduction to an Exemplary Zen Canon

Jeff Broughton

The Zen tradition commonly uses the term Zen forest (*ch'an-lin*) to refer to the gathering or clustering of its adepts. With some justification, we could apply this forest metaphor to the literature of Zen as well, because that literature is without doubt an immense woods of staggering expanse and diversity. The enormous printed Zen literature of the Sung Dynasty and beyond encompasses a wide range of genres: sayings records; biographical transmission of the lamp records, or sacred histories; kōan case collections providing topics for meditation practice and commentary on the part of trainees; codes for the regulation of the Zen community; rules for *zazen*; poetic inscriptions; oxherding pictures that illustrate the stages of Zen practice; poetry collections; lineage charts; and so on. When we include early Zen texts of the prior T'ang Dynasty that were retrieved by scholars from the cache of manuscripts discovered in the cave complex near the desert oasis of Tun-huang and carried off to libraries around the world, our Zen corpus grows considerably. The Tun-huang Zen manuscripts show some of the same genres as the Sung and Yüan printed books and some new ones as well: transmission of the lamp records, cultivation treatises, imaginary sayings, encounter dialogues, apocryphal works attributed to Bodhidharma, inscriptions, exhortations, praises, verses, apocryphal Zen sutras, sutra commentaries by Zen figures, and so on.

Within this entire Zen corpus, one text can fairly be described as unique: the *Prolegomenon to the Collection of Expressions of the Zen Source* (*Ch'an-yuan chu-ch'uan-chi tu-hsu*; abbreviated as *ZP* for *Zen Prolegomenon*) of the T'ang Dynasty Zen master and exegete Kuei-feng Tsung-mi (780–841).¹ The *ZP* does not fit into any of the above genres; it stands alone and should be approached with this singularity in mind. It literally has no predecessor texts.

Biography

I will provide here not a complete biography of Tsung-mi but simply an ab-breviated treatment of his life.² Those familiar with the biographies of T'ang Zen masters will immediately note two striking differences in the case of Tsung-mi. Given his early educational credentials, he could easily have become a proper Confucian literatus; after becoming a Zen monk he attained a very high level of erudition, not just in Zen literature but also in Buddhist literature as a whole. These traits do not fit the usual profile. Typical T'ang Zen masters in their youth did not attend Confucian academies in preparation for the official examination system, and they did not become erudite commentators on the sutra and *śāstra* literature. The following biography is broken down into six phases.

Youthful Classical Education (780–804)

Tsung-mi was born into a provincial elite family, the Ho, in what is today central Szechwan Province (Hsi-ch'ung County in Kuo Prefecture) in 780. His family was affluent and powerful but not part of the national elite. From the age of six to fifteen or sixteen he worked at typical Confucian studies, and from seventeen to about twenty-one he studied Buddhist texts, perhaps because of the death of his father. From twenty-two to twenty-four he was enrolled at the Righteousness Learning Academy (I-hsueh Yuan) in nearby Sui Prefecture, where he deepened his exposure to Confucian texts. His later writings show a deep familiarity with the standard works of the classical canon.

A Young Man's Commitment to Zen Practice (804–810)

In 804, at the age of twenty-four, he encountered the Zen master Sui-chou Tao-yuan and left home, training under Tao-yuan for two to three years until he received Tao-yuan's seal in 807. It is also during this phase that Tsung-mi encountered a copy of the apocryphal *Perfect Enlightenment Sutra* (*Yuan-chueh ching*)³ and had an enlightenment experience.

Tsung-mi traces his Zen lineage as follows: Hui-neng, the sixth patriarch, to Ho-tse Shen-hui, the seventh patriarch; next to Tzu-chou Chih-ju; then to I-chou Nan-yin, who is also known as Wei-chung; and finally to Sui-chou Tao-yuan. He refers to this line as the Ho-tse. Tsung-mi's accuracy has been questioned, due to some confusion over Nan-yin's genealogy. It happens that

Nan-yin trained under two different Shen-huis: the Ho-tse mentioned above (perhaps through the intermediary of his disciple Tzu-chou Chih-ju); and Ching-chung Shen-hui, a mainstay of the Ching-chung (Pure Assembly) lineage of Zen that flourished in Szechwan. Tsung-mi sometimes refers to the latter Shen-hui as I-chou Shih. Nan-yin first trained under Ho-tse Shen-hui, or perhaps his disciple Tzu-chou Chih-ju, before going to Szechwan and becoming one of Ching-chung Shen-hui's disciples.

Later, while abbot of Sheng-shou Monastery in Ch'eng-tu in Szechwan (technically a branch of the Ching-chung school), Nan-yin must have stressed his connection to Ho-tse. As Peter Gregory states, "The identification of the Sheng-shou tradition [of the Ching-chung school] with Ho-tse Shen-hui did not originate with Tsung-mi."[4] In other words, Tao-yuan must have continued his master's emphasis on Ho-tse rather than Ching-chung, and passed this on to his student Tsung-mi.

Inheritance of Ch'eng-kuan's Hua-yen in His Thirties (810–816)

In 812 Tsung-mi left for the western capital Ch'ang-an in order to meet Ch'ing-liang Ch'eng-kuan (738–839), the great Hua-yen exegete and preeminent scholar of the day in virtually all fields of Buddhist studies. For two years (812–813) he studied under Ch'eng-kuan and later remained in consultation with him. Ch'eng-kuan wrote voluminous commentaries on the *Avataṁsaka-sūtra* and had some experience with Zen. The Hua-yen lineage considers Ch'eng-kuan and Tsung-mi its fourth and fifth patriarchs.

Production of Technical Buddhist Exegesis in His Maturity (816–828)

Tsung-mi took up residence on Mount Chung-nan southwest of the imperial capital Ch'ang-an, eventually settling at Ts'ao-t'ang Monastery beneath Kuei Peak on that mountain. Hence he became known as Kuei-feng Tsung-mi. In 828 he was summoned to the court of Emperor Wen-tsung, where he received such honors as the purple robe and the title *bhadanta* (worthy). During this phase Tsung-mi, now a Zen master, produced many technical Buddhist works; this makes him unique among major Zen masters of the T'ang. A list of extant and nonextant exegetical works that can be dated with some certainty to this period includes:

1. a commentary on the *Awakening of Faith* (*Ch'i-hsin lun*)
2. a commentary and subcommentary on the *Vajracchedikāprajñāpāramitā-sūtra* that draws on passages from the *śāstras* of Vasubandhu and Asaṅga, a range of other commentaries on the sutra, and one on the *Treatises of Seng-chao* (*Chao-lun*)

3. an abridged commentary to the *Perfect Enlightenment Sutra*
4. a subcommentary to the above abridged commentary
5. an enormous procedural manual based on the *Perfect Enlightenment* (first part on the conditions for praxis; second on methods of worship; and third on *zazen*)
6. a commentary on the *Perfect Enlightenment*
7. a subcommentary to the above commentary (contains a section that gives the histories and teachings of seven houses of Zen, each discussed in terms of its idea and praxis)
8. a work on the *Avataṃsaka-sūtra*
9. a commentary on the *Dharmagupta-vinaya*
10. a compilation of passages from commentaries to the *Perfect Enlightenment*
11. a commentary on Vasubandhu's *Thirty Verses* (*Trimsika*) that draws from Hsuan-tsang's *Treatise on the Establishment of Vijñāna Only* (*Ch'eng wei-shih lun*) and his disciple K'uei-chi's commentary on his master's work
12. a commentary on the *Nirvāṇa-sūtra* that may be datable to this phase.[5]

Association-with-Literati and Zen-Works Phase: Compilation of the Zen Canon, ZP, and P'ei's Inquiry (828–835)

At this time Tsung-mi was in contact with numerous literati and politicians, composing works in response to their requests.[6] The central figure in Tsung-mi's circle, and without question his most important Zen disciple, was P'ei Hsiu (787?–860). During this phase, and perhaps well before it, Tsung-mi was in the process of collecting copies of every Zen text in circulation, for he envisioned compiling nothing less than a Zen canon. We know the title of this lost treasure: *Collection of Expressions of the Zen Source* (*Ch'an-yuan chu-ch'uan chi*; abbreviated as *Zen Canon*). P'ei Hsiu caught the nature of his master's *Zen Canon* more incisively than its actual title when he referred to it as a "Zen pitaka" (*Ch'an-tsang*).[7] P'ei meant that the *Zen Canon* was nothing less than a wholly new section of the Buddhist canon, a Zen addition to the traditional three *pitakas*. In doing this, Tsung-mi strove to bring Zen books into the Buddhist canon. Although the Zen canon itself has been lost to us, his efforts did eventually come to fruition. The standard modern scholarly edition of the Chinese Buddhist canon, the Taishō canon, includes a substantial selection of Zen books in two of its first fifty-five volumes.

Tsung-mi composed three works on Zen, and they are without doubt our most valuable sources on T'ang dynasty Zen. There is no other extant source even remotely as informative, and no evidence that anybody else ever compiled one. These three sources show considerable intertextuality. One must read all three as one in order to apprehend the panorama of Tsung-mi's picture of T'ang Zen. Each of the three makes an especially strong contribution to filling in one aspect of that picture—the first in supplying an overall theoretical framework, the second in supplying critiques of the schools, and last in supplying descriptive data on their teachings and practices.

The first of the three is Tsung-mi's lengthy introduction to the Zen canon, the *ZP*, which was written around 833. It provides the theory underlying his vision of the relationship between Zen and the canonical teachings. For a long time I referred to this text as the *Zen Preface*, always aware that calling a text of about 25,000 Chinese logographs, approximately 120 double-spaced pages in English translation, a preface was a serious misnomer. Most prefaces, needless to say, are considerably shorter than this work, which has one preface of its own in every edition by P'ei Hsiu. One edition has a total of four prefaces. If we are forced to find some niche in terms of genre, it can best be described as a prolegomenon, a formal essay or critical discussion serving to introduce and interpret an extended work, in this instance the Zen canon.

The second is a letter Tsung-mi wrote to P'ei Hsiu sometime between 830 and 833, in response to a letter from P'ei Hsiu. This work provides a critical apparatus evaluating each of the Zen schools. It has been known by numerous titles in China, Korea, and Japan, and much confusion has ensued. Recently a Kamakura-period manuscript was discovered in Japan entitled *Imperial Redactor P'ei Hsiu's Inquiry* (*Hai Kyu shui mon*; *P'ei Hsiu shih-i wen*), and this version appears to be the most complete. I shall for the sake of convenience refer to this text as *P'ei's Inquiry*.[8] P'ei, citing his dread about making a mistake when taking up the Zen records, requests that Tsung-mi compose a brief piece that lays out the histories of the Zen lineages and classifies them. Tsung-mi replies that he will specify the collateral and straight transmissions and will discuss the relative depth of their teachings. He then organizes four houses of Zen: Niu-t'ou (or Ox Head), Northern, Ho-tse, and Hung-chou.

The third is a detailed set of notes on seven Zen houses, including the above four, buried in one of Tsung-mi's subcommentaries on the *Perfect Enlightenment Sutra* (*Yuan-chueh ching ta-shu ch'ao*; abbreviated as *Subcommentary*).[9] The *Subcommentary* provides us with a wealth of descriptive data, some of it clearly deriving from firsthand observation, on the teachings and practices of the schools plus a slogan for each encapsulating its idea and practice. These notes must have been compiled about a decade earlier than the *ZP* and *P'ei's Inquiry*, since the *Subcommentary* as a whole is datable to 823–824.

Implication in the Sweet Dew Incident and Forced Retirement (835–841)

In 835, through his association with the politician Li Hsun, Tsung-mi became implicated in a failed attempt to oust the eunuchs from court power. He was arrested but released; apparently his forthright testimony and personal courage in the face of possible execution impressed a general of the eunuch forces. He passed his last years in obscurity, and his final act was that of a Zen master, dying in *zazen* posture at the Hsing-fu Yuan within the capital Ch'ang-an on the sixth day of the first month of Hui-ch'ang 1 (February 1, 841). The onslaught of the Hui-ch'ang Suppression of foreign religions was about to begin. On February 17 his body was returned to Kuei Peak and on March 4 cremated. When, twelve years later, P'ei Hsiu became a chief minister, Tsung-mi was awarded the posthumous title Samādhi-Prajñā Zen Master and a stupa called Blue Lotus was erected to hold his remains.

The Master Metaphor of the *ZP*: The Meshing of Two Sides of a *Fu* (Tally)

The *ZP* is filled with metaphors, similes, and analogies, but one main metaphor buttresses the two foundational concepts of the text. Those two concepts are the *identity* of Zen mind along with its expression in Zen texts and the Buddha's intention along with its expression in the sutras, and the *complementariness* between all-at-once (or sudden) awakening and step-by-step (gradual) practice. The master metaphor is the *fu* ("tally") and how its two halves fit together perfectly as testimony in a contract. Such tallies were made of bamboo or wood on which characters or symbols were written. The bamboo or wooden piece was then cut in half and each person came into possession of one side. When later the two parties assembled, each bearing his side of the bamboo or wooden slip, they were able to put them together to prove their bona fides. A match was proof of sincerity and authenticity. Other meanings of *fu* that are probably latent when Tsung-mi uses the term are seal or signet as well as charm or amulet.

The term *fu* occurs nine times in the *ZP*, not really a great number when we consider the size of the text, but it is the contexts in which the *fu* metaphor shows up that make it central to the metaphorical architecture of the *ZP*.[10] We find the following *fu* pairs:

The three canonical teachings/three Zen theses
Bodhidharma's robe/the Dharma
Zen mind or what the Zen masters say/the Buddha's intention
Zen texts/sutras
all-at-once awakening/step-by-step practice
all-at-once teaching/Zen all-at-once gate
step-by-step teaching/Zen step-by-step gate
real/unreal

The *ZP*'s *Fu* (Tally) of the Canonical Teachings and Zen

The *ZP* says of the Zen canon:

> It is not solely an aid to the [Zen] gate of forgetting words. It equally
> hands down the benefits of the teachings along with Zen. It not only
> makes the [Zen] ideas tally with that of the Buddha. I also desire to
> make the [Zen] texts coincide with the sutras. Since the [Zen] texts
> seem to contradict each other, it is impossible to consider all of
> them the real [teaching]. I must classify the entire canon into Hinay-
> āna and Mahāyāna, into provisional principle and real principle, into
> explicit meaning and nonexplicit meaning. Then I should critically
> evaluate the Zen gates of the various lineages. Each of them has a
> purport; none is in conflict with the intention of the Buddha. I
> mean by this that the sutras and *śāstras* of the entire canon consist
> of just three types, and the spoken teachings of the Zen gate consist
> of just three theses. [When the three types of teachings and three
> Zen theses] are matched up like a tally, they become the perfect
> view.[11]

The relationship between the teachings and Zen, in short, is one of identity,
perfection, fulfillment, and completion. No form of Zen is in conflict with the
intention of the Buddha; each form has a target audience of practitioners for
which it is effective.

The three teachings, actually the third subdivision of the first teaching plus
the second and third teachings, are: the teaching of cryptic meaning that takes
vijñāna to negate *visayas*, the teaching of cryptic meaning that negates *lakṣaṇas*
to reveal *dharmatā*, and the teaching that openly shows that the true mind is
dharmatā. The three Zen theses are: the stop-*abhūtaparikalpa*-and-cultivate-
cittamātra thesis, the be-extinguished-with-nothing-to-rely-upon thesis, and the
directly-reveal-the-*cittadharmatā* thesis.[12] The three theses could be dubbed Cittamātra Zen, Śūnyata Zen, and Dharmatā Zen. The first teaching, based on
such sutras as the *Saṃdhinirmocana* and such *śāstras* as the *Yogācārabhūmi* and
the *Treatise on the Establishment of Vijñāna Only* (*Ch'eng wei-shih lun*), tallies
with the *cittamātra* thesis of Zen. The second teaching, based on the
Prajñāpāramitā-sūtras and such *śāstras* as the *Mādhyamaka* and the *Catuḥśataka*, tallies with the *śūnyatā* thesis of Zen. The third teaching, based on such
sutras as the *Avataṃsaka, Ghanavyūha, Perfect Enlightenment, Śūraṅgama, Śrī-
mālā, Tathāgatagarbha, Saddharmapuṇḍarīka*, and *Nirvāṇa*, and such *śāstras* as
the *Ratnagotravibhāga, Buddhagotra, Awakening of Faith, Daśabhūmika, Dhar-
mādhatvāviśeṣa*, and *Nirvāṇa*, tallies with the *dharmatā* thesis of Zen.

This *fu* is simultaneously a seal or signet that authenticates Zen and a charm or amulet that serves as a magical protection against polemics, biases, and criticisms, whether from scholastic partisans or Zen partisans. Tsung-mi was well acquainted with such things. He encountered profound doubts about Zen on the part of scholars, various hostilities within the Zen camp, criticisms of both his scholasticism and of his exhortations to practice *zazen* from Zen people, and so forth.

The *Subcommentary's* Notes on the Seven Zen Houses

The ZP lists four houses under Cittamātra Zen: Ching-chung, Northern, Pao-t'ang, and South Mountain Nembutsu Gate, all of which with the exception of the Northern were centered in Tsung-mi's native region of Szechwan.[13] In the short section on seven houses in his *Subcommentary*, for each Tsung-mi gives a six-to eight-character slogan. The first half encapsulates the idea or view of the house in question; the second half distills its practice. In each case, an account of the house's genealogy and an insightful description of its idea and practice follow the slogan. The division into two parts, doctrine and praxis, is not unique to Tsung-mi; we find it in Tibetan Buddhism as a formula for dividing up the three turnings of the wheel of Dharma.[14] What is unique is the application of such a distinction to Zen. This shows creativity and considerable research on Tsung-mi's part.[15]

Tsung-mi's reports in the *Subcommentary* on the contentious world of Zen of his time are quite astounding for their unbiased and accurate reporting. It is clear that he actually visited Zen establishments, talked to the Zen adepts, and took notes on their answers and his observations. Though one may charge him with bias in elevating the Ho-tse house to the pinnacle of the Zen genealogy as the only "straight" transmission and relegating the other houses to "offshoot" or "collateral" status, in his accounts of the ideas and practices of the other houses he seems never to have engaged in active distortion. Given the occasionally acrimonious climate of Zen at the time, much credit is due.

ZP's Cittamātra Zen No. 1: Ching-chung's Three-Topic Zen

The *Subcommentary* tells us that Ching-chung followed a rigorous variety of disciplinary formalism much like the South Mountain Vinaya School, which was recognized by the state as an ordination center and which propagated Zen at periodic, nighttime assemblies that included monks and nuns as well as laypeople who practiced *zazen* at these mass gatherings.

> "Exertion in the three topics is *śīla, samādhi,* and *prajñā*" is the second house. At its origin it is an offshoot from the fifth patriarch [Hung-

jen] through one monk named Chih-shen. He was one of the ten
disciples [of Hung-jen]. He was originally a man of Tzu-chou [in
Szechwan], and after [his stay on East Mountain under Hung-jen] he
returned to Te-ch'un Monastery in his native prefecture to begin
teaching. His disciple Ch'u-chi, whose family name was T'ang, received the succession. T'ang produced four sons, the preeminent of
which was [the Korean] Preceptor Kim of Ching-chung Monastery in
the superior prefecture of Ch'eng-tu, Dharma name Wu-hsiang [Ko-
rean Musang]. He greatly spread this teaching. (As to Kim's disciples, Chao of that monastery [i.e., Ching-chung], Ma of Mount
Ch'ang-sung, Chi of Sui-chou, and Chi of T'ung-ch'uan county all
succeeded him.) "The three topics" are: no remembering, no
thought, and do not forget. The idea is: do not recall past *visayas*; do
not anticipate future glorious events; and always be yoked to these
insights, never darkening, never erring. This is called do not forget.
Sometimes [the three topics run]: no remembering of external *visayas*, no thinking of internal mind, dried up with nothing to rely
upon. "*Śīla, samādhi, and prajñā*" correspond respectively to the
three topics. Even though [Ching-chung's] *upāya* discussions surrounding its thesis are numerous, the purport of its thesis is dis-
tilled in these three topics. Their teaching rituals are a little like the
upāya of receiving the full precepts on an official ordination platform at the present time in this country. That is, in the first and second months, they first pick a date and post notices, summoning
monks, nuns, and laypeople. They arrange a Mahāyāna practice site,
worship [the three treasures] and confess [transgressions]. Sometimes it is three to five weeks long. Only after this do they hand over
Dharma. All of this is performed at night. Their idea is to cut off
external [*visayas*] and reject confusion. The Dharma having been
handed over, immediately beneath the words [of the master] they are
made to stop thoughts and do *zazen*. Even those who come from
distant parts, sometimes nuns and lay types, must not tarry for long.
Directly they must do one or two weeks of *zazen*. Only afterwards
do they disperse according to their conditions. It is like the method
of mounting the ordination platform [to receive the precepts] in the
Vinaya lineage. It is obligatory to have a group. Since they use a tablet with an official statement [i.e., an official license] on it, it is called
"opening conditions." Sometimes once in a year, sometimes once in
two or three years, it is irregular in its opening.[16]

The Tun-huang text entitled *Record of the Dharma Treasure down through
the Generations* (*Li-tai fa-pao chi*) independently confirms the major points of
Tsung-mi's report in its entry for Wu-hsiang. There are the three topics and

their correlation with *śīla*, *samādhi*, and *prajñā*, the disciplinary formalism, the ordination ceremonies, and the mass assemblies with laypeople present. The one element in the *Record of the Dharma Treasure down through the Generations* entry that is missing in the *Subcommentary* report is Preceptor Kim's singing *nembutsu*. The *Record* states: "Preceptor Kim, annually in the first and twelfth months, for the sake of thousands of monks, nuns, and laypeople, [held a ceremony] of receiving conditions. At the ornamented practice site he took the high seat [on the platform] and spoke Dharma. He first taught chanting *nembutsu* as a gentle [or slow] song, exhausting one breath's thoughts. When the sound [of the *nembutsu* tune] died down and thoughts were stopped, he said: 'No remembering, no thought, and do not forget. No remembering is *śīla*. No thought is *samādhi*. Do not forget is *prajñā*. These three topics are the *dharani* gate."[17] Tsung-mi's portrait of Ching-chung as a conservative Zen securely contained within the confines of the vinaya can be taken at face value.

ZP's Cittamātra Zen No. 2: Northern's Gazing-at-Purity Zen

The *Subcommentary* is critical of the Northern house, saying that it is caught up in the dichotomy of impurity and purity within dependent arising, and therefore misses the innate purity of the *dharmatā*. Its practice involves the five *upāyas*, each of which is grounded in a Mahāyāna sutra:

"Sweep away dust [i.e., *visayas*] and gaze at purity; the *upāyas* penetrate the sutras" . . . is the first house. It is descended from the fifth patriarch [Hung-jen]. The Great Master [Shen-]hsiu is the fountainhead of this lineage. His disciple P'u-chi and others greatly spread it. "Sweep away dust" refers to their basic gatha: "From time to time we must polish [the mirror of the mind]; do not let dust collect." The idea is: from the outset sentient beings have an awakened nature that is like the brightness of a mirror. The depravities cover it, just like the dust on a mirror. One extinguishes false thoughts. When thoughts are exhausted, then the original nature is perfectly bright. It is like rubbing off the dust until the mirror is bright; then all things reach an extreme. This [house deals] only with the *lakṣaṇas* of the dependent arising of impurity and purity. It has not yet seen that false thoughts from the outset are nonexistent and the one nature from the outset pure. Since it has yet to penetrate awakening, how can its practice be called true? Since its practice cannot be called true, [even] over numerous kalpas how could one reach realization? In "*upāyas* penetrate the sutras," *upāyas* refers to the five *upāyas*. The first totally displays the Buddha substance and relies on the *Awakening of Faith*. The second opens the gate of *prajñā* and relies on the *Saddharmapuṇḍarīka-sūtra*. The third reveals inconceivable liberation and relies on the *Vimalakīrti-sūtra*. The fourth clarifies the true nature of all Dharmas and relies on the *Viśeṣācintī-sūtra*. The fifth realizes the liberation of nondifference, spontaneity, and nonobstruction and relies on the *Avataṁsaka-sūtra*.[18]

This encapsulation seems to be a blend of Ho-tse distortion and accurate reporting. The distortion involves the so-called basic gatha about sweeping away dust on the mirror. Tsung-mi cites this gatha in *P'ei's Inquiry* and paraphrases it in the *ZP*, both times without mentioning a source.[19] It does not appear in any text produced within the "Northern" lineage, however, which in any case never used that name but called itself the Bodhidharma lineage or the East Mountain Dharma Gate. Tun-huang manuscript materials corroborate the remainder of the slogan or the parts about gazing at purity and the *upāyas*. A Shen-hsiu saying in a very brief East Mountain collection of sayings found on a Tun-huang manuscript runs: "In the pure locus gaze at purity."[20] And among the Tun-huang Zen manuscripts we have a set that could be called the five-*upāyas* series.[21]

ZP's Cittamātra Zen No. 3: Pao-t'ang's Stripped-Down Zen

The *Subcommentary*'s picture of the Pao-t'ang house is perhaps the most curious of all. Tsung-mi tells us that Pao-t'ang was a Zen totally devoid of Buddhist practices, precepts, rituals, iconographic paraphernalia, textual study, teaching lectures, begging rounds, and so forth. Pao-t'ang monks apparently shaved their heads, put on the robes, did *zazen*—and that was about it. This Zen lineage is probably the most radical in the history of Zen. The *Subcommentary* relates:

> "Bound by neither the teachings nor praxes and extinguishing *vijñāna*" is the third house. At its beginning it is also an offshoot from the fifth patriarch [Hung-jen], through Preceptor "Old Mother" An. An was his given name. At sixty years of age he left home and received the precepts. When he expired sixty summers later, he was one hundred twenty years old. Therefore, at the time he was styled "Old An." He was honored as a master by the Noble Empress [Wu] Tse-t'ien. His power in the path was deep and thick, his determination and integrity singular. None of the famous worthies could compare to him. He had four disciples, all of whom were high in the path and famous. Among them there was a lay disciple Ch'en Ch'u-chang (the other three were T'eng T'eng, Tzu-tsai, and P'o-tsao To), at that time styled Ch'en Ch'i-ko. There was a monk named Wu-chu. He met Ch'en, who instructed him and guided him to awaken-

ing. [Wu-chu] was also singular in his determination. Later he traveled within Shu [i.e., Szechwan] and encountered Preceptor Kim's
instruction in Zen, even attending his assembly. [Wu-chu] merely
asked questions and seeing that it was not a matter of changing his
previous awakening, wanted to transmit it to those who had not yet
heard it. Fearing that it was improper to have received the succession from a layman [i.e., Ch'en Ch'i-ko], he subsequently recognized
Preceptor Kim as his master. Even though the Dharma idea of [Wu-
chu's] instruction was just about the same as that of Kim's [Ching-
chung] school, [Wu-chu's] teaching rituals were completely different.
The difference lies in the fact that [Wu-chu's Pao-t'ang house] practices none of the phenomenal *laksanas* of Buddhism. Having cut
their hair and donned robes, they do not receive the precepts. When
it comes to doing obeisance and confession, turning and reading
[the canonical scrolls], making paintings of Buddha figures, copying
sutras, they revile all such things as *abhūtaparikalpa*. In the halls
where they dwell they set up no Buddhist artifacts. This is why [I say
the Pao-t'ang's idea is] "bound by neither the teachings nor praxes."
As to "extinguishing *vijñāna*," this is the path that [Pao-t'ang] practices. The meaning is: All samsaric wheel-turning causes the arising
of mind. Arising of mind is the unreal. They do not discuss good
and bad. Nonarising of mind is the real. [Their practice] shows no
resemblance whatsoever to [ordinary Buddhist] practices in terms of
phenomenal *laksanas*. They take *vikalpa* as the enemy and *avikalpa*
as the wondrous path. They do transmit Preceptor Kim's three-topic
oral teaching, but they just change the graph for "forget" to the one
for "unreal," saying that fellow students [i.e., Ching-chung] are making a mistake in the oral teaching of the former master [i.e., Preceptor Kim] entrusted to them. The meaning is: No remembering and
no thought are the real. Remembering thoughts is the unreal, [so]
remembering thoughts is not allowed. Therefore, they say "do not
[allow the] unreal" [rather than the original Ching-chung formulation "do not forget"]. Moreover, their idea in reviling all the *laksanas*
of the teachings lies in extinguishing *vikalpa* and [manifesting] the
completely real. Therefore, in their dwellings they do not discuss
food and clothing, but leave it to people to send offerings. If sent,
then they have warm clothing and enough to eat. If not sent, then
they leave matters to hunger and cold. They do not seek to transform [beings], nor do they beg for food. If someone enters their
monastery, they do not discuss whether he is highborn or villainous.
In no case do they welcome him. They do not even stand up [when
he enters]. As to singing hymns and praises, making offerings, rep-
rimanding abuses, in all such things they leave it to other. Indeed,

because the purport of their thesis speaks of *avikalpa*, their gate of practice has neither right nor wrong. They just value no mind as the wondrous ultimate. Therefore, I have called it "extinguishing *vi-jñāna*."[22]

The image of Pao-t'ang presented in the *Record of the Dharma Treasure down through the Generations*, which is a product of the Pao-t'ang house, echoes this report. There the founder of Pao-t'ang is depicted as "not allowing obeisance, confession, mindfulness, and chanting, but just doing *zazen* in the midst of voidness and quietude."[23] Even the *Subcommentary*'s remarks about not welcoming someone and the attitude of "leaving it to other" find an echo in the *Record of the Dharma Treasure down through the Generations*.[24] Surely Tsung-mi had set foot within a Pao-t'ang establishment.

ZP's Cittamātra Zen No. 4: South Mountain Nembutsu Gate's Transmission-of-the-Incense Zen

The *Subcommentary*'s description of the South Mountain Nembutsu Gate indicates that it was a highly ritualized form of Zen that employed singing a *nembutsu* that consisted of just one syllable. We do not know what the one syllable was, as Tsung-mi (who is the only source) does not say. A special feature of this singing *nembutsu* was a lowering of the pitch, much like the conclusion of the four vows as they are chanted in Zen today. We have no source for this house beyond the following report in the *Subcommentary*:

> "Taking the transmitting of the incense to make the Buddha live on" is the sixth house, that is, the South Mountain Nembutsu Gate Zen lineage. At its beginning it is also an offshoot from the fifth patriarch [Hung-jen], through one with the Dharma name Hsuan-shih. Preceptor Wei of Kuo-chou, Yun-yu of Lang-chou, and the Nun I-ch'eng of Hsiang-ju county all spread it. I do not clearly know the father-and-son ancestral temples of the masters and disciples of this succession. As to "transmitting the incense," when they first gather the community and [conduct such] rituals as obeisance and confession, it is like Preceptor Kim's [Ching-chung] school. When they are about to hand over Dharma, they take transmitting the incense as faith between disciple and master. The preceptor transfers [the incense] by hand. The disciple hands it back to the preceptor. The preceptor hands it back to the disciple. They do this three times. It is the same for every person [attending the ceremony]. As to "making the Buddha live on," just as they hand over Dharma, [the preceptor] first speaks on the path principles of their Dharma gate and the significance of practice. Only afterwards does he enjoin the one-syllable

nembutsu. First they chant this *nembutsu* as a gentle [or slow] song. Later they gradually lower the sound to a finer and finer sound, until there is no sound at all. They are sending the Buddha to thought, but [initially] the thoughts are still coarse. They also send [the Buddha] to mind, from moment to moment making such thought live on. [Thus] there is always the Buddha inside mind, until they arrive at no thought, at which point they have attained the path.[25]

By placing Ching-chung, Northern, Pao-t'ang, and South Mountain houses under the heading of *cittamātra* Zen, the ZP is making the case that these houses share a focus on the negation of *visayas*. For the ZP, the ideas of these four Zen houses are identical to classical Yogācāra teachings, the teachings of the *Samdhinirmocana-sūtra*, and the *śāstras* of Asaṅga and Vasubandhu. These teachings lay out the path for the elimination of *abhūtaparikalpa*, which is the basis or locus of the duality of grasped and grasper. In the words of the ZP, trainees in these houses are following this Yogācāra program, for "relying on the spoken teachings of the Zen masters, they turn away from *visayas*, discern mind [only], and extinguish *abhūtaparikalpa*."[26]

ZP's Śūnyatā Zen: Niu-t'ou's Having-Nothing-To-Do Zen

The ZP classifies two Zen houses as Śūnyatā Zen, the Shih-t'ou and the Niu-t'ou, but Tsung-mi seems to have known virtually nothing of the former. Nowhere in his three Zen writings does he give any information on its genealogical background or its teachings and praxis, simply classifying Shih-t'ou in the ZP as part of the *śūnyatā* thesis of Zen. These two houses go beyond the houses of Cittamātra Zen in the same way that the second teaching supercedes the first: Whereas the first teaching denies *visayas*, the second denies both *visayas* and *vijñāna*. Cittamātra Zen negates *visayas*, and these two houses of Śūnyatā Zen, Niu-t'ou and Shih-t'ou, negate both *visayas* and *vijñāna*. Their idea is identical to the *Prajñāpāramitā-sūtras* and the *śāstras* of Nāgārjuna and Āryadeva. The *Subcommentary* says of Niu-t'ou:

"From the outset nothing to do and forgetting feelings" is the fifth house. It is an offshoot from the fourth patriarch [Tao-hsin]. Its beginning is the Great Master Niu-t'ou Hui-yung. He was a fellow student of the fifth patriarch, the Great Master [Hung-]jen. Just after the fourth patriarch entrusted the succession to the Great Master [Hung-jen], he and [Hui-]yung met. [Hui-]yung's nature of comprehension was lofty and simple, his spirit *prajñā* marvelous and sharp. He was long skilled at the *prajñā*-and-*śūnyatā* thesis. He was already without calculation or grasping toward dharmas. Later he encountered the fourth patriarch. Because he dwelt in the substance of *śūn*-

yatā and no-*lakṣaṇas* [and yet] openly produced the absolute original awakening of the marvelous mind, his awakening was clear without the need of lengthy training. The fourth patriarch told him: "This Dharma from ancient times has been entrusted to only one person at each generation. I already have a successor [i.e., Hung-jen]. You may set yourself up [separately]." Subsequently at Mount Niu-t'ou he stopped conditions, forgot thoughts, and practiced the principle of no-*lakṣaṇas*. He served as first patriarch [of Niu-t'ou]. Chih-yen was the second, Hui-fang the third, Fa-ch'ih the fourth, Chih-wei the fifth, and Hui-chung the sixth. Chih-wei's disciple was Preceptor Ma-su of Ho-lin Monastery in Jun-chou. [Ma-]su's disciple Preceptor Tao-ch'in of Mt. Ching inherited. They transmitted the purport of this lineage. "From the outset nothing to do" is the principle they awak-ened to. This means that mind and *visayas* from the outset are *śūnya*; and that quiescence is not something that has just commenced. Be-cause one is deluded about this and holds that things exist, one pro-duces such feelings as hatred, love, etc. When feelings are engen-dered, then one is bound by various sufferings. These are created in a dream, perceived in a dream, and so [Niu-t'ou] comprehends from the outset that there is nothing to do. Then they must lose self and forget feelings. Because forgetting feelings is crossing over suffer-ing, [Niu-t'ou] takes "forgetting feelings" as its practice.[27]

There is a Tun-huang text that may afford us some independent confir-mation of this report on Niu-t'ou teachings—the *Treatise on Cutting off Ex-amining (Chueh-kuan lun)*.[28] This treatise has long been attributed to Niu-t'ou Hui-yung because material from it is quoted under Niu-t'ou's name in two tenth-century Zen texts, the *Record of the Patriarchal Hall (Tsu-t'ang chi)* and the *Record of the [Ten-thousand Dharmas] Mirror of the [One-Mind] Thesis (Tsung-ching lu)*.[29] Whether or not we accept this attribution is not crucial, for the important point is that Tsung-mi's assessment of Niu-t'ou emphasizes Mād-hyamaka, and the *Treatise on Cutting off Examining*, an authentic early Zen treatise, represents a Mādhyamaka trend in early Zen. Perhaps Niu-t'ou is not the author of the *Treatise on Cutting off Examining*, but it is a reasonable guess that someone within what Tsung-mi considered Śūnyatā Zen was. On the other hand, the traditional attribution is not weakened by the fact that the treatise discusses "having nothing to do,"[30] which the above report considers to be the essential idea of the Niu-t'ou house.

ZP's Dharmatā Zen No. 1: Hung-chou's Naturalism Zen

The *ZP* classifies two Zen houses, the Hung-chou (i.e., Kiangsi) and the Ho-tse, to which Tsung-mi belonged, within the third thesis of Zen, Dharmatā

Zen. Hung-chou teaches that all actions without exception are the functioning of the Buddha nature, that is, *dharmatā*. In short, everything one experiences or comes into contact with is the real, it being impossible to step outside the real. Thus Hung-chou eschews all picking and choosing—whatever you touch is the path. The *Subcommentary* says of Hung-chou:

> "Whatever you touch is the path and leave it to mind" is the fourth house. Its beginning is an offshoot from the sixth patriarch [Hui-neng]. This means that Preceptor [Hui-]jang of Avalokitesvara Terrace in Nan-yueh was a disciple of the sixth patriarch. Never opening a Dharma, he just dwelled in the mountains practicing the path. In this connection there was a *śramana* from Chien-nan [i.e., Szechwan] Tao-i. His lay family name was Ma. He had been a disciple of Preceptor Kim [of the Ching-chung house in Szechwan]. He was lofty in the extreme path. Wherever he was, he did *zazen*. He dwelled for a long time on Mount Ming-yueh in Chien-nan. Later, when he was on a pilgrimage to [sites of] the traces of *āryas*, he arrived at Preceptor [Hui-]jang's place. They had a dialogue concerning the logic of the thesis and contended about the extreme principle. [Tao-i's] principle did not measure up to that of [Hui-]jang. [Tao-i] also realized that Ts'ao-ch'i [Hui-neng] was the legitimate successor who had received the robe and Dharma. He immediately relied on this to practice. He went to Kan-chou, Hung-chou, and Hu-chou. In both the mountains and towns he widely practiced worship and guided followers of the path. He greatly spread this Dharma. An arising of mind, a movement of thought, a snapping of the fingers, a tinkling of musical chimes, a spreading of a fan, all action and all doing are the totalistic functioning of the Buddha-nature. There is no second controller. By analogy, one prepares many types of drinks and foods out of flour, but every one of them [continues to be] flour. The Buddha-nature is also that way. Passion, hatred, stupidity, the creation of good and bad [karma], the receiving of suffering and joy— in their totality every one of them is the [Buddha-nature]. If one uses this [Hung-chou] idea to examine [this physical body, it becomes apparent that] the four elements, bones, flesh, tongue, teeth, eyes, ears, hands, and feet cannot by themselves speak, see, hear, move, or act. By analogy, at the moment of death, before any decomposition of the whole body, the mouth cannot speak, the eyes cannot see, the ears cannot hear, the feet cannot walk, and the hands cannot perform. Therefore, we know that speech and action must be the Buddha-nature. If we examine the four elements and the bones and flesh carefully one by one, [it becomes apparent that] not a one

of them understands passion and hatred. Therefore, the depravities, passion and hatred, are the Buddha-nature. The Buddha-nature is not [in a substantialist sense] all differentiated things, and yet it has the potential to create all differentiated things. The [Hung-chou] idea accords with the *Laṅkāvatāra-sūtra* when it says: "The *tathāgatagar-bha* is the cause of good and non-good. It has the potential to create all beings in the rebirth paths, receive suffering and joy, to be the cause of everything."[31] Furthermore, [the chapter entitled] "The Mind behind the Words of the Buddhas" [of that sutra] says: "A Buddha land, a raising of the eyebrows, a movement of the pupils of the eyes, a laugh, a tinkling of chimes, a bit of agitation, etc., are all Buddha events."[32] Therefore, [the Hung-chou idea] is "whatever you touch is the path." "Leave it to mind" refers to their practice gate of stopping karma and nourishing the spirit (sometimes it is "stopping spirit and nourishing the path"). This means that one should not rouse the mind to cut off bad or practice good. One does not even cultivate the path. The path is mind. One should not use mind to cultivate [the path in] mind. Bad is mind. One should not use mind to cut off [the bad in] mind. When you neither cut off nor create and leave it to luck and are spontaneous, then you are to be called a liberated person. You are also to be called a person who surpasses the measure. There are no dharmas to be bound up in, no buddhas to become. Why? Outside the *cittadharmatā* there is not one dharma to be apprehended. Therefore, I have said that "just leaving it to mind" is their practice.[33]

Confirmation of what Tsung-mi says about Hung-chou can be found in two Hung-chou works, the *Essentials of the Dharma of Mind Transmission* (*Ch'uan-hsing fa yao*) and *Wan-ling Record* (*Wan-ling lu*), both by P'ei Hsiu. In 842, within a year of Tsung-mi's death, P'ei was stationed in the south and made contact with the eminent Hung-chou master Huang-po Hsi-yun, and in 848 P'ei had a second encounter with Hsi-yun. P'ei's notes on Hsi-yun's talks on these two occasions, with considerable editorial help from Hsi-yun's monks on Mount Huang-po, resulted in the two works listed above. They show some of the same themes as this *Subcommentary* encapsulation of Hung-chou: "Do not take mind to pursue mind," "*as it is* everything is right," "leave it to luck and ascend energetically," "the *cittadharmatā* is without difference," and so forth.[34] Further evidence of P'ei's interest in Hung-chou is shown in *P'ei's Inquiry* when Tsung-mi mounts a sustained critique of the Hung-chou position, and P'ei rises to its defense.[35]

ZP's Dharmatā Zen No. 2: Ho-tse's *Jñāna* Zen

Ho-tse's distinctive idea is *jñāna*, the complete and constant *jñāna* of the third teaching. The third teaching openly shows that this *jñāna* is the true nature, no different from buddhahood.[36] According to the *ZP*, Bodhidharma did not transmit the word *jñāna*, even though it was the basis of his teaching.[37] He simply waited for beings to awaken on their own, and thus his teaching was a silent transmission. Silence here means only that he was silent about the word *jñāna*, not that he eshewed all speech. This pattern was followed for six generations, until the seventh patriarch Shen-hui. Shen-hui desired to propagate such a silent bond, but encountered inopportune conditions and so spoke the line "the one word *jñāna* is the gate of all wonders." This open transmission was easily comprehensible. The *Subcommentary* says of Ho-tse:

> "The *jñāna* of calmness points to the substance, and no thought is
> the thesis" is the seventh house. It was transmitted by the Great
> Master Ho-tse [Shen-hui], the seventh patriarch of the Southern
> lineage. It says that since the ten thousand dharmas are *śūnya*, the
> mind substance from the outset is calmed. Calmness is the *dhar-
> makāya*. Calmness—that is *jñāna*. *Jñāna* is true knowing. It is also
> called *bodhi* or *nirvāṇa*. . . . This is the pure mind that is the original
> source of all sentient beings. It is Dharma that has spontaneously
> existed from the outset. As to "no thought is the thesis," having
> awakening [to the realization that] this Dharma from the outset is
> calmness and *jñāna*, by principle one must praise exerting mind
> from the outset. One should not subsequently rouse false thoughts.
> "Just having no false thoughts" *is* practice.[38]

Once again we can locate confirmation of the *Subcommentary*'s descriptive analysis in a work produced within the Zen house in question. Here it is the *Platform Talks* (*T'an-yu*), a Shen-hui work discovered among the Tun-huang manuscripts. In the *Platform Talks* we find such statements as: "From the substance of *śūnyatā* and calmness there arises *jñāna*," "no thought is the thesis," and so on.[39]

The theoretical framework of the *ZP* emphasizes what the Hung-chou and Ho-tse houses have in common—they both bring *lakṣaṇas* back to *dharmata* and thus are of a single thesis.[40] They are identical to the third teaching, the teaching that shows that the true mind is *dharmatā*. These two Zen houses do not reveal *dharmatā* in terms of *lakṣaṇas* (as in the case of Ching-chung, Northern, South Mountain Nembutsu Gate, and Pao-t'ang) houses; nor do they reveal *dharmatā* by negating *lakṣaṇas* (as in the case of Niu-t'ou and Shih-t'ou). With no cryptic intention, both Hung-chou and Ho-tse openly reveal *dharmatā*. In contrast, the first two teachings and hence the previous six Zen houses are all of the cryptic type. In other words, Hung-chou and Ho-tse are *nitartha* forms of Zen—they are of clear, explicit, definite, well-established meaning that can be taken as it stands. One does not have to infer their intention. The other six Zen houses are *neyartha* Zen, Zen in which a meaning is not clearly established and has to be determined.

P'ei's Inquiry, in contrast to the *ZP*, emphasizes what separates the Ho-tse from the Hung-chou, that is, how the Ho-tse teaching is superior to that of the Hung-chou. This is nicely illustrated by a *maṇi* (jewel) simile.[41] When a black object is placed before the *maṇi* it reflects the blackness. The limitation of Hung-chou lies in its saying that the blackness *is* the bright *maṇi*, the substance of which is never seen—Hung-chou fails to recognize the bright *maṇi* with no colors in front of it. Ho-tse, of course, knows that the bright *maṇi* is simply the potential for manifesting all the colors of the rainbow.

The *ZP*'s *Fu* (Tally) of the Sequential Processes of Delusion (the Unreal) and Awakening (the Real)

In the *ZP*, the relationship between delusion and awakening is one of neither identity nor difference and is expressed in the concept of the *ālayavijñāna*. Each of the two opposing sequences has ten levels:

> I will next explain the [step-by-step] practice and realization [awaken-
> ing] that come after [all-at-once understanding] awakening. It too
> has ten levels. Overturn the unreal and it is the real, because they
> are not separate dharmas. However, the principles of delusion and
> awakening are separate, the flow and counterflow sequences differ-
> ent. The former is to be deluded about the real and pursue the un-
> real. It arises in sequence from the fine and subtle [characteristics of
> root *avidyā*], revolving toward the coarse [characteristics of branch
> *avidyā*]. This [awakening sequence] is to awaken to the unreal and
> return to the real. Proceeding from the coarse and heavy, in the op-
> posite sequence it cuts off [each successive level of delusion], revolv-
> ing toward the subtle. The *prajñā* necessary to overturn [each suc-
> cessive level of delusion] proceeds from shallow to deep. The coarse
> hindrances are easily eliminated because shallow *prajñā* can over-
> turn them. The subtle depravities are more difficult to get rid of, be-
> cause only deep *prajñā* can sever them. Therefore, these ten [levels
> of awakening] begin at the end [of the delusion sequence] and work
> backward, overturning and annulling the former ten. It is just that
> there is a small discrepancy involving the first level of this [awaken-
> ing sequence] and the first two levels of the former [delusion se-
> quence]. Later I will show this.[42]

The ten levels of the delusion sequence (with a dream simile beneath each level) are:

1. All sentient beings possess the true mind of original awakening. (Wealthy nobleman, endowed with both virtue and wisdom, is inside his own house.)
2. Having not yet met a good friend as a guide, inevitably from the outset there is nonawakening. (He falls asleep in his own house and forgets who he is.)
3. As a natural consequence of nonawakening, thoughts arise. (The dream that arises as a natural consequence of sleep.)
4. Because thoughts have arisen, there is a seer *lakṣaṇa*. (Thoughts in a dream.)
5. Because there is a seeing, an organ body and world falsely manifest themselves. (In his dream he sees himself in another place in a condition of poverty and suffering, and he sees all sorts of likable and dislikable phenomenal *viṣayas*.)
6. Unaware that the organ body and world have arisen from one's own thoughts, one grasps them as real existents—this is called Dharma grasping. (While in the dream he inevitably grasps the things he sees in the dream as real things.)
7. Because one has grasped dharmas as really existent, just at that very moment one sees a distinction between self and others—this is called self-grasping. (While dreaming, he inevitably believes that the person who is in another place in a condition of poverty and suffering is his own person.)
8. Because one clings to the notion that the four elements of earth, water, fire, and air constitute a self-body, naturally one comes to love *viṣayas* that accord with one's feelings, wanting to adorn the self, while one comes to despise those *viṣayas* that are contrary to one's feelings, fearing that they will vex the self. Feelings of stupidity make all sorts of calculations and comparisons. (In his dream he also desires agreeable events in the other place and hates disagreeable events.)
9. From these come the creation of good and bad karma. (In his dream he either steals and murders or practices kindness and spreads virtue.)
10. Once karma comes into existence, it is impossible to escape. It is like a shadow trailing a form or an echo trailing a voice. And so one receives a form of karma bondage suffering in the six rebirth paths. (If in his dream he steals and murders, then he is apprehended, put into a wooden collar, and sent to prison. On the

other hand, if he practices kindness and obtains rewards, he is recommended for office and takes his position.)[43]

The ten levels of the awakening sequence are:

1. The good friend shows a sentient being the true mind of original awakening.
2. The sentient being produces *karuṇā*, *prajñā*, and the vow, resolving to realize *bodhi*.
3. He practices the gates of giving, morality, forbearance, striving, and calming-discerning.
4. The great thought of *bodhi* arises.
5. He realizes that in the Dharma-nature there is no thought of stinginess, passion, hatred, lethargy, distraction, and stupidity.
6. Flowing along, he practices the six *pāramitās*. By the power of *sāmadhi* and *prajñā*, self and dharmas are both done away with.
7. There is master over forms, and everything is in fusion.
8. There is mastery over mind, and everything is illuminated.
9. Full of *upāyas*, in a moment one is in conjunction. Mind is eternally abiding, awakened to the origin of delusion.
10. The mind having no thought, there is no separate initial awakening. From the outset it is sameness, a single awakening, and so it is mysteriously in the basic, true, pure mind source.[44]

The relationship between these two sequences is likely to confuse the reader to some degree, and Tsung-mi was aware of this danger. The *ZP* tries to ensure that the schema is clear:

The first level of this [awakening sequence] corresponds to the first and second levels of the former [sequence of delusion], while the tenth level of this corresponds to the first level of the former. Of the remaining eight levels [of the awakening sequence], each in reverse order [successively] overturns and annuls the eight levels of the former [running from level ten down to level three]. In the first level, one awakens to the original awakening of the first level of the former, overturning the nonawakening of the second level of the former. Previously, nonawakening perverted original awakening, real and unreal contradicted each other, and so they opened into two levels. Now, having awakened, they mysteriously tally. Mysteriously tallying, they are in accord with one another, and because there is no separate initial awakening, they combine into one. Also, if we were to adhere [strictly] to the flow and counterflow sequences, the first level of this would correspond to and overturn the tenth level of the former. At present within the gate of all-at-once awakening, by principle one must directly recognize the original substance, overturning the original delusion of the former, and so [the first level of awakening] corresponds to levels one and two of the former. (This is the discrepancy I mentioned earlier.) In the second level, because of fear of suffering in *saṃsara* one produces the three minds to cross oneself and others over. Therefore, it corresponds to the tenth level of the former, *saṃsara* of the six rebirth paths. The third level, cultivation of the five practices, overturns the ninth level of the former, creation of karma. In the fourth level the three minds open up, overturning the eighth level of the former, the three poisons. (The mind of *karuṇā* overturns hatred; the mind of *prajñā* overturns stupidity; and the mind of the vow overturns passion.) The fifth level, realization that self is *śūnya*, overturns the seventh level of the former, selfgrasping. The sixth level, realization that dharmas are *śūnya*, overturns the sixth level of the former, Dharma-grasping. The seventh level, mastery over forms, overturns the fifth level of the former, *viṣayas*. The eighth level, mastery over mind, overturns the fourth level of the former, a seer. The ninth level, divorcing from thoughts, overturns the third level of the former, the arising of thoughts. Therefore, at the tenth level, becoming a buddha, a buddha is not a separate substance. It is just initial awakening, overturning the second level of the former, nonawakening, and combining with the first level of the former, original awakening. Initial and original are nondual. They are just manifestations of *tathatā* and are called *dharmakāya* and great awakening. Therefore, [level ten, becoming a buddha,] and initial awakening are not two substances. The discrepancy between the flow and counterflow sequences is right here. At level one causes include the sea of effects; at level ten effects penetrate to the source of causes.[45]

The "all-at-once awakening" of level one of the awakening sequence refers to *understanding* awakening, which is an intellectual understanding of the teaching of original awakening (i.e., the true mind), pointed out by the good friend or teacher; the "becoming a buddha" of level ten refers to *realization* awakening, *bodhi*. So we have the sequence of all-at-once *understanding* awakening, followed by step-by-step practice, followed by all-at-once *realization* awakening. All-at-once *understanding* awakening is equivalent to awakening to original awakening and overturning nonawakening. Having attained all-at-once *understanding* awakening, nonawakening (which refers to level two of the delusion sequence as well as to the delusion sequence as a whole) and original awakening form a *fu*. Also, all-at-once *realization* awakening (level ten of the awakening sequence) overturns nonawakening and combines with original awakening. The seeming contradiction between all-at-once awakening and

step-by-step practice collapses here. As in the case of the *fu* between the canonical teachings and Zen, this *fu* between all-at-once and step-by-step is a
charm or amulet. It functions to ward off the objections of both subitist and
gradualist partisans, who felt, for different reasons, that all-at-once awakening
and step-by-step practice were contradictory and incompatible. In the *ZP*
Tsung-mi shows their utter complementariness.

The Literary Style of the *ZP*

The *ZP* is not in what might be called native Buddhist Chinese, that is, the
language of native works on technical Buddhist subjects. ("Buddhist Chinese"
here is perfectly analogous to "Buddhist Tibetan.") Such native works are classified in the Taishō canon under *shoshu-bu*, the section of writings of the various
lineages—San-lun, Hua-yen, T'ien-t'ai, and so forth. With the exception of the
writings of the Zen lineage, they take the Chinese translations of Indic Buddhist texts as their prototype in vocabulary and style. Tsung-mi did write technical works in such Buddhist Chinese, numerous commentaries and subcommentaries on sutras and *śāstras*. But a few works that are oriented to a
sophisticated lay audience rather than monastic scholiasts—the *ZP*, *P'ei's Inquiry*, and *On the Origin of Man* (*Yuan-jen lun*)[46]—are in "secular" literary Chinese, even as they utilize considerable technical Buddhist vocabulary and quotations from sutras and *śāstras*.

In literary style, the elegance of the *ZP* towers over other works of early
Zen literature. I would even go so far as to say that the *ZP* ranks alongside
examples of the literature of antiquity (*ku-wen*) of Tsung-mi's contemporary
Han Yu.[47] In this regard, it is noteworthy that Tsung-mi's essay *On the Origin
of Man* derives its title from one of Han Yu's essays and serves as a Buddhist
answer to Han Yu's Confucian position. In the early 830s, when Tsung-mi was
composing his *ZP* and *P'ei's Inquiry*, he clearly felt that to reach a literati
audience he had to present Zen in an elegant prose style.

The *ZP*'s style is a sort of Buddhist *ku-wen*. In the following example, a
literal word-for-word rendering is followed by analysis and translation; the
numbers at the end of lines give the total number of graphs for that line:

Teachings 3
All Buddhas enlightenment beings left behind sutras *śāstras* 9
Zen 3
All good knowledge ones composed lines gathas 9
But Buddha sutras open outward 5
Catching great thousands eight classes of beings 7
Zen gathas pinch up abridgment 4
Oriented to this land one type of ability 7

Catching beings broad vast difficult rely upon 7
Orienting to ability points bull's-eye easy use 7
Present's compiling collection intention lies here 8[48]

If we drop the extraneous conjunction "but" (*tan*) in the fifth line and represent full words (*shih-tzu*), that is lexical words, by "x" and empty words (*hsu-tzu*),[49] that is, grammatical words that indicate the relationships of lexical words, by "o," the alternating pattern of ABABCDCDEFEF emerges:

xoo
xxxxoxxxo
xoo
xxxxoxxxo
xxxx
xxxxxox
xxxx
xxxxxox
xxoxxxx
xxoxxxx
xoxxxxxo

The teachings are the sutras and *śāstras* left behind by the buddhas
and bodhisattvas. Zen is the poetic lines and gathas composed by
the various good friends. The Buddha sutras open outward, catching
the thousands of beings of the eight classes, while Zen gathas pinch
up an abridgment, being oriented to one type of ability found in this
land [of China]. [The teachings,] which catch [the thousands of] beings [of the eight classes], are broad and vast and hence difficult to
rely upon. [Zen], which is oriented to [Chinese] abilities, points to
the bull's-eye and is easy to use. Herein lies my intention in making
the present collection.

This passage does not exhibit the almost mechanical nature of much native Buddhist Chinese, its lack of rhythm, opaqueness, and what seems to those steeped in Chinese literature and without exposure to Buddhist materials to be generally artless and to have an alien aroma. An example would be an exegetical passage from a typical T'ien-t'ai or Hua-yen treatise. The widely varying rhythms and liberal use of empty words seen here are characteristics of *ku-wen*.[50] The origin of Tsung-mi's flowing style is probably to be found in his early training at home and at the Righteousness Learning Academy.

Editions of the *ZP*: The Wan-li 4 (1576) Korean Edition

Students of the *ZP* in modern times have based their work on two editions, a 1576 Korean edition, known as the Wan-li 4; and the Ming Canon edition

(1601), as found in the Taishō Canon and its supplement *Zoku zōkyō*, both published in Japan in the early twentieth century.[51] The Wan-li 4 is divided into two fascicles, the Ming Canon edition into four. The differences between the two editions are found primarily in the chart; the most obvious to the eye is the Ming Canon edition's utilization of white and black circles to diagram headings.[52] The Wan-li 4 chart has no circles, and Tsung-mi's original chart probably did not use them either.

The Wan-li 4 has two colophons, the first originally added at the time of the Sung printing and undated. Given that the Wan-li 4 reproduces the Sung edition colophon, it clearly transmits the original form of the Sung edition—in fact, it is certain that it is a reprint of the Sung edition.[53] A specialist in old Korean books has argued that the Wan-li 4 "should be evaluated quite highly in bibliographical terms."[54] Japanese and Western scholarship on the ZP have subsequently preferred to work from that Korean edition. From the Sung colophon we can trace the ZP down to the mid-tenth century:

> In Ta-chung 11 *ting-ch'ou* year of the T'ang [857] Minister P'ei personally copied out a manuscript. He handed it over to Lao-su of T'ai-i yen-ch'ang Monastery on Mount Wu-tang in Chin-chou [in Shensi]. [Lao-su] kept it in his possession for fifty years. In the *jen-shen* [year] of the Great Liang [912] Lao-su transmitted it to Zen Master Wei-ching, who took it back to Hunan. And then twenty-three years later in the *chia-wu* [year; 934] the Zen Master transmitted it to Ch'i-hsuan, who took it back to Min [i.e., Fukien]. And then after twenty-two years in the *chia-yin* and *i-mao* [years; 954–955] in possession of it he entered Wu-yueh [i.e., Kiangsu and Chekiang]. [There he had] copies made and disseminated them.
>
> Recorded by the Fu-chou Sramana Ch'i-hsuan Yen K'ai, the son of Yen Ming of Ch'ien-t'ang [i.e., Hangchow in Chekiang] of the Great Sung took charge of the carving [of the blocks] and printing.[55]

This is quite a pedigree. P'ei Hsiu had a reputation as an extraordinarily gifted calligrapher. His biographical entry in the *Old T'ang History* (*Chiu T'ang-shu*) describes him as "perfected in the art of the brush."[56] The year he copied out the ZP is the same year he wrote the preface to his twofold Zen classic *Essentials of Mind Transmission* and *Wan-ling Record*, sixteen years after Tsung-mi's death.[57] A copy of the ZP in his hand would have been not only a valuable Buddhist text but an artistic treasure, as well. Just over a century later this copy wound up in the hands of the layman Yen K'ai in Hangchow, and he arranged for a printing. Hangchow was the epicenter of Zen. Many Zen monasteries were clustered in its environs. Surely copies of Yen K'ai's printed ZP ended up in the libraries of some of the local Zen establishments and eventually made their way to Korea and Japan.

The second colophon, the Korean colophon, closes with a line to the effect that "the printing was carried out at the Kwanum Monastery on Mount Songi [in Ch'ung ch'ong-do] in the summer of Wan-li 4 [1576]."[58] The slightly earlier Hung-chih 6 (1493) Korean edition, a reproduction of which has been published,[59] has the same Sung colophon by Ch'i-hsuan and shows other similarities to the Wan-li 4. These points of similarity set the Wan-li 4 and the Hung-chih 6 apart from other Korean editions and suggest they are very close in the stemma.[60] The following comment by the bibliographer of old Korean books provides us with perspective on the position of the *ZP* in the history of Buddhist books in Korea: "Over time in Korea the *ZP* was one of the Buddhist books with the highest number of printings at monasteries in the various regions."[61]

Editions of the *ZP*: The Ming Canon Edition

The Ta-te edition published by Zen Master Hsueh-t'ang P'u-jen, which dates to Ta-te 7 of the Yuan Dynasty (1303), is the basis of the Ming Canon edition. In addition to the P'ei Hsiu preface, three other prefaces, by Wu-wai Wei-ta, Teng Wen-yuan, and Chia Ju-chou, were appended to the Ta-te edition, appearing also in the Ming Canon edition as found in the Taishō canon. Teng Wen-yuan's preface states:

> In the Ta-chung era of the T'ang [847–860] the Chief Minister P'ei Hsiu did a preface for it and personally copied out the *Chart*. He handed them over to Yen-ch'ang Monastery in Chin-chou. Afterward they were transmitted to Master Wei-ching. Once again they were transmitted to Master Hsuan-ch'i [i.e., Ch'i-hsuan], and the *Chart* circulated in Min, Hsiang, and Wu-yueh [i.e., Fukien, Hunan, Kiangsu, and Chekiang]. In Chih-yuan 12 [1275] at the court of the nation Shih-tsu [i.e., Kublai] in the Kuang-han Hall wished to inquire about the essential meaning of the teachings of Zen. The Imperial Teacher and various venerable worthies took the *Expressions of the Zen Source* [i.e., the *ZP*] as their reply. The emperor was pleased and ordered a wood-block printing for the world. Twenty-nine years later in the Ta-te era *kuei-mao* year [1303], the Zen Master Hsueh-t'ang [P'u-]jen, successor in Dharma, received an imperial decree to go to Mount Wu-t'ai and on the return journey passed through Ta-t'ung. He obtained the *Chart* copied by Zen Master Ch'ien-an Chueh-kung of the Chin period and did a collation.[62]

Zen Master Hsueh-t'ang P'u-jen's lay friend Teng Wen-yuan had the *ZP* printed. Though it is not entirely clear what Teng means here by *Chart*, it seems to refer to one or more of a number of charts drawn up by Tsung-mi. The preface by Chia Ju-chou lists a Ch'ing-ning edition dating to Ch'ing-ning 8 (1062) of the liao dynasty.[63] The relationship of this edition to the Sung edition is unclear.

In addition, in the National Center Library in Taipei, Taiwan, there is a *ZP* fragment on a Tun-huang manuscript that at the end gives a date of Kuang-shun 2 of the Later Chou during the Five Dynasties period (952).[64] It contains the chart as well as some text. Interestingly, this chart is in general quite similar to the one in the Wan-li 4 Korean edition—for instance, no circles. As for Japanese editions, we have the Embun edition, a Gozan printing of 1358; an undated Tahara edition; and the Genroku edition of 1698.[65] Perhaps the most mysterious of all *ZP*s is to be found in St. Petersburg, Russia. It is a printed book, a translation of the *ZP* into the Hsi-hsia or Tangut language with its puzzling orthography, which looks like a caricature of Chinese script.[66] The Tanguts translated their Buddhist books from both Chinese and Tibetan, and Tsung-mi works seems to have been quite influential. There are also Tangut renderings of a digest of the *ZP*, two commentaries on the *ZP*, and *P'ei's Inquiry*.[67]

The *ZP* and the Third Patriarch of the Fa-yen House of Zen

After the T'ang Dynasty, the *ZP* exercised its greatest influence within the Fa-yen house of Zen, one of the five houses of the Five Dynasties and Sung periods, via the third patriarch of Fa-yen, Yung-ming Yen-shou (903/4–976). One has only to read the preface and opening lines of the first fascicle of his compendium in one hundred fascicles entitled the *Record of the Mirror of the Thesis* to sense that one is walking in the garden of Tsung-mi's *ZP*. Yen-shou commences the *Record of the Mirror of the Thesis* with a sketch of its tripartite structure:

> The patriarchs make known the principles of Zen, transmitting the true thesis of silent alignment. The Buddhas extend the gate of the teachings, setting up the great purport of the canonical explanations. What the former worthies have stated later [Zen] students take refuge in. Therefore, I will first lay out the section that makes known the [One-Mind] thesis [i.e., the first half of the first fascicle]. . . . Next I will set up the question-and-answer section [i.e., from midpoint of the first fascicle through the ninety-third fascicle]. Lastly I will arrange the quotation-and-authentication section [i.e., seven fascicles, 94–100].[68]

The opening line is clearly a paraphrase of the *ZP*.[69] The tripartite structure and overall size of the *Record of the Mirror of the Thesis* sounds very much like what we know of the structure and size of the Zen canon. Tsung-mi in the *ZP* tells us that the *Zen Canon* consists of Bodhidharma's one thesis (i.e., the One-Mind thesis); writings of the various Zen houses, many in question-and-answer format; and ten-plus fascicles of *sutra* and *śāstra* passages sealing the three Zen theses.[70] The *Zen Canon* is usually described as one hundred or so fascicles in length. All this suggests strongly that Yen-shou's compendium is related somehow to the *Zen Canon* and may preserve some of the Zen materials gathered by Tsung-mi.[71]

Yen-shou was at the right place at the right time to encounter a copy of the *ZP*, virtually as soon as it arrived from the North. Yen-shou was a Hangchow native.[72] In the early 930s he took ordination under a student of Hsueh-feng I-tsun, who may well have been a fellow student of the Wei-ching, who handed over the *ZP* to Ch'i-hsuan. The undated Sung colophon to the Wan-li 4 Korean edition relates that in the 930s, a Wei-ching, who may be Nan-yüeh Wei-ching, a disciple of Hsüeh-feng I-tsun (822–908), transmitted the copy in P'ei Hsiu's hand to one Ch'i-hsuan. Ch'i-hsuan, in the 950s, brought it to Wu-yüeh and disseminated it. The layman Yen K'ai, a native of Hangchow, provided for the carving of blocks and a printing, probably at one of the local Zen monasteries. All of the monasteries that Yen-shou was associated with, throughout his career, were in the Hangchow vicinity.

The *Record of the Mirror of the Thesis* was influential in both Koryo Korea and Kamakura Japan. A Koryo king admired it and dispatched monks to study it.[73] It is extensively quoted in the works of the famous Koryo Son (Zen) master Chinul (1158–1210).[74] Dainichi Nonin, founder of the Daruma school of Japanese Zen, used it also. The Dharma school, which spread widely throughout the Nara and Kyoto areas during the late 1100s, constitutes the first Zen school in Japan. Nonin's entry in the *Biographies of the Eminent Monks of Japan* (*Honchō kōsōden*) mentions that, after his Daruma school took off, "Shōkō of Chinzei visited Nonin's assembly and studied the essentials of the *Record of the Mirror of the Thesis* with him."[75] In fact, it is possible that Nōnin got the inspiration for his radical approach to Zen from his immersion in the *Record of the Mirror of the Thesis*. Perhaps his Zen stance derives from quotations from authentic early Zen texts that are buried in the last section of the *Record of the Mirror of the Thesis*.[76]

The *ZP* and *P'ei's Inquiry* in Korean Son

Son's absorption of the other traditions of Korean Buddhism was complete after the fifteenth century.[77] This fusion of the teachings and Son coincides with Tsung-mi's orientation. No more explicit evidence of Tsung-mi's influence in Korea is to be found than a seminary curriculum of the modern Chogye school as described by an American scholar.⁷⁸ That curriculum, which goes back to the Son master Hwan-song Chian (1664–1729), is divided into a recitation track and a textual-study track. The former is subdivided into a novice course, consisting of the study of monastic etiquette and edifying tracts, and a more rigorous fourfold collection course (*sajipkwa*).

The four collections consist of the *Letters of Ta-hui* (*Ta-hui shu*), the *Essentials of Zen* (*Ch'an-yao*) of Kao-feng Yuan-miao, Tsung-mi's *ZP*, and Chinul's *Excerpts from the Separately Circulated Record of the Dharma Collection with the Insertion of Personal Notes* (*Popchip pyorhaeng nok choryo pyongip sagi*).⁷⁹ The last work, Chinul's magnum opus, consists of most of Tsung-mi's *P'ei's Inquiry*, here called the *Separately Circulated Record of the Dharma Collection*, cut up, rearranged, and supplied with extensive comments by Chinul. Thus, the theoretical half of this fourfold course involves study of the *ZP* and *P'ei's Inquiry*. Even the three courses of the textual-study track include a number of canonical works closely associated with Tsung-mi: *Awakening of Faith*, *Perfect Enlightenment Sutra*, *Avataṁsaka-sūtra*; and a commentary on *Avataṁsaka* by Ch'eng-kuan, Tsung-mi's Hua-yen teacher.

Quotations from the *ZP* are sprinkled throughout Chinul's works.⁸⁰ He was literally steeped in the *Platform Sutra of the Sixth Patriarch*, *Avataṁsaka-sūtra*, Li T'ung-hsuan's commentary entitled *Treatise on the New Avataṁsaka-sūtra* (*Hsin hua-yen ching lun*); *Recorded Sayings of Ta-hui* (*Ta-hui yü-lu*), and Tsung-mi's *ZP* and *P'ei's Inquiry*. Even a detractor of Chinul and champion of the gazing-at-the-topic (*kanhwa*) purist T'aego Pou (1301–1382), such as the late Son master Songch'ol of Haein Monastery, who tried to eliminate Chinul's influence from the Chogye school,⁸¹ resorted to Tsung-mi categories in the process. Songch'ol strongly criticized Chinul's, that is, Tsung-mi's, favored position of all-at-once awakening and step-by-step practice (*tono chomsu*), claiming that the only correct position is all-at-once awakening and all-at-once practice (*tono tonsu*). Both positions are presented as viable options in the *ZP*, which says of the latter: "In terms of cutting off hindrances, this is like cutting a piece of silk; a myriad of silk threads are all-at-once severed. In terms of cultivating virtue, this is like dyeing a piece of silk; a myriad of silk threads all-at-once take on the color."⁸² The *ZP* associates this position with the Niu-t'ou lineage.

It would be hard to dissent from the following comment on the role of the *ZP* in Korea, by the Japanese scholar Kamata Shigeo: "[The *ZP*] is one of the most highly regarded books in Korean Buddhism."⁸³ It is not a coincidence that the only commentaries extant on the *ZP*, with the exception of the two Tangut translations of commentaries mentioned earlier, are Korean.⁸⁴ Unfortunately, Korean Son, with its roots deep in the soil of Tsung-mi's *ZP* and *P'ei's Inquiry*, has not received much attention in Western scholarship until fairly recent decades.

The *ZP* and *P'ei's Inquiry* in Japanese Kegon

Two articles in the possession of the author—a book and a transparency of a painting—reflect a major aspect of the role of the *ZP* and *P'ei's Inquiry* in Japan. The book is a copy of the *ZP*, apparently executed with an ordinary pen in some sort of mimeograph process; it was published in Showa 30 (1955).[85] This *ZP* was clearly intended for study purposes, with each page providing room for notes at the top; the copy has many such notes. The transparency is a portrait of Tsung-mi in color mounted on a brown and black *kakemono* or hanging scroll.[86] Tsung-mi sits in *zazen* posture in a high-back chair that is draped in blue-green silk with a lotus pattern. His shoes are on a low stool before him. He holds a fly whisk in his right hand, the symbol of authority of a Zen master. A cursory perusal of the book and the portrait give one the impression of a Zen book and Zen *chinzō*, a portrait used in Zen for transmission purposes. One feels they are in the presence of traces of T'ang Dynasty Zen in modern Japan.

Zen recedes, however, when one takes a look at the book's colophon and the description of the painting in an exhibition catalogue. Tsung-mi wore two hats: a Zen hat as successor to Tao-yüan in the Ho-tse lineage, and a Hua-yen hat as successor to Ch'eng-küan in the Hua-yen lineage. The colophon to the book states that it was published by the Kangaku-in of Tōdai-ji in Nara, the ancient center of Kegon (Hua-yen) studies, and clearly takes the *ZP* as an expression of "Kegon Zen." In fact, the scholar who copied it out, Takamine Ryōshū, was a Kegon scholar. In parallel the museum catalogue makes it clear that the portrait, which is found in the collection of Kumida-dera, a Shingon temple in the Osaka area, is not a Zen *chinzō*. The catalogue presents this Tsung-mi portrait as the last in a set of four portraits of the Chinese patriarchs of the Kegon lineage: Tu-shun, Fa-tsang, Ch'eng-kuan, and Tsung-mi.[87] The description in the catalogue dates the set to sometime from the period of the Northern and Southern courts to the early Muromachi, that is, from the late fourteenth century into the fifteenth. In medieval times, Kumida-dera was a center of Shingon, Kegon, and Ritsu (Vinaya) studies, and hence a wide variety of Buddhist paintings were transmitted. The catalogue, for instance, also includes a eightfold set of portraits of the Shingon patriarchs.[88]

The roots of Kegonistic Zen, or perhaps more accurately, Zenistic Kegon, lie in the Kamakura period, when Kegon was very old in Japan and Zen was a "new religion." One disciple of the Kegon master Kōben or Myōe shōnin (1173–1232) stands out: Shojō (1194–?). Shojō was the author of the *Outline of the Zen Lineage* (*Zenshū komoku*), which dates to Kenchō 7 (1255), the initial period of the introduction of Sung Zen to Japan.[89] Shojō received the teachings of Ch'eng-küan, Tsung-mi, and Li T'ung-hsüan from Myōe, and experienced the new Zen being disseminated from Sung China. It was rather natural that he came to employ Tsung-mi's Zen writings to advocate the identity of the teachings and Zen from a Kegon standpoint. The *Outline of the Zen Lineage* does not really explicate Zen, but melts Zen into Kegon. Shojō's authorities are Ch'eng-küan and Tsung-mi, particularly Tsung-mi, as opposed to the standard Kegon reliance on Fa-tsang and Ch'eng-küan as found in the writings of someone like Gyōnen (1240–1321). Almost all of quotations in the *Outline of the Zen Lineage* are Ch'eng-küan and Tsung-mi quotations, but, while accepting Tsungmi's identity of the teachings and Zen, as well as Kataku (Ho-tse) Zen, the *Outline of the Zen Lineage* does not accept the former as is. Shojō's work deletes the structure of the three teachings and three Zen theses developed in the *ZP*, and utilizes instead the simpler presentation of *P'ei's Inquiry*. This is precisely because *P'ei's Inquiry* does not utilize that structure. Shojō did not face the same situation as Tsung-mi—there was no need for a classification of Zen in Shojō's time.

Tsung-mi as an Exemplar of the *ZP*'s Themes

As for a final assessment, we can make do with a poem dedicated to Tsungmi by Po Chu-i, one of the greatest of the T'ang poets. Po mixed *zazen* and poetry, once musing that he must have been a poet monk in a past birth.[90] His poem presents the author of the *ZP* as a living embodiment of the themes of the *ZP*, such as the complementariness of the sutras and Zen mind, and the assertion that Zen is not talking about a liberation that has nothing to do with the written word. Po presents Tsung-mi's mouth as a *pitaka* that transmits the sutras; Tsung-mi's mind as a blazing Zen mind-platform that hands down the torch of the Zen patriarchs. Rejection of the sutras and śāstras on the part of Zen partisans is a sort of Hinayānistic floating in the vacuity of outer space, in Buddhist technical terms, the extreme of annihilationism (*ucchedavāda*):

To the Superior Man Ts'ao-t'ang Tsung-mi:

My master's path is bonded with buddhahood,
Moment after moment no concerted action, dharma after dharma
  pure potential,
His mouth *pitaka* transmits the twelvefold canon,
His mind platform shines like a hundred thousand torches,
The middle path does not lie in jettisoning the written word,
Taking up perpetual residence in the nothingness of space is Hinay-
  ānistic,
Few are those aware of the bodhisattva praxis,
In the world he is the only one truly to be esteemed as an eminent
  monk.[91]

NOTES

1. The following are indispensable for the study of the *Zen Prolegomenon* (hereafter cited as *ZP*):

- Kamata Shigeo, ed. and trans., *Zengen shosenshū tōjō*, Zen no goroku 9 (Tokyo: Chikuma shobō, 1971). One of 17 volumes published in the projected 20-volume *Zen no goroku* series, all of which were done by Zen scholars except this one by Kamata, a Kegon scholar. Includes an edition of the Wan-li 4 (1576) Korean edition of the *ZP* with a *kambun kakikudashi* (no modern Japanese translation), a short summary of each section in modern Japanese, and notes. All translation and paraphrase from both the *ZP* and *P'ei's Inquiry* (see note 8) are from this edition, hereafter abbreviated as *K*.
- Ui Hakuju, ed. and trans., *Zengen shosenshū tōjō* ([1939] reprint Tokyo: Iwanami bunko, 1943). Based on the Ming Canon edition ZZ 2, 8; with a *kambun kakikudashi* and notes.
- Urs App, ed., *Concordance to the "Preface" by Zongmi*, Hanazono Concordance Series Vol. 11 (Kyoto: International Research Institute for Zen Buddhism Hanazono University, 1996). Generated by computer from electronic text. Based on T no. 2015 as newly punctuated by Xiaohong Liang. Includes T text (the Ming Canon edition) minus the chart.
- Tanaka Ryōshō, *Tonkō zenshū bunken no kenkyū* (Tokyo: Daito shuppansha, 1983), pp. 424–443. An edition of the Five Dynasties Tun-huang manuscript fragment of the *ZP* (Taipei collection no. 133) dated 952.
- Lin Shih-t'ien, ed., *Tun-huang ch'an-tsung wen-hsien chi-ch'eng* (Beijing: Xinhua shudian, 1998), vol. 1, pp. 479–489. A reproduction of the Tun-huang manuscript fragment.

2. The biographical treatment below, including the division into phases, is based on the excellent biography in Peter N. Gregory, *Tsung-mi and the Sinification of Buddhism* (Princeton: Princeton University Press, 1991), pp. 27–90. Gregory's biography is now the best available in any language.

3. T no. 842. Yanagida Seizan, ed. and trans., *Chūgoku senjutsu kyōten 1 Engaku-kyō*, Bukkyō kyōten-sen 13 (Tokyo: Chikuma shobō, 1987) has text, *kambun kakikudashi*, modern Japanese translation, and notes. This work could be called a "Zen sutra."

4. Gregory, *Tsung-mi*, p. 48. Gregory has solved the vexing problem of Tsung-mi's Ch'an filiation. Some have charged him with fudging his lineage in order to claim descent from Ho-tse Shen-hui.

5. Gregory, *Tsung-mi*, pp. 315–325, lists 31 works by Tsung-mi, though some are listed twice under different titles. The Tun-huang manuscript fragment of the *ZP* (Taipei no. 133) has a list of 25 Tsung-mi works at the end (Lin, *Tun-huang ch'an-tsung wen-hsien chi-ch'eng*, pp. 488–489, and Tanaka, *Tonkō zenshū bunken no kenkyū*, pp. 437–442). Titles of five charts appear: *San-chiao t'u* in one fascicle (Chart of the three teachings); *Ch'i-hsin t'u* in one fascicle (Chart of the *Awakening of Faith*); *Chin-kang ching shih-pa chu t'u* in one fascicle (Chart of eighteen commentaries on the *Vajracchedika-sūtra*); *Yuan-chueh liao-i ching t'u* in one fascicle (Chart of the *Perfect En-*

lightenment Sutra); Lei-tai tsu-shih hsueh-mo t'u (Chart of the blood veins of the patriarchal masters from generation to generation). The last is probably *P'ei's Inquiry.*

6. For information on all of these figures, including P'ei Hsiu, see Gregory, *Tsung-mi,* pp. 73–85. The Tun-huang manuscript of ZP lists a *Tao-su ch'ou-ta wen-chi* (Collection of [Tsung-mi's] responses to [questions from] monks and laypeople) in ten fascicles. Among the works in this posthumous collection were *P'ei's Inquiry* and *Yuan-jen lun* (On the origin of man). A number of works in this collection, such as these two, also circulated as independent works. See Jan Yun-hua, "Tsung-mi chu *Tao-su ch'ou-ta wen-chi* te yen-chiu," *Hwakang Buddhist Journal* 4 (1980): 132–166.

7. P'ei's preface to the ZP opens: "Zen Master Kuei-feng collected the expressions of the Zen source into a Zen *pitaka* and did a prolegomenon to it. Ho-tung P'ei Hsiu says: 'There has never been such a thing!'" Kamata, *Zengen shosenshū tōjō,* p. 3.

8. The following are indispensable for the study of *P'ei's Inquiry:*

- Kamata, *Zengen shosenshū tōjō,* pp. 267–341. Based on the *Chung-hua ch'uan hsin-ti ch'an-men shih-tzu ch'eng-hsi t'u* (Chart of the master-disciple succession of the zen gate that transmits the mind ground in China in one fascicle) in ZZ 2, 15. This text was only discovered in 1910 at Myōken-ji of the Nichiren school and put into ZZ. In section 22 (pp. 340–341) on the clarification of the two gates of all-at-once awakening and step-by-step practice, Kamata follows Chinul's *Popchip pyorhaeng nok choryo pyongip sagi* for a missing portion.

- Ui, *Zengen shosenshū tōjō,* pp. 175–225. Based on the text in ZZ 2, 15; in the section on the clarification of the two gates of all-at-once awakening and step-by-step practice (p. 222), Ui indicates a missing section by ellipsis points. Ui Hakuju, *Zenshūshi kenkyū* ([1943] reprint Tokyo: Iwanami shoten, 1966), vol. 3: pp. 490–491, was the first to supply the missing section of several hundred logographs from Chinul's *Popchip.*

- Ishii Shūdō, "Shinpuku-ji bunkō shozō no *Hai Kyu shui mon* no honkoku," *Zengaku kenkyū* 60 (1981): 71–104. Contains an edition of the manuscript of the *P'ei Hsiu shih-i wen* (Imperial redactor P'ei Hsiu's inquiry) found at Shinpuku-ji, a Shingon temple in Nagoya. It is dated Ninji 2 of the Kamakura (1241). In the section on the two gates (96) it includes nineteen logographs not found in Ui (ZZ), Chinul's *Popchip,* or Kamata, *Zengen shosenshū tōjō.* At the end it has Tsung-mi's responses to Hsiao Mien, Wen Tsao, and Shih Shan-jen. The *P'ei Hsiu shih-i wen,* which I shall for the sake of convenience simply call *P'ei's Inquiry,* has been known by many titles. Even the collection containing it, the *Tao-su ch'ou-ta wen-chi,* has gone under more than one title. Sorting all this out and determining the "original" title is probably impossible and surely not very profitable. Ui Hakuju suggested long ago, in 1943, that it was a letter, and hence there originally was no title (Ui, *Zenshūshi kenkyū,* vol. 3, p. 489). Titles under which it has circulated or been quoted in China, Korea, and Japan include the following.

- *Lei-tai tsu-shih hsueh-mo t'u* (Chart of the blood veins of the Patriarchal masters from generation to generation). A title appearing in the list of Tsung-mi works at the end of the Tun-huang manuscript fragment of the *ZP*.

• *Kuei-feng hou-chi* (Later collection of Kuei-feng). The T'ien-t'ai figure Chih-li (960–1028) in a letter contained in the *Szu-ming tsun-che chiao-hsing lu* (T 46.895a1–9) edited by Tsung-hsiao (1151–1214) gives this title as the source of the opening section of *P'ei's Inquiry* (in paraphrase). He goes on to say that a printed edition is in circulation. It may be another title for the *Tao-su ch'ou-ta wen-chi* or a similar posthumous collection.

• *Kuei-feng ta P'ei hsiang-kuo tsung-ch'u chuang* (Kuei-feng Answers Minister Pe'i's Note on the Purports of the [Zen] Lineages). The *Lin-chien lu* (1107) by Chüeh-fan Hui-hung cites this work as "arranging the six successors of Ma-tsu, the first of which is said to be Chiang-ling Tao-wu." ZZ 2B, 21, 4, 296d. It is referring to the Hung-chou Ma section of the chart in *P'ei's Inquiry*.

• *Ts'ao-t'ang ch'an-shih chien-yao* (Essentials of Zen Master Ts'ao-t'ang's Letter[s]). The *Lin-chien lu* quotes this work (ZZ 2B, 21, 4, 296d–297a). The quotation consists of the *mani* simile of *P'ei's Inquiry*. Whether the title refers to just Tsung-mi's response to P'ei's letter or a collection of Tsung-mi letters is unclear.

• *Popchip pyorhaeng nok* (*Fa-chi pieh-hsing lu*; Separately Circulated Record of the Dharma Collection). The title of *P'ei's Inquiry* for Chinul's magnum opus—a Korean title of the time. "Dharma collection" apparently refers to either the collection entitled *Tao-su ch'ou-ta wen-chi* in which the *Record* was embedded or to a similar collection under another title.

• *Nok* (*Lu; Record*). Quotations from *P'ei's Inquiry* in Chinul's work are introduced by "the *Record* says"; Chinul's expositions are introduced by "I say."

• *Keizan to Hai Kyu monshō* (*Kuei-shan ta P'ei Hsiu wen-shu*; Kuei-shan Answers P'ei Hsiu's Letter of Inquiry). The *Zenshū komoku* of the Kegon scholar Shojō (1194–?, see note 89), a disciple of Myōe, cites the simile of the *mani* in *P'ei's Inquiry* under this title.

• *Chung-hua ch'uan hsin-ti ch'an-men shih-tzu ch'eng-hsi t'u* (Chart of the Master-Disciple Succession of the Zen Gate that Transmits the Mind Ground in China). See Kamata, *Zengen Shosenshū tōjō*, above.

• *P'ei Hsiu shih-i wen* (Imperial Redactor P'ei Hsiu's Inquiry). The existence of a 1241 manuscript under this title at the Shingon temple Shinpuku-ji in Nagoya was already pointed out in a 1936 catalogue of the temple's holdings, but it was not introduced to the scholarly world until the publication of an edition in 1981 by Ishii Shūdō (see above). This title and *Keizan to Hai Kyu monshō* above are very similar. They have in common the elements *Hai Kyu mon* (P'ei Hsiu's inquiry), and some such title is probably the one under which the text circulated in Kamakura Japan.

9. The following are indispensable for the study of the *Subcommentary* notes:

• *Yuan-chüeh ching ta-shu ch'ao*, ZZ 1, 14, 3, 277c–279d. Contains numerous misprints, some of which can be corrected by consulting parallel passages in the Kamata, *Zengen shosenshū tōjō* edition of *P'ei's Inquiry*.

• Kamata, *Zengen shosenshū tōjō*, pp. 273–320. Cuts up the *Subcommentary* notes and inserts them piecemeal into *P'ei's Inquiry*. Divides notes on Niu-t'ou, Northern, Ho-tse, and Hung-chou into two pieces (history and teachings), but gives Ching-chung and Pao-t'ang notes in complete form. Omits note on South Mountain Nembutsu Gate. Followed by a *kambun kakikuda-shi* only.

10. App, ed., *Concordance to the "Preface" by Zongmi*, p. 191. Kamata, *Zengen sho-senshū tōjō*, pp. 103–132. The first teaching is the teaching of cryptic meaning that relies on *dharmatā* to speak of *lakṣaṇas*. Its three subdivisions are the karmic cause-and-effect teaching that allows rebirth as a human or a *deva*; the teaching that cuts off the depravities and extinguishes suffering (i.e., Hinayāna); and the teaching that takes *vi-jñāna* to negate *viṣayas*. The four *Āgamas* (corresponding to the first four Pali *Nikāyas*) and such *śāstras* as the *Mahāvibhāṣa* and *Abhidharmakośa* discuss the first two. Only the third has a Zen analogue. The *ZP* uses the term *tsung* in two meanings: "thesis" and "lineage." Zen has many lineages, that is, houses, and those houses on the basis of their ideas can be grouped into three theses. The usage here is equivalent to the "theses" or "tenets" of the four tenet systems (Sanskrit *siddhānta* = Tibetan *grub mth'a* = Chinese *tsung*) in Tibetan Buddhism: Madhyamaka, Cittamātra, Sautrāntika, and Vaibhāṣika.

11. Kamata, *Zengen shosenshū tōjō*, p. 40.

12. Ibid., pp. 103–132.

13. Ibid., p. 87.

14. Alex Wayman, "Nāgārjuna: Moralist Reformer of Buddhism," in Alex Wayman, ed., *Untying the Knots in Buddhism: Selected Essays*, Buddhist Tradition Series, vol. 28 (Delhi: Motilal Banarsidass, 1997), pp. 75–76: "Native Tibetan works make a distinction of the 'doctrinal part' (*darśana-bhaga*) and the 'practical part' (*caryā-bhaga*) for classifying Buddhist treatises. The 'doctrinal part' can be called the 'viewpoint'; and the 'practical part' can be called 'context of practice.' These Tibetan works apply this classification to what are called the three 'wheels of Dharma,' which are: (1) that of early Buddhism, the 'wheel of the four noble truths'; (2) that of the Mādhyamika, the 'wheel of lack of characteristics,' i.e., voidness; (3) that of the Yogācāra, the 'wheel of intensive analysis.'" For the first wheel, the doctrinal part is the *Abhidharma* and the practice part the *Vinaya*. For the second wheel the doctrinal part is the five or six *śāstras* of Nāgārjuna, beginning with the *Mādhyamaka-kārikā*, and the second eight chapters of the sixteen-chapter *Catuḥśataka* by Āryadeva; the first eight of the *Catuḥś-ataka* are the practice part. For the third wheel, the *Sūtralamkara* equally expounds doctrine and practice, and the *tattva* chapter of Asaṅga's *Bodhisattvabhūmi* teaches doctrine, the remaining chapters practice. The Sanskrit terminology here is very similar to Tsung-mi's terminology in his three Zen writings: *chien-chieh* (view-understanding), *so-chien* (view), *chieh* (understanding), *chih* (purport), *chih-ch'u* (purport-meaning), *tsung-chi chih* (thesis purport), *i* (idea), *i-ch'u* (idea-meaning), and *fa-i* (Dharma idea) for the doctrinal part and *hsing, hsiu,* or *hsiu-hsing* for the practice part.

15. In *P'ei's Inquiry*, Tsung-mi speaks of his research and the evasive reaction his questioning elicited from Zen people: "I, Tsung-mi, have an innate disposition toward comparative analysis. I visited each and every one [of the Zen houses] and found their purports to be like this. If you were to question those [Zen] students about these en-

capsulations, none of them would have any part of it. If you ask about existence, they answer with śūnyatā. If you [ask for] proof of śūnyatā, they acknowledge existence or say that both are to be negated. Or they say that nothing can be apprehended. It is the same in the matter of what they practice or do not practice. In their idea they are always fearful of falling into the written word, always afraid of being obstructed by having something to apprehend. This is why they dismiss verbal formulations." Kamata, *Zengen shosenshū tōjō*, pp. 315–316.

16. ZZ 1, 14, 3, 278b–c.

17. Yanagida Seizan, ed. and trans., *Shoki no zenshi* II, *Zen no goroku* 3 (Tokyo: Chikuma shobo, 1976), 143; T 51.185a11–15. Szechwan must have been a center of *nembutsu* Zen, since in addition to Wu-hsiang we find *nembutsu* in his co-student under Ch'u-chi, Ch'eng-yuan, and in Hsuan-shih (Nan-Shan Nembutsu Gate Zen). Ch'eng-yüan after serving Ch'u-chi studied under the Pure Land teacher Tz'u-min, and Ch'eng-yüan's disciple Fa-chao composed the *Ching-t'u fa-shen tsan* (Praises on the Pure Land dharmakāya). For Ch'eng-yuan, see Ui, *Zenshūshi kenkyū*, vol. 1, pp. 175–177.

18. ZZ 1, 14, 3, 277c–278b.

19. ZZ 1, 14, 3, 277c–278b.

20. It is the last saying in the *Hsien-te chi yu shuang-feng shan t'a ko t'an hsuan-li* (Former worthies gather at the Mount Shuang-feng stupa and each talks of the dark principle), a collection of short sayings for twelve figures at an imaginary memorial gathering for Hung-jen. For a reproduction, see Yanagida Seizan, *Shoki zenshū shishō no kenkyū* (Kyoto: Hozokan, 1967), pl. 15B; for an edition, see Yanagida Seizan, "*Dembōhōki* to sono sakusha: Pelliot 3559go bunsho o meguru hokushu zen kenkyu shiryo no satsuki, sono ichi," *Zengaku kenkyū* 53 (1963): 55.

21. For reproductions, see Lin, *Tun-huang ch'an-tsung wen-hsien chi-ch'eng*, vol. 1, pp. 598–677; for editions, see Suzuki Daisetsu, *Suzuki Daisetsu zenshū* (Tokyo: Iwanami shoten, 1968), vol. 3, pp. 161–235.

22. ZZ 1, 14, 3, 278c–d.

23. Yanagida, *Shoki no zenshi* II, 170; T 51.187a10–11.

24. Yanagida, *Shoki no zenshi* II, 199; T 51.188c26–189a4: "[A group of officials] came ahead and addressed preceptor [Wu-chu]: 'The president [Tu Hung-chien] is coming to visit you.' He replied: 'If coming, then follow other [*ts'ung-t'a*] in coming.' The imperial guard captain and others addressed the preceptor: 'The president is a distinguished guest. You must go out to welcome him.' The preceptor replied: 'One should not welcome him. Welcoming is human feeling. Not welcoming is the Buddhadharma.' As the imperial guard was about to speak again, the president entered the courtyard and saw that the preceptor's facial expression did not change and was sternly composed. The president bent deeply at the waist, descended the stairs, bowed, did *gassho* [i.e., put his hands flat together in respectful greeting], and inquired about how they were getting along. The secretaries and officials had never seen such a thing. They saw that the preceptor did not get up to welcome him. By pairs they looked at each other and asked: 'Why does he not get up to welcome [the president]?'" The "follow other" or "yield to other" (*ts'ung-t'a*) here is equivalent to the *Subcommentary*'s "leave it to other" (*jen-t'a*).

25. ZZ 1, 14, 3, 279c.

26. Kamata, *Zengen shosenshū tōjō*, p. 87.

27. ZZ 1, 14, 3, 279b–c.

28. For an edition and reproductions of the manuscripts, see Tokiwa Gishin and Yanagida Seizan, ed. and trans., *Zekkan-ron* (Kyoto: Zen bunka kenkyūjō, 1973).

29. Using the numbering system of the above edition of the *Chueh-küan lun*, sections II.1–6 are quoted in Yanagida Seizan, ed., *Sōdōshū*, Zengaku sōshō 4 (Kyoto: Chubun shuppansha, 1974), pp. 52b–53a, within the Niu-t'ou Hui-yung entry. Section II.8 is quoted in Yen-shou's *Tsung-ching lu*, T 48.463b10–13, with the introduction "the first patriarch of Niu-t'ou said." The last part of II.8 is quoted in Yen-shou's *Wan-shan t'ung-kuei chi* (Collection on the reversion to sameness of the myriad good actions), T 48.974b5–6, with the introduction "the Great Master Niu-t'ou Yung said."

30. Sections X.7–8 of the *Chueh-küan lun* (see previous note) run: "Question: 'Having something to do—what hindrance would that be?' Answer: 'No hindrance is having nothing to do. Having nothing to do—what hindrance could there be to become a problem?' Question: 'If you delete having something to do and seize having nothing to do, how can you call that walking on a no-path?' Answer: 'Reality itself is having nothing to do. You deliberately send forth something other to produce something to do, and this creates something.'" "Nothing to do" (*wu-shih*) here is the *Sub-commentary*'s "from the outset nothing to do" (*pen wu-shih*).

31. Two quotations have been fused here: T 16.510b4–5 and 512b16–17.

32. Paraphrase of T 16.493a28–b1.

33. ZZ 1, 14, 3, 279a–b.

34. Iriya Yoshitaka, ed. and trans., *Denshin hōyō, Enryō-roku, Zen no goroku* 8 (Tokyo: Chikuma shobō, 1969), pp. 20, 30, 61, 19, 90, 135, 71, and 97.

35. In *P'ei's Inquiry*, Tsung-mi argues that Ho-tse unites the negative expressions of the Mahāyāna sutras with jñāna by speaking of the *jñāna* of *śūnyatā* and calmness and that the Hung-chou and Niu-t'ou speak only in terms of negative expressions, thus missing the *bodhi* aspect. P'ei Hsiu mentions that Hung-chou does in fact speak of marvelous awakening and mirror illumination, which do not seem to differ from Ho-tse's *jñāna*. A paraphrase of Tsung-mi's reply runs:

These Hung-chou terms do not apply to a deluded person, who in spite of his delusion is still in a state of constant *jñāna*. Hung-chou and Niu-t'ou merely take sweeping away traces as the ultimate, and thus they have merely apprehended the intention behind the negative teaching, true *śūny-atā*. This just completes substance and misses the intention behind the teaching that reveals the meaning of wonderful existence. This omits the functioning. P'ei Hsiu challenges this formulation, and Tsung-mi replies that the true mind's original substance has two types of functioning, intrinsic functioning (the brightness of a mirror) and responsive functioning (the reflections that the brightness gives off). Mind's constant *jñāna* is the intrinsic functioning. Hung-chou says that the potential for speech and action must be the Buddha-nature, but this potential is just the responsive functioning. Hung-chou omits the intrinsic functioning. Hung-chou's saying that the mind substance should not be pointed out, that it is just by means of this potential that we can verify it, is only revealing by inference. Ho-tse's revealing mind in terms of *jñāna* is revealing by direct perception. Hung-chou omits this. Tsung-mi provides a simile for step-by-step practice: Wind stirs the water (true mind) to produce waves, and in cold weather it coagulates into ice. Constant *jñāna* is like the unchanging wetness of the water. Hung-chou says that passion, hatred, goodness, etc., are all the Buddha-nature, but this is like a person who just discerns that wetness from beginning to end is undifferentiated but does not realize that the merit of supporting a boat and the fault of overturning it are widely divergent. Thus, Hung-chou is close to the gate of all-at-once awakening but runs completely counter to the gate of step-by-step practice. (Kamata, *Zengen shosenshū tōjō*, pp. 332–336)

36. Ibid., pp. 131–132.

37. Ibid., p. 141.

38. ZZ 1, 14, 3, 279d.

39. Hu Shih, ed., *Shen-hui ho-shang i-chi* (Taipei: Hu Shih chi-nien kuan, 1968), pp. 239 and 241.

40. Kamata, *Zengen shosenshū tōjō*, p. 95. In Fa-tsang's Hua-yen system, this corresponds to the fifth gate of the tenfold *cittamātra*. His *Hua-yen ching t'an-hsuan chi* (Record of a search for the profundities of the Avataṁsaka Sūtra; T 35.347a16–18) states: "Because of taking *lakṣaṇas* back to *dharmatā* [she-hsiang kuei-hsing] we speak of *cittamātra*. This means that these eight *vijñānas* lack any substance of their own. Just the *tathāgatagarbha* in sameness is manifested. All other *lakṣaṇas* are exhausted." Thus, the ZP is saying that Hung-chou and Ho-tse are based on the *tathāgatagarbha*.

41. Here is a paraphrase: It is like a *maṇi* (the one marvelous mind) that is round, pure, and bright (*jñāna* of *śūnyata* and calmness). It utterly lacks color *lakṣaṇas*. (*Jñāna* from the outset lacks *vikalpa*.) When the *maṇi* reflects black, it is black all the way through, with no brightness visible. (When the mind of *jñāna* is in the common person, it is delusion, stupidity, passion, and desire.) If an ignorant child sees it, he will say that it is just a black *maṇi*. Even those with a belief in the *maṇi*'s brightness will assert that the *maṇi* is wrapped in obscurity by the black, and they will try to wipe and wash it to eliminate the blackness. Only when they succeed in making the brightness reemerge do they say that they see a bright *maṇi* (the view of the Northern house). There is a type of person who points out that the blackness itself *is* the bright *maṇi* and that the substance of the bright *maṇi* is never to be seen. Upon seeing a *maṇi* that is not facing any colors, one that is just bright and pure, they resist and do not recognize it. They fear being limited to the one *lakṣaṇa* of the bright *maṇi* (the view of Hung-chou). There is a type of person who, upon reading in the *Prajñāpāramita-sūtras* that the various colors on the *maṇi* are unreal and that it is *śūnya* all the way through, deduces that this one bright *maṇi* is nothing but *śūnyatā* and is not to be apprehended. This type is not awakened to the realization that the locus wherein the color *lakṣaṇas* are all *śūnya* is precisely the non-*śūnya maṇi* (the view of Niu-t'ou). The sparkling purity and perfect brightness *are* the *maṇi*. Ho-tse recognizes that the bright *maṇi* *is* the substance with the potential for manifesting all the colors and that it is eternally unchanging. Kamata, *Zengen shosenshū tōjō*, pp. 322–330.

42. Ibid., p. 222.

43. Ibid., pp. 217–218.

44. Ibid., p. 222.

45. Ibid., p. 223.

46. The last is T no. 1886. For an edition with a modern Japanese translation, see Kamata Shigeo, ed. and trans., *Gennin-ron* (Tokyo: Meitoku shuppansha, 1973).

47. On Han Yu's *ku-wen*, see Charles Hartman, *Han Yu and the T'ang Search for Unity* (Princeton: Princeton University Press, 1986), pp. 211–275.

48. Kamata, *Zengen shosenshū tōjō*, p. 33.

49. This is the fundamental distinction of the grammar of literary Chinese. The classic work on empty words is Lu Shu-hsiang, *Wen-yen hsu-tzu* (Shanghai: Hsin chih-shih ch'u-pan she, 1957).

50. Hartman, *Han Yu*, p. 240.

51. For the Wan-li 4, see note 1 above. The Ming Canon edition is T no. 2015 and ZZ 2, 8.

52. There are small discrepancies in the headings and in the text beneath the headings, as well as in the arrangement of the Buddha bodies. Under the awakening heading, Wan-li 4 gives step-by-step practice and all-at-once awakening, which are further subdivided, whereas the Ming Canon edition provides a ten-stage awakening sequence that parallels the ten-stage nonawakening sequence. The Ming Canon edition's circles include a white circle for sentient-being mind, a black circle for the unreal, a small black circle within a white circle for the conditioned, a small white circle within a black circle for nonawakening, and a very intricate circle for the *ālayav-ijñāna*. Sequences of circles that look like phases of the moon diagram the ten stages of awakening and nonawakening. Note that the *ālayavijñāna* circle appears in the *Great Ultimate Chart* (*T'ai-chi t'u*) of the Sung dynasty neo-Confucian Chou Tun-i, where it illustrates the relationship between the two energies of *yin*, or quiescence, and *yang*, or movement.

53. Kuroda Ryo, *Chosen kyusho ko* (Tokyo: Iwanami shoten, 1940), pp. 117 and 120.

54. Ibid., p. 120.

55. Kamata, *Zengen shosenshū tōjō*, p. 260.

56. Liu Hsu-teng et al., eds., *Chiu T'ang-shu* (Beijing: Chung-hua shu-chu, 1975), vol. 7, p. 4,594. For an example of P'ei's powerful hand, see the reproduction of a rubbing of his funerary inscription for Tsung-mi in P'ei Hsiu, *T'ang P'ei Hsiu shu Kuei-feng ch'an-shih pei* (Taipei: Hsin-shih ch'u-pan she, 1981).

57. For the preface, see Iriya, *Denshin hōyō*, p. 3.

58. Kamata, *Zengen shosenshū tōjō*, p. 262.

59. Yanagida Seizan, ed., *Korai-bon*, Zengaku sosho 2 (Kyoto: Chu-bun shuppan-sha, 1974), pp. 123–149.

60. Kamata, *Shūmitsu kyōgaku no shisōhi-teki kenkyū*, p. 239.

61. Kuroda, *Chosen kyusho ko*, p. 122. Kuroda (pp. 122–125) lists ten Korean editions he has personally seen, three of them in his own collection. Komozawa Daigaku tō/ōkan, ed., *Shinsan zenseki mokuroku* (Tokyo: Komozawa Daigaku tō/ōkan, 1962), p. 253, lists thirteen Korean editions.

62. T 48.397c18–25.

63. T 48.398a19–20.

64. See note 1 above.

65. Kamata, *Zengen shosenshū tōjō*, p. 373.

66. Nishida Tatsuo, *Seikabun Kegon-kyō* (Kyoto: Kyoto Daigaku Bungaku-bu, 1977), vol. 3, pp. 26. It is listed as no. 091 (Leningrad Cat. 227). See also vol. 1, p. 18.

67. Nishida, *Seikabun Kegon-kyō*, vol. 3, pp. 26 and 30. They are listed as nos. 092, 093, 094, and 119.

68. T 48.417b3–14. At the beginning of the ninety-fourth fascicle of the *Tsung-ching lu* (T 48.924a14–16), Yen-shou states: "Now I will for the sake of those whose faith power is not yet deep and whose minute doubts are not yet severed further quote 120 Mahāyāna sutras, 120 books of the sayings of the [Zen] patriarchs, and 60 collections of the worthies and *āryas*, altogether the subtle words of 300 books." Perhaps at least some of the quotations from 120 Zen books derive ultimately from Tsung-mi's collecting efforts.

69. Kamata, *Zengen shosenshū tōjō*, p. 33. This is the passage used above as an example of the literary style of the *ZP*.

70. Ibid., p. 254.

71. Yun-hua Jan, "Two Problems Concerning Tsung-mi's Compilation *of Ch'an-tsang*," *Transactions of the International Conference of Orientalists in Japan* 19 (1974): 46, remarks that Sekiguchi Shindai first suggested in a conversation that Tsung-mi's Zen canon had been absorbed into Yen-shou's *Tsung-ching lu*.

72. Biographical entries at *Sung kao-seng chuan*, T 50.887a29–b16, and *Ching-te ch'uan-teng lu*, T 51.421c8–422a20.

73. *Sung kao-seng chuan*, T 50.887b12–14.

74. For references, see the index of Robert E. Buswell, Jr., *The Korean Approach to Zen: The Collected Works of Chinul* (Honolulu: University of Hawai'i Press, 1983), p. 465.

75. Bernard Faure, "The Daruma-shū, Dōgen, and Sōtō Zen," *Monumenta Nipponica* 42 no. 1 (Spring 1987): 28.

76. See particularly T 48.939b–943a. A step forward in research on the immense *Tsung-ching lu* is the publication of the text in electronic form: Urs App, ed., *ZenBase CDI* (Kyoto: International Research Institute for Zen Buddhism, 1995).

77. Robert E. Buswell, Jr., *The Zen Monastic Experience: Buddhist Practice in Contemporary Korea* (Princeton: Princeton University Press, 1992), p. 22.

78. Ibid., pp. 95–99.

79. For the four works, see ibid., p. 96 (no. 25). According to Buswell, the best edition of the fourfold collection is Kim T'anho, ed. and trans., *Sa chip*, 4 vols. (Seoul: Kyorim, 1974). Buswell, *The Korean Approach to Zen*, pp. 262–374, contains an annotated translation of Chinul's *Popchip*.

80. For references, see the index of Buswell, *The Korean Approach to Zen*, p. 444.

81. Buswell, *The Zen Monastic Experience*, p. 100.

82. Kamata, *Zengen shosenshū tōjō*, p. 191.

83. Kamata, *Gennin-ron*, p. 25.

84. See Kamata, *Zengen shosenshū tōjō*, p. 374, and Komozawa Daigaku tōshō-kan, *Shinsan zenseki mokuroku*, p. 254. Both are eighteenth-century works. The first, a printed edition, is Komozawa University Library no. 121–4. The second (printed edi-

tion in Seoul University and handwritten copy in Komozawa University Library as *kotsu-*
1195) is reproduced in Kamata, *Shūmitsu kyōgaku no shisōhi-teki kenkyū* (Tokyo: Tōkyō
Daigaku shuppansha, 1975), pp. 267–292.

85. Tsung-mi, *Zengen shōsenshu tōjō* (Nara: Todai-ji Kangaku-in, 1955). I would
like to thank Professor Ueyama Daishun of Ryūkoku University in Kyoto for allowing
me to make a copy.

86. For use of this portrait, I am grateful to Aoki Hideo, the Jushoku of Kumida-
dera in Osaka, and to Yamanaka Goro, Arts Member of the Kishiwada City Museum.
The museum held an Autumn Special Exhibition in 1999 titled "History and Art of
Kumida-dera Centering on Buddhist Paintings and Medieval Documents." I would
also like to thank Yoshioka Nobuko for her efforts in obtaining the transparency.

87. Kishiwada-shiritsu kyōdō shiryōkan, *Kumida-dera no rekishi to bijutsu: But-
suga to chūsei bunsho o chūshin ni* (Kishiwada-shi: Kishiwada-shiritsu kyodo shiryokan,
1999), pp. 14–15. The catalogue describes the four paintings as "In color on silk, 95
cm × 53 cm. Nambokucho to early Muromachi." It is stated that originally the set
must have included a portrait of the second patriarch Chih-yen, but by the time of a
restoration in Meiwa 2 (1765), it was missing.

88. Kishiwada-shiritsu kyōdō shiryōkan, *Kumida-dera no rekishi to bijutsu*, pp. 3
and 8–9.

89. Kamata, *Shūmitsu kyōgaku no shisōhiteki kenkyū*, p. 610. The following is
based on pp. 629–637.

90. *Ch'uan T'ang-shih*, ([1960] reprint Beijing: Chung-hua shu-chu, 1979), vol.
13, p. 5,010.

91. Ibid., vol. 14, p. 5,137.

2

Mazu yulu and the Creation of the Chan Records of Sayings

Mario Poceski

Over recent decades, the study of medieval Chan literature made considerable progress, which enabled scholars working in this area to reassess important issues and events in early Chan history. They have been able to focus attention on topics that have not been addressed by traditional Buddhist scholarship. This was possible in part due to an increased access to Chan texts and other relevant documents, which included the Dunhuang manuscripts and other texts such as *Zutang ji* (Hall of the Patriarchs collection), which were rediscovered after having been lost for a number of centuries. Chan scholarship also benefited from the application of modern research methodologies adopted from relevant academic disciplines. As a result, Chan/Zen scholars have been able to rewrite important chapters of the story about the early formation of the Chan tradition and its subsequent emergence as a major school of East Asian Buddhism. Notwithstanding the substantial progress made so far, however, there is still much work that needs to be done in a number of areas pertinent to the historical study of classical Chan. Major areas that require further research include the origins, contents, and functions of important Chan texts that are used as sources of historical data, and the provenance and main characteristics of the distinct literary genres in which such texts were composed.

The lack of meaningful consideration of basic problems pertaining to the formation and functions of individual genres is a case in point that highlights the fragmented nature of scholarly approaches to the study of early Chan literature. There seems to be no clear set of criteria for defining the basic features that constitute a particular

Chan genre, even though various terms that refer to specific genres are widely used in both popular and scholarly writings about Chan literature and history. A pertinent example of the tendency to blur the distinctions between different Chan genres is the use of the term "records of sayings" (*yulu*). Although the term is the name of a specific Chan genre, very often it is used in broad and vague manner, so the meaning roughly corresponds to such general terms as "Chan literature" or "Chan text."[1] Such lack of precision obscures the prolific variety of writings that form classical Chan literature, and imputes uniformity to a wide array of diverse texts composed over a long period of time. The imprecision implicit in this usage is to a certain extent based on a problematic assumption that there are widely accepted and self-evident, albeit unstated, criteria for identifying given texts as belonging to a supposedly homogeneous corpus of Chinese religious writings that we associate with the Chan school. Even though the boundaries that delimit the Chan canon are not clearly artic- ulated, it is at least tacitly assumed, and not infrequently explicitly asserted, that its texts clearly stand apart from the literary artifacts of the rest of Chinese Buddhism.

As a result of the dearth of exactness in regard to the classification of the different types of texts that constitute the larger body of classical Chan litera- ture, often there is a marked lack of differentiation among dissimilar genres and insufficient awareness of the diverse origins, contents, and literary formats of texts that belong to them. Texts written in completely different genres are often mixed together as equally representative records of Chan religiosity, which is typically construed as a coherent spiritual universe centered on uni- form yet deeply personal experiences of timeless truth(s). That is usually done despite the fact that the great differences in the literary format, contents, and dating of individual texts indicate that they are products of quite different re- ligious and social milieus. To further complicate matters, despite the pretense of being coherent and homogeneous narratives, most classical Chan texts are somewhat unwieldy compilations formed from several different types of earlier textual and oral sources, all of which had independent origins.

Some of the issues that were at play in the creation of Chan literature come more clearly into focus through closer analysis of specific texts, set against the backdrop of the conventions of the genres in which they were written. In this chapter I examine one such text, *Jiangxi Mazu Daoyi chanshi yulu* ("Record of the sayings of Chan Master Mazu Daoyi of Jiangsi," hereafter referred to as *Mazu yulu*), one of the most influential texts of the records of sayings genre.[2] This text purports to be a record of the life and teachings of Mazu Daoyi (709–788), the renowned leader of the Hongzhou school and arguably one of the most important monks in the whole history of Chan. By the early ninth century, the various fragmented schools of early Chan were replaced by a new orthodoxy centered on the Southern school, which for all practical purposes came to be identified with Mazu's Hongzhou school. He was thus a central figure in a key phase of Chan history, which retroactively came to be recognized as the tradition's "golden age," and in that role he was remembered as one of the main protagonists in the incipient ascendancy of Chan as the elite tradition of Chinese Buddhism. Consequently, he is still widely esteemed as one of the most important Chan/Zen "patriarchs," and his record is held in high esteem as an authoritative source of authentic Chan teachings.

The examination of Mazu's record presented in the following pages has two objectives. First, in accord with the general tenor of the present volume, this chapter is meant to offer general information about the *Mazu yulu*. That includes information about the text's provenance, literary structure and style, contents, and status and function within the later Chan/Zen traditions. Second, by using Mazu's record as an example of the record of sayings genre, the chapter also engages in preliminary consideration of broader issues about the creation of texts that belong to this genre and their use as historical sources about the Chan religious movement in the Tang dynasty (618–907).

Compilation of Mazu's Record of Sayings

Although *Mazu yulu* is usually regarded as the main record about Mazu's life and teachings, the texts is of a quite late provenance. It was first published during the Northern Song dynasty (960–1126) as a part of *Sijia yulu* (Records of the sayings of four masters), the earliest version of which is now extant only in a late Ming (1368–1644) edition. In addition to Mazu's record, this collection also includes the records of Baizhang Huaihai (749–814), Huangbo Xiyun (d. 850?), and Linji Yixuan (d. 866), who represent the first three generations of Mazu's direct spiritual descendants. The date of the compilation of *Sijia yulu* can be established on the basis of Yang Jie's preface, a portion of which is preserved in a Ming edition of the text. This preface is dated the first day of the eleventh month of the eighth year of the Yuanfeng period, which corresponds to November 20, 1085.[3] According to Yang, the collection was edited by Huanglong Huian (1002–1069), a noted Chan teacher in the Linji lineage, presumably during the final years of his life.[4]

The different texts that comprise the *Sijia yulu* collection have varied histories. Mazu's record of sayings does not have a documented history as an independent text prior to its inclusion in this collection, and in all probability it appeared as a whole text for the first time as a part of *Sijia yulu*. That means that the text was compiled almost three centuries after Mazu's death. Like Mazu's text, Linji's record of sayings, *Linji yulu* (Record of the sayings of Linji), is also of a relatively late date. Though this text seems to have existed independently before the compilation of *Sijia yulu*, it first appeared only during the Northern Song period, not long before its inclusion in the collection.[5]

Compared to the records of the sayings of Mazu and Linji, Huangbo's two records—*Chuanxin fayao* (The essentials of the transmission of mind) and *Wanling lu* (Wanling record)—and Baizhang's *Baizhang guanglu* (Baizhang's extensive record) are much older. Although there are no surviving manuscripts from the Tang period, it is known that parts of *Chuanxin fayao* and *Wanling lu* were recorded by the prominent official Pei Xiu (787–860) during the late 840s. The texts are based on Pei's personal notes taken during two periods when he served as a government official in the south, where he met Huangbo and studied Buddhism with him.[6] The final versions of both texts seem to have been compiled from Pei Xiu's notes and the notes of other disciples not long after the death of Huangbo (discussed in chapter 4 below), although additional materials might have crept into later editions of the text.[7] In a similar vein, there is evidence that *Baizhang guanglu*, which consists of transcripts of Baizhang's talks and conversations with his students, was compiled soon after Baizhang's death.[8]

Although these two texts are regularly referred to as "records of sayings," they were created before the evolution of the mature records of sayings genre, and they lack many of the features that are characteristic of texts composed in this genre.[9] In both texts the omission of biographical sketches is conspicuous; these are a common feature of the records of sayings genre. Even more significant is the fact that neither text contains any examples of classical "encounter dialogues."As we will see shortly, the Hongzhou school was an iconoclastic tradition that introduced that novel mode of religious communication and practice.[10] In contrast, the second of Baizhang's two records included in the *Sijia yulu* collection, the *Baizhang yulu*, which is much shorter than the *Baizhang guanglu*, is clearly a product of the Song period. Its contents and literary format are closer to Mazu's and Linji's records, which are typical Song *yulu* texts. It is interesting to note that the earlier of these texts, the two records of Huangbo and Baizhang's *Guanglu*, are noticeably more conservative in their approach to Chan soteriology than the later texts included in *Sijia yulu*.

Given that *Sijia yulu* was compiled by the Song Linji school, its main ideological function was to buttress that school's claim that Linji, the school's putative founder, was the orthodox heir of Mazu's Chan lineage, and by extension that the Linji lineage was the authentic transmission of Chan. The collection is of undoubtedly great historical importance, since it includes materials about the four best-known monks associated with the Hongzhou school. At the same time, *Sijia yulu*'s late date of compilation and the diverse literary and historical origins of the texts that constitute it indicate that we must exercise caution in using the collection as a source for the historical study of Tang Chan. That is especially the case with the three texts that were compiled during the Song, the records of the sayings of Mazu, Baizhang, and Linji. Concerning Mazu's record, the three-century gap between Mazu's death and the compilation of *Mazu yulu* is a very long period, which makes the authenticity of the text suspect.

The late provenance of *Mazu yulu* and other similar texts should not, however, be used hastily as "evidence" that they are works of fiction whose contents are inadmissible as sources of information about Tang Chan. It is of course, patently naïve to accept the contents of these texts at face value as records of the sayings and deeds of the great Chan teachers from the Tang period. Historical research on Tang Chan should primarily be based on the earliest strata of epigraphic and other pertinent textual sources. At the same time, we should also be apprehensive about falling into the kind of unwarranted historical revisionism that is predicated on a notion that the records of Tang Chan teachers are merely products of Song Chan ideology. We should not presume, following Griffith Foulk's suggestion, that these texts constituted "a body of religious mythology, a sacred history that served polemical, ritual, and didactic functions in the world of Song Chan," and thus deduce that their contents are directly relevant for studies of Chan during the period when they were compiled and bear little (if any) relevance to the study of Tang Chan.[11]

A prudent approach to the study of these texts should avoid both forms of reductionism, naïve acceptance of their contents as authentic historical records and the characterization of them as products of Song Chan ideology that invented the mythical "golden age" ushered by Mazu and his followers and thereby "drew attention away from its own creativity."[12] Although the compilation of a records of sayings such as *Mazu yulu* was undeniably influenced by concerns and issues unique to the eleventh-century Chan milieu, in fact virtually all of the materials that were used by the text's compiler(s) can be found in earlier texts. The Song editor(s) merely collected all materials about Mazu they could lay their hands on, ostensibly without making serious attempts to establish the provenance and historical accuracy of the various sources they were drawing from. In the following pages I will examine the various pre-Song sources that contain earlier versions of the materials that constitute Mazu's record and trace the earliest appearance of the contents of each of its constituent parts. Before doing that, it will be helpful to provide a brief overview of the *Mazu yulu*.

Structure and Contents

The structure and content of *Mazu yulu* described below are representative of the recorded sayings genre. A text composed in this genre was originally meant to serve as an inclusive record of the life and teachings of a noted Chan teacher, whose words and deeds were presented as paradigmatic models of authentic religiosity unique to the Chan school. These texts typically include biographical information, short sermons and conventional dialogues, encounter dialogues and other stories that illustrate a Chan teachers' lively manifestations of their spiritual insights, and occasional poems. Although there are some variations in terms of literary format and style among the various texts that belong to this genre, for the most part those differences are minor. For instance, in *Linji yulu* the biographical material is placed at the end, instead at the beginning, where it is usually found.[13] Such somewhat unusual placement of the *xinglu* (lit., "record of acts") at the end of the text can also be found in *Yunmen guanglu* (The Extensive Record of Yunmen), which was compiled at about the same time as *Linji yulu*.[14] Notwithstanding slight variations of this sort, we can say that the records of the sayings of Mazu and other late Tang Chan teachers, most of which were initially compiled during the Northern Song period, constitute a collection of texts that is quite homogeneous in literary structure and contents.

The structure of the *Mazu yulu* consists of three distinct parts: a biographical sketch of Mazu's life, numerous transcripts of his sermons, and thirty-two short dialogues between him and his disciples. Although the three parts follow each other in this order, in the original text they are presented together as a single continuous narrative in which there are no structural boundaries or explicit markings that set the three sections apart. Yet the contrast in their literary structure and, even more important, the differences in their contents are quite striking. As we will see shortly, these disparities point to the distinct origins of each of the three literary formats in which they were composed, a crucial point that has wide-ranging ramifications for the study of medieval Chan literature. The production of a text such as *Mazu yulu* was a process of editing and combining different kinds of materials, which the editors presented together as a homogeneous record of Mazu's life and teaching in a way that obscured the diverse origins of the sources on which the different parts of the text were based.

The first part of the text, Mazu's biographical sketch, follows the traditional pattern of Chinese Buddhist hagiography. Mazu's brief biography is typical of normative depictions of the life and career pattern of a noted Chan teacher. Following an established literary model, the biography mentions Mazu's youthful predisposition toward religious life, and then goes on to note the main events in his religious career, such as his ordination and early study of Buddhism, training under a Chan teacher, spiritual awakening, teaching of disciples, and gradual rise to fame. Although biographies of Chan monks such as Mazu were products of a specific Chan milieu and were informed by the internal dynamics of Chan's religious, historical, and institutional developments, they clearly reflected earlier Chinese traditions of biographical writing, both secular and Buddhist. Like the secular biographies, individual Chan biographies are not to be read as independent examinations of their subject's personal character, or even of his life.[15] They are to be read, rather, as formulaic depictions of his performance of a specific function or role that is defined by the larger social and religious contexts in which an individual biography is presented. Whereas in the secular biographies the role is typically that of an exemplary official, as is to be expected, Chan biographies focus on their subjects' roles as enlightened monks and charismatic Chan teachers.

The information about Mazu's life presented in *Mazu Yulu* is brief. It follows the basic conventions of biographical writing such as narrative sequence, and it covers his whole life, from his birth in Sichuan until his death in Hongzhou (northern Jiangxi). In between, we are provided with concise data about his ordination, meeting and study with his teacher Huairang (677–744) at Nanyue Mountain in Hunan, establishment of monastic communities in Jiangxi, first at Gonggong Mountain and later at Kaiyuan Monastery in Hongzhou, and an exceptionally successful teaching career, during which he had 139 distinguished disciples, more than any other Chan teacher before or after him. As is customary in the biographies of noted Chan monks, Mazu's biographical sketch ends with information about his imperially bestowed posthumous title and his stupa, thus placing his life in relation to the established sociopolitical order. The life pattern presented in *Mazu yulu* has a dual point of reference and can be read at two levels: as a source of information about the historical reality of Mazu's life as a Buddhist monk and noted Chan teacher, and as an idealized depiction of his function as an archetype of a particular type of religious personality.

The second part of the *Mazu yulu* consists of transcripts of three of Mazu's sermons. The first and the third sermons are prefaced by the phrase "[Mazu] instructed the assembly, saying" (*shihzhong yun*). Together with the term *shangtang*, which literaly means to "ascend the [Dharma] hall," *shizhong* is an expression that is commonly used at the beginning of the transcripts of sermons of Chan teachers. In Chan texts the two terms are used interchangeably, and they both refer to a formal occasion during which a Chan teacher would address his disciples in the main hall of the monastery for the purpose of elucidating the essentials of Buddhist soteriology—responding to the audience's questions, resolving their doubts about the Buddhist teachings, and inspiring and encouraging them to persevere in their religious practice. The second sermon is initiated by a question from an anonymous monk, another common feature of this kind of text.

In his sermons Mazu seamlessly weaves in numerous quotations from and allusions to Buddhist scriptures, usually without identifying his sources. Judging from their contents, the sermons' main function seems to have been to instruct disciples in the teachings of Buddhism and provide them with religious guidance and inspiration. The format of the sermons is traditional, and their contents do not fit the radical image of the Hongzhou school's leader, who is often depicted in modern secondary sources as a sort of religious revolutionary who was bent on overturning established traditions and transgressing conventional norms of monastic behavior. Although the three sermons exhibit a conception of religious doctrine and a direct rhetorical style that were characteristic of the Hongzhou school, they belong to a hallowed tradition of Buddhist discourse that existed in China long before the emergence of the Chan school. As a matter of fact, much of the sermons' contents is little more than a string of canonical quotations and allusions, accompanied by Mazu's further elaboration of the cited passages. Let me give an example (with the information about the canonical sources added in brackets):

> [The *Vimalakīrti Scripture* says,] "Those who seek the Dharma
> should not seek for anything." [As it is taught in the *Huayan Scrip-
> ture*,] Outside of mind there is no other Buddha, outside of Buddha
> there is no other mind. Not attaching to good and not rejecting evil,
> without reliance on either purity or defilement, one realizes that the
> nature of offense is empty: it cannot be found in each thought be-
> cause it is without self-nature. Therefore [as explained in the
> *Huayan* and *Laṅkāvatāra* scriptures], "the three realms are mind-
> only," and [as stated in the *Faju jing*] "all phenomena in the universe
> are marked by a single Dharma." Whenever we see form, it is just
> seeing the mind. The mind does not exist by itself; its existence is
> due to form. Whatever you are saying, it is just [what Dushun's *Fajie
> guanmen* refers to as] "a phenomenon, which is identical with the
> principle." They are all without obstruction, and the fruit of the way
> to awakening is also like that.[16]

The use of sermons as a medium of religious instruction was a tradition that was not unique to Chinese Buddhism. As can be seen from the earliest Bud-dhist scriptures, like those preserved in the Pali canon, the sermon was one of the main forms of religious instructions practiced by the Buddhist community ever since its early inception in northern India. During the medieval period, sermons of eminent monks often drew large audiences and were a ubiquitous feature of Chinese Buddhism. Very often the sermons consisted of the exegesis of Mahāyāna scriptures, delivered by erudite monks identified as *jiangshi* (lit., "lecturer"), or by some similar title.[17] Closer to the teaching format used by Chan monks were the sermons of a class of Buddhist teachers called *chang-daoshi*, who propagated Buddhist teachings without relying on a specific text.[18] Some *changdaoshi* presented their sermons in a simple language that was ac-cessible to the masses, whereas some were adept at presenting Buddhist teach-ings in ways that were appealing to the educated elites, both lay and monastic. The sermons of Chan monks such as Mazu were therefore presented in a format that was highly conventional and widely recognized by the mainstream traditions of medieval Chinese Buddhism.[19] In his sermons, Mazu assumes the traditional function of a Dharma teacher (*fashi*), as many Chinese monks—such as the renowned Tiantai "patriarch" Zhiyi (538–597), for example—had done before him, and as many continued to do after him.

The picture changes dramatically when we come to the third part of the *Mazu yulu*, which consists of dialogues between Mazu and his monastic and lay disciples. The thirty-two dialogues that appear in the text are brief records of Mazu's interaction with his disciples, many of whom entered the ranks of the most distinguished Chan teachers of their time. In pithy exchanges that have been made by far the best-known part of Chan lore by both popular and scholarly works on Chan/Zen, Mazu answers his disciples' questions in un-usual ways and uses unconventional pedagogical techniques, such as shouting and beating, to lead them to awakening. The stories are written in a manner suggestive of actual speech. Although we are dealing with written narratives, they are presented as bare transcripts of oral narratives, which supposedly capture the essence of actual events. The impression/illusion of oral narrative is further reinforced by the employment of a vernacular style of rhetoric. The interlocutors are directly relating not only to each other but also to the situation, surroundings, and circumstantial milieu of their discourse, with brief descrip-tions of everyday scenes from medieval monastic life serving as a backdrop for the actual dialogues. Their communication becomes fully meaningful in re-lation to the milieu.[20] All this is done without the author of the story revealing any traces of his identity or agenda. The author is obscured, and we are only left with the story as a verbatim record of a putative event/dialogue, with no clues about its origins.

The dialogues are written in such a way as to suggest that together they represent a pious record of a great teacher's enlightened activity, which is pre-sented as a direct expression of the essence of the Buddhist way in the midst of everyday situations typical of medieval monastic life. In these short ex-changes, traditional Buddhist discourse is completely forsaken, and there is hardly any mention of common Buddhist doctrines and practices. Instead, the text presents brief stories that depict Mazu's lively and unpredictable, osten-sibly spontaneous interaction with his disciples. A classic example is the short story that supposedly depicts Shuilao's awakening as a direct result of Mazu's unusual "teaching."

> When Rev. Shuilao of Hongzhou came to see the Patriarch (i.e.,
> Mazu) for the first time, he asked, "What is the meaning of [Bodhid-
> harma's] coming from the West?" The Patriarch said, "Bow down!"
> As soon as Shuilao went down to bow, the Patriarch kicked him.
> Shuilao had great awakening. He rose up clapping his hands and
> laughing heartily, and said, "Wonderful! Wonderful! The source of
> myriad samādhis and limitless subtle meanings can all be realized

on the tip of a single hair." He then paid his respects to the Patriarch and withdrew. Later he told the assembly [at his monastery],
"Since the day I was kicked by Master Ma, I have not stopped laugh-
ing."[21]

In this and other similar stories, instead of being portrayed as an abbot of a
public monastery and an exemplar of proper moral behavior to a large monastic
community, Mazu is depicted as an iconoclast par excellence. In most stories
that supposedly recount the interaction between him and his disciples, Mazu
comes across as a radical religious leader who challenged established norms
of conventional behavior and introduced new forms of religious expression
that were at conspicuous variance with the prevalent monastic mores of his
time.

Contrasting Images of Patriarch Ma

The contrast between the images of Mazu conveyed by his sermons and dialogues is quite striking. In the sermons he assumes a somewhat traditional
role of a teacher of Buddhist doctrine (albeit of the Chan variety). There he
comes across as a fairly conventional religious figure, someone who is well
versed in canonical texts and traditions and who adopts a time-honored mode
of religious instruction. In the dialogues, on the other hand, he seems to be a
strikingly unconventional figure and assumes the role of an iconoclastic Chan
master who engages in spontaneous and often seemingly eccentric exchanges
that subvert the established mores of his time. Under the influence of popular
lore about the ancient "Zen masters," both Zen adherents and scholars have
so far chosen to focus on the image of Mazu depicted in the dialogues. They
have also tended to gloss over or ignore the discrepancies between the iconoclastic character depicted in the dialogues and the conservative disposition
evidenced in the sermons. As a result, the popular image of Mazu conveyed
in numerous Zen books is that of an iconoclast, a radical figure who embodies
a classical Chan tradition that to a large extent was created by him.

   Since iconoclastic Chan dialogues appear in the records of Mazu and other
monks who belonged to the Hongzhou school, but do not appear in the records
of other Chan monks who lived prior to Mazu, Japanese scholars have assumed
that the encounter dialogue format that figures so prominently in Song Chan
text was invented by Mazu and his followers. In keeping with prevalent notions
about the central role of the encounter dialogues as essential records that ep-
itomized a new type of Chan religiosity, the evidence behind such attribution
to Mazu and his Hongzhou school of the historical origins of what is probably
the best-known feature of classical Chan has received relatively little scrutiny.

According to Yanagida Seizan's widely accepted interpretation, having rejected all established forms of Buddhist practice, including the practice of formal meditation that characterized early Chan, under Mazu's leadership the Hongzhou school developed the new encounter dialogue (also referred to as "question and answer") model of practice, which became the centerpiece of its bold new approach to religious training. According to this explanation, also reflected in the writing of other Japanese scholars, the spontaneous patterns of interaction between Chan teachers and their disciples become the main or perhaps even exclusive foci of spiritual discipline. This putative paradigm of religious training supposedly freed Chan teachers to communicate directly the deepest truths of enlightenment in ways that often defied reason and logic. As a result, the focus shifted away from the teachings and practices that typified canonical Buddhism, and toward the actual human words and actions of enlightened Chan teachers. That new approach stood in sharp contrast to the *mārga*-centric soteriological schemata of all earlier Indian and Chinese Buddhism, and was tantamount to radical remaking of the basic character of Chinese Buddhism.[22]

But is there really any convincing proof for the putative link between the encounter dialogue model of religious communication and practice on the one hand, and Mazu and the rest of Tang Chan on the other hand? Can the copious presence of encounter dialogues stories in Mazu's record be taken as adequate evidence in support of Yanagida's theory? Because the encounter dialogue stories dominate current (mis)interpretations of classical Chan as a unique Sinitic religious movement with strong iconoclastic tendencies, if these questions were to be answered in the negative that would have important ramifications for our understanding of key elements of Chan history, doctrine, and practice.

We can assume that stories such as the one about Shuilao's awakening tell us something about Chan Buddhism at the time they were created, but *when* was that? Should the contents of stories of this kind be taken at face value as revealing anything about the views and practices of the monks who appear in them, or could it be that they are reflections of later images of classical Chan that might not have much to do with what monks such as Mazu and Shuilao actually did in the course of their religious careers? To rephrase the question slightly: are both traditional and contemporary writers about Chan justified when they use these stories as historical records about the classical Chan tradition, or are they perhaps mistakenly basing their interpretations on apocryphal textual materials that bear no direct relevance to the tradition they are supposed to describe? In order to answer these questions, and try to solve the already noted incongruity that arises from the contrasting images of Mazu conveyed by his sermons and dialogues, we have to examine the origins of the records where these divergent images first appear.

Origins of the Three Parts of the Text

Closer examination of Chan literature reveals, among other things, the composite structure of the texts that were composed in the main Chan literary genres. Despite their compilers' best efforts to construct seemingly coherent narratives that illumine a Chan monk's search and realization of religious awakening, texts such as Mazu's record of sayings bear a resemblance to quilts. They are essentially like multicolored patchworks, collections of miscellaneous and often incongruous parts. That is the case with all texts composed in the recorded sayings genre and the large historical chronicles written in the transmission of the lamp genre. In fact, there is substantial correspondence and overlap between the two genres, since the editors and compilers of texts composed in both genres used much the same materials, albeit in somewhat distinctive ways and for slightly different purposes. The basic materials used for the composition of both the transmission of the lamp chronicles and the recorded sayings primarily consisted of biographical sketches, transcripts of sermons, and stories that feature encounter dialogues. There was substantial direct borrowing between texts that belong to the two genres, as well as utilization of the same primary sources. For that reason, it is possible to say that in terms of their contents, the transmission of the lamp chronicles are compilations of abbreviated records of sayings of individual masters that are organized in a genealogical form that tracks the various Chan lineages of ancestral transmission.

Once we let go of normative notions of classical Chan records consisting of coherent and homogeneous accounts of Chan teachers' lively and spontaneous communications of ineffable truths, it becomes possible to seriously examine the Chan genres as composite narratives created from diverse literary formats. As it turns out, each of the different literary formats had its own separate history prior to its use as a building block for the construction of a specific genre. In order to better understand these texts we must determine the specific historical origins of each of the main literary formats that compose them. In the following pages I will address this issue by tracing the oldest textual sources that contain versions of the materials that compose each of the Mazu record's three constituent parts (biographical sketch, sermons, dialogues), and by tracking down the earliest appearance of the contents of each of the three parts.

First, Mazu's biography in *Mazu yulu*, as well as his biographies in other Chan texts, were primarily based on the two inscriptions composed by Quan Deyu (759–818) and Bao Ji (d. 792), two renowned literati and officials. Both men, who were good friends, became personally acquainted with Mazu during tours of government duty in Jiangxi. Quan's stele inscription, *Tang gu Hongzhou Kaiyuansi Shimen Daoyi chanshi beiming bingxu*, was composed in 791, only three years after Mazu's death, and Bao's memorial inscription soon thereafter.²³ In addition, a short stone inscription was discovered in 1966 underneath Mazu's memorial pagoda located on the grounds of Baofeng monastery in Jingan county, Jiangxi province. This inscription was also composed in 791, on the occasion of the formal opening of the memorial pagoda.²⁴ Bao's inscription is no longer extant, but its existence is mentioned in Mazu's biography in *Song gaoseng zhuan* (Song biographies of eminent monks), which was probably in part based on it.²⁵ Since Quan was on familiar terms with Mazu and his close disciples, he knew well the basic biographical details about his life.²⁶ Notwithstanding the presence of formulaic topoi and hagiographic embellishments of the kinds that are common in commemorative inscriptions written for medieval religious leaders, we can assume with reasonable certainty that the basic outline of Mazu's life presented in these almost contemporary sources is fairly accurate.

Although there are no extant manuscripts from the Tang period that contain Mazu's sermons, on the basis of substantial circumstantial evidence it is possible to infer that the extant sermons are based on early editions of edited transcripts of various talks Mazu gave during his long teaching career. Due to space constraints, it is not possible to provide copious quotations and detailed textual analysis of the relevant documents, but the evidence used to arrive at this conclusion can be summarized as follows. First, there are various quotations from Mazu's sermons in the records of his disciples, including mention of the existence of a record of Mazu's teachings (*yuben*) in biographies by Dongsi Ruhui (744–823) and Yangshan Huiji (807–883) in *Zutang ji*. Ruhui is recorded as saying that Mazu's *yuben* included discussion about the well-known maxim "Mind is Buddha," whereas Yangshan is cited as stating that in his sermons Mazu quoted the *Laṅkāvatāra* Scripture (*Lengqie jing*).²⁷ Both of these appear in Mazu's extant sermons. Mazu's sermons are also quoted or alluded to in other early texts, such as Huangbo's *Chuanxin fayao*, one of Wuye's sermons quoted in *Zongjing lu*,²⁸ and in the record of Baizhang.²⁹ Furthermore, a close textual comparison of the description of Mazu's teachings presented in the writings of the famous Chan historian Guifeng Zongmi (780–841), composed during the 830s, with the extant version of Mazu's sermons indicates that Zongmi read Mazu's sermons during the early ninth century and drew on them in his depiction of the Hongzhou school's teachings.³⁰ Finally, in terms of their literary structure, terminology, use of canonical quotations, and doctrinal contents, Mazu's sermons closely resemble the records of his disciples' teachings that were compiled during the ninth century, such as Baizhang's *Guanglu* and Huangbo's *Chuanxin fayao*. Although each of the points above is inconclusive on its own, taken together they make a strong case for establishing the early provenance of Mazu's sermons as edited transcripts of his talks and lectures.

In conclusion, as far as the provenance of the dialogues is concerned, there is no evidence to suggest that *any* of the dialogues that appear in *Mazu yulu* existed during the Tang period. The earliest extant text where a few of them appear, *Zutang ji*, was compiled in 952, 164 years after Mazu's death. Moreover, Mazu's biography in this text contains only five of the thirty-two dialogues that appear in *Mazu yulu*, and on the whole its contents are quite different from those of *Mazu yulu*.[31] *Zongjing lu*, the other Five Dynasties (907–960) Chan text that includes Tang materials contains all of Mazu's sermons (as well as excerpts from two additional sermons), but it contains only one of his dialogues.[32] A large number of Mazu's dialogues, including some of the best-known, appear for the first time in *Chuandeng lu*, compiled in 1004. Although there are only minor differences between these versions and the ones from *Mazu yulu*, on the whole it seems probable that the compiler of *Mazu yulu* used *Chuandeng lu*, a text composed well over two centuries after Mazu's death, as one of his main sources.

The origins of the materials that constitute the three parts of *Mazu yulu* are summarized in Table 2.1.

TABLE 2.1. Origins of the Materials that Constitute the Three Parts of *Mazu yulu*

Sources[a]	Section[b]		
	Biography	Sermons	Dialogues
Baofeng monastic stone inscription (791)	2/7	0	0
Quan Deyu's inscription (791)	7/7	0	0
Biography in *Baolin zhuan* (801)[c]	1/7 (7/7?)	0 (more?)	0
Chanyuan duxu and Pei Xiu sheyiwen (c. 830)[d]	2/7	3/3	0
Biography in *Zutang ji* (952)	5/7	1/3	5/32
Zongjinglu (961)	2/7	3/3 (+2)	1
Biography in *Song gaoseng zhuan* (988)	7/7	0	0
Biography in *Chuandeng lu* (1004)[e]	7/7	1/3 (+1)	11/32
Mazu Yulu (c. 1085)	7/7	3/3	32/32

[a]The approximate dates of the compilation of each text are given in parentheses.
[b]The subdivision of each section is based on the following criteria: (1) the biographical sketch is divided into seven parts, each of which consists of essential information about Mazu's life—years of birth and death, birthplace, study with Huairang, teaching at Gonggong Mountain, stay in Hongzhou, association with literati/officials, and training of disciples; (2) the number of sermons given as basis of comparison is three, based on the sermons contained in *Mazu yulu*; (3) the extant dialogues are divided into thirty-two sections, following the division introduced in *Sun-Face Buddha*, my translation of *Mazu yulu*. The correspondences between the contents of a particular text and the relevant section of *Mazu yulu* are expressed as fractions.
[c]The last (tenth) fascicle of *Baolin zhuan*, which included Mazu's biography, is lost and only a few brief fragments from Mazu's biography are still extant. My guess about the presence of additional biographical data and excerpts from the sermons is based on the inclusion of this kind of materials in the biographies that are preserved in the extant fascicles from this text. The contents of the last two missing fascicles of *Baolin zhuan* are discussed in Shiina Kōyū's two articles, "*Hōrinden* itsubun no kenkyū," *Komazawa daigaku bukkyōgakubu ronshū* 11 (1980): 234–257; and "*Hōrinden* makikyū makiju no itsubun," *Shūgaku kenkyū* 22 (1980): 191–198.
[d]T 48.402c XZJ 110.434b–d. In these two texts, Zongmi is not quoting directly from Mazu's sermons; rather, he is alluding to or paraphrasing short passages from each of the sermons. See also his discussion of the Hongzhou School in *Yuanjuejing dashuchao*, XZJ 14.279a–b.
[e]*Chuandeng lu* 6, pp. 104–106. The second sermon is presented as an independent text, rather than part of his biography, in *Chuandeng lu* 28, pp. 581–582.

As we examine the data presented in the table, it is obvious that none of the early sources from the Tang period contains a single dialogue. The fact that the encounter dialogues were nonexistent during the early ninth century is also corroborated by the contents of *Baolin zhuan*. Although the crucial tenth fascicle that included Mazu's biography is lost, on the basis of the materials presented in the extant fascicles it is apparent that this important text, which depicts the recently deceased Mazu as the inheritor of the orthodox Chan transmission, was composed before the onset of the encounter dialogue age.

After the dialogues made their appearance in *Zutang ji*, their numbers gradually increased in later transmission of the lamp texts. Mazu's biography in *Chuandeng lu* contains only about 34 percent of the number of dialogues found in *Mazu yulu*. If we add the other eleven dialogues that appear in the biographies of Mazu's disciples, that brings the number of dialogues to twenty-two, or approximately 69 percent of the total found in *Mazu yulu*. It is apparent that the inclusion of dialogues as part of Mazu's record started with Mazu's biography in *Zutang ji*, and was significantly expanded in *Chuandeng lu*. From then on, virtually all later Song collections of Chan materials, such as *Tiansheng guangdeng lu* (compiled in 1029) and *Gu zunsu yulu* (compiled in 1178), continued to include the dialogues as the largest part of Mazu's record.[33] We can therefore conclude that it was only from the second part of the tenth century onward that stories that contain Mazu's and his disciples' iconoclastic dialogues came to shape the understanding of their religious thought and teaching methods, and the history of the Hongzhou school.

Literary Transmutations

The analysis of *Mazu yulu* presented in the preceding pages offers a simple resolution to the problem posed by the contrasting images of Mazu evidenced in his sermons and dialogues. The existence of the two sharply divergent images can be explained by the simple fact that each of the two types of literary subgenres in which they are presented originated at different times and in response to different sets of religious and social predicaments. The two distinct types of literary narratives reflected the changing images of Mazu, his Hongzhou school, and the rest of classical Chan. Those images were continually refashioned in light of the distinct conceptions of Chan orthodoxy prevalent during the periods of their creation and among the groups that produced them. The sermons' conservative image of Mazu as a somewhat traditional Buddhist teacher, which is confirmed by the available biographical materials, reflects the historical reality of his actual position as an abbot of a large official monastery in the southern part of the Tang empire. The iconoclastic image that we find in his dialogues, on the other hand, reflects later semi-mythologized portrayals of Mazu as a radical leader of a growing novel movement that challenged the hallowed traditions of medieval Chinese Buddhism and charted a path for the establishment of new Chan orthodoxy.

One of the notable differences between the sermons and the dialogues, which is directly related to their diverse origins, is the level of variation among different editions and versions of the same stories and sermons. Whereas there were no significant changes in the different versions of Mazu's sermons and the sermons of other Chan monks from the Tang period, the situation with the dialogues was quite the opposite. Careful comparison of different editions of Chan records reveals that often there are great changes and significant differences between variant versions of the same encounter dialogue.[34] In some instances, identical or similar stories are attributed to completely different monks. It is apparent that because many of the dialogues were originally created and transmitted as oral narratives, at the early stage of their historical development their contents had considerable fluidity and flexibility, which accounts for the proliferation of different versions of the same stories.

To illustrate the changes introduced in different versions of an encounter dialogue, let us examine the story of the initial meeting between Mazu and his disciple Wuye (761–823). Below there are translations of two extant versions of this story presented next to each other, divided into sections for an easy comparison. Parts of the story that are identical in both versions (or differ only in unimportant details) are italicized. The version on the right is from *Mazu yulu*[35]; the version on the left from Wuye's biography in *Song gaoseng zhuan*.[36] When comparing the two versions, it is useful to bear in mind that even though the exact origin of either is impossible to establish, the *Song gaoseng zhuan* version is earlier, and it appears in a nonsectarian text that is a more reliable source of historical information.

[A1] Later, [when *Wuye*] heard that *Daji* (i.e., Mazu) of Hongzhou was the leader of the Chan School, he went there to see him and pay his respects. Wuye's *body* was six feet tall and it stood magnificently like a mountain. His gaze had a determined expression, and the sound of *his voice was like a bell.* As soon as he saw him, Daji smiled and *said, "Such an imposing Buddha hall, but no Buddha in it."*

[A2] When Chan teacher *Wuye* of Fenzhou went to see the *Patriarch* (i.e., Mazu), the Patriarch noticed that his *appearance* was extraordinary and that *his voice was like* [the sound of] *a bell.* He *said, "Such an imposing Buddha hall, but no Buddha in it."*

[B1] *Wuye respectfully kneeled down, and said, "As to the texts which contain the teachings of the three vehicles, I have been able to roughly understand their*

[B2] *Wuye respectfully kneeled down, and said, "I have studied the texts that contain the teachings of the three vehicles and have been able to roughly un-*

meaning. I have also heard about the teaching of the Chan school that mind is Buddha, and this is something that I have not yet been able to understand."

[C1] Daji said, "This very mind that does not understand is it; there is nothing else. When there is no realization, it is ignorance; with realization it is awakening. Ignorance is sentient being; awakening is the Buddha's Way. Without leaving sentient beings, how could there be any Buddha? It is like making a fist with one's hand—the fist is the hand!"

[E1] On hearing this, *Wuye experienced awakening.* He wept sorrowfully, and told Daji, "Before I used to think that the Buddha's Way is broad and distant, and that it can be realized only after many eons of effort and suffering. Today for the first time I realized that the true reality of the *dharmakāya* is originally completely present in oneself. All the myriad dharmas are created by the mind and are names only, devoid of any reality."

[F1] *Daji said,* "That is so. The nature of all dharmas is neither born nor perishable. All dharmas are fundamentally empty and quiescent. The sutras say that 'all dharmas are from the very beginning of the character of extinction [nirvāṇa].' They also say that they are 'the house of ultimate

derstand their meaning. I have also often heard about the teaching of the Chan school that mind is Buddha, and this is something I have not yet been able to understand."

[C2] *The Patriarch said,* "This very mind that does not understand is it. There is no other thing."

[D2] Wuye further asked, "What is the mind-seal that the Patriarch [Bodhidharma] secretly transmitted from the West?" The Patriarch said, "The Reverend looks rather disturbed right now. Go and come some other time."

[E2] As Wuye was just about to step out, the Patriarch called him, "Venerable!" Wuye turned his head and the Patriarch asked him, "What is it?" [On hearing this] *Wuye experienced awakening.*

[F2] He bowed to the *Patriarch,* who *said,* "This stupid fellow! What is this bowing all about?"

emptiness and quiescence,' and that 'emptiness is the seat of all dharmas.' This is to say that all the buddhas, *tathāgatas*, dwell in this abode of nondwelling. If one has this understanding, then one dwells in the house of emptiness and quiescence, and sits on the seat of emptiness. Whether lifting the foot or putting it down, one never leaves the site of enlightenment. If upon receiving instructions one has realization, then there is no gradualness; without moving the foot, one ascends to the mountain of nirvāṇa."

The basic "plot" of the story is typical of this sort of Chan writings. The young Wuye goes to visit Mazu's monastery with an intent to receive religious instructions from the famous Chan teacher, perhaps in the hope of becoming enlightened by him. Until the beginning of section C both versions of the story are very similar. From that point on, however, they present two contrasting images of the Chan search and experience of spiritual awakening. The earlier version, from Wuye's biography in *Song gaoseng zhuan*, presents a fairly conservative description of Mazu's teachings, which accords with the earliest sources. This version of the story lacks the dramatic pathos we expect to find in classical Chan stories. It simply presents Mazu as a skilled teacher who instructs his new student by offering him rather commonplace doctrinal explanations, complete with scriptural quotations, very much in the style of a traditional Buddhist teacher. This version of the story depicts Wuye as having become awakened (*kaiwu*) upon hearing Mazu's short discourse on the essential identity of the Buddha and sentient beings, without clarifying the epistemological status of Wuye's realization. Nonetheless, Wuye is portrayed as equally prone to verbosity, and in section E1 we are provided with information about the intellectual content of Wuye's spiritual realization, which consists of a realization of the immanence of the true reality of *dharmakāya* (the true body of the Buddha) within oneself. All of these are standard Chinese Buddhist ideas, and they hardly represent notions that were unique to the Chan school. In its form and contents, this transcript of the dialogue between Mazu and Wuye is similar to conventional dialogues found in other Hongzhou school texts from the Tang period, such as the records of Huangbo and Baizhang; its format is also akin to some of the dialogues featured in other early Chan texts, such as the *Platform Sutra* and the records of Shenhui.

In contrast, the later version of the story from *Mazu yulu* portrays Wuye as being enlightened by Mazu in a direct and immediate way without resort to traditional forms of religious instruction. Here there is no trace of doctrinal explanations, very much in keeping with latter-day expectation that a Chan teacher would eschew the kind of profuse verbosity that was characteristic of the doctrinal schools. Instead, Chan teachers such as Mazu were supposed to discard conventional Buddhist teachings in favor of more direct methods of communication that, we are told, went directly to the heart of the matter. The unusual form of religious "training" presented in this story accords with popular notions about the distinctive teaching methods of classical Chan, which supposedly included beating, shouting, asking enigmatic questions, remaining silent in response to a question, and the like. The calling of student's name as a means to induce religious insight featured in this version of the story was another of the unconventional teaching methods, which according to D. T. Suzuki, Yanagida, and other scholars, were developed by the Hongzhou school as an expression of its novel style of uniquely Chinese form of profound spirituality.

Even without taking into account its late origin, the contents of the second version of the story give rise to doubts about its authenticity. It is strange, for example, that Wuye, who in section B describes himself an outsider to the Chan school, asks for religious instruction by employing the question about Bodhidharma's mythic transmission of the mind-seal of enlightenment to China. This formulaic question is an alternative and probably earlier version of the famous question about the "meaning of [Bodhidharma's] coming from the West," which appears as a set expression in numerous Song Chan texts. That is a typical example of the Chan "insider talk" that was popularized by Northern Song texts and took its full force with the offset of the age of *gongans*, not a question of somebody like Wuye who comes to meet a Chan teacher for the first time. It is also strange that Wuye, who prior to his coming to Mazu's monastery had undertaken extensive study of the Buddhist canon, would be unfamiliar with the doctrine about the identity of mind and Buddha. Though the authors of this and other similar stories tried to appropriate this doctrine as being unique to the Chan school, the theory of the intrinsic identity of the mind of the Buddha was by the mid-Tang period very much an integral part of the mainstream doctrinal outlook of Chinese Buddhism. It is highly improbable a monk as well versed in Buddhist doctrine as Wuye would have been unfamiliar with it, or that he would have been startled by its theoretical and practical ramifications.

It is apparent that the later version of the story presented in *Mazu yulu* is not a record of an encounter between two eighth-century monks. Rather, it should be read as a record that reflects the transformation of the images of classical Chan that was taking place during the tenth and eleventh centuries. The central feature of that process was the refashioning of Mazu and his disciples into radical iconoclasts, a process that reflected the changing beliefs of the Chan school and the sectarian needs of certain Chan factions. To a large extent, these changes were enacted as part of unstructured growth and transmission of popular lore that centered on the spiritual exploits of the great Tang Chan teachers. But at least to some degree, they also reflected the attempts of later Chan groups to transform existing or invent new religious narratives that would lend support to their claims about the spiritual legitimacy of their lineage. Often the image of a noted Chan teacher from the Tang period was recreated in a manner that conformed to a new pattern of "exemplary" Chan religiosity that reflected the religious concerns and ideological requirements of these later Chan factions. An easy way to achieve that transformation was to rewrite earlier dialogues in which that particular Chan teacher was a participant, or to create entirely new fictional dialogues in which he acted and spoke in ways that accorded with the religious ideas and sectarian predilections of much later Chan factions. In the case of Mazu, we are of course talking of the Linji school, which after its slow start by the early Song was successfully positioning itself as the orthodox Chan tradition that traced its spiritual ancestry back to Mazu.

Canons, Texts, and Interpretations

As we saw, the three main styles of narrative discourse found in Mazu's record of sayings (his biographical sketches, sermons, and encounter dialogues) were products of different sets of historical circumstances, had different literary histories, and revealed different dimensions of the Chan school's constantly evolving conceptions of religious doctrine, practice, and experience. The analysis presented above demonstrates that although it can be substantiated that Mazu's sermons and his biography were recorded during the mid-Tang period, there is no evidence that any of his encounter dialogues were extant before the mid-tenth century or that any of them had any direct connection with Mazu. This finding about the varied provenance of the constituent parts of *Mazu yulu* is also applicable to other records of prominent Chan teachers from the middle and late Tang periods.

    In light of popular belief about the central role of the encounter dialogue model in the religious discourse and practice of classical Chan, it is important to note that the lack of any evidence about Tang-period origins of any of the dialogues that appear in *Mazu yulu* is in no way unique to this text. Despite the fact that later Chan collections include many stories that contain iconoclastic dialogues in which Mazu and his disciples are the main protagonists, not one of them appears in a text from the Tang period (i.e., before the tenth century). Indeed, I have not been able to find a single piece of contemporary evidence to indicate that during the Tang period there was any awareness of such a thing as encounter dialogue, let alone that it was Chan's main medium of religious instruction, as is often assumed. None of the extant records from the Tang convey any sense of recognition of the encounter dialogue model. That is true of the numerous stele inscriptions and other epigraphic evidence, the transcripts of the teachings of Mazu's spiritual descendants (such as the records of Baizhang and Huangbo mentioned above), Zongmi's writings on Chan, and the poems and miscellaneous writings of Tang literati and historical chronicles such as *Baolin zhuan*. It is also true of texts actually written by Chan monks, such as the treatise by Dazhu Huihai (fl. 8th c.) on Chan doctrine, *Dunwu rudao yaomen lun*, and the tract on monastic life by Guishan Lingyou (771–853), *Guishan jingce*.

It was only from the middle part of the tenth century onward that stories containing Mazu's iconoclastic dialogues with his disciples came to shape the (mis)understanding of his religious thought and teaching methods. At present, the situation is further exacerbated by the uncritical acceptance of the somewhat biased interpretation of sectarian Japanese scholarship, not to mention popular vulgarizations of the tradition's teachings and history. That does not preclude the possibility that some of the dialogues might echo an orally transmitted lore that was at least partially based on events that took place during the lives of Mazu and other Chan monks, even if they were taken out of context and recast in the light of sentiments and concerns that were not present during the late Tang period. But such tenuous connections are impossible to unravel, and even if there was anything of that sort, it is still clear that the encounter dialogue model of religious communication and practice, as presented in Song texts and interpreted by modern commentators, was not in vogue during the Tang period. In the same vein, it is apparent that encounter dialogue stories should in no way be used as historical sources for the study of the Hongzhou school's history, teachings, and practices.

The establishment of religious canons, such the Chan canon of which *Mazu yulu* became a part, is usually an act of defining the basic identity of a religious tradition and establishing the parameters of its orthodoxy. The writing of texts that turn out to be parts of an emerging canon typically involves a somewhat arbitrary demarcation of the historical origins and essential teachings of a specific tradition. That obscures the complex historical processes that led to the creation of the contents of the canon. That a major portion of the Chan canon is in a sense forgery—which in the present case applies to the numerous apocryphal stories that feature encounter dialogues of noted Chan teachers from the middle and late Tang periods—should perhaps not come as a surprise to students of Buddhism (or more generally to students of religious literature).

The history of Buddhism in both India and China was a history of production of new texts whose complex origins were obscured by attributing them to the Buddha or to other noted leaders and thinkers of various Buddhist traditions. Such were the origins of the Indian Mahāyāna scriptures that were translated into Chinese, as well as the numerous apocryphal scriptures and treatises composed in China. The proliferation of new texts that openly aspired to canonical status, or unwittingly and gradually become accepted as such, was made possible by the fact that the Chinese Buddhist canon was an open one. As it set to create its own body of religious literature—some of which was eventually canonized as prized repository of quasi-historical lore and authoritative religious teachings—the Chan school simply inherited and adapted tendencies that were an inherent part of the broader Buddhist tradition from which it evolved.

The reading and interpretation of canonical texts such as *Mazu yulu* is greatly enhanced when it is grounded in an understanding of their genesis, literary structure, and the ideological and institutional contexts that shaped their creation. All of these, in turn, can be situated in relation to the characteristics of the genre to which a specific text belongs. The creation of distinctive Chan genres was a gradual process of codification of discursive properties characteristic of the Chan school that took place over an extended period of time.[37] Each new genre, including the records of sayings of noted Chan teachers that were briefly examined in the proceeding pages, grew out of what existed before it. The codification of a genre such as the Chan records of sayings was the result of a prolonged process that involved the transformation—through "combination, displacement, or inversion"—of one or more earlier genres.[38] By combining elements from earlier texts and introducing new models of narrative structure, the Chan school developed original types of literature that reflected its continuously evolving religious and institutional concerns.

Comprehending the process that led to the creation of a specific Chan genre and its subsequent institutionalization is of great help in understanding, to use Tzvetan Todorov's terminology, the "models of writing" utilized by the ancient authors of Chan works, as well as the "horizons of expectation" of their medieval readers.[39] Like firmly rooted social institutions, established genres transmit certain sets of religious and social attitudes by which they are shaped, and on which in turn they act and affect.[40] Since genres, like other institutions, are reflections of the dominant ideology and reveal the major constitutive traits and values of the social groupings or religious traditions that created them, understanding the formation and function of Chan genres sheds light on the forces that shaped the historical development of the tradition(s) that produced them.[41]

As far as the historical emergence of the encounter dialogue model is concerned, unfortunately at this point we do not know how and why these stories were created.[42] We also do not understand the impulses and circumstances that led to the canonization of those texts that created and popularized the iconoclastic image of classical Chan, as conveyed by the encounter dialogues of Mazu and other great Chan teachers from the Tang period. Although it is possible to speculate about the ways various aspects of changing religious, social, and political milieus influenced this development, in order to be able to respond to these questions in a meaningful and productive way we must undertake a systematic study of the history and literature of Chan Buddhism during the period that covers the late ninth and the tenth centuries, that is, the final decades of the Tang dynasty, the Five Dynasties period, and the early Song. Unfortunately, that period has received little attention from Chan scholarship.

The present analysis highlights some of the serious problems that arise from the prevalent tendency to use the encounter dialogues as sources of information about Mazu, his Hongzhou school, and the rest of the classical Chan tradition. Most of the prevalent misunderstandings of the doctrines, practices, and institutions of the Hongzhou school stem from the fact that studies of Tang Chan place undue emphasis on the apocryphal dialogues found in later strata of Chan literature, and gloss over or ignore those earlier sources that do not accord with entrenched views about classical Chan. That does not mean that the dialogues are of no value for our understating of Chan's historical evolution. They are of immense importance for understating the religious and social milieus that produced them, and the later traditions that transmitted and employed them. But none of that has anything to do with the Hongzhou school and Tang Chan, but pertains to the religious history of the Song and the subsequent periods.

One of the key issues here is the need to establish sound criteria for distinguishing elements of Chan narratives that are pertinent to the study of Tang Chan from those that are more useful for understanding the social and religious milieus of Song Chan. This is not a case where we must adopt a historiographic approach that privileges earlier texts and narratives over later ones. Religious meaning is produced not only with the emergence of great religious leaders, new traditions, and texts produced by them. New meaning is constantly produced in light of changing religious sentiments and diverse local conditions, often disguised as a restatement or clarification of meaning initially articulated by individuals who are perceived as tradition's founding figures. A text such as *Mazu yulu* should therefore be read in relation to at least two points of reference: the historical contexts of the life and teachings of the religious leader who dominated the Chan tradition during the mid-Tang period, and the subsequent transformations of his image in light of the prevailing religious attitudes and ideological agendas of later Chan milieus and traditions. Both are valid areas of historical research, but we must not confuse the two. Such multivalence makes the study of this and other comparable texts a much more complex undertaking. But even as that calls for a prudent consideration of the convoluted questions of origin, genre, and interpretation that were briefly touched upon in the preceding pages, it also makes these documents valuable sources that shed light on a broader array of issues that shaped the ongoing evolution of a key tradition in Chinese religious history, as reflected in the lives (both actual and fictional) of its great patriarchs.

NOTES

1. An example of this tendency is Judith Berling's "Bringing the Buddha down to Earth: Notes on the Emergence of Yü-lu as a Buddhist Genre," *History of Religions* 27 no. 1 (1987): 56–88, a rare study of one of the Chan genres. In what is supposed to be a discussion of the evolution of the "records of sayings" (*yulu*) genre, Berling does not distinguish between different Chan genres. For example, *Jingde chuandeng lu*, which belongs to the genre of "lamp histories," and *Biyan lu*, a Northern Song *gongan* collection, are both assigned to the *yulu* genre, whereas the *yulu* genre itself is basically reduced to one of its elements, the popular encounter dialogue stories. Berling's somewhat indiscriminate mixing of different genres and lack of appreciation of their complex origins is by no means unique; as a matter of fact, it is typical of both traditional and modern Chan/Zen scholarship.

2. The record forms a part of *Sijia yulu* (Record of the sayings of four masters), which can be found in XZJ 119.405c–409a (discussed in the next section). An English translation by Cheng-chien can be found in my *Sun-Face Buddha: The Teachings of Mazu and the Hongzhou School of Chan Cheng-chien* (Berkeley: Asian Humanities Press, 1993), pp. 59–94. For a good Japanese translation, which also includes the original Chinese text, see Iriya Yoshitaka, trans., *Baso no goroku* (Kyoto: Zen bunka kenkyūjo, 1984), pp. 1–119.

3. Yanagida Seizan, "Goroku no rekishi: Zen bunken no seiritsu shiteki kenkyū," *Tōhō gakuhō* 57 (1985): 474.

4. Ibid., p. 476.

5. The extant editions of Linji's record go back to an even later version of the text, produced at Gushan, Fujian, in 1120. See Akizuki Ryomin, trans., *Rinzairoku* (Tokyo: Chikuma shobō, 1972), p. 251.

6. For Pei Xiu's association with Huangbo, see Yoshikawa Tadao, "Hai Kyū den: Tōdai no ichi shidaifu to bukkyō," *Tōhō gakuhō* 64 (1992): 140–50. For the compilation of Huangbo's records, see Yanagida's comments in Iriya Yoshitaka, trans., *Denshin hōyō, Enryōroku* (Tokyo: Chikuma shobō, 1969), pp. 172–76.

7. Iriya, trans., *Denshin hōyō, Enryōroku*, pp. 172–76.

8. The compilation of Baizhang's record is mentioned in his stele inscription, which was written by Zhen Xu shortly after his death. A text entitled *Baizhangshan heshang yaojue* (The essential teachings of the reverent from Baizhang Mountain), presumably an early version of this text, is listed in Enchin's (814–891) catalogues of texts he brought to Japan from China in the 840s. See T 55.1,095a, T 55.1,101a, T 55.1,106c, and Yanagida, "The 'Recorded Sayings' Texts of Chinese Ch'an Buddhism," translated by John McRae, in Whalen Lai and Lewis Lancaster, eds., *Early Ch'an in China and Tibet* (Berkeley: Asian Humanities Press, 1983), pp. 191–92.

9. The very term "record of sayings" is not attested before the beginning of the Song Dynasty. It first appears in the biographies of Huangbo and Zhaozhou (778–889) in *Song gaoseng zhuan*, T 50.842c23 and T 50.775c17–8, respectively. For a dis-

cussion of the antecedents to this term, see Yanagida, "Goroku no rekishi," pp. 229–246.

10. For a definition of "encounter dialogue," a term coined by Yanagida, see John McRae, "The Antecedents of Encounter Dialogue in Chinese Ch'an Buddhism," in Steven Heine and Dale S. Wright, eds., *The Kōan: Texts and Contexts in Zen Buddhism* (Oxford: Oxford University Press, 2000), pp. 47–48.

11. T. Griffith Foulk, "Myth, Ritual, and Monastic Practice in Sung Ch'an Buddhism," in Patricia Buckley Ebrey and Peter N. Gregory, eds., *Religion and Society in T'ang and Sung China* (Honolulu: University of Hawai'i Press, 1992), pp. 149–150.

12. Ibid., p. 149.

13. T 47.504b–506c.

14. T 47.575a–576a. See also Yanagida, "Goroku no rekishi," p. 576. New revised editions of both *Linji lu* and *Yunmen lu* were published together in 1267; see Akizuki, trans., *Rinzai roku*, p. 252. For the compilation of *Yunmen lu*, see Nagai Masashi, "Unmon no goroku no seiritsu ni kansuru ichi kōsatsu," *Shōgaku kenkyū* 13 (1971): pp. 111–116.

15. For the format of official biography, see Denis Twitchett, "Problems of Chinese Biography," in Arthur F. Wright and Denis Twitchett, eds., *Confucian Personalities* (Stanford: Stanford University Press, 1962), p. 28.

16. *Mazu yulu*, XZJ 119.406a; translation adapted (with minor modifications) from Cheng-chien in Poceski, *Sun-Face Buddha*, p. 62.

17. See Kenneth Ch'en, *The Chinese Transformation of Buddhism* (Princeton: Princeton University Press, 1973), pp. 240–241. The image of the erudite but spiritually unaccomplished lecture master is a standard trope in Chan literature, where the subject is unflatteringly contrasted with the enlightened Chan teacher. One such example that comes from Mazu's records is the story about the abbot of Daan monastery in Hongzhou and a ghost, recounted in *Zutang ji* (Changsha: Yuelu shushe, 1996), vol. 14, pp. 304–305. A more flattering picture of this type of monk can be found in the numerous biographies assigned to the category of exegetes (*yijie*) that are included in the collections of biographies of eminent monks, such as *Gaoseng zhuan*.

18. Ch'en, *The Chinese Transformation of Buddhism*, pp. 243–244.

19. Yanagida has argued that Chan sermons were markedly different from the conventional sermons that were in vogue at the time. See Yanagida, "Goroku no rekishi," pp. 513–514. His contention is based more on his heartfelt convictions about the uniqueness of Chan teaching methods—indeed, the uniqueness of the whole Chan experience—than on any sound textual evidence. There is insufficient data to ascertain the exact format and ritual setting in which Chan sermons were delivered during the mid-Tang period. The earliest description of the format of a Chan sermon is a brief passage from *Chanmen guishi* (composed toward the end of the tenth century), which is appended to Baizhang's biography in *Chuandeng lu* 6 (Taipei: Xinwen feng, 1988), p. 117; English translation by Cheng-chien in Poceski *Sun-Face Buddha*, p. 34. Though conclusive evidence is lacking, it seems probable that the ritual context in which Chan monks presented their sermons was not much different from the one used in most Tang monasteries. Descriptions of ritual settings for Buddhist sermons can be found in monastic texts such as Yuanzhao's *Sifenlü xingshichao zichiji*, T 40.404b, quoted in Ch'en, *The Chinese Transformation of Buddhism*, p. 247. See also

Edwin O. Reischauer, trans., *Ennin's Diary: The Record of a Pilgrimage to China in Search of the Law* (New York: Ronald, 1955), pp. 154–55, for a translation of a passage from Ennin's diary that describes a public lecture which Ennin heard in 839.

20. Paul Ricoeur, *Hermeneutics and the Human Sciences: Essays on Language, Action, and Interpretation* (Cambridge: Cambridge University Press, 1981), p. 148.

21. *Mazu yulu*, XZJ 119.408a; Cheng Chien, in Poceski, *Sun-Face Buddha*, p. 16. There is a different version of this story in *Gu zunsu yulu*, XZJ 118.80d, also translated in *Sun-Face Buddha*, p. 92 n. 58.

22. See Yanagida is three articles, "Basozen no sho mondai," *Indogaku bukkyōgaku kenkyū* 17 no.1 (1968): 37–38; "Chūgoku zenshū shi," in Suzuki Daisetsu and Nishitani Keiji, ed., *Zen no rekishi: Chūgoku*, pp. 53–56; and "Zenshū goroku no keisei," *Indogaku bukkyōgaku kenkyū* 18 no.1 (1969): 40. For a further discussion of the encounter dialogue model that is influenced by Yanagida's views, see John McRae, "Encounter Dialogue and the Transformation of the Spiritual Path in Chinese Ch'an," in Robert E. Buswell and Robert M. Gimello, eds., *Paths to Liberation: The Mārga and Its Transformations in Buddhist Thought* (Honolulu: University of Hawai'i Press, 1992), pp. 339–369.

23. There are three extant editions of Mazu's stele inscription, preserved in the following collections: *Quan Tangwen* 501.5106a–5107a, *Tang wenzui* 64.1058–1059, and *Quanzai zhi wenji* 28.167a–168a. The three editions are quite similar, and the minor differences between them appear to be mostly due to copyists' errors.

24. For brief information about the discovery of this inscription and its contents, see Chen Baiquan, "Mazu chanshi shihan tiji yu Zhang Zongyan tianshi kuanji," *Wenshi* 14 (1982): 258.

25. *Song gaoseng zhuan* 10, T 50.766c. See also Nishiguchi Yoshio, "Baso no denki," *Zengaku kenkyū* 63 (1984): 117.

26. Quan also wrote a stele inscription for Zhangjing Huaihui (756–815), one Mazu's main disciples who taught in Changan, the Tang capital. For this inscription, titled *Tang Zhangjingsi Baiyan dashi beiming bingxu*, see *Quan Tangwen* 501.2260b–c and *Wenyuan yinghua* 866.4568a–b.

27. *Zutang ji* 15.338 and *Zutang ji* 18.410, respectively.

28. For Mazu's quotation, see *Zongjing lu* 14, T 48.492a; for Huangbo's passage, see T 48.381a (Iriya, *Denshin hōyō, Enryō*, p. 30); and for Wuye's, see *Zongjing lu* 98, T 48.942c. These correspondences are pointed out in Yanagida, "Goroku no rekishi," p. 494.

29. See *Mazu yulu*, XZJ 119.406c, and *Baizhang guanglu*, XZJ 118.85.

30. For more details, see my "The Hongzhou School of Chan Buddhism during the Mid-Tang Period" (Ph.D. dissertation, University of California at Los Angeles, 2000), pp. 98–101.

31. *Zutang ji* 14.304–309.

32. T 48.418b, 492a, 550c, and 940b.

33. For a convenient summary of the inclusion of Mazu's dialogues in these texts, see the table in Okimoto Katsumi, "Zen shisō keiseishi no kenkyū," in *Kenkyū Hōkoku* (Kyoto: Hanazono Daigaku gokusai zengaku kenkyūjō, 1998), pp. 351–353.

34. Yanagida, "Goroku no rekishi," p. 545.

35. XZJ 119.407d; translated by Cheng-chien in Poceski, *Sun-Face Buddha*, p. 74.

36. *Song gaoseng zhuan* 11, T 50.772b–c; translated by Cheng-chien in Poceski, *Sun-Face Buddha*, p. 90 n. 52. Two additional version of the same dialogue can be found in *Zutang ji* 14.308 and *Zongjing lu* 98, T 48.942c–43a.

37. See Tzvetan Todorov, "The Origin of Genres," *New Literary History* 8 no.1 (1976): 162.

38. Ibid., p. 161.

39. Ibid., p. 163.

40. Heather Dubrow, *Genre* (London: Methuen, 1982), p. 4.

41. See Todorov, "The Origin of Genres," p. 162.

42. For discussion of different types of Chan discourses that might be construed as antecedents to the encounter dialogues, see McRae, "The Antecedents of Encounter Dialogue."

3

The *Lidai fabao ji* (Record of the Dharma-Jewel through the Ages)

Wendi Adamek

The *Lidai fabao ji* is a long-lost Chan/Zen Buddhist text, recovered from among the manuscripts discovered in 1900 in the hidden library at the Mogao caves, near the Silk Road oasis of Dunhuang.[1] Until then, it was remembered only as a fraudulent history produced by a dubious branch of Chan, the Bao Tang (Protect the Tang dynasty) school of Jiannan (modern-day Sichuan).[2] Previously, this sole work of the Bao Tang was known only through critical comments found in the writings of two Sichuan contemporaries, the Jingzhong Chan master Shenqing (d. 814), and the Chan/Huayan master Zongmi (780–841).[3]

The *Lidai fabao ji* fabrication most frequently singled out for criticism is the story that the founder of their school, the Chan master Wuzhu (714–774), was in possession of the key Chan talisman, the robe that the fifth patriarch Hongren (602–675) was said to have conferred upon the sixth patriarch Huineng (638–713). The *Lidai fabao ji* author or authors claim that the robe had been given by the empress Wu Zetian (r. 684–705) to a master in the lineage claimed by the Bao Tang school. In contrast, the accepted belief was that the robe was enshrined at Huineng's temple in Shaozhou, far to the south.[4] At the same time, in the *Lidai fabao ji* the most prominent of Wuzhu's teachings is anti-institutional antinomianism, and the text ends with no indication of the fate of the robe or the succession at Wuzhu's death.

The Background of the *Lidai fabao ji* Texts

The *Lidai fabao ji* was probably composed sometime between 774 and 780 at the Bao Tang monastery in Zizhou by an anonymous disciple or disciples of Master Wuzhu. Wuzhu claimed Dharma descent from the charismatic Korean Chan master Wuxiang (684–762), who was well known as the founder of the Jingzhong school of Chengdu, but the Bao Tang cannot be traced as an independent line beyond the generation of Wuzhu's immediate disciples. The *Lidai fabao ji* is preserved in a surprisingly large number of manuscripts and fragments from the Dunhuang materials.[5] The complete or nearly complete texts are: P 2125, S 516, P 3717, and Jinyi 304.[6] The fragments are: S 5916, S 1611, S 1776, S 11014,[7] part of P 3727, Jinyi 103,[8] the manuscript from the collection of Ishii Mitsuo,[9] Chapter 3934r,[10] and Fragment 261.[11] Other Dunhuang texts that quote from or show the influence of the *Lidai fabao ji* include P 2776, P 2680, a separate text included in P 3727, P Tib. 116, P Tib. 121, P Tib. 813, P Tib. 699.[12]

Except in one instance, there is no way to know the circumstances in which the text survived until the early eleventh century, when the cave-temple cache was sealed.[13] The large number of texts and fragments of the *Lidai fabao ji* in the Dunhuang cache, and the evidence of its dispersion into Turfan and Tibet, shows that it was far from being a negligible work. Moreover, Rong Xinjiang has effectively challenged the theory, promulgated by Stein and later scholars, that the Dunhuang deposit was a repository of "sacred waste." Instead, he argues that the cache held the library collection of Sanjie Monastery, which included valuable texts and paintings collected and repaired by the monk Daozhen until late in the tenth century.[14] Among the apocrypha and Chan works popular in ninth- and tenth-century Dunhuang, the *Lidai fabao ji* appears to have been considered worthy of frequent reproduction, and its subsequent disappearance thus becomes all the more puzzling. This disappearance means, however, that the *Lidai fabao ji* provides us with a rare opportunity to shed light on the historical contingencies that shape sectarian identity. The fact that the Bao Tang school was so short-lived and its remains were hermetically sealed makes it for all its fabrications a more accurate reflection of the Buddhist world of the eighth and ninth centuries, the so-called golden age of Chan, than the authoritative eleventh- and twelfth-century accounts. Indeed, the canonical accounts may be no more truthful than the *Lidai fabao ji*—merely more successful.

The *Lidai fabao ji* is one of a scant handful of Chan texts from roughly the same period, each possessing unique features that were absorbed and/or superseded by the official Chan genealogy, the *Jingde chuandeng lu* (Record of the transmission of the lamp compiled in the Jingde era) compiled in 1004.[15] The lore of the Chan patriarchy was reworked in numerous iterations over the course of several centuries, so that most traces of the particular historical valuations and tensions from which it had originally emerged were erased or submerged. The historicity of the biographies and lineages of renowned Chan masters has been undermined not only by Dunhuang finds but also by scholarly recognition that these biographical genealogies are by and large products of the Song dynasty (960–1279), when Chan enjoyed the prestige of an established religious and cultural institution, and the privilege of canonizing a romanticized view of its origins.[16] Examination of the Dunhuang cache and subsequent reexamination of earlier materials have given scholars a glimpse of lost sketches and a few of the cruder attempts, such as the *Lidai fabao ji*, that nevertheless contributed to the polished and confident style of Song Chan literature.

The *Lidai fabao ji* authors' romanticized view of the origins of their school retains many traces of the historical tensions from which it emerged, which contributes to its interest for scholars today. Unlike later treatments of the masters of Chan's golden age, the *Lidai fabao ji* is not stylistically consistent, and the narrative is sometimes disjointed and unpolished. Themes and texts associated with disparate modes of Buddhist discourse are juxtaposed within the *Lidai fabao ji*, and I suggest that this in part reflects a broader social and religious transition.

The shift was signaled most dramatically by the 755 rebellion of the general An Lushan against the Tang ruling clans, but is discernible even before this critical turning point. Warring agendas in the *Lidai fabao ji* can be seen as a reflection in microcosm of a more extensive crisis of faith in the religious and secular structures of authority inherited from the early Tang. Rhetoric regarding patriarchal robes thus becomes a window on the complex relationship between Tang politics and Chan sectarian rivalries in the latter half of the eighth century.

During the century preceding the An Lushan rebellion, the Buddhist monastic establishments clustered in and around the two Tang capitals of Changan and Luoyang had grown into a collective force to be reckoned with. The power of the Buddhist church was maintained through relations of sometimes strained interdependence with the imperial court, in a milieu of rivalry with court Daoism, and successive emperors struggled to co-opt and/or control its increasingly pervasive influence. This kind of institutional, esoteric/scholastic Buddhism reached the height of its power under the empress Wu Zetian, who created a network of monasteries to promulgate Buddhist teachings in support of her reign and continually invited exemplary monks to court in order to pay her respects to them. After Empress Wu, the next ruler to have a significant impact on institutional Buddhism was Emperor Xuanzong (r. 712–756), whose reign effectively ended with the An Lushan rebellion. Even though the Tang forces subsequently rallied, the war effort resulted in the strengthening of the peripheries at the expense of the center.[17]

Politically as well as culturally, the eighth century saw a great deal of oscillation between the time-honored and the experimental. In particular, the nonhereditary bureaucratic class fostered by the exam system began to make inroads into the labyrinth of privilege previously negotiated by the imperial household, Buddhist and/or Daoist monastic institutions, and aristocratic factions. More significantly, with the disintegration of periphery-center tribute relations, decrease in central control of the military, and greater freedom for interprovince commerce, the middle-level officials and military governors became increasingly independent administrators in the provinces. Before the end of the dynasty in 907 there were several attempts to reinforce imperial authority, but some provincial centers such as Chengdu, the birthplace of the *Lidai fabao ji*, became nearly autonomous. There was also a trend toward secularization of social values within the newly powerful and increasingly competitive bureaucratic class. These factors all contributed to create a milieu in which received genres and cultural paradigms were seen as inadequate or decadent.[18]

The shifting of the balance of power from center to peripheries also weakened the influence of the Buddhist monastic complexes of the capitals, which were heavily implicated in Tang imperial politics. Decrease in resources for the older institutions of the central region, combined with new opportunities for patronage in the provinces, clearly had much to do with the development of the so-called Southern school of Chan to which the *Lidai fabao ji* claimed allegiance. Discussion of sudden awakening (*dunwu*) in Chinese Buddhist texts predates the appropriation of this soteriology as the hallmark Southern school doctrine. However, the polemical context that gave birth to the Southern school has been linked to the Chan master Shenhui's (684–758) attacks, beginning in 730, against the successors of the Chan master Shenxiu (d. 706), who had been highly revered by Empress Wu and the entire Changan/Luoyang establishment.[19]

Shenhui had a decisive role in creating the symbolism and the narratives that were to change what it meant to be a Chan master (*chanshi*) in the eighth century. Claiming to represent the teachings of Huineng, Shenhui advocated direct realization of the truth of one's own Buddha-nature and (falsely) contended that the teachings of Shenxiu's Northern school followers were gradualist and nurtured the delusion that awakening was a condition to be achieved, rather than one's inherent reality. Implicated in Shenhui's claims was the centuries-old struggle over Buddhist elitism, an elitism that engendered and was engendered by imperial and popular enchantment with the mystique of the adept who gained numinous power through asceticism, ritual worship, and scriptural recitation.

Although Shenhui himself did not go so far as to disavow any form of Buddhist activity whatsoever, he and subsequent Chan masters became increasingly attentive to the contradiction involved in teaching and practicing (which are inherently gradualistic) according to the orthodoxy of the "sudden." This sudden/gradual doctrinal divide is key to understanding the hybrid nature of the *Lidai fabao ji*. Although it has features usually associated with the so-called gradual or Northern school trends that flourished through court patronage in the eighth century, it is most heavily influenced by Shenhui's Southern school writings. Conspicuously, it is the only text to take Shenhui's doctrine to its logical extreme by advocating radically antinomian "formless" practice.[20]

The *Lidai fabao ji* was also the only text in which Bodhidharma's robe continued to play a role beyond the sixth generation of patriarchs. Shenhui had fused historical and doctrinal claims into an exclusive notion of patriarchal succession in which only one patriarch in each generation received mind-to-mind transmission of the true Dharma from the previous patriarch, linking back to Buddha Śākyamuni's transmission to his disciple Mahākāśyapa. According to Shenhui, when Bodhidharma (d. ca. 530), the Indian patriarch who came to China, passed this unique mind-to-mind transmission to his Chinese disciple Huike (487–593), he concomitantly transmitted his robe as verification. Shenhui claimed that the Dharma and robe had then been passed through three more generations to the sixth patriarch, Huineng (638–713).

Widespread cultural acceptance of the power of talismanic objects helped the early Southern school movement establish the authority of its patriarchs, but at times the ingenious stories of the objects threatened to overshadow the teachings of those who laid claim to them. The *Lidai fabao ji* authors were not the only ones entangled in this dilemma. Any criticism of the *Lidai fabao ji* version of succession inevitably raises the inconvenient question: where *did* true patriarchal power lie? The doctrinal, ideological, and historical aspects of this question cannot be addressed separately, for each implicates the others. Doctrinally, the reconciliation of inherent Buddha-nature and temporal transmission of spiritual authority is as slippery as the reconciliation of the theory of *anātman* (no-self) and the theory of karma (the morally charged momentum of past action that shapes the actor). Spiritual lineage and spiritual discipline became theoretically equally problematic for so-called Southern school Chan, and yet the relative attention given these two aspects was the inverse of previous Buddhist discourse. Among Chan schools of the late Tang, the rhetoric of genealogy was increasingly developed, while the hagiographic value of accounts of spiritual athleticism slowly atrophied.

Reflecting Stylistic Trends, Anticipating Genres

From the eighth through thirteenth centuries, Chan doctrinal issues were closely related to the development of distinct literary and artistic forms. In Southern school Chan texts, sutra commentary, discursive explanation, and eventually even the standard question-and-answer format all gave way to new genres. By the eleventh and twelfth centuries, the quintessential Chan genre had become the *yulu* (discourse record), collections of anecdotal "records" of interaction between a master and his disciples that were designed to convey a sense of everyday encounter as the true Buddhist teaching. The format clearly had antecedents in pre-Han classics such as the *Lunyu* and the *Zhuangzi*, but rather than simply reflecting the oft-cited "sinification of Buddhism," this can be associated with a vogue in intellectual classicism, a rejection of ornate commentarial prose in favor of a terser style, as exemplified in the *guwen* (old writing) movement of Han Yu (768–824). In his prose, Han Yu favored the archaic to the point of severity, but he and other writers of the period also began to include colloquial elements in their poetry and fiction. In Chan *yulu*, champions of the "sudden"—which was increasingly identified with the quotidian immanent, as we shall see—were part of an intellectual milieu that favored skillful use of colloquial language and a deftly rendered personal immediacy.

The *yulu* were usually appended to the biographies of masters, and Chan hagiography developed, and was used, in ways distinctly different from earlier typologically arranged Buddhist biographical collections. In the eleventh century, biographies arranged as lineages, called *chuandeng lu* (lamp transmission record), became the standard means of advancing a particular school's claim to inheritance of perfect mind-to-mind transmission from master to disciple through the generations. In the *yulu* and *chuandeng lu* genres themselves we can thus recognize a tension between the absolutely unique encounter and the genealogy of perfect replication.

The *Lidai fabao ji* is prototypical of both Chan genres, being rather neatly divided into two parts; the first is in a format analogous to *chuandeng lu* and the second analogous to *yulu*. Through the *Lidai fabao ji* we may thus gain glimpses of an earlier stage of the hagiographical sensibilities that shaped Song Dynasty Chan's distinctive literary styles and its images of exemplary practice, which were in turn the styles and images adopted by Japanese monks who founded the Zen schools of the Kamakura period. The early texts do not, however, help greatly to establish any firmer historical basis for the Chan masters who figured most prominently in the thirteenth-century *gongan* (public case) genre, which currently enjoys widespread cultural recognition in its Japanese form, *kōan*. These short Chan anecdotes were culled from *yulu* and *chuandeng lu*, and were used as meditative aids to exemplify teaching points.

In the late Tang, both Chan literature and secular fiction developed in new directions, and the second part of the *Lidai fabao ji* reflects these trends. As with Tang *chuanqi* (transmitted marvels) fiction, what were once preparatory sketches and notes in the margins of official literature became the features of a new genre. In both Chan lore and *chuanqi*, interactions in ordinary settings are used to establish the relative spiritual or moral standing of the characters, and in Chan literature, displays of supernormal powers and extraordinary acts of virtue almost disappeared.

It is significant that the adoption of a sparser and more colloquial mode in Chan literature coincided with similar stylistic experiments formulated and practiced by late Tang literati such as Han Yu, mentioned above. Like these experimenters, Chan writers were at pains to present innovation as excavation, or to establish reform on ancient foundations. And indeed, the new Chan genres of *yulu*, *chuandeng lu*, and *gongan* are consistent with previous patterns of development in stylistic convention.[21] Chan genres are unique, yet complement and refer to each other in a familiar manner. Just as accounts of the bizarre (*zhiguai*) complemented official didactic "arrayed" biographies (*liezhuan*), and the brevity and wit of *qingtan* (pure conversation) characterizations were related to the more formal dialogical treatises of the third and fourth centuries, so too did the turning words, scatological references, and shouts of Chan depend on daily recitation of the sutras.[22] The appeal of the *Lidai fabao ji* is that the sutras and the scatology are not yet divided into separate genres.

Content and Structure

The *Lidai fabao ji* could be called a history of origins, beginning with a legendary account of the introduction of Buddhism to China, and ending with the record of the Bao Tang school founder, Wuzhu. As the title indicates, the *Lidai fabao ji* is meant to be a record "through (successive) ages/generations." In the presentation of the text, key successive moments in Chinese Buddhist history radiate inward like spokes of a wheel that converge upon the cardinal importance of Wuzhu and the core concerns of the Bao Tang school. Narrative choices, scriptural quotation as commentary, and occasional overt commentary all repeatedly orient one back to Chengdu in the eighth century, even as one is brought steadily forward from the first century.

The *Lidai fabao ji* constitutes seventeen pages of the Taishō shinshū daizōkyō edition of the Buddhist canon, or approximately twenty-five thousand Chinese characters.[23] It begins with a list of thirty-seven titles that the authors claim as sources. The narrative then opens with a version of the legend of the dream of Emperor Ming of the Han (r. 57–75) and his subsequent embassy to bring Buddhist scriptures and monks to China. This is followed by a description of a contest of magical powers between Buddhists and Daoists, a brief account of Śākyamuni Buddha, and a quotation from a work in the genre of Buddhist rebuttal to the third-century Daoist *Hua hu jing* (Scripture of conversion of the barbarians). A second version of the legend of Emperor Ming ensues. The narrative shifts to a quasi-historical anecdote involving the famous Jin dynasty monk Huiyuan (334–417). Then, quotations from two well-known sutras are followed by a quotation from a putative fifth-century "translation" of a work (probably a Chinese compilation) chronicling the transmission from the Buddha up until the twenty-third generation in India and Kashmir. A passage from this work is altered and supplemented by the *Lidai fabao ji* authors in order to bring the transmission up to the twenty-ninth generation, to "Bodhidharmatrāta," founder of the Chan lineage claimed by the Bao Tang school. The authors then dispute a rival claim made in an early eighth-century Chan text, the *Lengqie shizi ji* (Record of the masters and disciples of the *Laṅkā [vatāra-sūtra]*).²⁴ This is followed by polemics over the origins of the *Laṅkā* transmission.

For all its diversity, the rather disjointed introductory section summarized above makes up a mere tenth of the text as a whole. The *Laṅkā* transmission discussion forms a segue for a more orderly but no less lively section, the biographies of the six successive Chan patriarchs: Bodhidharmatrāta (d. ca. 530), more commonly known as Bodhidharma; Huike (487–593); Sengcan (d. 592); Daoxin (580–651); Hongren (602–675); and Huineng (638–713).²⁵ The text then jumps abruptly back to the fourth century with a passage on the monk Daoan (312–385), followed by a long series of quotations from Indian sutras and from apocryphal Chinese scriptures. The biography of Huineng includes an account of the transmission of the robe and the Dharma from Hongren to Huineng; immediately following the scriptural quotations, however, the Hongren-Huineng robe transmission episode is repeated in greater detail.

Next follows the robe transmission episode set in the court of Empress Wu Zetian, which leads to short biographies of Zhishen (609–702) and his disciple Chuji (669–736). The genealogical implications are complicated by the fact that although Zhishen is actually a disciple of Hongren, he receives Huineng's robe of transmission from the empress and passes it on to Chuji. The biography of Chuji's disciple, the Korean monk Wuxiang (684–762), is given in some detail, including quotations from his Dharma sermons. This is followed by passages purporting to record dialogues between the above-mentioned Southern school advocate Shenhui and various interlocutors. These passages are certainly based on extant works related to Shenhui, but the *Lidai fabao ji* authors spuriously interpolate a commentary on Sichuan Chan figures into Shenhui's discourses. The section on these various figures constitutes approximately another 30 percent of the whole.

The remaining 60 percent of the text is devoted to the Bao Tang founder Wuzhu (714–774). He is introduced giving a dramatic Dharma sermon. There follows an extended account of his early years and wanderings, his encounter with Wuxiang, the robe transmission from Wuxiang, and his ultimate recognition as the legitimate heir after Wuxiang's death. The rest of the text is taken up by sermons and dialogues with disciples and visitors on various topics, and it concludes with Wuzhu's death.

In a manner quite common to Tang-dynasty historical and exegetical literature, at least a quarter of the *Lidai fabao ji* is composed of freely altered quotations from a multiplicity of other works, some marked by direct reference and most not. Source materials from different times and places, changes in writing style, and strikingly innovative passages are all loosely held together by the author-compilers' arguments for formless practice as a necessary corollary to the Southern school doctrine of no-thought.

The first part of the *Lidai fabao ji* is largely a pastiche of earlier material or imitations of traditional Buddhist scholarship. In the second part of the *Lidai fabao ji*, the use of other Buddhist material is confined to Wuzhu's quotations from sutras. The impressive effect with which Wuzhu deploys his quotations reveals the *Lidai fabao ji* authors' reverence for treasures from the storehouse of Buddhist lore, but it also reveals a certain sense of editorial license to be less than exact in reproducing the originals. The quotations have an almost talismanic function, in that they are not always clearly related to the topic at hand yet invariably produce awe in the succession of Wuzhu's interlocutors. Moreover, they are imbedded in other modes characteristic of Wuzhu's discourse underlining the telegraphic, almost hypnotic, recurring *wunian* (no-thought) phrases, which we cannot help but think of as pompous, and the earthy, piquant stories.

The *Lidai fabao ji*'s Unique Version of the Indian Patriarchy

There were several different lists of Indian patriarchs produced by various factions of the nascent Chan school. A good summary is provided in the first chapter of Philip Yampolsky's study on the *Platform Sutra*.[26] Yampolsky made a chart of the patriarch lists found in eighth-century Chan works and compared these with the two main source texts, the *Fu fazang [yinyuan] zhuan* (Traditions [of the Causes and Conditions] of Transmission of the Dharma Treasury)[27] and Buddhabhadra's (359–429) preface to his translation of the *Damoduoluo chan jing* (The Dhyāna-sūtra of Dharmatrāta).[28]

The *Fu fazang zhuan* is a major source for the version of the patriarchal lineage that is found in the *Lidai fabao ji*. The *Fu fazang zhuan* identifies transmission of the Dharma with a single line of transmission from master to disciple, beginning with Śākyamuni and ending with the murder of the twenty-third patriarch Siṃha bhikṣu in Kashmir, but the *Lidai fabao ji* authors rewrote Siṃha's biography in the *Fu fazang zhuan* in order to create an unbroken lineage.

The *Lidai fabao ji* authors were not the first to use lineage in Buddhabhadra's preface in order to overcome the unsatisfactory ending of the *Fu fazang zhuan*. However, the *Lidai fabao ji* is the earliest extant Chan text that tries to respond to the obvious insufficiency of Shenhui's notion of "unbroken transmission." In Shenhui's list, the gap between the five Indian "patriarchs" from the popular *Aśokarāja-sūtra* (*Ayu wang jing*)²⁹ and the Chinese patriarchs is bridged by names derived from the Sarvāstivāda lineage: 6) Śubhamitra, an unknown figure who may be a scrambling of Vasumitra from Buddhabhadra's list, and 7) Saṅgharakṣa, who is the figure between Vasumitra and Dharmatrāta in Buddhabhadra's list.³⁰ Shenhui replaced Dharmatrāta with 8) Bodhidharma, but the *Lidai fabao ji* authors tried to retain both with the unique coinage Bodhidharmatrāta. The *Lidai fabao ji* uses the entire *Fu fazang zhuan* list, and interpolates the names Sāravasa and Upagupta in between Siṃha and Shenhui's (or his source's) "Śubhamitra," making for a total of twenty-nine Indian patriarchs. Sāravasa and Upagupta are the fourth and fifth figures in the *Aśokarāja-sūtra* account of the initial transmissions, but the *Lidai fabao ji* authors distinguish the traditional fourth and fifth Indian patriarchs Sāravasa and Upagupta from the newly minted twenty-fifth and twenty-sixth patriarchs Sāravasa and Upagupta by using alternative transliterations.³¹

The *Baolin zhuan* (801) list of twenty-eight Indian patriarchs was to become the canonical version that was incorporated into the *Jingde chuandeng lu*. Its author duplicated most of the *Lidai fabao ji* list but eliminated Madhyāntika and substituted three different names after Siṃha, ending with Bodhidharma. The *Lidai fabao ji* list was thus a key source for the standard version of the Chan lineage of Indian patriarchs. In the final analysis, the *Lidai fabao ji* authors appear to have drawn from Shenhui's ideology and his list, Buddhabhadra's tradition linking the Indian and Kashmiri masters, and the *Fu fazang zhuan* list without its ideology.

The fifth- or sixth-century sensibilities that shaped the *Fu fazang zhuan* could conceive the continuity of the Dharma, though weakened, through preservation of the formal practices and traditional roles of the Saṅgha alone. This reflects a long-standing tendency in the Saṅgha to rely on orthopraxy rather than orthodoxy as the basis for continued viability of the Dharma. In marked contrast, eighth-century Chan sectarians' increasing dependence on lineage as the source of continuity made the *Fu fazang zhuan* account of a broken patriarchal lineage difficult either to ignore or to accept unaltered. The story of how the lineage was saved from extinction begged to be told, just as traditional Buddhism's wanton extinction of fully realized arhats had begged for the resuscitating doctrine of the bodhisattva path. The *Lidai fabao ji* authors' oft-cited freedom with sources qualified them well for the task. They included the story of the martyrdom of Siṃha, but claimed that the crucial Dharma transmission was accomplished before Siṃha's death.

> Siṃha bhikṣu had transmitted [the Dharma] to Saravasa, and so he went from central India to Kashmir. The king there was named Mihirakula.³² This king did not believe in the Buddha-dharma. He destroyed stupas, demolished monasteries, and slaughtered sentient beings to serve the two heretics Moman (Mani) and Mishihe (Mes-

siah, i.e., Jesus).³³ At that time Siṃha bhikṣu purposely came to convert this kingdom, and the pathless king with his own hands took up a sharp double-edged sword and swore an oath: "If you are a sage, the [other] masters must suffer punishment." Siṃha bhikṣu then manifested a form whereby his body bled white milk. Moman and Mishihe were executed like common men, and their blood spattered over the ground. The king resolved to take refuge in the Buddha, and he ordered the disciple of Siṃha bhikṣu (the Dharma had already been transmitted to Sāravasa) to enter south India to preach extensively and liberate beings.³⁴

In the *Fu fazang zhuan* there is no mention of the heretic masters and no conversion of the king. The martyrdom is summary and graphic: the king beheads Siṃha, and the story ends thus: "in his head there was no blood, only milk flowed out. The persons who had transmitted the Dharma from one to the other were in this manner severed."³⁵ In contrast, the *Lidai fabao ji* authors appear to have been somewhat anxious to make their main point, repeating that the transmission had already passed to Sāravasa.

The implicit message of the *Fu fazang zhuan* is that the true current of Dharma transmission runs in a narrow and hidden channel, encompassing the paradox of its destructible human vessels and its perpetual pure nourishment. The *Fu fazang zhuan*, with or without emendations, was clearly compelling to those who were engaged in spreading the Dharma in the sixth through eighth centuries. I would argue that the *Fu fazang zhuan* mystique of the "holy ones" was one of the forces in the negotiation of the relative identities of lay and ordained, state and Saṅgha, in Chinese terms. It places the "holy ones" who transmit the Dharma in a special category, precisely the special category appropriated in the "Chan master" rhetoric of the late eighth century. Like the "holy one," the Chan master is an ordinary man in recognizable circumstances, not exactly an arhat or buddha, not bound by karma and yet preordained to carry on the transmission.

The Portrait of Wuzhu in the *Lidai fabao ji*

The *Lidai fabao ji* contains the only known biography of the Bao Tang founder Wuzhu. In this biography it is claimed that he was originally of a military family in the north and intitially attained some success in a military career. However, he became disillusioned and sought out various Buddhist masters, eventually becoming a monk.³⁶

As the story unfolds, Wuzhu is not content to stay long with any master, but then he meets a merchant who is astounded at his physical resemblance to the famous Master Wuxiang, prompting Wuzhu to travel to Sichuan to meet him. In the midst of an assembly that has gathered to hear Wuxiang preach, Wuzhu understands a mysterious command that Wuxiang addresses to him, telling him to go into the mountains. In the mountains he practices an asceticism even more radical than Wuxiang's, and there we see him preaching, for the first time, a formless practice more absolute than his fellow monks can stomach. Wuzhu is deserted by the other monks because his refusal to carry out any recognizable Buddhist activity besides sitting in meditation is, it is implied, responsible for the dearth of donations to their remote temple.

> Master Daoyi, [Wuzhu's] fellow inmate [at the mountain hermitage], practiced chanting, worship, and recitation of the Buddha's name, while the Venerable [Wuzhu] wholeheartedly cut through thinking and ceased all restless anxiety, and entered into the field of self-mandating [enlightenment].
>
> Daoyi, accompanied by all the minor masters who were their fellow inmates, addressed the Venerable, saying, "I, together with all our fellow inmates, want you to join us in the daily six repetitions of the ritual of repentance. We humbly beg the Venerable to listen and accede."
>
> The Venerable said to Daoyi and the others, "Here we are altogether cut off from provisions, [which must be] transported on foot deep into the mountains. We cannot depend on legalistic practice. You want to learn deranged [behavior], but this is not the Buddhadharma at all." The Venerable quoted the Śūraṅgama-sūtra, "'The deranged mind is not at rest. At rest, it is bodhi (awakening). Peerless pure bright mind fundamentally pervades the dharmadhātu.' No-thought is none other than seeing the Buddha. Thinking is none other than birth-and-death. If you want to practice worship and recitation, then leave the mountains. Below the mountains there are gracious and easeful temple-quarters, and you are free to go. If you want to stay with me, you must utterly devote yourself to no-thought. If you can, then you are free to stay. If you cannot, then you must go down from the mountains."[37]

Daoyi does leave the mountain to go down to the Jingzhong monastery and bear tales of Wuzhu to Wuxiang. However, Wuxiang is delighted rather than dismayed by reports of Wuzhu's behavior, saying that he himself practiced thus in his youth, "When I was at the stage of learning I wouldn't get around to eating, I just sat empty and unoccupied. I didn't even make an effort to shit or piss. You lot don't realize that when I was at Mount Tiangu I didn't worship or recite, either. All my fellow students became angry with me and left the mountain. No one sent provisions and I had only smelted earth (liantu) for food."[38]

The Lidai fabao ji authors thus defended their own standards for distinguishing those worthy of offerings and those not. Bao Tang survival depended on wider acceptance of these standards, yet they must have been aware that their manifesto, the *Lidai fabao ji*, would draw even more critical attention to the group. It is possible that even sympathizers might have been hard put to explain the basis of the Bao Tang claim for support as Buddhist clergy, since they did not retain the forms of monastic practice.

Beginning with the passage above and reinforced in subsequent passages featuring encounters with various challengers and followers, Wuzhu's signature teaching was no-thought (*wunian*) and nonattachment to the forms of practice. Nothing was to be set apart as Buddhist practice, and yet nothing was not Buddhist practice. It seems that Wuzhu's followers did achieve some measure of success in living up (or down) to this standard. According to the Bao Tang's ninth-century critic Zongmi, the Bao Tang were notorious for not maintaining any monastic observances, or even basic etiquette, and for tonsuring and conferring robes on people without requiring of them any evidence of Buddhist practice. Given this radical designification of the monastic robe, it becomes all the more surprising that the plot of the first half of the *Lidai fabao ji* is wrapped up in the convoluted story of how Bodhidharma's robe came into Wuzhu's possession.

In the second part, concerning Wuzhu's dialogues with antagonists and disciples, one of the more intriguing passages concerns the nun Liaojianxing (Completely seeing the [Buddha]-nature), who receives one of the most detailed treatments of any of the ordained disciples.[39] In this passage, it is said that Liaojianxing became a nun simply by donning robes and tonsuring herself, flaunting both Buddhist and imperial authority in a perfect enactment of Wuzhu's teachings.[40] There is no other record of this person, and we can only speculate as to why neither she nor any other disciple was named as Wuzhu's successor. Was it because his closest disciples were laypersons and women, or was it because his radical interpretation of sudden practice was incompatible with any form, including that of transmission? If the latter, then why is so much of the *Lidai fabao ji* invested in establishing a claim to legitimacy in conventional and fabricated terms?

The final talismanic evocation in the text concerns Wuzhu's portrait, not his robe. The last section of the *Lidai fabao ji* is set off by these words: "Portrait Eulogy (*zhenzan*), with Preface, for the Venerable of the Dali Bao Tang Monastery, a Disciple of Chan (*chanmen menren*) Who Transmitted Sudden Awakening in the Mahāyāna."[41] It was common for an eulogy or epitaph to include a preface. Here the preface praises Wuzhu's teachings and gives the reasons for having a portrait made, and the eulogy itself praises the Buddha-dharma and the portrait. The piece echoes Wuzhu's sermons as given in other sections of the *Lidai fabao ji*, but it is written in a more polished style than that of the person or persons who wrote the rest of the text. In the preface Wuzhu is referred to as "our teacher," so the writer (who refers to himself as "the mountain man Sun Huan") identifies himself as a Bao Tang follower. Sun Huan is otherwise unknown, but he seems to have been a retired scholar and lay disciple with a Daoist background. Following the preface and eulogy, there is a short concluding description of Wuzhu's death in the classic manner of a Buddhist master, and the style of this concluding passage seems to revert to that of the authors of the main body of the *Lidai fabao ji*. It is possible that the preface and eulogy are earlier than the rest of the text, if they were in fact written soon after his death. Below, I include the last paragraph of the preface and the last paragraph of the eulogy:

> Accordingly, we secretly summoned a fine artist to paint [our master's] portrait (*zhenji*). His appearance [in the portrait] is lustrous, his features are fine and successfully realized. Those who gaze at this rendering are able to destroy evil, those who rely on his Dharma are able to attain the mystery. The deeper places [of his Dharma] I have not yet fathomed. Bowing my head to the ground and raising my gaze with reverence, I exert my strength to write this eulogy.[42]
>
> Accordingly we summoned the fine artist; secretly he made the painting. [The artist] pushed the brush and produced the form, and gazing at the majestic response-body separate from characteristics and emptied of words, we see the expansive vessel of the Dharma. His virtue is like a gift from Heaven, his bones are not like those of this world. How silently mysterious and fine! [The portrait] seems to be truly breathing, the face quivers and wants to speak, the eyes dance and are about to see. "I look up and it is ever loftier, I venerate and it is ever more dear."[43] Without our master, this Dharma will sink.[44]

The eulogy for Wuzhu ends with a chilly breath of the "decline of the Dharma" sensibility that wafts through the *Lidai fabao ji* as a whole: "Without our master, this Dharma will sink." At the same time, the preface claims that the portrait has magical and soteriological effect. This claim is all the more striking because much of the *Lidai fabao ji* has to do with the drama of patriarchal transmission and the story of Wuzhu's inheritance of the true Dharma and Bodhidharma's robe. Yet at the scene of Wuzhu's death, no Dharma heir is named and the robe is conspicuously absent. Instead, the manifestation of Wuzhu's Dharma becomes this painted likeness.

It may be appropriate that the Dharma of a master named Wuzhu, nonabiding, should be considered to abide in his portrait. As noted, one of the recurrent themes in the autograph inscriptions of Song Chan abbots is the idea that the true form of no-form is representation. The representation signs that it is impossible to render the true image of enlightenment, and at the same time it functions as emptiness functions, as the multifaceted transformations of *upāya*, or skillful means. Griffith Foulk and Robert Sharf write:

"According to the ritual logic of Sung Buddhist monasteries, the icon of the Buddha, the living person of the abbot, and the abbot's portrait were largely interchangeable. It would seem that the body of the living abbot, like his portrait, had come to be regarded as the 'simulacrum' (*hsiang*) of Buddha-hood."[45]

The notion that the abbot and his image are equally similacra, virtual buddhas, has roots in the ninth-century notion of the Chan master as a "living Buddha." This was a sacralization of the "sudden" teaching of intrinsic Buddha nature, the realization of the ultimate truth of the contingent, expressed in the *Platform Sutra* teaching that the self is the *Trikāya*, the three bodies of the Buddha.[46]

The mysterious portrait of Wuzhu balances on the same crux that characterizes the *Lidai fabao ji* as a whole, because those responsible for creating it treated it both conventionally and absolutely, both gradually and suddenly, as an icon and as a representation of iconoclasm. It combined many qualities and abided in none—it was at once an ancestral shrine tablet, a sacred relic, a response-body, representation as the true face of the Dharma, and the unique and ephemeral image of a unique and ephemeral religious community. Wuzhu became for his followers the form of the formless practice he taught, and whether this was the revenge of supressed devotionalism or a demonstration of his disciples' true understanding of the emptiness of reverence, we must leave it for Mañjuśrì, the bodhisattva of wisdom, to decide.

The Legacy of the Bao Tang and the *Lidai fabao ji*

It is perhaps impossible to tell how long the Bao Tang school survived as an independent Chan line. Most of the ninth-century traces involve its closely related rival, the Jingzhong school. As mentioned above, not long after the *Lidai fabao ji* was written the Jingzhong master Shenqing produced his *Beishan lu* (Record of North Mountain) and discredited the *Lidai fabao ji* claim that Wuzhu was a disciple of Wuxiang, criticized its account of the patriarchy, and condemned the antinomian practices of the Bao Tang.[47] Shenqing advocated the "unity of the three teachings" (*sanjiao yizhi*, i.e., Buddhism, Daoism, and Confucianism) as well as defending the Jingzhong lineage. In fact, the eulogy for Wuzhu shows elements of the "unity of the three teachings" trend as well.

Following the persecution of Buddhism in the mid-ninth century, the reconstructed Jingzhong sect and temple devoted to Wuxiang developed a syncretic and popular character. Sources for the Wuxiang "cult" include Wuxiang's biography in the *Song gaoseng zhuan* and a piece written by the literatus Li Shangyin (813–858).[48] In a stele for the Korean monk Langkong, it is said that in 875 he went on foot to Chengdu to pay his respects at Wuxiang's memorial hall at Jingzhong temple.[49]

In the *Lidai fabao ji*, it is said that Wuxiang had a special method of chanting the *nianfo* (J. *nembutsu*) at the beginning of his precepts assemblies:

> The Venerable Kim, every twelfth and first month, administered the "receiving of conditions" for countless numbers of people of the four assemblies. The teacher was magnificently arranged, and occupying the high seat [Wuxiang] would expound the Dharma. First, he would lead the vocal repetition of the Buddha's name. When he had exhausted a single breath in recitation [of the Buddha's name], the intoning broke off, the recitation stopped, and then he spoke: "Nonrecollection, no-thought, and not forgetting: Nonrecollection is the precepts, no-thought is meditation, and not forgetting is wisdom. These three phrases are the gate of perfectly maintaining [the precepts]."[50]

There may be a connection between Wuxiang's style of chanting and that of the monk Fazhao (d. 820). Fazhao was a disciple of the Pure Land devotee Chengyuan (712–802), who was a disciple of Wuxiang's master Chuji, and Fazhao developed a special method of chanting that was linked with visualization of Amitābha.[51] The Jingzhong Monastery was primarily associated with Pure Land practices in the ninth century, so Wuxiang's legacy contributed to Pure Land as well as Chan developments.

Wuxiang's Dharma heir Jingzhong Shenhui (720–794) became abbot of Jingzhong Monastery after Wuxiang's death. Jingzhong Shenhui's patron Wei Gao, the military governor of Jiannan West from 785 until his death in 805, was even more powerful in Chengdu in his day than Wuzhu's patron Du Hongjian (709–769) had been. Wei Gao seems to have been a devout believer in *nianfo* practice and probably helped to promote it.

Wuxiang and Wuzhu were also known in Tibet. Dunhuang was part of Tibetan-occupied territory from 786 to 848, and Chengdu and its environs were under Tibetan occupation during the tenth century. In the period between the composition of the *Lidai fabao ji* and its entombment in the eleventh century, there was a complex pattern of military, commercial, and religious interaction, interspersed with periods of isolation, among the cultural centers of western Sichuan, Nanzhao, Tibet, and Gansu. This interaction is attested by the Dunhuang Tibetan manuscripts; a surprising number of them include elements of the *Lidai fabao ji* version of Chan history. Moreover, the chronicle of Samye (bSam yas) Monastery in Lhasa includes a story of the meeting between Wuxiang and the Tibetan envoy to China.[52]

There are also links between the *Lidai fabao ji* and one of the two post-Huineng lineages that continued (or were constructed) into the Song dynasty and beyond. Two Sichuan Chan texts that give evidence of connections between the *Lidai fabao ji* and the Hongzhou lineage of Mazu (709–788), namely, Zhiju's *Baolin zhuan* (Transmission of the Baolin [Temple]) and the *Yuanjue jing dashu chao* of the Chan/Huayan master Zongmi. The *Baolin zhuan*, compiled in 801, is incomplete, but its extant sections prove it to be closely related to the *Lidai fabao ji* in its style and ideology of transmission. The reputation of the Bao Tang school probably had some degree of influence on the Hongzhou school, which was the Chan school that best survived the Buddhist persecution of the Huichang era (841–846).[53] The Hongzhou founder Mazu was also a native of Sichuan, and there is some controversy over whether Mazu was more influenced by the Korean master Wuxiang or by his putative master, Huairang (677–744). The biographies of Korean monks included in the mid-tenth-century *Zutang ji* (Anthology of the Patriarchal Hall) show evidence that Korean monks believed Mazu's lineage to have stemmed from Wuxiang.[54] Discussion of this controversy becomes more complex when one takes into account issues of national bias among the twentieth-century scholars (Chinese, Korean, and Japanese) who have written about it.[55]

Mazu was the common patriarch of the Linji and Guiyang schools, two of the "Five Houses" of the Song. The paradigm of Mazu as presented in his biography and the style of his "recorded sayings" reflects, like the *Lidai fabao ji*, a need to find an appropriate form for the sudden teaching, but the Mazu material mediates between poles of traditional and radical styles that are at once less extreme and also more clearly and confidently on the side of the new. Mazu was said to have stressed immanence, nondual everyday function such as simply eating and wearing clothes as an expression of Buddha-nature. This neither privileged nor precluded ordination and left more room to adapt existing monastic institutions, unlike the *Lidai fabao ji* denial of formal precepts and practices. The later Chan schools' choice of immanence rather than antinomianism as the foundation of orthopraxy allowed reclamation of the conventional, whereas Wuzhu's absolutism was bound to fall back to dualism on the symbolic level, due to its investment in the inversion of symbols.

In the ninth century, there were several competing versions of symbols of authentic transmission. As Bernard Faure has shown, the role of mummies and relics was much greater than classic Chan literature would lead us to believe.[56] The *Baolin zhuan* instituted transmission verses, and these verses were included in later biographies even though their esoteric use was abandoned. The *Jingde chuandeng lu* became the accepted history of eighth-and ninth-century Chan transmission: it has more or less the version of transmission of the robe that is in the *Caoqi dashi biezhuan*, the patriarchal biographies and transmission verses from the *Baolin zhuan*, and an inclusive notion of Chan affiliation. It represents a coalition among the main Chan "houses" and the absorption of the patriarchal lineages into a genealogy. Thus the tensions inherent in the linear "one patriarch per generation" model of the late eighth century were resolved in a more traditional genealogical mode in which the transmission was vested in the structure of the well-defined gnostic community rather than in the realization of any single individual.

Conclusion

All of the elements touched upon in the previous section—syncretic doctrines and popular devotional practices, connections with Korea and Tibet, post-persecution opportunities, the rise of the Hongzhou lineage and the development of Chan genealogies—contributed to the unique character of Sichuan Chan Buddhism. Sichuan Chan became an important source for the styles, traditions, and practices of mainstream Chan of the Song dynasty. Therefore, these regional developments would leave their imprint upon Chinese society as a whole during the era of Chan Buddhism's greatest political and cultural influence. The influence of the Bao Tang upon Sichuan Chan was not negligible. What, in the end, is the transmission of the Bao Tang school?

The huge repository of Chan lore owes much to Wuzhu's disciples, one or several of whom created the written portrait of the master whose spirit lives on in the *Lidai fabao ji*. The *Lidai fabao ji* modified received genres or introduced new stylistic features in ways that would shape the standard genres of Song Chan literature—*chuandeng lu*, *yulu*, and *zhenzan*. Furthermore, the *Lidai fabao ji* version of the Indian line of patriarchs was the source for the version that became official. Many anecdotes that have their origins in the *Lidai fabao ji* found their way into the official annals of Chan. Yet the *Lidai fabao ji* itself was repudiated and all but forgotten.

Some of the creative fabrications of the *Lidai fabao ji* made their way into more acceptable works and passed into the realm of revered Chan lore. However, the elements that were incorporated into the mainstream of Chan underwent a trimming process in which the fervent and eccentric qualities, particularly the antinomianism, were excised. In this process, what was lost?

Due in part to a late-twentieth-century Western fascination with *kōan* literature, Chan writings are often approached, in both popular and scholarly works, as spare renderings of the spontaneous expression of realized self-presence. By presenting the *Lidai fabao ji* with its anxious and loquacious fictions exposed, I do not want to end at the other extreme and reduce it to an example of as-yet-unskilled Chan propaganda. I have no wish to imply that traces of mundane concerns and expedients necessarily invalidate the originality of insight or the purity of the motives of the unknown author or authors. To do so would merely replicate the ideological hypostasis of the tradition while attempting to unsettle it; by taking issue with the fabrications of the Chan histories one joins in the reification of a separate and unwritten transmission of Chan. In a tribute to the creativity of Wuzhu and his followers, I would like to end with a consideration of the vexed nature of Buddhist transmission itself. The very time- and place-bound paradoxes of eighth-century Chan that produced the *Lidai fabao ji* and the unique experiments of the Bao Tang school also exemplify a perennial Buddhist dilemma—the dilemma of the necessary instability of the transmission of a specific yet unclosed canon of teachings (Dharma) by an ordained community (Saṅgha) that is predicated upon the ultimacy of the individual's experience of truth (Buddha/*bodhi*). At the heart of this "Triple Jewel" there is always already a tension between the continuity of received forms and the formless fecundity of insight.

NOTES

1. This article consists of excerpts from various sections of my book in progress: *The Mystique of Transmission: On an Early Chan History and its Contexts*. The primary sources for this study are as follows: Dunhuang manuscripts in the Pelliot collection, Bibliothèque Nationale, Paris, are cited as P, and Dunhuang manuscripts in the Stein collection, British Library, London, are cited as S.

- *Ayu wang jing* (*Aśokarāja-sūtra*, Sutra of King Aśoka). Translated in 512 by Saṃghapāla. T 50 (2043).
- *Baolin zhuan* (Transmission of the Baolin [Temple]) [801], by Zhiju. In Yanagida, ed., Sodōichin Hōrinden (Tokyo: Chūbun Shuppasha, 1975).
- *Beishan lu* (Record of North Mountain) [ca. late 8th c.], by Shenqing. T 52 (2113).
- *Caoqi dashi bie zhuan* (Separate biography of the Master at Caoqi) [781]. ZZ 146, 483–488.
- *Chu sanzang ji ji* (Collection of notes on the translation of the tripitaka) [515], by Sengyou. T 55 (2145).
- *Damoduoluo chan jing* (The Dhyāna-sūtra of Dharmatrāta). Translated by Buddhabhadra (359–429). T 15 (618).
- *E cang Dunhuang wenxian* (Dunhuang documents held in Russia [at the Institute of Oriental Studies of the Russian Academy of Sciences, St. Petersburg Branch]) (1995–1999). 9 vols. Shanghai: Shanghai guji.
- *Fu fazang [yinyuan] zhuan* (Traditions [of the causes and conditions] of transmission of the Dharma Treasury). T 50 (2058).
- *Jian yiqie ruzangjing mulu* [934], by Daozhen. In Oda Yoshihisa, "Tonkō Sankaiji no 'Ken issai nyūzōkyō mokuroku,'" *Ryūkoku Daigaku ronshū* 434–435 (1989): 555–576.
- *Jingde chuandeng lu* (Record of the transmission of the lamp [compiled in] the Jingde era) [1004], by Daoyuan. T 51 (2076).
- *Lengqie shizi ji* (Record of the masters and disciples of the Laṅka [*vatāra-sūtra*]) [ca. 720], by Jingjue. T 85 (2837); P 4564, P 3294, P 3537, P 3436, P 3703, S 2054, S 4272.
- *Lidai fabao ji* (Record of the Dharma-Jewel through the ages) [ca. 780]. T 51 (2075).
- *Lidai sanbao ji* (Record of the triple jewel through the ages). T 49 (2034).
- *Liuzu tanjing* (Platform sutra of the sixth Patriarch) [ca. late 8th cent.]. S 5475.
- *Putidamou nanzong ding shifei lun* (Treatise determining the true and false

about the Southern school of Bodhidharma). Record of Shenhui's 732 debate, by Duhu Pei. P 3047; in Hu Shih, Xingjiaa ding de Dunhuang xie-
ben Shen hui heshang yizhu liangzhong (Taibei: Hu Shih jin ianguan,
[1958] 1970); Suzuki and Koda, eds., 1934.

* *Song gaoseng zhuan* (Song Dynasty biographies of eminent monks) [988],
  by Zanning. T 50 (2061).
* *Tang Zizhou huiyijingshe nanchanyuan sizhengtang beiming* (Stele inscrip-
  tion for the four exemplars hall of the Southern Chan cloister of the Huiyi
  Monastery in Zizhou, Tang dynasty), by Li Shangyin (813–858). *Sibu bei-
  yao*, Fannan wenji bubian, vol. 10. pp. 1–24.
* *Tianjinshi yishu bowuguan cang Dunhuang Tulufan wenxian* (Dunhuang and
  Turfan documents held at the Tianjin Art Museum) (1997–1999). 7 vols.
  Shanghai: Shanghai guji.
* *Yuanjue jing dashu chao* (Subcommentary to the Scripture of Perfect En-
  lightenment) [823], by Zongmi (780–841). ZZ 14, 3–5 and 15, 1.
* *Zutang ji* (Anthology from the Patriarchal Hall) [952]. In Yanagida Seizan,
  Sodō shū (Chodangjip) (Kyoto: Chūbun shuppansha, 1974), pp. 1625–1631.

2. The designation derives from the name of the temple occupied by the group,
the Dali Bao Tang si. Chan scholar Yanagida Seizan surmises that Wuzhu's patron,
the imperial minister Du Hongjian (709–769) may have been responsible for installing Wuzhu in a temple with an imperial designation, and possibly imperial support.
See Yanagida Seizan, *Shoki zenshū shisho no kenkyū* (Tokyo: Hōzōkan, 1967), pp. 286–
287. The Bao Tang monastery was situated in Zizhou in Jiannan, the southwest frontier region of China. Use of the term "school" for the loosely defined affiliations of
the eighth century is vexed; the designations are usually retrospective and often motivated by later sectarian considerations. Nevertheless, this convention is difficult to
avoid entirely.

3. Shenqing's criticisms of Wuzhu and the Bao Tang occur in his *Beishan lu*, T
52 (2113) 611b. Zongmi's critique occurs in his summary and evaluation of the different Chan schools of his day. He first describes Bao Tang ordination and practices, or
lack thereof, and characterizes the Bao Tang as a school that preaches "extinguishing
consciousness" (*mieshi*). *Yuanjue jing dashu chao*, ZZ 14, 278d. See Kamata Shigeo,
Zengen shosenshū tōjō, Zen no goroku no. 9 (Tokyo: Chikuma shobō, 1971), pp. 306–
307. The Bao Tang school is then included in Zongmi's more extensive criticism of
the nihilistic and antinomian tendencies of the Hongzhou and Niutou schools (ZZ
14, 279a–c; Kamata, *Zengen shosenshū tōjō*, pp. 312–315. For a description of Zongmi's
commentaries on the *Yuanjue jing*, see Peter N. Gregory, *Tsung-mi and the Significa-
tion of Buddhism* (Princeton: Princeton University Press, 1991), pp. 320–321.

4. The earliest extant text claiming that Huineng received the robe is the *Putidamou nanzong ding shifei lun* by Dugu Pei, which purports to be a record of the con-
frontation of Shenhui (684–758) with the "Northern school" disciples in 732. In this
text, Shenhui states that it was not necessary to transmit the robe after Huineng, and
that the robe was in Shaozhou. See Hu Shi, *Shen hui heshang yizhi* (Taibei: Hu Shi
jinian guan, [1930] 1970), pp. 280–281.

5. On the discovery and publication of the *Lidai fabao ji* texts and fragments

known before 1997, including fragments newly identified by Rong Xinjiang, see Rong Xinjiang, "Dunhuang ben Chanzong dengshi canjuan shiyi," in *Zhou Shaoliang Xiansheng xinkaijuzhi qingshou wenji* (Beijing: Zhonghua shuju, 1997), pp. 235–242. On the more recently discovered Tianjin and Berlin texts, see notes 6 and 10 below. My translation of the *Lidai fabao ji* is based on Yanagida Seizan's redaction of P 2125, which includes corrections based on comparison with the other *Lidai fabao ji* manuscripts, in *Shoki no zenshi II: Rekidai hōbōki* (Early Chan history II: *Lidai fabao ji*). However, I will cite the page and line numbers in the Taishō edition, T 51 (2075) 179a–196b. I do so because it is the standard source for the Chinese canon, and the most readily available, although its *Lidai fabao ji* is not the best redaction. The Taishō editors claim that P 2125 is the base text, with notes on the variations in S 516, but there are many places where the text was changed without annotation, and a number of misprints. See Kondō Ryōichi, "Rekidai hōbō ki no shōshahon ni tsuite," *Indogaku bukkyōgaku kenkyū* 21 no. 2 (1974): 313–318. I would like to revise and publish my annotated English translation of the *Lidai fabao ji*, but for the time being it is held hostage by the "this is not a book" prejudice against translations that is endemic to the current tenuring system of U.S. academic institutions. See David J. Haberman and Jan Nattier, "Whatever Became of Translation?" *Religious Studies News* (1996): 13.

6. Jinyi designates Dunhuang and Turfan manuscripts in the Tianjin Art Museum, cited by document number in *Tianjinshi yishu bowuguan cang Dunhuang Tulufan wenxian*. Jinyi 304 is in vol. 4, pp. 324–349.

7. This is the title only; see Rong, "Dunhuang ben Chanzong dengshi canjuan shiyi," pp. 241–242.

8. *Tianjinshi yishu bowuguan cang Dunhuang Tulufan wenxian*, vol. 2, p. 199.

9. Described by Tanaka Ryosho, *Tonkō Zenshō bunken no Kenkyū* (Tokyo: Daitū Shuppansha, 1983). An article in the *Mainichi Shimbun* in 1976 revealed that the manuscript was in the possession of a Mr. Hamada Noriaki. His collection was subsequently divided between the Tōyō Bunkō and the National Diet Library, but part of it ended up in a bookstore. The current whereabouts of the *Lidai fabao ji* manuscript is still unknown. See Rong, "Dunhuang ben Chanzong dengshi canjuan shiyi," p. 237.

10. A fragment from Turfan collected during the German expeditions of 1902–1914, now in the Staatsbibliothek in Berlin, identified by Nishiwaki Tsuneki. See Nishiwaki Tsuneki, "Guanyu Bolin suo zang Tulufan shoujipin zhong de Chanji ziliao," *Suyuyan yanjiu* 4 (1997): 138–139.

11. A fragment at the Institute of Oriental Studies of the Russian Academy of Sciences, St. Petersburg Branch, published in *E cang Dunhuang wenxian* vol. 5, pp. 42–43. See Rong, "Dunhuang ben Chanzong dengshi canjuan shiyi," pp. 237–241.

12. See Rong Xinjiang, "*Lidai fabao ji*" *zhong de Momanni he Mishihe* (Beijing: Beijing chubanshe, 1999), pp. 136–137.

13. The *Lidai fabao ji* is listed in the catalogue of the library of the Sanjie Monastery at Dunhuang, the *Jian yiqie ruzangjing mulu* written by Daozhen in 934. One copy of the catalogue is now in the Beijing Library collection; see published edition in Oda Yoshihisa, "Tonkō Sankaiji no 'Ken issai nyūzōkyō mokuroku,'" *Ryūkoku Daigaku ronshū* 434–435 (1989): 555–576 (the entry of the title *Lidai fabao ji* occurs on p. 560). Rong Xinjiang and other scholars have raised the question of whether or not

the Dunhuang Chan manuscript listed therein can be considered a part of the lost "Chan Canon" (*Chan zang*) compiled by Zongmi; see Rong, "Dunhuang ben Chanzong dengshi canjuan shiyi," p. 242. On the *Chan zang*, see Gregory, *Tsung-mi and the Sinification of Buddhism*, pp. 322–323.

14. See Rong Xinjiang, "The Nature of Dunhuang Library Cave and the Reasons for Its Sealing," *Cahiers d'Extrême-Asie* 11 (1999–2000): 247–275, on the nature of the materials in the library cave. Rong also advances the theory that the cave was sealed due to fear of invasion by the Islamic Karakhanids, who destroyed Khotan in 1006, resulting in a wave of refugees to Dunhuang; ibid., pp. 272–275.

15. T 51 (2076). This and other Song-dynasty Chan texts drew from the following eighth- and ninth-century Chan sectarian histories (see note 1 above): the *Baolin zhuan* of 801; the *Beishan lu* by Shenqing; the *Caoqi dashi biezhuan* of 781; and early versions of the *Liuzu tanjing*. Also relevant is the recently discovered manuscript at the Dunhuang museum edited by Yang Cengwen, (Shanghai: Shanghai guji, 1993). See Philip B. Yampolsky, *The Platform Sutra of the Sixth Patriach* (New York: Columbia University Press, 1967).

16. For Yanagida's extensive work on this and related topics, I refer the reader to Bernard Faure's "Bibliographie succincte de Yanagida Seizan" in the *Cahiers d'Extrême-Asie* 7 (1994): 45–50. For relevant works in Western languages, see Bernard Faure, *The Will to Orthodoxy: A Critical Genealogy of Northern Chan Buddhism*, translated by Phyllis Brooks (Stanford: Stanford University Press, 1997); John McRae, *The Northern School and the Formation of Early Ch'an Buddhism* (Honolulu: University of Hawai'i Press, 1986); Jeffrey L. Broughton, *The Bodhidharma Anthology: The Earliest Records of Zen* (Berkeley: University of California Press, 1999); T. Griffith Foulk, "The Ch'an School and Its Place in the Buddhist Monastic Tradition" (Ph.D. dissertation, University of Michigan, 1987).

17. For an excellent overview of institutional Buddhism in the Tang, see Stanley Weinstein, *Buddhism under the T'ang* (Cambridge: Cambridge University Press, 1987).

18. See Denis Twitchett, "The Composition of the Tang Ruling Class: New Evidence from Tunhuang," in Arthur F. Wright and Denis Twitchett, eds., *Perspectives on the Tang* (New Haven: Yale University Press, 1973), pp. 47–85; Charles Peterson, "Court and Province in Mid- and Late-T'ang," in Denis Twitchett, ed., *The Cambridge History of China*, Vol. 3, *Sui and T'ang China, 589–906* (Cambridge: Cambridge University Press, 1979), pp. 464–560; Michael T. Dalby, "Court Politics in Late T'ang Times," in Denis Twitchett, ed., *The Cambridge History of China*, Vol. 3, *Sui and T'ang China, 589–906*, pp. 561–681; Charles Hartman, *Han Yü and the T'ang Search for Unity* (Princeton: Princeton University Press, 1986).

19. See Hu Shi, "The Development of Zen Buddhism in China," *Chinese and Political Science Review* 15 no. 4 (1932): 475–505; Jacques Gernet, *Entretiens du maître dhyana Chen-houei du Ho-tsö (668–760)* ([1949] Paris: École Française d'Extrême-Orient, 1977); John McRae, "Shen-hui and the Teaching of Sudden Enlightenment in Early Ch'an Buddhism," in Peter N. Gregory, ed., *Sudden and Gradual: Approaches to Enlightenment in Chinese Thought* (Honolulu: University of Hawai'i Press, 1987), pp. 232–237. The dates for Shenhui are based on the recently discovered Longmen stele of 765. See Kōdō Takeuchi, "Shinshutsu no Kataku Jinne tōmei ni tsuite" *Shūgaku kenkyū* 27 (1985): 313–325.

20. See Bernard Faure, *The Rhetoric of Immediacy: A Cultural Critique of Chan/Zen Buddhism*. (Princeton: Princeton University Press, 1991), pp. 63–65.

21. For a discussion of the emergence of the Chan *yulu* genre and its relation to earlier Buddhist genres, see Judith Berling, "Bringing the Buddha down to Earth: Notes on the Emergence of *Yu-lü* as a Buddhist Genre," *History of Religions* 21 no. 1 (1987): 56–88. For a related discussion of the "encounter" versus "marga" paradigms of cultivation, see John McRae, "Encounter Dialogue and the Transformation of the Spiritual Path in Chinese Ch'an," in Peter N. Gregory, ed., *Paths to Liberation: The Marga and Its Transformations in Buddhist Thought* (Honolulu: University of Hawai'i Press, 1992), pp. 339–369. On Neo-Confucian *yulu*, see Daniel K. Gardiner, "Modes of Thinking and Modes of Discourse in the Sung: Some Thoughts on the *Yü-lu* (Recorded Conversations) Texts," *Journal of Asian Studies* 50 no. 3 (1991): 574–603.

22. For a fascinating study of connections among early medieval genres, see Robert Ford Campany, *Strange Writing: Anomaly Accounts in Early Medieval China* (Albany: State University of New York Press, 1996). On the relationship between *qingtan* and Buddhist treatises, see Erik Zürcher, *The Buddhist Conquest of China: The Spread and Adaptation of Buddhism in Early Medieval China*, 2 vols. (Leiden: Brill, 1959), pp. 93–94.

23. T 51 (2075) 179a–196b.

24. T 85 (2837).

25. The *Lidai fabao ji* gives these specific dates for Daoxin, Hongren, and Huineng, but does not give dates for Bodhidharma, Huike, or Sengcan. Dates for Bodhidharma's death vary from text to text; see Chen Yuan, *Shishi yinian lu Jiangsu: Jiangsu guangling guj* (Jiangsu: Jiangsu guangling guji, [1939] 1991), p. 38. Huike's dates are based on the *Jingde chuandeng lu*; see Chen, *Shishi yinian lu*, p. 42. The date for Sengcan is from the memorial inscription reported by Chen Hao in *Wenwu* 4 (1985): 8. The inscription states that it was written by Daoxin, thus corroborating their master-disciple relationship.

26. Yampolsky, *The Platform Sūtra of the Sixth Patriarch*, pp. 8–9.

27. T 50 (2058). The origins of the *Fu fazang zhuan* are unclear. In the *Chu sanzang ji ji* it is listed as a translation completed in 472 by Tanyao (d. ca. 485) and the Indian monk Kinkara. *Chu sanzang ji ji*, T 55 (2145) 13b6–12. The compiler of the *Lidai sanbao ji* refers to the mention of a *Fu fazang zhuan* in an earlier catalogue, for which the *terminus ad quem* of 481 has been established. The *Lidai sanbao ji* notice on Tanyao claims that after the persecution Tanyao regretted leaving the mountains where he hid during the persecution. Therefore he sequestered himself in a cave temple with a group of monks and retranslated a number of sutras, including the *Fu fazang zhuan*, in order to restore the integrity of Dharma transmission that the persecution had damaged. *Lidai sanbao ji*, T 49 (2034) 62b–63a. On dating the text, see Henri Maspéro, "Sur la date et l'authenticité du fou fa tsang fir yuan tchovan," *Melanges d'Indianism (offeots à S. Lev. par ses élèves* Paris: E. Leroux, 1911); on the use of the text in later Chan lineages, see Elizabeth Morrison, "The *Fufazang yinyuan zhuan* and the Ancestry of Genealogy in Medieval Chinese Buddhism" (seminar paper, Stanford University, 1995).

28. T 15 (618).

29. T 50 (2043), translated in 512 by Samghapala.

30. For Shenhui's version of the Indian patriarchs, see Hu, *She-hui heshang yizhi*, p. 179. In spite of the use made of it, the *Aśokarāja-sūtra* is not a generational lineage as conceived by sixth-century Chinese exegetes such as Guanding or the unknown author of the *Fu fazang zhuan*, for the first two figures, Mahākāśyapa and Ānanda, are both presented as disciples of the Buddha, although Ānanda does succeed Mahākāśyapa in authority. Likewise the third and fourth figures, Madhyāntika and Sāravasa, are both presented as disciples of Ānanda, and Sāravasa transmits the Dharma to the fifth figure, Upagupta. Following the *Aśokarāja-sūtra*, the *Fu fazang zhuan* retains Madhyāntika as a co-disciple to Sāravasa, but Shenhui, who was probably following Buddhabhadra's list, has Madhyāntika as the third Indian patriarch.

31. *Lidai fabao ji*, T 51 (2075) 180a16–b15.

32. Mihirakula was the second ruler of the conquering Hura people (related to the Hepthalites) who ruled northwest India and Kashmir from the end of the fifth century and well into the sixth. The exceptional cruelty of this ruler and his known persecution of Buddhists has led to speculation that his reign, and the consequent exodus of monks, may have been responsible for the late sixth-century development of the "decline of the Dharma" theme in China. Nattier argues that although this may have been a factor, the literature of decline is also strongly associated with the very prosperity of the saṅgha during the peaceful Kushan rule of the second and third centuries. See Jan Nattier, *Once upon a Future Time: Studies in the Buddhist Prophecy of Decline* (Berkeley: Asian Humanities Press, 1991), pp. 110–117, 224–227. If the "Miduoluojue" of the *Fu fazang zhuan* is indeed Mihirakula, then this is another indication of its sixth-century origins.

33. The *Lidai fabao ji* is the only account of Siṃha's murder in which these identifications are made. Rong Xinjiang discusses the possible influence of this *Lidai fabao ji* passage on the attitude of the Tibetan king Tri Songdetsen (r. 754–797) toward Manichaeism, and suggests that this is but one effect of Chinese xenophobia following the An Lushan rebellion. Since the Tang restoration depended on Uighur armies, the central government was forced to adopt tolerant policies (in contrast to Xuanzong's edict of 732 criticizing Manichaeism and barring Chinese from practicing it). Rong argues, however, that the similar northern military backgrounds of Wuzhu and his patron Du Hongjian would probably have created a Bao Tang prejudice against foreign religions. See Rong, "The Nature of the Dunhuang Library Cave and the Reasons for Its Sealing." See also G. Uray, "Tibet's Connections with Nestorianism and Manichaeism in the 8th–10th Centuries," *Wiener Studien zur Tibetologie und Buddhismuskunde* 10 (1983): 399–429; Samuel N. C. Lieu, *Manichaeism in the Later Roman Empire and Medieval China* (Tubingen: J. C. B. Mohr, 1992); David Scott, "Buddhist Responses to Manichaeism: Mahāyāna Reaffirmation of the 'Middle Path,'" *History of Religions* 35 no.2 (1995): 148–162; Paul Pelliot and Antonino Forte, *L'inscription nestorienne de Si-ngan-fou* (Kyoto and Paris: Italian School of East Asian Studies and Collège de France, 1996); Antonino Forte, "The Chinese Title of the Manichaean Treatise from Dunhuang" (paper at the International Conference on Dunhuang Studies, Dunhuang, July 2000).

34. *Lidai fabao ji*, T 51 (2075) 180a29–b9.

35. *Fu fazang zhuan*, T 50 (2058) 321c14–18.

36. *Lidai fabao ji*, T 51 (2075) 186a15–b8.

37. Ibid., T 51 (2075) 186c28–187a8.

38. Ibid., T 51 (2075) 187a16–19.

39. The *Lidai fabao ji* also highlights Wuzhu's relationship with the prominent imperial minister in Sichuan, Du Hongjian (709–769). Although he is considered to have been Wuzhu's follower, his role is that of primary patron rather than close personal disciple.

40. *Lidai fabao ji*, T 51 (2075) 192a24–b20.

41. Ibid., T 51 (2075) 195c14–15.

42. Ibid., T 51 (2075) 196a10–13.

43. Adaptation of Yan Hui's praise of virtue in the *Lunyu*; see Arthur Waley, trans., *The Analects of Confucius* (London: George Allen and Unwin, 1938), p. 140.

44. *Lidai fabao ji*, T 51 (2075) 196a22–26.

45. T. Griffith Foulk and Robert Sharf, "On the Ritual Use of Ch'an Portraiture in Medieval China," *Cahiers d'Extrême-Asie* 7 (1994): 195.

46. See Yampolsky, *The Platform Sūtra of the Sixth Patriarch*, pp. 141–143.

47. *Beishan lu*, T 52 (2113) 611b and 612c.

48. *Song gaoseng zhuan*, T 50 (2061) 832b–833a; *Tang Zizhou huiyijingshe nanchanyuan sizhengtang beiming*.

49. Minn Young-gyu, "Shisen kōdan shūi," *Chūgai Nippō* (1991): 24509: 1; 24510: 1; and 24511: 1–2.

50. *Lidai fabao ji*, T 51 (2075) 185a11–15.

51. Tsukamoto Zenryū, *Chūgoku jōdo kyōshi kenkyū*, Tsukamoto Zenryū chosakushū 4 (1976), pp. 559–565; Jeffrey L. Broughton, "Early Ch'an Schools in Tibet," *Studies in Ch'an and Hua-yen* (Honolulu: University of Hawai'i Press, 1983); Stanley Weinstein, *Buddhism under the Tang* (Cambridge: Cambridge University Press, 1987), pp. 73–74; Daniel Stevenson, "Visions of Manjusri on Mount Wutai," *Religions of China in Practice* (Princeton: Princeton University Press, 1996), pp. 203–222.

52. See Giuseppe Tucci, *Minor Buddhist Texts*, II ([1958] Delhi: Motilal Banarsidass, 1986); Paul Demiéville, "L'introduction au Tibet du Bouddhisme sinise d'après les manuscrits de Touen-houang," Michel Soymie, ed., *Contributions aux Études sur Touen-houang*, (Geneva: Librairie Droz, 1952); Yamaguchi Zuihō, "Tora o tomonau daijūhachi rakanzu no rairek," *Indō koten kenkyū* 13 (1984): 1–10; Obata Hironobu, "Pelliot tib. No. 116 bunken ni mieru sho Zenshi no kenkyū," *Zenbunka kenkyūjo kiyō*, 8 (1974): 33–103; Ueyama Daishun, *Tonkō bukkyō no kenkyū*, (1974): vol. 13, 1–10; Ryūtoku Kimura, "Le dhyana chinois au Tibet ancien après Mahayana," *Journal Asiatique* 269 (1981): 183–192; Broughton, "Early Ch'an Schools in Tibet"; Guilaine Mala and Ryūtoku Kimura, "Une traite tibetain de dhyana chinois," *Bulletin de la Maison Franco-Japonaise*, 11 no. 1 (1988): 1–103. For an excellent bibliography of Japanese scholars' work on Tibetan Chan texts, see Ueyama Daishun, "Études des manuscrits tibetains de Dunhuang relatifs au bouddhisme de dhyana. Bilan et perspectives," *Journal Asiatique* 269 (1981): 287–293.

53. See Mario Poceski's dissertation on the Hongzhou school, "The Hongzhou School of Chan Buddhism during the Mid-Tang Period" (Ph.D. dissertation, University of California at Los Angeles, 2000).

54. Minn, "Shisen kōdan shūi." The biographies of the Korean monks are in

juan 17 of the *Zutang ji,* Yanagida Seizan, *Sodō shū (Chodangjip)* (Kyoto: Chūbun shuppansha, 1974), pp. 1,625–1,631.

55. See Minn, "Shisen kōdan shūi," where he discusses the writings of Hu Shi and of Japanese scholars on the subject. See also Yanagida Seizan, "Shinzoku tōshi no keifu: jo no ichi," *Zengaku kenkyū* 59 (1978): 1–39.

56. See Faure, *The Rhetoric of Immediacy,* pp. 132–178.

4

The Huang-po Literature

Dale S. Wright

The classic literature presenting the ninth-century Zen master Huang-po holds an especially significant position in the Zen canon. Its significance is attributable to two primary factors. From a traditional Zen point of view, its importance is simply that of its central figure, the Zen master Huang-po Hsi-yun, an early lineage holder in the Hung-chou style of Zen that descends from Ma-tsu, and the teacher of Lin-chi, the historical founder of Rinzai Zen. From the perspective of contemporary Buddhist studies, its importance derives from the fact that this literature is the best example of the state of the Zen tradition in China during what has traditionally been regarded as the "golden age." What is unique about the Huang-po literature is that it is precisely dateable, thus providing a crucial historical marker in the Zen tradition. What in this essay will be called the "Huang-po literature" consists of two early "recorded sayings" texts compiling the teachings of Huang-po; one is the *Essentials of Mind Transmission (Ch'uan-hsin Fa-yao)* and the other is the *Record of Wan-ling (Wan-ling lu).*

The preface to these texts, written by their primary composer and editor, P'ei-hsiu, was dated September 857, thus providing a clear and specific example of Hung-chou Zen teachings as they existed in the middle of the ninth century, when the Zen tradition was coming to prominence in China. The teachings of the Huang-po literature demonstrate the emergence of a unique and powerful Zen teaching style that would provide an important basis for the subsequent development of the classical Zen of the Sung period. This essay will describe the Huang-po literature by developing four primary dimensions: the origins of the texts, the literary structure and style of the texts, the teachings of the texts, and the appropriation of the Huang-po texts in Zen history.

The Origins of the Huang-po Literature

The development and rise to prominence of Chinese Ch'an Buddhism aligns with larger historical developments in the powerful T'ang dynasty (618–906). Midway through T'ang, signs of dynastic weakness and social/political deterioration were evident. The An Lu-shan rebellion (755–763) devastated the political structures of the government to such an extent that central authority of the kind held in the earlier regime would not be restored. The implications of the historical shift for Chinese Buddhism were profound. Prior to this time, Buddhism had been sponsored and supported by the imperial government. Buddhist temples were also "government" temples, and the control of the clergy was ultimately in the hands of central authorities. Since patronage in the form of financial support assumed or mandated some degree of compromise between the Buddhist establishment and the central government, Buddhism would develop in China as the central authority would dictate or encourage. In the second half of the T'ang dynasty, this situation changed dramatically as the rise of the Zen tradition developed. Although one might say that Chinese Ch'an benefited from this historical situation, it would be more accurate to say that the decentralization of power and authority in China is a condition without which Zen as we know it would never have come into being. Under the conditions of decentralization, local authorities, military leaders, and wealthy patrons began to support alternative forms of Buddhism, and as the recipients of these new sources of support, Zen came to be the leading edge of innovation and religious power in the later T'ang.

As it is now possible to understand this development, the career of Zen master Huang-po Hsi-yun corresponds with the height of this decentralization of religious authority in China, and to the rise of local patronage in south central China. Born perhaps sometime in the 780s in Fu-chien province,[1] Huang-po entered the monastic life at an early age on Mount Huang-po and was given the Buddhist name Hsi-yun. Zen tradition maintains that he later studied under the renowned Zen master Pai-chang Huai-hai, the reputed organizer of a distinctly Zen monastic system, who had himself studied under the great Ma-tsu Tao-i, to whom the Hung-chou lineage of Zen is traced. Although these lines of genealogy are extremely important in the Zen tradition, in fact sources cannot verifiably say anything about what Huang-po studied as a young postulant in the Buddhist tradition, or with whom. Nevertheless, it is clear that the Zen tradition of the Hung-chou area was rapidly rising to prominence, and Huang-po's reputation as a Zen master was well known in his time.

At the time when the great Buddhist scholar Tsung-mi wrote about Hung-chou Zen in the 830s, Huang-po would have been its best-known current figure. Although Tsung-mi does not mention Huang-po by name, instead focusing his attention on Ma-tsu, the founder of this style of Zen and its most reknowned figure, it is highly probably that Tsung-mi had Huang-po in mind as he surveyed the teachings of this new sect of Zen.[2] At some point—perhaps not long after the death of his teacher[3]—Huang-po would have opened his own monastery in the mountains of Kiangsi province, naming it Huang-po shan after the temple in Fukien where he had first entered the monastic life.[4] Biographical records tell us nothing about Huang-po's life during this period.

What is known with considerable precision is that in 841 Huang-po attracted a very important disciple—the scholar/official P'ei-hsiu—who would over the next twenty years compose and publish the Zen teachings of Huang-po. The story of the relationship between Huang-po and P'ei-hsiu is very important, and provides us with a great deal of information on what the Huang-po literature is, and how it came to be.[5] P'ei-hsiu (787 or 797–860) was born into a well-known and politically influential family in Hunan province. Like his brothers, he passed the Chinese civil service examination at the highest level (chin-shih) and served in a series of official posts until being elevated to the position of chief minister in 853, which would have been sometime close to the death of Huang-po. Throughout his life, P'ei-hsiu was an avid scholar and intellectual. As he grew into positions of power and prominence, he more and more focused on the study and practice of Buddhism, making a point of seeking out the most famous Buddhist teachers in China. In the middle of his career he became a disciple of the great Hua-yen and Zen scholar, Tsung-mi, who would guide him in the study of Buddhist philosophy and Zen.[6]

As an ardent student of Tsung-mi, P'ei-hsiu studied the teachings of the various lines of Zen that were emerging in south central China at that time. Because it was beginning to receive a good deal of attention in China, P'ei-hsiu was especially curious about the kind of Zen being developed in the Hung-chou area. Tsung-mi, however, himself a teacher in the Ho-tse line of Zen, was somewhat critical of the Hung-chou style. For him, this excessively rural school of Buddhism lacked the comprehensive vision that he found in Ho-tse Zen and in the Hua-yen philosophical school of Buddhism.[7] As we have seen, however, P'ei-hsiu pressed his teacher with questions, unwilling to yield so easily to the critique of Hung-chou Zen.[8]

Then, in 841, just after the death of Tsung-mi, P'ei-hsiu received a government assignment in Kiangsi province, and took the occasion to seek out the foremost representative of Hung-chou Zen, the famous master Huang-po, about whom P'ei-hsiu would have learned from Tsung-mi and others. In the preface to the text of Huang-po's teachings that he later compiled, P'ei-hsiu explains how in 842 he invited Huang-po to come down from his mountain monastery to take up residence at Lung-hsing Monastery in the prefectural seat at Chung-ling in order to teach there. P'ei-hsiu explains how "day and night" he questioned Huang-po and received his Dharma teaching. Much of the *Ch'uan-hsin fa-yao* derives directly from P'ei-shiu's notes on this historic occasion. As it turned out, the first meeting between P'ei-hsiu and Huang-po would also occur just prior to the historic Hui-chang (841–846) suppression of Buddhism in China in which thousands of Buddhist monks would be under attack by the government. Although no documents allude to Huang-po's situation and whereabouts during this government persecution of Chinese Buddhism, scholars assume that, like others in his time and place, Huang-po would have gone into hiding in the mountains to evade the punitive attention of government officials.

Following the gap in Huang-po's life, we read in P'ei-hsiu's preface to the Huang-po literature that in 848 P'ei-hsiu once again went to his teacher, inviting him out of the mountains to join him where he was now assigned the government duty of serving as examiner in the Wan-ling district. Huang-po took up residence at K'ai-yuan Monastery and begin to instruct P'ei-hsiu in his Zen teachings. P'ei-hsiu wrote, "day and night I received the Dharma and withdrew to write it down. I was able to write just one or two of each ten statements he made. I received this as a mind-seal and did not presume to publish it."⁹

P'ei-hsiu's account of receiving Huang-po's teachings in Wan-ling is the last reference we have to any event in Huang-po's life. Sometime, perhaps shortly after this, the great Zen master died (in the *Ta-chung* period, sometime between 849 and 857) on Mount Huang-po and, if the grave marker at his old temple site is accurate, was buried there. He received posthumous titles from the government, probably under P'ei-hsiu's encouragement, and was honored at court. What happened to P'ei-hsiu at that historic juncture is especially important, and helps to make possible the enormous prestige of Huang-po from that time on. In 853 P'ei-hsiu was called to the capital to take the central government position of chief minister, from which he served the country for several years. Then, upon retirement from that prestigious position, he began to work on composing the teachings of Huang-po from the notes that he had compiled while studying under the Zen master on those two occasions in the Hung-chou area. Having written in the preface that he "had not presumed to publish" these notes from Huang-po, P'ei-hsiu had second thoughts on the matter. "But now I fear," he writes, "that the essential teachings of the great master will not be heard by future generations."¹⁰ Rather than assume, however, that his notes contained a complete and accurate account of the teachings of Huang-po, P'ei-hsiu decided to elicit the aid of the elder monks on Mount Huang-po, who had heard the great master teach the Dharma for many years.

"So," P'ei-hsiu writes in the preface, "I gave the manuscript to the monks T'ai-chou and Fa-chien, who took it to Kuang-t'ang monastery on Huang-po Mountain and asked the elder monks of the monastery whether it accords with what they had heard in the past."[11]

We can imagine that the arrival of former Chief Minister P'ei-hsiu's manuscript account of their master's teaching must have created quite a stir on Mount Huang-po. Monks there must have been aware that this was an extraordinary opportunity for Huang-po's teachings to be disseminated to a significantly large and prominent audience; after all, P'ei-hsiu would have been one of the most famous and influential Buddhists of the day, and his close link to the most highly educated level of Chinese society would have been something of a breakthrough for the Zen tradition at that time. But P'ei-hsiu had sent the manuscript to the monastery for a reason—that is, so that the monks could edit, correct, and perfect the manuscript to better represent the overall teachings of the Zen master. He assumed that the elders at the monastery would have an even better sense than he did of what the master had taught, and thus he invited the possibility of addition and emendation to his handwritten manuscript. For the most part, historians today follow the lead of Zen historian Yanagida Seizan in thinking that the elder monks at Huang-po had in their possession "private notes" written and collected over the years of studying under the Zen master. The arrival of P'ei-hsiu's manuscript would therefore have been the occasion for the monks to bring their own notes out to compare with those collected by P'ei-hsiu.[12]

There is irony in the very existence of these notes, since much of Huang-po's teachings focus on a critique of textual practices in Chinese Buddhism, including the practice of writing secret notes containing the "sayings" of the master. Nevertheless, there is good reason and plenty of evidence to think that many of the monks would have done this anyway as an aid to their own Zen practice.[13] Even P'ei-hsiu, the highly cultured literati scholar, expressed reservations in his preface about creating a text of the teachings of Huang-po, though in the end the thought of their being lost to posterity persuaded him to bring them out into the open. In view of the strong Zen criticism of textual practices, however, we might wonder why monks might have disobeyed the advice of the teachings on this point. Yanagida provides one explanation of the process: "The greater the number of disciples that surrounded a great teacher became, the smaller each student's opportunities for individual instruction. Hence, moments of direct contact with the teacher became prized experiences for the disciples involved, some of whom soon began making secret notes of the events. Eventually certain monks prone to such activity started making anthologies of the teacher's words and actions based on what they heard from other students in addition to their own experience. This was a perfectly natural development."[14] The practice of writing secret notes of meetings with the Zen master was "perfectly natural," given the importance of these meetings for the spiritual quest, especially since China had by that time in its history become a highly literate culture.[15] On the one hand, Huang-po's utterances must have warranted memorization and reflection. After all, he was the enlightened master and the state of his mind was what the monks sought. His were considered enlightened expressions, words that in some way captured the deeper sense of the Dharma. Getting these words right, and making them available for later reflection, would have led monks to seek some means of preservation. And on the other hand, the fact that writing skills were widely disseminated in monastic life and in Chinese society generally meant that the most natural response to the situation would have been to jot these notes down and to save them for later meditation.

Considering these individual textual practices and P'ei-hsiu's request for help on the manuscript, it seems very likely that additions were made to the basic text that P'ei had recorded, edited, and sent to the monastery. How much the manuscript grew with the aid of the Huang-po monks, no one knows. It is possible, however, to see a variety of perspectives in the kinds of questions brought to Huang-po in the text. Some of these clearly show the internal workings of monastic practice, and seem to reflect the mentality of monks. Other questions posed to Huang-po ask how Zen practice for the laity ought to be undertaken. This diversity in point of departure indicates clearly enough the range of interests evident in the final manuscript.

Although printing had been invented considerably before this time, China was still largely a "manuscript" culture in which handwritten manuscripts of Buddhist texts were still the most common. In order to get a copy of the Huang-po literature, monks would need to copy their own or get someone else to do it. In writing one's own record, there are two ways in which manuscripts undergo change. One is simply error; you can make a mistake copying a long text. Indeed, it would be virtually impossible not to make mistakes. Second, changes can be intentional. You can decide not to copy, for example, the fourth scroll, if you think that the first three would be enough, or if you think that the fourth might not contain the specific teaching that you seek. You may also decide to alter the way a particular story is presented, just to embellish it or make it accord with the way you had heard it earlier. Or you might add another story about Huang-po that you had heard but which, so far, had not yet made its way into the text. The distinction between written text and verbal text was not as clear as it would become in the era of printing. In any case, we know that when manuscripts "circulate" as they did in medieval Buddhist culture, a range of different versions come into being. It is only when an official version is printed and widely disseminated that these practices of variation begin to slow or come to an end. In the case of the Huang-po literature, this would have been in 1004, when the *Ching-te ch'uan-teng lu* was printed, including in its massive contents one version of the Huang-po literature, which became in effect the official version of Huang-po.

We can speculate that at some point the manuscript was sent back to P'ei-hsiu, now edited and corrected by the monks on Mount Huang-po.[16] Judging the manuscript fit for publication, P'ei-hsiu composed a preface, dated October 8, 857, explaining what the text is and how it came to be. For that reason it is a historical document of considerable significance. We can also imagine that at least one copy of the original remained in the possession of the monks on Mount Huang-po, probably circulating in handwritten form in south China for a long time. This version would have lacked P'ei's preface. P'ei-hsiu's version, preface included, no doubt circulated among the literati in Ch'ang-an, and was later selected as the most authoritative version for printing. In any case, here we have a rare case of an important Buddhist manuscript, exact date included, that incorporates writing on its own origins, an opportunity from which a lot has been learned about how Zen texts came into being.

Literary Style, Structure, and Authorship

A cursory look at the Huang-po literature shows two distinct literary forms, one structured as a sermon or direct teaching and the other as a dialogical question-and-answer format. Looking more closely at the sermons, however, we notice that they are introduced in several different ways. A small number of didactic sermons are introduced in a personal way with the words, "The master said to me," or, "On September first, the master said to me." These passages appear to represent the original form of the Huang-po literature as it comes from the handwritten notes of P'ei-hsiu following his personal meetings with Huang-po. They encourage us to picture a setting in which Huang-po is meeting privately with P'ei-hsiu to teach him the Dharma. A greater number of sermons are not introduced at all; they just begin the teaching by moving directly to the issue at hand.

Some of the sermons duplicate or repeat teachings already given in the text. These would appear to be versions of the same sermon contributed by two different people. Either the editor did not notice the repetition, or he simply included everything that he had received. A small number of sermons are prefaced by a very familiar Zen phrase, *shang t'ang* or "ascending the platform." This phrase simply means that the occasion for the sermon to follow is that of a formal lecture given by the master in the main hall of the monastery, when he enters the room and climbs up unto his elevated platform to sit before the assembly of monks and speak. The earliest extant code of rules for a Zen monastery prescribes the ritual of ascending the platform to give a sermon as follows: "The community of the whole monastery should gather in the Dharma hall for the morning and evening discussions. On these occasions the Elder 'enters the hall and ascends his seat.' The monastery officers as well as the ordinary monks stand in files and listen attentively to the discussion. For some of them to raise questions and for the master to answer, which invigorates and clarifies the essence of Zen teaching, is to show how to live in accord with the Dharma."[17] At some point in the history of Zen, these Dharma rituals had become standard daily routines, and we see evidence of their pervasiveness in the Huang-po literature. Sermons were clearly the primary form in which most monks and most Buddhists of all kinds received the teachings. Although later Zen literature tended to abandon this form of textual presentation, it is unlikely that this literary change reflects a transition in the oral form in which most people encountered the teachings. Recall in this case that even the earliest Buddhist literature, the sutras, took the form of sermons. They are sermons of the Buddha himself as remembered and committed to memory by close disciples. As sutras evolved over many centuries, many becoming exceedingly long and complex, they ceased to be plausible as sermons. In spite of that obvious fact, however, Buddhist *sutras* have always taken the formal structure of a sermon of the Buddha. It is not surprising that later Zen masters followed this pattern.[18]

In addition to the sermons attributed to Huang-po, roughly half of the Huang-po literature consists in dialogue between the master and his disciples, both monks and lay people. These are easily identifiable in the text, since in each case they are introduced by the Chinese words for *question* and *answer*. In each case, the question posed is very brief, typically one short sentence. This probably reflects the fact that neither notetaker nor editor was interested in the words of the inquirer; they wanted to get to the teachings of Huang-po as directly as possible. Answers to these questions vary in length from one sentence to several paragraphs. As we can see from the above description of the ritual of "ascending the platform," it was the custom of the time to allow question-and-answer periods to follow the formal sermons. In this sense it may be that the distinction between the sermon and the question-and-answer style is not significant, since both occurred on the same occasion and entered into the Huang-po texts at the same time through the memories of disciples who had observed the rituals.

One of the themes in the Huang-po literature is the necessity of direct spiritual experience and the related idea that traditional Buddhist textual practices are more likely to block or prevent direct experience than to support or evoke it. Frequently, the texts present Huang-po as ridiculing monks who are intent on conceptual or doctrinal points but who lack the vision to see how these are subsidiary to the real point of Zen. As the Zen tradition developed over time, these images of Huang-po were accentuated and extended so that the image of Huang-po would more clearly accord with his position in the Rinzai sect as the teacher of his radically iconoclastic student, Lin-chi I-hsuan. With these extreme antitextual and antidoctrinal images in view, we might easily miss the extent to which the Huang-po literature displays familiarity with a wide range of Buddhist doctrines and texts. Indeed, in spite of railing against improper monastic and meditative uses of texts, the image we get of the master is one of widespread literacy and a long-standing textual practice that appears to extend to the very end of Huang-po's life.

Evidence for this is the way in which the Huang-po literature quotes and alludes to other Buddhist texts. Because this literature had its origin in the notes and memories of P'ei-hsiu and the monks on Mount Huang-po, we have good reason to believe that when the literature has Huang-po quoting a particular Buddhist text, this may very well show us the actual textual references of the master Huang-po. In any case, even in the process of making its frequent anti-textual point, the Huang-po literature draws its backing and its content from earlier Buddhist texts. The sermons as well as the question-and-answer sections have Huang-po supporting his points with references to Buddhist sutras as well as to earlier Chinese Buddhist teachers. Sometimes these are named explicitly, "as so and so says" or "as the *Diamond Sutra* says," and sometimes the language of an earlier text is simply borrowed without citation. But in both cases we are shown very clearly that the Zen tradition in Huang-po's time still considered the literature of the Buddhist tradition to be crucial to the development of an enlightened Buddhist, in spite of the critique that Huang-po so powerfully articulates.

The literary style of the Huang-po literature is also interesting. Although the doctrinal sophistication of early T'ang dynasty Buddhist literature is clearly evident here, the formal character of the written language is missing. What we find instead is a rhetorically effective colloquial style that gives us the impression that we are listening to an actual speech event, a ninth-century monastic sermon directly from Huang-po. The forcefulness of this colloquial language makes Huang-po emerge in the text as a real person rather than as a figure put forth to symbolize the Zen tradition. The manner of the written language suggests actual speech situations of Zen players whose personalities we can imagine. The overall effect of this stylistic transformation in Zen literature is very powerful, and would subsequently be taken up in virtually all Zen literature of the "recorded sayings" (*yü-lu*) genre.

The style of the literature, in other words, gives the Zen master personality, and this concretization of the Zen master adds efficacy to the tradition's self-impression. The fact that P'ei-hsiu, the one most responsible for writing these texts, was a member of China's elite literati class, whose education, therefore, would have been in the formal and elegant prose style of that class, presents us with an intriguing puzzle. How is it that P'ei-hsiu, in his effort to present Huang-po to the literati audience of the capitol, could have allowed Huang-po's colloquial style of speaking to emerge so forcefully in this literature? Of course we don't know the answer. But a good guess might focus our attention on broader transformations that were already under way in late T'ang dynasty China, including the breakdown of central authority, the dissemination of cultural leadership to other previously unknown parts of China, and the fact that transformation from one cultural style to another is always the long-term theme of any human history. In any case, it is clear that by the end of his life, the style of thinking and speaking that we can now attribute to Huang-po was having a powerful effect on Chinese culture at all levels.

The question of how to situate the Huang-po literature in an appropriate genre is also perplexing. Traditionally, because these texts have been placed into the larger *Transmission of the Lamp* collections, the *Ch'uan-hsin Fa-yao* and the attached *Wan-ling lu* of Huang-po and P'ei-hsiu have been taken to be examples of the "recorded sayings" literature. And insofar as these texts purport to be records of the "sayings" of Huang-po as they were received by P'ei-hsiu in two prolonged sessions with the master, perhaps that is exactly where they belong. Nevertheless, a closer examination of the texts shows that they lack certain features that are characteristic of that genre.[19] In the Huang-po literature, there is no biographical sketch of the Zen master at the beginning of the text, where, judging from virtually all other examples of *yü-lu* texts found in the *Transmission of the Lamp* literature, we would expect to find it. P'ei-hsiu appears not to have been interested in or concerned with his master's biography; after introducing the texts with an account of how it came into existence, he moves directly to the teachings themselves in both sermon and question-and-answer mode. Only later, it seems, after the death of the great masters, was it important to gather the biographical facts needed to place the master in an elaborate genealogy. Typical of these "facts" are date and place of birth, family names, place of ordination, names of teachers, stories demonstrating early signs of religious brilliance and, usually at the end of the text, an account of the master's death and the poetry associated with his transmission. All these are missing from the Huang-po literature, although some of this information is supplied by later biographies elsewhere.

Moreover, the fit of the earliest Huang-po literature into the "recorded sayings" genre is complicated by another missing element, examples of "encounter dialogue" between Huang-po and other Zen masters, monks, or government officials.[20] "Encounter dialogue," as we get the term from Yanagida Seizan, tells Zen stories about what happens when a Zen master came into Dharma encounter with others, the kinds of actions and speech that a master performed in view of the actions or speech of others. These dialogues are typical of later, mature Zen texts, and are by now the stories best known about the great Zen masters. The early Huang-po texts do not contain any of these stories.[21] What we can see in them, however, is a prototypical form of it. When the texts show Huang-po in dialogue with a monk or layperson in a question-and-answer session, and when the authors and editors display that encounter in powerful colloquial language, we are only an evolutionary step or two away from "encounter dialogue." Poceski is correct that the extant materials from the Zen tradition in the T'ang dynasty do not include evidence of the encounter dialogue model.[22] What we see instead in the Huang-po literature is that the foundations have been laid for the emergence of that literary form over the next several centuries. The fact that later published editions of the Huang-po literature include "encounter dialogue" episodes shows the perceived necessity of that element in the "recorded sayings" texts. Huang-po, a centrally important Zen master in the Rinzai lineage, required subsequent updating in order to keep the account of his life and teachings both current and powerful, and "encounter dialogue" episodes were the form that this revision would take.[23]

On the basis of the foregoing account of how the Huang-po literature came into being, it is clear that the "authorship" of the text is an extremely complicated matter. Although Huang-po himself is certainly not the writer of the text, it may very well be that the language and the rhetorical style of the documents are indeed his. Although P'ei-hsiu was the initial author, he regarded himself as writing just what Huang-po had said. Furthermore, others besides P'ei-hsiu contributed to the text at his invitation. When P'ei-hsiu sent the documents to Mount Huang-po, he invited the dissemination of authorship to any number of monks and teachers who had known Huang-po. They, too, contributed "sayings" to the text and helped shape its form and style. Even then the texts were not fixed, however. Circulating as handwritten documents, we will never know what was added or deleted by whom and to what effect. Nor will we know how many versions of these texts circulated and how it was that one of them was eventually selected to be printed in the official versions of the Sung dynasty. "Communal composition" is our best way to understand authorship for Zen literature of this era, and even though it took an unusual and early form, the Huang-po literature is no exception. Although the texts do place before us a powerful image of Huang-po as a paradigm for Zen practice and thought, this image is best conceived as an ideal projection of the larger Chinese Buddhist monastic world over a significant period of time.[24]

Teachings in the Huang-po Literature

The teachings of the Huang-po literature live up to the innovative standards of the newly formed Hung-chou sect of Zen, and provide an early basis from which to see the rise and development of the Lin-chi Ch'an or Rinzai Zen tradition in East Asia. Most of the teachings in these texts, or close approximations of them, can also be found in the older sections of the literary remnants of Ma-tsu Tao-i and Pai-chang Huai-hai, as well as in the descriptive, and at times, critical accounts of Tsung-mi[25] written in the 830s.[26] This is not to say that the Huang-po literature was not innovative, but rather that its innovation was set in a larger tradition of Buddhist thought. As in any era of any culture, a great teacher will teach the most authoritative ideas of the time. Nevertheless, the image of Huang-po symbolized the creative act of pushing the Zen tradition forward, overcoming and transcending its past form. By the self-evaluation of the Zen tradition, Huang-po stood at the height of the "golden age" of Zen as one of its exemplary figures.[27] In outlining and describing the teachings of Huang-po, we will take up ten different ideas that are characteristic of the texts, and then address the question of innovation in teaching methods.

1. The Idea of Transmission and the Concept of the Zen School

It is very clear in the Huang-po literature that "Zen" was regarded as a distinct sect of Buddhism, and that this sect could already be identified in terms of its origins, history, stories, and symbols. Although not all the slogans and symbols that developed at the height of the Zen tradition in the Sung dynasty can be found in Huang-po, enough of them are present to warrant attributing to its authors a clear sense of a distinctive lineage. Huang-po refers to Bodhidharma, the legendary "founder" of Zen, to Hui-neng, the brilliant but uneducated "sixth partriarch" and to a line of descent going all the way back to the Buddha through Mahākāśyapa's receipt of the "wordless Dharma." On occasion, the texts have Huang-po proclaim what is distinctive about "our sect," differentiating what would be identified as "Zen" from other Buddhist groups at that time.

Although the name of the primary text, *The Essentials of Mind Transmission* (*Ch'uan-hsin fa yao*), was affixed to the writings some time after its first public appearance, given the doctrine found in the text the title could not have been more appropriate. The teachings of the text focus on the mind and the way the awakened mind is transmitted from one Zen master to the next generation. The issue of a single line of transmission—one master to one master in the next generation—as opposed to a more complex and escalating transmission, or one Zen master who awakens a number of subsequent masters, does not surface in the Huang-po literature. But this must have been an issue not too far away, since Huang-po is supposed to have awakened twelve disciples and Ma-tsu many more. Nevertheless, the doctrine of transmission is an essential idea in the texts, and serves to solidify a distinct and separate "Zen" identity that had accumulated in China for at least a century.

2. The Concept of Mind

Hsin or "mind" is the single most important concept in the Huang-po literature. In fact, P'ei-hsiu opens his preface with the claim that Huang-po only taught about mind, and that in the final analysis there wasn't anything else to teach.[28] Although the rhetoric of that statement sounds radical indeed, the basic idea is far from exceptional, since this concept had already been the focal point of Chinese Buddhist practice and philosophy for at least two centuries. So central was this word to the identity of Chinese Buddhism that, by the time of the Huang-po literature, *hsin* is really as much a symbol as a concept. By that

I mean that mind was less the object of conceptual reflection than it was the focal point of meditative religious practice.

In this regard Huang-po was simply accentuating a primary point of mature Chinese Buddhism, which is that mind cannot be successfully sought by the mind, and that direct apprehension of mind is the only possible means of awakening. In spite of the admonition against conceptualizing mind, much of the Huang-po literature consists in an effort to do just that, although clearly with the intention of deepening spiritual practice. The *Ch'uan-hsin fa yao* begins in an effort to say what "one mind" is: "All Buddhas and all sentient beings are nothing but one mind, beyond which nothing exists. This mind is without beginning, unborn, and imperishable. . . . It neither exists nor does not exist . . . it transcends all boundaries, measurements, traces, and distinctions. It is directly before you; when you begin to conceptualize it you immediately fail in grasping it. . . . The one mind is just the Buddha."[29]

Much of the text works on preventing errors in the conceptualization of mind. Mind cannot, by definition, be an object of experience; it is not something to which a practitioner of Zen could come into relation. Mind is also not something within the totality of things, since it is the formless background against which all things can be experienced. The Huang-po texts are skillful in insisting that this mental background is essentially "open" or "empty"; every effort to put yourself before it excludes you from it. Nor is mind the subject of experience. Therefore the texts claim that in "mind" there is "no subject, no object, no self, no other."[30] Mind and objects of mind "co-arise" and are therefore undifferentiated. Since, as P'ei-hsiu writes, Huang-po taught nothing but "mind," we will have occasion in explaining the ideas that follow to say more about this elusive Zen symbol.

3. Everything We Do Is the Functioning of the Buddha-nature

If nothing exists but mind, and mind is the Buddha, as Huang-po claims, then every action in which we can be engaged is the acting of the Buddha. When Tsung-mi sought to classify the various types of Zen in his era, he placed Hung-chou Zen, at that time personified in Huang-po, in the category of Dharmatā Zen, the teaching that everything we do is the function of the Buddha-nature, thus singling this doctrine out as the most significant feature of the Hung-chou school. It had been clear for some time, however, that this was the direction in which Chinese Buddhist teachings were going. The only question was how far Zen teachers could extend this idea without falling into self-contradiction or ethical absurdity.

Tsung-mi thought that, although admirable, Hung-chou Zen might have crossed that line, and that Ma-tsu's path may have been too "extreme."[31] It is very clear, however, that Huang-po sought to stretch this idea as far as it would take him, and the subsequent history of Chinese Buddhism proved that this would be a very successful tactic. Earlier forms of this teaching can be traced back to the Indian and central Asian teaching of the *tathāgatagarbha*, the "womb of the Buddha," the idea that within all people and all things is the nature of the Buddha. Seeking for it, therefore, was an internal matter, simply an act of discovering within yourself what has always been there, whether in potentiality or actuality. Therefore, the texts proclaim that "when, in a sudden opening, you are awakened, you will simply be realizing the Buddha nature that has always been within you."[32] This explanation would justify the *Wan-ling lu* in saying, "Your true nature is never lost to you even in delusion, nor is it gained in the moment of awakening."[33]

4. The Concept of Sudden Awakening

The idea that awakening entails a sudden breakthrough into a mode of consciousness that has always been fundamental to your being but never truly seen is basic to the Huang-po literature. Reference to it appears numerous times in the text, even though little time is spent dwelling on the idea. Conscious reflection on this theme would not have been necessary in Chinese Buddhism of the ninth century because the mainstream of the tradition had several centuries before this period to come to a consensus—enlightenment is a sudden, unexpected, unplanned, and incomprehensible event that befalls the practitioner even though he or she may have spent an entire career striving to attain it.

The only question that remained was how exactly to account for it, or how to connect it to Buddhist practice and to the other concepts of the tradition. This is where Huang-po was innovative, and rhetorically powerful. In working with sudden awakening, Huang-po and the Hung-chou tradition of Zen took up the Taoist theme that since you already reside within the Way, and cannot escape it, there is "nothing to do." Enlightenment, therefore, is simply awakening to this fact. Therefore, the text says, "Awakening suddenly, you realize that your mind *is* the Buddha, that there is nothing to be attained, nor any act to be performed. This is the true way, the way of the Buddha."[34]

There were a number of cultural and spiritual forces behind the emergence of the Chinese doctrine of sudden awakening, but an important one was the philosophical realization that it did not make sense to claim that something truly transcendent emerged out of the world in incremental stages, as if enlightenment were just more of the many phenomena things found in the world of unenlightenment. Ideas about "stages of practice," therefore, which were vital to early T'ang-dynasty Buddhist thought, came under heavy critique in the Zen tradition. Thus, the Huang-po texts explain how "the six perfections and other similar practices, which seek buddhahood through advancement along stages,"[35] are simply misguided; they fail to understand what kind of a realization buddhahood might be. "The real Buddha is not a Buddha of stages!"[36]

If one's own mind is the Buddha-nature that is sought, then ordinary religious practices, which assume a dichotomy between oneself and the goal of practice, will in fact prevent awakening. Therefore Huang-po advocates quieting the mind, stilling all the thought processes that split the mind from reality. "Realize," the *Wan-ling lu* proclaims, "that sudden awakening occurs when the mind has been cleared of conceptual and thought processes."[37] At the moment when these are cleared, suddenly, there is awakening. This sudden opening is presented by way of numerous metaphors; it is a "sudden leap" and "occurs with the suddenness of a knife thrust."[38]

5. Critique of Conceptual Thinking

Fundamental to the Huang-po texts and to Hung-chou Zen is that processes of conceptual thinking are inimical to spiritual practice and Zen awakening. Understanding this critique is difficult, since it is obvious that the author of the text was ignoring his own advice as he wrote, but it helps to put this theme in historical context. Because China inherited Buddhism largely in the form of a vast collection of sophisticated texts, it was natural over the first half millennium of Chinese Buddhism that textual practices would dominate the tradition. Through the early part of the the T'ang dynasty, the most revered and the most famous Chinese Buddhists were scholars who had worked hard to master this vast canon of religious texts.

The rise of Zen Buddhism marks the arrival of impatience with this scholarly tradition; from this point on, focus on practice and simplification of doctrine would be leading concerns. Reconceiving enlightenment meant restructuring Chinese Buddhism from the ground up, and Zen texts like Huang-po led the way in this new emphasis. If awakening was a sudden breakthrough into a domain of consciousness that was so close that you have always resided within it, then ordinary thinking processes would be of no avail. Therefore, Huang-po claims that "If you stop conceptual thinking, and let go of its anxiety, then the Buddha will appear because mind *is* the Buddha."[39] "The mind is no mind of conceptual thought . . . if you eliminate conceptual thinking, everything will be accomplished."[40]

Conceptual thinking is here considered a kind of activity that is imposed upon the world as we experience it. Eliminating it is not thought to eliminate the varieties and movements of experience, but rather to enhance it. The "emptiness" of Buddha-nature is experienced within the form of ordinary life rather than abstracted from it conceptually. Therefore, the *Ch'uan-hsin fa yao* sets up a distinction between eliminating thought and eliminating phenomena experienced in the world such that getting rid of thought is not getting rid of the world. "The ignorant eliminate phenomena but not thinking, while the wise eliminate thinking but not phenomena."[41] Huang-po helps develop the iconoclastic dimension of the Zen tradition in his claim that even sacred thoughts are obstructive: "If you conceive of a buddha, you will be obstructed by a buddha!"[42]

6. No Attachment, No Seeking

The Huang-po texts take the ideas of nonattachment and nonseeking to their logical and radical conclusions. Although nonattachment was a prominent theme in early Buddhism, "seeking" nirvana was considered the only way to attain it. What many Buddhists came to see over time, however, is that the spiritual quest is itself laden with attachment, including overt attachments to a goal and an implied attachment to the one who pursues it. In Huang-po's understanding of the matter, awakening is itself an awakening from the attachment of seeking to be awakened. The radical implications of this teaching will be clear if we remind ourselves that most of the people to whom Huang-po would have been talking in these sermons were monks who had dedicated their lives to seeking enlightenment. For them, as for us, not to seek would have been as perplexing an admonition as could be imagined.

The problem, as Huang-po puts it, is attachment: "In speaking or in simply blinking an eye, do it without attachment."[43] "When you attain a state of no attachments, your functioning will be like the Buddha's."[44] Pictured as a form of seeking without attachment, Huang-po instructs his disciples to "learn not to seek or be attached to anything. . . . Letting go of everything is the Dharma, and one who understands this is the Buddha."[45] One powerful effect that these teachings have is that they force you to reconsider what it is that you are seeking. Huang-po ridicules, "seeking the Buddha outside of yourself."[46] He asks sarcastically, "What kind of 'true Dharma is there to go seeking for?"[47] And he exclaims that, "by your very seeking you lose it."[48] This is so, he claims, because "Awakening is no state; the Buddha did not attain it, and ordinary people do not lack it."[49] The spiritual tensions created by the paradoxical state of seeking a kind of life that is devoid of seeking was thought very useful for the purposes of awakening!

7. Nondualism

All of the foregoing ideas suggests the importance of nondualism in Huang-po's Zen. Mind encompasses all things, all of which possess the Buddha-nature. Overcoming conceptual thought, attachment, seeking for what you think you do not possess, lead to a sudden awakening because there is nothing new to attain. The world, conceived in this manner, is not dualistically separated from the one who perceives it and dwells without anxiety within it. All of the themes outlined so far come to fruition in a nondualistic understanding in Zen. Thus, the Huang-po texts proclaim: "Rid yourselves of dualism, your likes and dislikes. Everything is one mind."⁵⁰ "If you realize that all sentient beings are already awakened, you will no longer need to attain it."⁵¹

Although the idea of life in *saṃsāra*, the world of suffering, was basic to Buddhist practice, several schools of Buddhist thought, including Zen, concluded that this concept led to dualistic thinking, and that it entrapped the mind of the practitioner in the thought that enlightenment was far away. More suited to attainment through practice, they thought, is the realization that we already possess what we are seeking, but simply need to realize that we've already got it. Huang-po's way of addressing this issue is to identify the practitioner as he already is with the Buddha by breaking down the distinction between them. Thus the texts say: "When you extinguish the concepts of 'ordinary' and 'enlightened,' you will see that there is no Buddha besides the Buddha in your mind";⁵² and "Buddha and sentient beings are both your own false conceptions. . . . All dualistic concepts such as 'ignorant' and 'enlightened,' 'pure' and 'impure,' are obstructions."⁵³ As religious concepts are no less a threat to awakening than are secular ones, "The way of the Buddha is as dangerous to you as the way of demons."⁵⁴

8. Spontaneity and Letting Go

The only clear alternative to "seeking" is to live spontaneously, that is, to live in accord with the world around you by seeing everything as a manifestation of the Buddha-nature. If the world is truly nondual, then to live naturally within it is the only reasonable response. This view is characteristic of Hung-chou Zen generally, and the version found in the Huang-po literature lives up to the expectations of the lineage. Although he may not have been in full approval of this dimension of Hung-chou Zen, Tsung-mi could only end his description of them by writing that "just leaving it to mind is their practice."⁵⁵ No doubt this theme in Hung-chou Zen alluded to its rural origins, its explicit rejection of the more socially stylized aristocratic Buddhism of the earlier T'ang dynasty.⁵⁶

Huang-po's critique of religious authority and their current values led his text to focus on the spirit of the "ordinary" in an effort to elevate it out of that debased status. Common Hung-chou sayings such as "everyday mind is the way" and "in chopping wood and carrying water, therein lies the wonderful way" show this unpretentious theme very clearly. Displaying the obvious Taoist roots of Hung-chou Zen, Huang-po valorizes the ancients who, "abandoning conceptual abstraction, come to dwell in spontaneity."⁵⁷ In this passage, the Huang-po texts allude to the Taoist *wu-wei*, or spontaneous action that accords with the larger world and is not distinct from it. Spontaneous action requires letting go, as we see in the following: "When everything inside and outside, body and mind, has been let go, when by way of emptiness no attachments remain, and when all action is shaped by situation and circumstance, and when subject and object are eliminated, that is the most exalted form of relinquishment."[58]

9. No Fear

It is fear, according to the texts, that holds us back from an awakened existence, that prevents our seeing directly the truth in which we live. The theme of fear appears throughout the Huang-po literature in a way that is unique to these texts. Nevertheless, this is a traditional Mahāyāna Buddhist theme, one that first appeared in the *Prajñāpāramitā* (*Perfection of Wisdom*) *Sūtras*. These sutras describe the reaction that new and inexperienced bodhisattvas have to the teaching of emptiness—they pull back in fear that the implications of this teaching are nihilistic and destructive. This theme is similar to the one we find in Huang-po, but in the Huang-po literature, partially as a result of the kinds of metaphorical language used, the threat is not conceptual so much as it is experiential.

In the *Ch'uan-hsin fa yao* we find the following: "Mind is empty in that it is without borders or limitations. It is neither subject nor object, has no place or form, nor is it perishable. Those who move toward it dare not enter; they fear falling into emptiness with nothing to grasp or save them. They approach the edge and pull back in fear."[59] It is almost as if the most important form that *saṃsāra* takes is fear and insecurity, and that these are what prevent our awakening rather than desire or craving, as we find it in early Buddhism. The texts bemoan the fact that "people are afraid to empty their minds, fearing that they will fall into emptiness. What they don't understand is that their mind *is* emptiness!"[60] The solution, for the Huang-po texts, is straightforward, although far from simple—a letting go of fear and insecurity by making a leap. Sudden awakening in this case amounts to a challenge to "open wide both hands like one who has nothing to lose."[61]

10. Skill-in-Means

Like much of the Chinese Buddhist philosophy from the first half of the T'ang dynasty, the Huang-po texts take a strong interest in the Indian Buddhist doctrine of *upāya*, "skill-in-means," the idea that the teachings of Buddhism are relative to the situation of whoever is being taught. References to the *Lotus Sutra*, perhaps best known for the development that it gives to the idea of "skill-in-means," are frequent in Huang-po, and the authors were eager to adapt this lucrative religious idea to the emerging Zen tradition. Unlike later Zen teachers, Huang-po could not simply ignore traditional Buddhist teachings and texts; in fact, the texts give strong evidence that the great master knew both texts and concepts very well. On the other hand, Huang-po's interest is clearly in denying their importance, so much so that a large part of the texts are spent explaining how and why it is that these time-worn teachings are no longer applicable to the spiritual situation in which they found themselves.

For example, after naming a series of complex teachings from Buddhist sacred texts, Huang-po is presented as saying: "If you adhere to the Buddha vehicle taught by Bodhidharma, you will take no interest in such teachings, but instead simply point to one mind which is beyond identity and difference, cause and effect."[62] Following that sentence, in an irony probably unrecogniz-able to the authors, the *Lotus Sutra*—part of the tradition being dismissed—is quoted to support the logic of setting the tradition aside. In another location in the texts, Huang-po provides his own rationale for taking an unattached relation to the Buddhist tradition: "Do not grasp for a particular teaching in-tended for a specific situation and, impressed that it is part of the sacred canon, take it as the absolute truth. Why? Because there is no permanent Dharma that the Buddha could have taught."[63]

What we can see in the Huang-po literature, as early Zen sermon doctrine, is the bold movement out of previous customs of Buddhist discourse in China and into a new form of religious language. Huang-po is clearly a transition figure.[64] After this time, as we see in early Sung dynasty Zen literature, teachers would no longer wrestle with the tradition as Huang-po and early Hung-chou masters did. Instead, they could simply presuppose the revolution in spiritual discourse initiated in the ninth century, and move ahead into creative ventures on their own terms. *Upāya* is perhaps the most effective enabling tool in pre-cipitating this historic development.

Teaching Methods in the Huang-po Literature

In terms of teaching methods, the Huang-po literature is very interesting and innovative. Examining both earlier Zen literature and later, we can notice move-ment from explicitly doctrinal teachings toward nondoctrinal discourse, from a traditional effort to instruct in religious ideas toward an audacious effort to evoke a transformative experience. The Huang-po literature stands in the midst of this historic change, and pushes the tradition along in substantial ways. In these texts, traditional doctrinal concepts are on the table for discussion, but the point of the discussion is their critique and reevaluation. In this regard, we can see that the personality of the Zen master Huang-po, which emerges so forcefully through the texts, is crucial. Overpowering in stature and exalted in status, Huang-po is presented in the texts as a powerful religious authority, one to whom even Chief Minister P'ei-hsiu would submit in humility. Huang-po is pictured as pressing right to the point, never allowing doctrinal garble to continue, always pointing directly to the "great matter" of Zen and demanding that his disciples either respond at that level or get out of the way. This is no ordinary teacher, and the resulting image of his teaching method is impressive. Briefly, here are five teaching techniques employed in the Huang-po literature.

1. Direct Pointing

This teaching technique, for which Zen is so well known, entails some form of spiritual action, either verbal or nonverbal, that "points directly" to the "great matter" of Zen without attempting to "teach" it or explain it or put it in objective language. As the Zen tradition developed over the centuries, these acts became more and more unconventional, ranging from absurd phrases to violent actions. The Huang-po literature is an early stage in this development. The phrase "direct pointing" comes up several times in the text, but always in association with Bodhidharma, the first patriarch of Zen, and always as a kind of slogan inherited from earlier texts. So whenever Huang-po wanted to provide an example of someone who set aside all the complex and abstruse doctrinal teachings in order to probe right to the heart of awakening, he called upon the image of Bodhidharma which had been developing in Chinese Buddhism for some time.

For example, in a challenging response to a question, Huang-po is quoted as saying: "When Bodhidharma came from the West, he 'pointed directly' to the identity between human nature and the Buddha. But you just go on in delusion, attached to concepts like 'ordinary' and 'awakened,' focusing your mind exteriorly where it races around like a horse. This is simply obscuring your mind."[65] Aside from helping to develop the idea of "direct pointing," passing the slogan and the concept down to future generations, Huang-po had several methods of teaching that would amount to a form of direct pointing, one of which is the kind of impatient, accusatory posture that he is pictured as taking in the quote above. We can only imagine him raising his voice, and losing his patience with doctrinal obfuscation.

2. Paradoxical Language

The use of paradoxical language in exalted spiritual discourse has a long history in Buddhism, and is not unknown in other religious traditions, as well. Two of Huang-po's favorite Mahāyāna texts, the Diamond Sutra and the Vimalakīrti Sūtra, are both exceptionally good at twisting language into paradoxical formulas as a way to demonstrate the ungraspability of the highest levels of Dharma. Although "emptiness" and "nirvana" are indeed concepts that must be grasped by Buddhist practitioners, failure to transcend those concepts and the acts of grasping implied in them constitutes failure to awaken. Huang-po stood firmly in this tradition of Buddhist thought, and made frequent use of paradox as a method of eliciting a deeper insight into Zen.

It is easy to see how this strategy of teaching fits with the various teachings outlined above. If the point of Zen practice is already within you and right there before you, even though in ordinary states of mind you cannot see it, then extraordinary language will be required to guide you to it. Here is just one example of Huang-po at his most paradoxical: "The most basic Dharma is that there is no Dharma, even though this Dharma of no Dharma is clearly itself a Dharma. Although we transmit this Dharma of no Dharma, how can a Dharma like this really be a Dharma?"[66]

3. Outrageous Rhetoric

Both "direct pointing" and "paradoxical language" are forms of outrageous rhetoric, unusual and unnerving ways of speaking that break out of any tradition of didactic discourse. But Huang-po has other forms. One of these is a method of turning the tables on someone who is asking a question, either by returning the question in a revised form that immediately shows the answer, or by making the questioner probe the false assumptions at the root of the question. Both of these seem to entail some element of ridicule; Huang-po appears in the textual images to have been able to draw the obvious out of the complex in such a way that the inquirer would have been made to look ridiculous. The effect, one might imagine, would be significantly more effective and more transformative than any patient act of explanation. Thus when someone piously asks about the "true Dharma," Huang-po immediately responds with another (rhetorical) question: "What kind of 'true Dharma' are you seeking?"[67] The obvious implication of the retort is that the questioner's assumptions about what the "true Dharma" is render the question preposterous. Or, in response to a question that assumes a dichotomy between "thoughts" and "the Buddha," Huang-po says: "At this moment you are aware of your thoughts. But your thoughts *are* the Buddha!"[68]

Another form of outrageous rhetoric is simply breaking monastic conventions. In this example, the Zen master ascends the lecture platform to give his regular sermon: "Ascending the platform, the master said: Possessing much knowledge is not as good as relinquishing the seeking altogether. This is the most exalted. A person of the way is someone 'without concerns.' There are not a variety of minds that can be sought, nor principles that can be put into words. Since, therefore, we have no concerns, the assembly is dismissed!"[69] These sections in Huang-po anticipate the subsequent arrival of the Zen tradition of "encounter dialogue."

4. Allegory

Although the use of allegory for the transmission of religious ideas is certainly not unique to Huang-po, its appearance in these texts amounts to a noteworthy and effective teaching tool. By "allegory" I mean the sense that important or sacred texts have various levels or depths of meaning, and that the literal, straightforward meaning is simply an initial entrance into the real or deeper meaning of the text. Buddhists, of course, were encouraged in this line of religious reasoning by the concept of *upāya*, the idea that the Buddha purposefully spoke at a variety of levels simultaneously as a means of communicating with human beings at a variety of levels and with a variety of spiritual problems.

Huang-po was clearly dissatisfied with and disinterested in literal renderings of traditional Buddhist doctrine. The texts show his impatience with traditional texts and ideas taking one of two forms: either he dismisses them as an inferior form of practice to the sudden apprehension of mind, or he allegorizes them in such a way that the inner meaning of these doctrines is itself the sudden apprehension of mind. For example, in response to an anxious questioner who asks about a traditional Buddhist story about violence and subsequent rebirth, Huang-po allegorizes the story out of its literal status and into what, for him, is the only issue worthy of attention: mind. "Answer: The holy men who were tortured were in fact your own mind, and the antagonist symbolizes the seeker within you."[70] Later Zen masters would for the most part simply drop allegory and either ignore or dismiss traditional doctrine. But the Huang-po literature stands at a turning point in Zen history where Zen is primarily understood in a "Buddhist" context and therefore requires reconciliation with the specifics of that tradition. It is worth noting that allegory appears in Huang-po primarily in the question-and-answer sections, where the topic of conversation is suggested by others, and Huang-po is presented as teaching them how to interpret traditional doctrine. In his sermons, where the topic of discourse is the master's own choice, these traditional doctrines are simply ignored. But when he is asked about them, Huang-po appears in the texts working to get them out of the way by one means or another, either through direct dismissal or circuitously through allegorical reinterpretation, where A "really means" B, or C "symbolizes" D.

5. Quotation and Allusion

Although the Huang-po literature presents the Zen master as a powerful critic of the Buddhist tradition, it also makes very clear that Huang-po was both intimately familiar with the sacred texts of the tradition and indebted to these texts as the source of his insight. Although later Zen texts present images of Zen masters who know much more about Huang-po than they do the sutras, Huang-po's own repertoire of stories is more tied to traditional Buddhist literature than it is to the emerging Zen sect. Huang-po is very selective, however. He naturally tends to quote and allude to texts that support his particular interest, texts that articulate the Buddhist theories of emptiness, mind, and skill-in-means.

Therefore the texts have him quote or cite the *Diamond Sutra,* the *Vimalakīrti Sūtra,* and the *Lotus Sutra,* or earlier Chinese Buddhist philosophers whose thought worked in the direction of Huang-po's. In the extensive footnotes to Iriya Yoshitaka's modern Japanese translation, we get a sense of how widely Huang-po's reading must have extended. Iriya finds in virtually every paragraph phrases and lines from other Buddhist texts, grafted together with others in innovative and insightful ways. Sometimes the text quotes directly from these Buddhist or Zen materials, but more often the language is simply borrowed, either consciously or unconsciously, and placed in the service of Hung-chou Zen's newly emerging spirituality. Although Huang-po is unique, an innovative work of religious literature, its interdependency with other texts is extensive. As a teaching method, however, this is extremely effective.

The Huang-po Literature in Zen History

With humble beginnings in the "notes" of a lay disciple in south central China in the 840s, the Huang-po literature has had a long and venerable history. We have seen how the text came together, the ways in which it was a communal product of P'ei-hsiu and the elder monks on Mount Huang-po. An early reference in the *Sung kao seng ch'uan* explains how Huang-po's "discourse record" circulated throughout the world. Although the world they would have imagined at this time would have been the monastic world of the Chinese empire, the text would soon circulate to other cultures, and eventually reach bookshelves in every nation in the world. What follows is a brief overview of this intriguing history.

It appears that the Huang-po literature was a great success from early in its history. This probably was due both to the fame and aristocratic status of P'ei-hsiu and to the emerging popularity of the Lin-chi sect of Zen. Huang-po's "sayings" were said to be in "circulation throughout the world."[71] It is known that the texts were particularly in favor among Chinese and Japanese aristocrats, the educated literati. This was true in China during the Sung dynasty, when Buddhism was especially in favor among the upper classes. In both northern and southern Sung, literati intellectuals were involved in the editing and publishing of the Huang-po literature. One version of the Huang-po texts was collected, edited, and published in the *Ching-te ch'uan teng lu* in 1004, which would be the first of many such publications. In fact, it was the only "discourse record" to be published independently as a text on its own in the *Ta tsang ching,* the Chinese "collected scriptures." As Yanagida claims, this seems to indicate a special status, indeed, a status that seems to be on par with the sutras, the words of the Buddha.[72]

In the Sung dynasty, however, two developments would have a major impact on the Huang-po literature, one negative and one positive. First, new forms of Zen literature emerged that would make Huang-po's discourse record look archaic. If we can consider the Huang-po texts as early, immature forms of *yü-lu* or "discourse record," then it was simply the full development of this genre that superseded Huang-po. Later *yü-lu* were shaped more like brief biographies; they included information about the birth, home area, and early studies of the famous Zen masters, along with other pertinent data such as where they studied, with whom, where they taught, when and to whom, as well and when and how they died. This quasi-biographical model became standard in the Sung, and it made the account of Huang-po seem shortsighted. More important, perhaps, is that later *yü-lu* featured anecdotal stories about the outrageous behaviors and saying of the masters. More and more, these texts downplayed or even abandoned the "sermon" or doctrinal development that is in effect the heart of the Huang-po texts.

To be a great master meant to have a wide variety of stories documenting unconventional speech and behavior, rather than a variety of doctrinal themes that are expounded in sermonic settings. Although Huang-po must have been radically unconventional in his own time, the image of him posted in the texts by P'ei-hsiu and the ninth-century monks came to appear conservative by contrast to later eccentrics. There is potent irony in this in that it was the antidoctrinal and antilogical emphases of Huang-po and others that would have persuaded later Zen Buddhists to abandon all efforts like Huang-po's to argue rationally for this conclusion. It was, in effect, Huang-po's logic that lured subsequent generations of Zen Buddhists into the nonlogical perspectives from which Huang-po would no longer be so interesting.

In addition to rendering the Huang-po texts less attractive, this shift in emphasis in Chinese Zen meant that reading would focus more on the question-and-answer sections of Huang-po than on the sermons, since these sections would have seemed more like the "encounter dialogue" texts that were in vogue in the Sung. On the other hand, at that very time another historical development was under way that would begin to turn the tables to some extent. It was at this time that a resurgent "neo-Confucian" tradition was beginning to form, and one of the ways these intellectuals attempted to stake their claim was to level a harsh critique of Buddhism. "Buddhism" to Chinese intellectuals at that historical moment meant Zen Buddhism, and this is exactly where they aimed their criticism.[73] Most vulnerable to critique would have been the newly emerging nondoctrinal Zen found in most Sung-dynasty "discourse records" and in the early kōan texts. Written in a slightly earlier era, however, the Huang-po texts seemed to have escaped this criticism because the Zen of Huang-po remained logical and doctrinal even while it submitted logic and doctrine to scathing criticism. For this reason, in the midst of this anti-Buddhism firestorm, the Huang-po texts continued to look sophisticated to the outside world and were employed by both neo-Confucian and Buddhist scholars in a variety of contexts.

Following the official publication of the Huang-po literature in the *Ching-te ch'uan-teng lu* in 1004, there were a series of important historical publications that included the Huang-po literature. In the next important Zen publication, the *T'ien-sheng kuang-teng lu* of 1036, the Lin-chi perspective rose to dominance, showing the ascendancy of this sect in the eleventh century. This text, including the Huang-po literature within it, was published in a full edition of the Buddhist canon printed in Fu-chou in 1148, and was deeply influential in promoting Huang-po and the Lin-chi sect. Because Huang-po was Lin-chi's teacher and on that account would necessarily be drawn into the most sacred lineage of the dominant sect, new stories about Huang-po began to appear in subsequent centuries and were gradually added to the earlier sections of the text. By the Ming dynasty, the Huang-po literature had grown to include a significant number of "encounter dialogue" stories about the master, and all of these are written in later styles that are amenable to the kōan focus of fully mature Chinese Zen. In the Ming edition of the *Ssu-chia yu-lu*, the *Four House Discourse Record*, Huang-po's "encounter dialogue" stories stand juxtaposed to the other three great masters of the founding of Lin-chi Zen—Ma-tsu, Pai-chang, and Lin-chi—and provide a full personality for Huang-po that matches the other Zen luminaries in style and depth.[74]

It is not clear when the first copy of the Huang-po literature appeared in Japan. It is quoted at great length in an early thirteenth-century text in Japan and therefore had clearly arrived by that time.[75] The Japanese Zen historian Ui Hakuju, thinks that the evidence points strongly to the possibility that Eisai, the founder of Rinzai Zen, brought the Huang-po literature back from China for use in Japan. The *Ch'uan-hsin fa yao* was first published in Japan in 1283, making it the very first "discourse record" to be published there. There is evidence that these texts were very popular in the late Kamakura period, both in Rinzai monastic settings and among the samurai who by then dominated the new social order in Japan.[76] Given its logical emphasis, even while undermining logic, the Huang-po literature would have been more easily understandable, and therefore accessible to a wider audience. One might speculate that the text may have played a role in Japan similar to the one it played in China, that is, through its logical analysis of the ways in which "awakening" transcends language and logic, it may have helped pave the way for the appreciation of later nonlogical "encounter dialogue" and kōan texts in the Muramachi period.

Finally, it is no doubt significant that the Huang-po texts were the first full-length Zen texts to be translated into English, or for that matter into any European language. Translated by John Blofeld with the assistance of his Buddhist teachers in China in the 1950s, *The Zen Teaching of Huang-po on the*

Transmission of Mind was published in 1959 and was immediately absorbed into the "Beat Zen" movement. At the same time, explanatory commentary and small segments of translation by D. T. Suzuki, focusing almost exclusively on Rinzai Zen, began to appear in his numerous English-language volumes. Many of these also featured Huang-po as the uproarious mentor of Rinzai himself. It is by means of these two sources that Huang-po has now spread throughout the world, and because of them that we might be justified in speculating that the story of the Huang-po literature is far from over.

NOTES

1. The date of birth for Huang-po is unknown. Yanagida guesses sometime between 766 and 783, but no known source alludes to this issue. Likewise, his date of death is unknown, but traditional texts date it during the Ta-chung period, from 847 to 859.

2. Yanagida Seizan and Iriya Yoshitaka, eds., *Denshin hōyō, Zen no goroku*, vol. 8 (Tokyo: Chikuma shobo, 1969), p. 151.

3. Ibid., p. 167.

4. Yanagida writes that Huang-po monastery was probably constructed in competition with the older government-sponsored Kai-yuan ssu, ibid., p. 165.

5. P'ei-hsiu is in fact our best source of information about Huang-po. Other sources old enough to contain some accurate account would include the *Tsu-t'ang chi* vol. 16, the *Sung kao sung-chuan* vol. 20, and *Ching-te ch'uan-teng lu* vol. 10.

6. Besides his association with Tsung-mi and Huang-po, P'ei-hsiu is also linked historically with the Hua-yen scholar Cheng-kuan and, later in his life, with Wei-shan Ling-yu, a well-known Zen master in Hunan and contemporary of Huang-po. P'ei-hsiu is perhaps best known in Chinese history for the artistic excellence of his calligraphy. His biographies are found in *Chiu T'ang shih* (177) and in *Hsin T'ang-shu* (182). For more information see Broughton, chapter one, above, and the formative work of Peter N. Gregory, especially *Tsung-mi and the Sinification of Buddhism* (Princeton: Princeton University Press, 1991).

7. See Yanagida, *Denshin hōyō*, p. 158.

8. See chapter one where Broughton writes that "further evidence of P'ei's interest in Hung-chou is shown in *P'ei's Inquiry* when Tsung-mi mounts a sustained critique of the Hung-chou position, and P'ei rises to its defense."

9. T 48.379c.

10. T 48.379c.

11. T 48.379c.

12. *Denshin hōyō*, p. 172.

13. The *Tsu T'ang chi* refers to "notes" about the activities of Huang-po that were in circulation at the time of its writing in the mid to late tenth century. See ibid.

14. Yanagida Seizan, "The 'Recorded Sayings' Texts of Chinese Ch'an Buddhism," in Whalen Lai and Lewis Lancaster, eds., *Early Ch'an in China and Tibet* (Berkeley: University of California Press, 1983), p. 187.

15. Records indicate that Huang-po had somewhere around one thousand monks

studying under his tutelage, which would have meant that private conversations would have been very rare for most individuals. We are also told that of these many monks, twelve received the "mind-seal" and were certified as masters themselves. Most notable among these would have been Lin-chi I-hsuan (J. Rinzai), the reputed founder of one of the schools of Zen that is prevalent today in China, Japan, and elsewhere.

16. My reason for thinking that it would have gone back to P'ei-hsiu before the preface was written is that he explains in the preface how he gave the manuscript to two monks traveling to Huang-po.

17. Martin Collcutt, *Five Mountains: The Rinzai Zen Monastic Institution in Medieval Japan* (Cambridge: Harvard University Press, 1981), pp. 138–145.

18. Mario Poceski is correct (in chapter two in this volume) when he says that this literary form reflects somewhat conservative tendencies in early Zen, tendencies that would be abandoned in the future when the Zen tradition became firmly established as the avant garde of Chinese culture, although it is important to recognize that their "conservatism" would only be visible in retrospect.

19. See Poceski, chapter two above.

20. For an overview of "encounter dialogue" in historical perspective, see John R. McRae, "The Antecedents of Encounter Dialogue in Chinese Zen Buddhism," in Steven Heine and Dale S. Wright, eds., *The Kōan: Texts and Contexts in Zen Buddhism* (New York: Oxford University Press, 2000), pp. 46–74.

21. Indeed, we can take this fact as further evidence for the early authorship of this literature.

22. See Poceski, chapter two above.

23. By the time of the *Ssu-chia yü-lu*, these stories had become a permanent part of the Huang-po texts.

24. On the issue of authorship in the Huang-po literature, see Dale S. Wright, *Philosophical Meditations on Zen Buddhism* (Cambridge: Cambridge University Press, 1998), chapter one.

25. Yanagida writes that the emergence of the Hung-chou sect of Zen was so forceful that Tsung-mi implied in his writing that this sect, of the several alive at that time, was the only real obstacle to the success of his own Ho-tse sect. See *Denshin hōyō*, p. 160.

26. Descriptions of these connections with Ma-tsu can be found in chapter two above, and connections to Tsung-mi can be found in chapter one.

27. It is likely that these texts demonstrate more creativity in the area of teaching method than they do in conceptual content.

28. T 48.379b–c.

29. T 48.379c.

30. T 48.384b.

31. See Jeffrey Broughton, chapter one in this volume.

32. T 48.380a.

33. T 48.387a.

34. T 48.381a.

35. T 48.380a.

36. Ibid.

37. T 48.385b.

38. T 48.383c.

39. T 48.379c.

40. T 48.380a.

41. T 48.382a.

42. T 48.384c.

43. T 48.383b.

44. Ibid.

45. T 48.381a.

46. T 48.380a.

47. T 48.382b.

48. T 48.379c.

49. T 48.385c.

50. T 48.381b.

51. T 48.385c.

52. T 48.383a.

53. T 48.384c.

54. T 48.385a. The nondualism of Hung-chou Zen is the focus of Tsung-mi's descriptive analysis in Broughton, chapter one above.

55. See Broughton, chapter one above.

56. This is an important thesis for Yanagida in *Denshin hōyō*, p. 158.

57. T 48.382c.

58. T 48.382a.

59. T 48.380a.

60. T 48.382a.

61. T 48.383b.

62. T 48.384c–385a.

63. T 48.383a.

64. One of the most effective techniques in Huang-po is the use of Taoist slogans to support the idea of "skill-in-means" in taking a relaxed and unattached relation to the Buddhist tradition. In one passage, Huang-po lectures on the word "Tao" as a skillful means that the ancient Buddhas had used to set people out on the "way." The texts then quote *Chuang-tzu's* famous last words that "once you have the fish, forget the fishtrap," T 48.382c.

65. T 48.383a.

66. T 48.383c. Although he did an admirable job in translating Huang-po in the late 1950s, when he got to this passage, John Blofeld wrote in a footnote that he had no idea what it meant! *The Zen Teaching of Huang Po: On the Transmission of Mind* (New York: Grove, 1959), p. 64.

67. T 48.382b.

68. T 48.385c.

69. T 48.383b. Iriya Yoshitaka traces this quote from Huang-po to the *Vimalakīrti Sūtra* and finds similar language in the *Lin-chi lu* (*Denshin hōyō*, p. 75). Although this story is found in the earliest versions of the *Ch'uan-hsin fa ya*, the nature of the story so resembles later Zen anecdotes that this might have been a later addition to the Huang-po corpus.

70. T 48.386b.

71. *Sung Kao seng ch'uan*, T 50.842bc.

72. Yanagida, *Denshin hōyō*, pp. 181–182.

73. It is interesting that Chu-hsi and other Sung neo-Confucians used Tsung-mi's analysis of Zen Buddhism in his time as a basis for their critique of Zen, which was useful to them precisely because Tsung-mi was involved in factional disputes against Hung-chou Zen, the precursor to the emerging Lin-chi sect.

74. ZZ 2, 24–25.

75. Yanagida, *Denshin hōyō*, p. 182.

76. Ibid., pp. 182–183.

5

Lineage and Context in the *Patriarch's Hall Collection* and the *Transmission of the Lamp*

Albert Welter

The development of transmission of the lamp records dedicated to the activities of famous masters constitutes one of the unique contributions of Ch'an to Chinese and world literature. The main purpose of these *teng-lu* (literally "Lamp [or flame] records") is usually depicted in terms of documenting the lineal relations among Ch'an masters to show where individual masters belong in the Ch'an "clan," tracing itself back to the "grand ancestor," Śākyamuni Buddha. One transmission record, the *Ching-te ch'uan-teng lu* (Ching-te era record of the transmission of the lamp), hereafter referred to as the *Ch'uan-teng lu*), is regarded as the prototype for the way in which the multibranched Ch'an tradition came to be regarded. It served as a model both for the way in which its contents were organized and for the style of the contents themselves. The *Tsu-t'ang chi* (Patriarch's hall collection) is similarly organized, and its contents are also comparably styled, but it was quickly overshadowed by the *Ch'uan-teng lu* and exerted little detectable influence. As a result, the *Ch'uan-teng lu* served as the acknowledged model for further developments in the production of the Ch'an *teng-lu* genre.[1]

It is hard to overestimate the influence that the contents of both the *Tsu-t'ang chi* and *Ch'uan-teng lu* had over subsequent Ch'an history. The origins of both *kung-an* (J. *kōan*) and *yü-lu* (J. *goroku*) may be traced to these texts. Considering the role that *kung-an* collections and *yü-lu* compilations came to assert, any discussion of Ch'an without taking the *Tsu-t'ang chi* and *Ch'uan-teng lu* into account will be found lacking. But why has scholarship on these texts progressed so slowly? The modern study of Ch'an, through much of its history, has been understandably consumed by the discovery of the Tun-huang documents and the effect that these have had in reforming our understanding of early Ch'an.[2] Yet, for all their importance, the Tun-huang manuscripts reveal almost nothing of Ch'an developments after the T'ang dynasty (618–906). All of our information regarding the so-called "golden age" of Zen comes from post-T'ang sources, beginning with the contents of the *Tsu-t'ang chi* and *Ch'uan-teng lu*.

In the following discussion, I review current scholarly opinion regarding the compilation of the *Tsu-t'ang chi* and *Ch'uan-teng lu*, before discussing what I consider as salient regarding the orientation of the documents themselves: what lineages were they compiled to promote, and what circumstances governed their compilation. Although the basic orientation of the documents is clear enough, recent scholarship suggests that the compilation process associated with each text was a complicated one, involving factors that are not transparent. Despite the reasonably straightforward intentions of the original compilers, evidence suggests that both texts were subject to further editing before being issued in their currently known forms. This implies that both texts represent multiple voices: the voices of the original compilers and the factional interests that they represented, as well as later voices representing other factional perspectives. If the voices of the multitude of students whose observances, anecdotes, musings, imaginings, and so forth, were committed to notebooks are added, the *Tsu-t'ang chi* and *Ch'uan-teng lu* contents reflect a cacophony of opinions about the nature of Ch'an, its essential message, style, and so on.

At this stage, it is not clear where one voice ends and another begins, even in the case of the *Ch'uan-teng lu*, where the compiler and editor's identities are clearly known. We do, however, know something of the basic orientation of some of the main speakers involved. My comments are simply an attempt to show where the different voices may be at work, and how these may have affected the arrangement of contents. The contents of both the *Tsu-t'ang chi* and *Ch'uan-teng lu* suggest that by the early Sung dynasty the various factions of the Ch'an movement were moving toward a consensus regarding its teachings and techniques (at least as represented in written form). Further speculation regarding this Ch'an consensus and how it shaped the contents of the *Tsu-t'ang chi* and *Ch'uan-teng lu* is included in my concluding remarks. Because of the nature of our current knowledge of the two texts and pending the outcome of ongoing investigations, the reader is advised to take many of the points raised here as tentative ones awaiting further validation or correction. Before the detailed discussion of the *Tsu-t'ang chi* and *Ch'uan-teng lu*, I offer a few preliminary comments as a way of approaching these texts.

One of the noteworthy features of the *Tsu-t'ang chi* and *Ch'uan-teng lu* is that they were the first Ch'an records to be compiled around a multilineal framework. This served as a convenient structure for diffusing the interfactional struggles that characterized earlier Ch'an transmission records, predicated on notions of a single orthodox transmission between a master and one disciple. The former unilineal model of transmission presupposed that each generation had only one recipient of the "true Dharma." Struggles ensued between factions to determine where true orthodoxy lay.[3] For Ch'an to thrive as a movement, it clearly needed a basis for wider recognition of legitimate transmission. The Tsu-t'ang chi and Ch'uan-teng lu provide this basis, documenting the spread of Ch'an through several lines of transmission, later codified as the "five houses" (or clans) of classical Ch'an.[4]

As instrumental as the Tsu-t'ang chi and Ch'uan-teng lu were in the formation of Ch'an identity, it is important to remember that they are documents of a tradition in transition. They emerged from a dark period of Chinese history, seeking acknowledgment and recognition at a time when the Buddhist presence in China faced unprecedented challenges. The compilation of the Tsu-t'ang chi and Ch'uan-teng lu represent significant steps in the process of winning an established place for Ch'an within Chinese culture. An important reminder of this can be seen in the way that transmission between Śākyamuni and Mahākāśyapa is explained in these two sources. While acknowledging that Śākyamuni is not the actual progenitor of the Ch'an Dharma, but the bearer of transmission that originated long before in the so-called seven buddhas of the past, the texts credit Śākyamuni with a crucial role in bringing the transmission into this world, where it is preserved through the unique line of Ch'an succession. Because of Śākyamuni's reputed role in instigating the transmission to Mahākāśyapa, this episode occupies an important place in Ch'an lore as the prototype for the silent, special transmission associated with the Ch'an Dharma. This story became one of the most famous kung-an in the Ch'an tradition. It relates how the Buddha's disciple, Mahākāśyapa, broke into a smile when the Buddha held up a flower to an assembly of the saṅgha on Vulture Peak. The classic formulation of the story is recorded in the Wu-men kuan (comp. 1228) as follows: "The World Honored One long ago instructed the assembly on Vulture Peak by holding up a flower. At that time everyone in the assembly remained silent; only Mahākāśyapa broke into a smile. The World Honored One stated, 'I possess the treasury of the true Dharma eye, the wondrous mind of nirvana, the subtle Dharma-gate born of the formlessness of true form, not established on words and letters, a special transmission outside the teaching. I bequeath it to Mahākāśyapa."[5]

This episode affirmed the cardinal feature of the Ch'an tradition, that is, the silent transmission between master and disciple as "a special transmission outside the teaching" (chiao-wai pieh-ch'uan/ J. kyōge betsuden). Regardless of its importance, it was a late development, devised by members of the Lin-chi lineage to bolster Lin-chi faction claims at the Sung court.[6] This explanation of the initial transmission between Śākyamuni and Mahākāśyapa, the cornerstone of all Ch'an lineages, is rendered quite differently in the Tsu-t'ang chi and *Ch'uan-teng lu.* Although both acknowledge the transmission from Śāk-yamuni to Mahākāśyapa of "the pure Dharma eye, the wondrous mind of nir-vana," there is no mention of Mahākāśyapa at the assembly when the Buddha holds up his famous flower.[7] The issue of the simultaneous dissemination of the public dharma (the word of the Buddha as reflected in Buddhist scriptures) and the secret spread of the private dharma (the mind of the Buddha as rep-resented by Ch'an transmission) was not resolved until the story of Śākya-muni's encounter with Mahākāśyapa at the famed assembly involving the flower emerged. It does not appear in Ch'an transmission records until the *T'ien-sheng kuang-teng lu,* compiled in 1036.[8] The appearance of the story is closely connected with the rise of Lin-chi factional supremacy at the Sung court and the attempt to legitimize factional claims as true representatives of Ch'an's "special transmission outside the teachings."At the time of the compilation of both the *Tsu-t'ang chi* and the *Ch'uan-teng lu,* the influence of the Lin-chi faction was keenly felt, but it had yet to gain unquestioned supremacy. The "classic" Ch'an perspective associated with this faction was in the process of formation and was exerting tremendous influence over Ch'an's emerging identity, but its dominance was far from monolithic. Other Ch'an factions claim supremacy in the *Tsu-t'ang chi* and *Ch'uan-teng lu.*

Another factor to reconsider before proceeding to the examination of the *Tsu-t'ang chi* and *Ch'uan-teng lu* is the alleged Ch'an and Zen aloofness from political entanglements. A staple of Ch'an's mystique is the text's enshrine-ment in legends, such as Bodhidharma's famous encounter with Emperor Wu of Liang, and Hui-neng's refusal to appear when summoned to the court of Empress Wu. This device is used to show where disavowal of political reality enhances spiritual character. Although this may suffice for the Ch'an master of legend, the reality is that Ch'an success was predicated on political patron-age. This patronage was forged through carefully cultivated relations between Ch'an monks and ruling officials, in what amounted to mutually beneficial associations. The story told in Ch'an *teng-lu* is of the lineages formed through master-disciple relations, the circumstances through which they were forged, and the unique Ch'an style engendered through them. This story is well known to all familiar with the contents of Ch'an *teng-lu,* through the standardized lineage charts that provide the framework for Ch'an lineage transmission. These lineage charts are the principal means by which individual masters are identified and regarded in the Ch'an tradition. Everyone familiar with Ch'an lineages is familiar with the formula: Master B is the disciple of Master A and the teacher of Master C; the three masters are part of lineage Y, x generations descended from Patriarch Z. This is the lineage framework that Ch'an *teng-lu* created, or at least consolidated.

This is an important aspect of my discussion of Ch'an *teng-lu* below, but I am also interested in examining another, often neglected aspect of the Ch'an story dealing with the patronage associations between ruling officials and

Ch'an monks. In addition to determining where particular lineages flourished, I am particularly interested in the patterns of political patronage that allowed Ch'an to flourish in those regions. In short, who built the temples and appointed the Ch'an monks to head them? This aspect of the story is little known and has often been ignored. My hypothesis here is that such relations were not simply material ones, but that the circumstances associated with the patterns of political patronage were determining influences upon the manner in which the classic Ch'an style was presented in *teng-lu* documents. In addition to recording master-disciple and other important Dharma relationships, *teng-lu* document the leading temples with which individual masters were associated and their relationships with government representatives. Thus, in addition to the master's Dharma lineage, *teng-lu* record the political associations of its most prominent masters: Master A was appointed to Temple/Monastery Y by official X, or Official X built Temple/Monastery Y and summoned Master A to head it.

The broader aim of *teng-lu* is to define Ch'an orthodoxy. The notion of orthodoxy is determined by the specific contexts of the documents themselves, by the individuals and circumstances that forged them. Ch'an *teng-lu* texts were retrospective in nature. They looked to the past as a means to justify the present. How they depict and shape the past must be viewed contextually, considering the concerns present during the period of compilation. Because *teng-lu* were forged and shaped to assert revisionist claims regarding Ch'an orthodoxy, they are best treated as historical fiction rather than truly biographical records.[9] Although they are constructed around historical circumstances, the records themselves are layered recollections of how the Ch'an tradition wished to remember their own champions. As such, they represent the constructed memory of Ch'an tradition expressing its most cherished aspirations. The biographical framework became the means to reveal the hallowed principles of a unique Ch'an identity. What is recorded using this framework are not so much the life stories of individual monks as the hallowed principles of this identity. The need to affirm these principles drove the interpretation of monks' lives. Through the filtered memory of successive generations and the exigencies associated with Ch'an's rising prominence, recollections of Ch'an's famed masters began to take on a life and character of their own. Less important than the facts of a Ch'an master's life was the way that the image of the master could be shaped according to the requisites of Ch'an's newfound identity and independence. As a result, Ch'an *teng-lu* serve the didactic purposes of Ch'an's own special version of hagiography, rather than anything approaching actual biography.

As indicated above, in Ch'an records compiled during the T'ang dynasty (*Ch'uan fa-pao chi, Leng-chia shih-tzu chi, Li-tai fa-pao chi, Pao-lin chuan*), transmission was predicated on a unilineal basis from a master to a single disciple. The nature of the transmission was of a variously conceived immaterial Ch'an essence, eventually reaching classic formulation as the "treasury of the true Dharma-eye" (*cheng fa-yen tsang*, J. *shōbōgenzō*).[10] The profusion of Ch'an lineages depended on a new, decentralized model. In order to understand how this model emerged, it is useful to review how Ch'an evolved through the T'ang and into the Five Dynasties and early Sung, in conjunction with the changing political climate.

The multilineal model provided by the *Tsu-t'ang chi* and *Ch'uan-teng lu* reflected new demands stemming from the deterioration of T'ang dynastic authority. Following the decentralization of Chinese authority in the wake of the An Lu-shan rebellion (755–763) and the decimation of the Buddhist establishment following the Hui-ch'ang suppression (c. 841–846), Ch'an proliferated in regional movements predicated on the support of local authorities. One pivotal result of the An Lu-shan rebellion was the increase in number of military commissioners (*chieh-tu shih*) and the autonomy with which they ruled. Originally, the title was given to T'ang military officers in charge of frontier defenses, appearing in records as a common variant to area commanders (*tu-tu*).[11] Prior to the An Lu-shan rebellion, the title began to be assumed by some prefects (*tz'u-shih*) not associated with frontier security, though this was still not common. Before An Lu-shan's insurgence, there were ten such commanders or prefects with the title of Military Commissioner. After An Lu-shan, their numbers increased greatly. During the *chen-yuan* era (785–805), the number grew to thirty. By the *yuan-ho* era (806–820), there were forty-seven.[12] The nature of Buddhism in China, usually aligned with and sanctioned by imperial authority, changed substantially through this process. Local Ch'an movements proliferated from these diverse bases of regional authority, relying on the support of local officials.

The suppression of Buddhism that followed during the Hui-ch'ang era served to augment the significance of the local Ch'an movements. On the one hand, imperial actions were aimed primarily at restricting the activities of Buddhist institutions related to the established schools like Hua-yen and T'ien-t'ai, which had assumed large public and economic roles in T'ang society. In addition, the sympathetic military commissioners protected Ch'an monks and monasteries from imperial sanction. Together, these factors contributed to the importance that Ch'an assumed as the leading representative of Chinese Buddhism, and as the major force for the spread of Buddhism throughout Chinese society. Against this was a growing wariness by members of the Chinese elite of the benefits that Buddhism in any form brought to China. The fall of the T'ang in 906 further exacerbated all these tendencies. The so-called Five Dynasties that rose and fell in rapid succession in the north in the short span of fifty-two years enacted varied policies toward Buddhism according to aims of individual rulers; imperial policy was generally unsympathetic toward Buddhism, and culminated in another suppression by Emperor Shih-tsung of the Latter Chou in 955.[13] The so-called Ten Kingdoms that prevailed throughout the rest of China, mainly in the south, functioned with a high degree of autonomy as de facto independent countries. Three became especially well known for their support of Buddhism: Nan (or Southern) T'ang, Min, and Wu-yüeh. These regions, relatively peaceful and prosperous, served as havens for Buddhist monks fleeing the harsh conditions of the north. As a result of the catastrophe that befell the T'ang and the continued havoc that raged throughout the Five Dynasties, rulers in these areas sought the revival of a vanishing civilization in their support of Buddhist monks and institutions.

The "five houses" of classical Ch'an, in effect, represent the profusion of Ch'an factions throughout a decentralized China during this period. Without the decentralization and eventual demise of T'ang authority, this profusion might never have occurred, and certainly would have taken a different form. Chinese imperial governments typically sought direct control over the Buddhist clergy and institutions, erecting the parameters for legitimate activity within its realm. They imposed imperial standards through which religious movements were legitimized. This pattern of imperial control was reasserted throughout China with the reunification of China by the Sung emperors. As Ch'an emerged as the major representative of Chinese Buddhism during the period of disunion, one of the first Buddhist-related matters for the new government to attend to was a systematic organization of regional Ch'an proliferation. The *Ch'uan-teng lu* was the officially sanctioned interpretation of the Ch'an movement. The *Tsu-t'ang chi*, as we shall see below, was compiled not through Sung auspices but under the sponsorship of one of the strong, independent regions in the south, a fact that may have hastened its disappearance once Sung authority was established.

As alluded to above, historical accuracy was not a major motivating factor in the compilation of the *Tsu-t'ang chi* and *Ch'uan-teng lu*. Lineal associations were creatively forged in order to maintain the cardinal principle of Dharma transmission. Similarly, the antics and enigmatic utterances of the Ch'an masters recorded in these transmission histories conformed to a predetermined style of appropriate "Ch'an-like" behavior. As a result, the records represent fictionalized accounts of a unique Ch'an persona. The persona itself is the affirmation of a uniform Ch'an style, constructed to meet the demands of a new orthodoxy. From the perspective of the Sung, regional Ch'an movements had developed virtually unchecked by the imperial government for nearly two hundred years. The *Ch'uan-teng lu* was the first opportunity to organize and systemize a burgeoning Ch'an movement.

Although various Ch'an movements are judiciously recognized in these records, if one probes beneath the surface of each record's generally harmonious transmission claims, one finds a preference for particular factions. These preferences are closely tied to the compilers of individual records and the lineages they are associated with—the regions where these individual lineages dominated and the patronage provided by the rulers of these regions. In the following, attention is turned toward these associations, especially as they reflect the motives and aspirations inherent in the records under review, the *Tsu-t'ang chi* and the *Ching-te Ch'uan-teng lu*.

The *Patriarch's Hall Collection*

Factors Associated with the Compilation of the Tsu-t'ang chi

The discovery of the *Tsu-t'ang chi* (Patriarch's hall collection) in the Korean monastery Haein-sa in the 1930s has had a large impact on the study of Chinese Ch'an. Prior to this, the text was believed to be nonextant, and no one had any idea of its contents. The rediscovery of the *Tsu-t'ang chi* underscores the power and aspirations of regional Ch'an movements during the Five Dynasties period. The text has clear parallels with the *Ch'uan-teng lu*. Although the information contained in the two texts is not necessarily the same, both texts drew from similar sources of information. They share many of the features of classical Ch'an: pithy dialogues, enlightenment verses, whimsical behavior, and so forth. Because the *Tsu-t'ang chi* was not subjected to the same kind of editorial standardization process as the *Ch'uan-teng lu* and later Ch'an transmission records, it contains an even greater wealth of idiomatic prose characteristic of the period. For reasons that are not entirely clear, knowledge of the *Tsu-t'ang chi* was quickly lost in China. It appears that because of the much greater scope and comprehensiveness of the *Ch'uan-teng lu*, not to mention the status of the *Ch'uan-teng lu* as an imperially sanctioned compilation involving the efforts of China's leading scholar-officials (see below), the *Tsu-t'ang chi* was largely overshadowed by it and was quickly forgotten.[14]

The most important research on the *Tsu-t'ang chin* to date has been that conducted by Yanagida Seizan.[15] Following information contained in the text of the *Tsu-t'ang chi* identifying the "present" as the tenth year of the *pao-ta* era of the Southern T'ang (952),[16] Yanagida determined this year as the date for the compilation as a whole. The preface by Sheng (or Wen)-teng of Chao-ch'ing temple in Ch'uan-chou, the master for whom the collection was compiled (see below), confirms that the text was gathered for use by Sheng-teng and his students. On the basis of this, it was assumed that the *Tsu-t'ang chi* was issued in a fairly complete form in 952, and subject to little alteration. The text discovered at Haein-sa was presumed to contain virtually unaltered materials from this original 952 compilation.

The identity of the *Tsu-t'ang chi*'s compilers, Ching and Yün, are otherwise unknown. In his preface, Sheng-teng identifies them simply as two virtuous Ch'an practitioners (*ch'an-te*), residents at Chao-ch'ing Temple.[17] Attempts have been made to affirm their identity.[18] Ishii Mitsuō attempted to identify Yün as T'a-kuan Ch'ih-yün (906–969), the Dharma heir of Fa-yen Wen-i.[19] Mizuno Kōgen identified Ching as Ku-yin Ch'ih-ching, Dharma heir of Lu-men Ch'u-chen, and Yün as Shih-men Yün, Dharma heir of Shih-men Hui-ch'e.[20] Because of the important role that Korean monks play in the *Tsu-t'ang chi*'s contents, Yanagida Seizan suggests that Ching and Yün were Korean émigré monks.[21] Shiina Kōyū attributes the ongoing significance of the *Tsu-t'ang chi* in Korea to the important role the Korean monks play in the text.[22] Shiina has also demonstrated the important connection of Korean monks who appear in the *Tsu-t'ang chi* to the founders of the "Nine Mountains" of Korean Son.[23]

The connection of the *Tsu-t'ang chi*'s contents with the Korean context, and the fact that it was preserved in Korea and not elsewhere figure prominently in a new theory regarding the *Tsu-t'ang chi*. A recent hypothesis proposed by Kinugawa Kenji challenges the perceived assumptions regarding how and when the *Tsu-t'ang chi* was compiled.[24] Kinugawa's theory suggests that the *Tsu-t'ang chi* originated as a slender compilation of a single fascicle in 952, the date hitherto associated with the compilation of the entire twenty-fascicle text. The rationale for Kinugawa's reassessment is in part based on the preface by Sheng-teng, mentioned above, stipulating that the *Collection* compiled by Ching and Yün consisted of a single fascicle (*chuan*). A second preface, presumably added by the Korean editor (whose name in Chinese is pronounced K'uang Chün) when the *Tsu-t'ang chi* was reissued in Korea in 1245, stipulates that the single fascicle text received in Korea was divided into twenty fascicles (*chuan*) for distribution in the new edition.[25] This is the twenty-fascicle text of the *Tsu-t'ang chi* known to us today. Although clearly puzzled by this, Yanagida surmises that the "received" Korean text was subjected to little alteration, and represented virtually the same text initially compiled by Ching and Yün in 952.

According to Kinugawa, it makes little sense to equate the initial one-fascicle compilation of Ching and Yün with the twenty-fascicle edition issued in Korea in 1245. From a reexamination of the original Haein-sa manuscript edition of the *Tsu-t'ang chi*, Kinugawa has concluded that in the second preface (attributed to K'uang Chün), the second character for "one" (in Chinese, a single horizontal line: −) should be read as "ten" (a single horizontal line plus a single vertical line: +).[26] On the basis of this, Kinugawa concludes that the *Tsu-t'ang chi* text developed over three stages: first, an original compilation in one fascicle; second, an enlarged ten-fascicle text completed by the early Sung dynasty; and third, the division of the ten-fascicle text into twenty fascicles in the 1245 Korean reissue.

Although final conclusions regarding this hypothesis await further research, it is worth noting that Kinugawa's proposal is also based on linguistic criteria, by examining the colloquial style of the *Tsu-t'ang chi* against the background of contemporary counterparts. The basis for Kinugawa's reevaluation based on linguistic criteria includes the appearance of terminology in the *Tsu-t'ang chi* clearly used only after the Sung assumed power.[27] Kinugawa's hypothesis would make Ching and Yün's compilation of the *Tsu-t'ang chi* a one-fascicle text, or outline, which was enlarged in the early Sung to ten fascicles.

This version was brought to Korea, where it was divided into the currently available twenty-fascicle edition. Significantly, Kinugawa suggests that the contents of the *Tsu-t'ang chi* were, for the most part, completed sometime in the presumed early Sung, ten-fascicle version. If proven correct, this would make the *Tsu-t'ang chi* roughly contemporary with its more famous counterpart, the *Ch'uan-teng lu,* or at least narrow the fifty-odd-year gap separating their compilation that has hitherto been assumed. At any rate, there are too many questions surrounding the compilation of the *Tsu-t'ang chi* to assert any position with complete confidence. The following description is offered provisionally on the basis of what, until recently, was assumed to be the case.

According to Yanagida, the *Tsu-t'ang chi* was compiled at the Chao-ch'ing Monastery in Ch'uan-chou (Fujian Province) in 952 by two Ch'an monks, Ching and Yün, disciples of Ch'an master Sheng (or Wen)-teng. Sheng-teng (884–972) was a major regional Ch'an figure during the Five Dynasties period.[28] According to the *Patriarch's Hall Collection,* Sheng-teng belonged in a lineage derived from Hsüeh-feng I-ts'un (822–908), a leading figure responsible for establishing Ch'an in the Min region.[29] Hsüeh-feng flourished under the support of the Min founder, Wang Shen-chih, and Hsüeh-feng's descendants continued to prosper under Wang family patronage. The Chao-ch'ing Monastery where the *Tsu-t'ang chi* was reputedly compiled was founded in 906 through the support of the Min ruler Wang Yen-pin for a follower of Hsüeh-feng, Chang-ch'ing Hui-leng (854–932). Following Hui-leng, Sheng-teng assumed control over the monastery. Although Sheng-teng is not regarded as Hui-leng's disciple in the *Tsu-t'ang chi,* Sheng-teng's master Pao-fu Ts'ung-chan (?–928) was also a direct heir of Hsüeh-feng, making Hui-leng a "Dharma-uncle." The *Tsu-t'ang chi* was conceived in the context of support provided to the descendants of Hsüeh-feng I-ts'un by the Min government. According to Yanagida, it was compiled expressly at the request of Li Ching (considered below, in the context of his support for Fa-yen Wen-i), the Southern T'ang ruler who assumed control of much of Min territory at its demise in 945.[30]

Sheng-teng was an unabashed supporter of the "new style" Ch'an attributed to Ma-tsu Tao-i (709–788). A Tun-huang manuscript attributed to Sheng-teng, the *Ch'uan-chou Ch'ien-fo hsin-chu-chuo tsu-shih sung,* commemorates the Ch'an patriarchs in verse form, covering the twenty-eight Indian patriarchs, the six Chinese patriarchs through Hui-neng, and the three generations of masters from the sixth patriarch to Ma-tsu.[31] The document infers that Sheng-teng (referred to here by his honorific title "Ch'an Master Ching-hsiu [Pure cultivator]") is the heir to the legacy of Ma-tsu's teaching. These verses have been incorporated into the *Tsu-t'ang chi,* indicating a close link between the two texts. As an example, Sheng-teng's verse commemorating Ma-tsu in the *Tsu-t'ang chi* reads as follows:

Ma-tsu Tao-i, his practice as hard as a diamond,
Awakened to the root and in a state of transcendence, strove
   assiduously in search of the branches.
With body and mind ever in meditation, he at once sacrificed all;
He converted widely in Nan-chang; [he stands like] a thousand foot
   pine tree in winter.[32]

Based on Sheng-teng's tributes, the *Tsu-t'ang chi* may be read as homage
to the enlightened patriarchs and masters who preceded Sheng-teng in the
Ch'an legacy. As a result, the *Tsu-t'ang chi* follows the *Pao-lin chuan*, linking
itself to the view of Ch'an orthodoxy championed there through the claim that
Nan-yüeh Huai-jang and Ma-tsu Tao-i represent the true heirs of the sixth
patriarch. The legitimization of Hsüeh-feng I-ts'un's Ch'an faction through its
supposed connection to the legacy of Ma-tsu Tao-i's Hang-chou faction seems
odd, given that Hsüeh-feng and his descendants belonged to a transmission
lineage traced to the sixth patriarch through a different route of transmission
(Ch'ing-yuan Hsing-ssu and Shih-t'ou Hsi-ch'ien) than Ma-tsu Tao-i. This suggests that lineage was not exclusively construed, and in any case need not be
considered as demarcating a specific ideology unique to a particular lineage.
Ch'an ideology was a common possession open to all who were legitimate
recipients of the transmitted Dharma.

The notion of *tsung,* or lineage, is not necessarily a determinant of ideology
in *teng-lu* texts, as if one lineage was committed to an exclusive interpretation
of Ch'an that excluded all others. It is true, as we shall see, that some regional
Ch'an movements did develop unique Ch'an interpretive schemes that contrasted and sometimes contradicted others. However, the affirmation of a multilineal tradition that Sung Ch'an *teng-lu* celebrate presupposes a common
Ch'an style and common propositions. I would suggest that agreement across
lineages, given Ch'an's bases in regionally defined movements, was not always
as free of rancor as *teng-lu* texts suggest. One of the main purposes of early
teng-lu collections is to present a harmonious picture of a fragmentary movement, a kind of "common front" or outward face that was easily understood
and accepted as Ch'an's public persona. Lineage affiliation thus is not intended
as a statement of a similar doctrinal affiliation; *teng-lu* assert that Ch'an has a
uniform heritage cutting across factional lines.

Nevertheless, the assimilation of the "Ma-tsu perspective" on Ch'an by
Sheng-teng in the *Tsu-t'ang chi* is noteworthy and merits our attention. By the
"Ma-tsu perspective," I am referring to a style and interpretation of Ch'an
attributed to the Ma-tsu lineage, including Ma-tsu and his more immediate
descendants. More than any other Ch'an group, this contingent of masters is
regarded in Ch'an lore as the instigators of the "classic" Ch'an style and perspective, which becomes the common property of Ch'an masters in Ch'an *teng-*

lu, including the *Tsu-t'ang chi* and *Ch'uan-teng lu*. This common style and per-spective represents the standardization of Ch'an as a uniform tradition dedicated to common goals and principles. Although factional differences may still have the potential to erupt into controversy, the standardization of the Ch'an message and persona tended to mask ideological differences. The stan-dardization of Ch'an also provided the pretext for the Ch'an orthodoxy to be no longer the sole property of a distinct lineage. This marked a departure from the perspective adopted in previous Ch'an transmission records. Tied exclu-sively to the promotion of a particular lineage, earlier Ch'an records champi-oned one lineage at the expense of all others.

In this atmosphere, orthodoxy was a war waged across strictly determined factional lines, whether real or not. It became a tricky proposition when one lineage was forced to usurp the orthodox claims of another. This is witnessed in the various machinations surrounding the possession of the robe as symbol of orthodox transmission in early Ch'an history.[33] The new structure proposed that Ch'an represented a common heritage. This common heritage, which takes the form of a tree-trunk-and-branches motif, is actually a façade imposed upon an entangled and by no means uniform snarl of vines.[34] The important point in the present context is that the presupposed common heritage allows descendants of other lineages to claim orthodoxy straightforwardly without resorting to convoluted intrigues for asserting how orthodoxy passed their way. Thus Sheng-teng is able to lay claim to Ma-tsu's legacy, even though he is not a descendant of Ma-tsu's lineage.[35]

Sheng-teng and his students were not alone in connecting the Hsüeh-feng lineage to the *Pao-lin chuan* heritage of Ma-tsu. Another student of Hsüeh-feng I-ts'un, a monk by the name of Wei-ching (dates unknown), compiled a work entitled *Hsü Pao-lin chuan* (Continued transmission of the treasure grove) sometime during the *k'ai-p'ing* era of the Later Liang (907–911), as a direct successor of the *Pao-lin chuan*. Wei-ching also compiled a work entitled *Nan-yüeh kao-seng chuan* (Biographies of eminent monks of Nan-yüeh), a successor to the Biographies of Eminent Monks (*kao-seng chuan*) series. Neither of these works survives. However, our knowledge of their existence shows that mem-bers of the Hsüeh-feng lineage consciously linked themselves to the Ch'an tradition of the *Pao-lin chuan*, and attempted to legitimize themselves in terms of the "eminent monks" tradition of Chinese Buddhism, as well.[36] More than anything, these developments indicate a sense of experimentation in the face of uncertainty within Ch'an and Chinese Buddhism following the collapse of the Buddhist establishment after the Hui-ch'ang suppression. Ch'an had yet to achieve legitimacy, while regional movements searched for alternate forms of justification with an eye toward past precedents. Similar attempts were made by monks connected with the Fa-yen faction in Wu-yüeh: Yan-shou with the *Tsung-ching lu* (Records of the source-mirror), Tsan-ning (though not a member of the Fa-yen lineage) with the *Sung kao-seng chuan* (Biographies of eminent monks compiled in the Sung) and the *Ta-Sung seng shih-lüeh* (Historical digest of the Buddhist order compiled in the Great Sung), and Tao-yüan with the *Ch'uan-teng lu*. What is interesting is that in both the Min and Wu-yüeh regions, monks experimented with traditional forms in addition to the innovative strategies adopted in the *Tsu-t'ang chi* and *Ch'uan-teng lu*.

Brief Analysis of the Tsu-t'ang chi's Contents

Fascicles one and two of the *Tsu-t'ang chi* contain the records of the seven buddhas of the past ending with Śākyamuni, the Indian Ch'an patriarchs ending with Bodhidharma, and the six Chinese patriarchs ending with Hui-neng. With the beginning of fascicle three, the *Tsu-t'ang chi* begins to document the separate lineages of Ch'an, taking into account regional and factional diversity, and acknowledging lineages other than those derived from the sixth patriarch Hui-neng. These include lineages stemming from Niu-t'ou Fa-jung, an alleged descendant of the fourth patriarch Tao-hsin, and lineages descended through three other disciples of the fifth patriarch (besides Hui-neng): Shen-hsiu, Preceptor of State Lao-an, and Tao (Hui)-ming.[37] Although these lineages generally do not receive much attention, they do acknowledge the situation in Ch'an prior to Shen-hui's successful assault. In the aftermath of Shen-hui, Ch'an factions increasingly legitimized themselves through lineages traced back to Hui-neng. This became the standard presumption of the surviving post-T'ang lineages documented in both the *Tsu-t'ang chi* and *Ch'uan-teng lu*.

Fascicle three of the *Tsu-t'ang chi* concludes with records for eight of Hui-neng's disciples, beginning with Ch'ing-chu Hsing-ssu and ending with Nan-yüeh Huai-jang (the two masters credited with descendants surviving the T'ang and responsible for the profusion of Ch'an codified in the "five houses"). The entry for Ch'ing-chu (a.k.a. Ch'ing-yüan) Hsing-ssu (d. 740) is meager, given his role in transmitting one of only two Ch'an lineages to survive the T'ang.[38] Moreover, this is the first recorded information that we have of this obscure figure. He is not mentioned among the list of Hui-neng's disciples in the *Platform Sutra*.[39] We have here the case of an influential Ch'an master, one on whom much of the future tradition rests, "exhumed from obscurity."[40] The information in the *Tsu-t'ang chi* records that after receiving Hui-neng's secret teachings, Hsing-ssu returned to his native Lu-ling (Chiang-hsi) and taught a large congregation. The *Sung kao-seng chuan*, compiled by Tsan-ning in 988, also contains a brief notice for Hsing-ssu, acknowledging Hui-neng's role in leading Hsing-ssu to "understand original mind" (*liao pen-hsin*).[41] In the *Tsu-t'ang chi*, a conversation between Hsing-ssu and Shen-hui is also recorded, but there is no independent verification for this, and it is not, in any case, very revealing.

What is more revealing is the verse by Sheng-teng (Ch'an Master Ching-hsiu) commemorating Hsing-ssu, which points directly to contemporary interest in Hsing-ssu's legacy.[42] This interest is also confirmed in the granting of a posthumous title to Hsing-ssu by emperor Hsi-tsung (r. 873–888) nearly one hundred and fifty years after Hsing-ssu's death.[43] The *Sung kao-seng chuan* also confirms a revival of interest in Hsing-ssu's legacy, by stipulating that Hsing-ssu's tomb was destroyed during the Hui-ch'ang era and reestablished by his later Dharma heirs.[44] From this it would appear that Hsing-ssu was an obscure figure to whom late-ninth-century Ch'an practitioners were drawn. Later Ch'an factions affirmed their own identity through linkage to the sixth patriarch, Hui-neng. Hsing-ssu served as a convenient link for this purpose. In terms of the *Tsu-t'ang chi*, the legitimacy of Sheng-teng's place in the lineage descended from Hsüeh-feng I-ts'un was predicated on Dharma transmission between Hui-neng and Hsing-ssu.

The disciple of Hui-neng with the last listed entry in the *Tsu-t'ang chi* was Nan-yüeh Huai-jang (677–744), the initiator of the other faction whose lineage survived the T'ang dynasty.[45] Several factors helped determine why the faction that decended from Huai-jang is less obscure: the prominence of Ma-tsu Tao-i and his disciples in the late eighth and early ninth centuries; the writings of Tsung-mi; and the missing fascicles of the *Pao-lin chuan* that presumably documented this lineage.[46] Still, Huai-jang has no presence in the *Platform Sutra*, and the inscription written for him by Chang Cheng-fu was probably written some fifty years after his death, during the heyday of Ma-tsu's disciples.[47] The *Tsu-t'ang chi* record of Huai-jang documents a legendary tale, common for important Ch'an figures with shadowy pasts. At the time of his birth, for example, a white vapor (or *pneuma*) (*qi*) was perceived throughout the six realms of sentient beings.[48] On the eighth day of the fourth month (commonly associated with the birth of Śākyamuni, and thus an important Buddhist memorial day), emperor Kao-tsung was made aware of this omen and sent an emissary to investigate. When the emissary returned, the emperor asked about it, and was informed: "It is the Dharma-treasure (*fa-pao*) of the empire (referring to Huai-jang), uncontaminated by vulgarity or high rank."[49]

Not only does this mark Huai-jang's auspicious beginnings, it does so under the sanction of imperial approval, and with the designation as "Dharma-treasure," the term for the secret essence of Ch'an transmitted in the *Ch'uan fa-pao chi* and *Li-tai fa-pao chi*. According to the *Tsu-t'ang chi*, Huai-jang was initially a student of Lao-an and attained enlightenment under him. Afterward, he is said to have linked up with Hui-neng, who predicts the proliferation of his teaching in the future with the activity of Ma-tsu. The whole tone of Huai-jang's record in the *Tsu-t'ang chi* smacks of legends concocted to lend credence to an ambiguous yet important figure. From this it is clear that Huai-jang's record was conceived through fabrication in an attempt to legitimize the contemporary motivations of Ma-tsu and his disciples.

The records of Hui-neng's disciples in the *Tsu-t'ang chi* provided important links to the world of Ch'an contemporary with the *Tsu-t'ang chi*'s compilers in the mid-tenth century. Primarily, it established lines of succession to the sixth patriarch for contemporary lineages descended from Ch'ing-yüan Hsing-ssu and Nan-yüeh Huai-jang. Also, it furthered the debate in Ch'an over the true nature of the teaching, between the accommodating, syncretic style that recognized strong links with Buddhist scholasticism and the scriptural tradition (represented by Tsung-mi and the *Leng-chia shi-tsu chi*), and the exclusive, antinomian approach that renounced Buddhist conventions as impediments to enlightenment (represented by Ma-tsu's Hung-chou-style Ch'an, the *Ch'uan fa-pao chi*, and its successors, the *Li-tai fa-pao chi* and *Pao-lin chuan*).[50] Among Hui-neng's disciples reviewed above, Hui-chung was regarded as a strong advocate of the former position, whereas Pen-ching and his insistence on the teaching of "no-mind" provided a link to the latter. Through these linkages to Hsing-ssu and Huai-jang on the one hand, and Hui-chung and Pen-ching on the other, the *Tsu-t'ang chi* maintained its balance between the different yet complimentary poles supporting Ch'an lineage and ideology.

Starting with fascicle 4, the *Tsu-t'ang chi* is divided into the two great Ch'an branches descended from Hsing-ssu and Huai-jang, the lineage of Shih-t'ou Hsi-ch'ien (fascicles 4–13) and the lineage of Chiang-hsi Tao-i (Ma-tsu) (fascicles 14–20). Shih-t'ou and Ma-tsu were regarded as the two great pillars of contemporary Ch'an, and it is to the legacy of their descendants that the *Tsu-t'ang chi* is devoted. Subsequent transmission records championed Ch'an as practiced by contemporary branches of lineages descended from Ma-tsu and Shih-t'ou.

A special feature of the *Tsu-t'ang chi* is the place it reserves for Sheng-teng and his contemporaries. No lineage is documented through the eighth generations of heirs from Hui-neng except for the generation of masters that Sheng-teng belongs to, descended from Shih-t'ou through his student T'ien-huang Tao-wu. For example, Sheng-teng's own lineage history as a descendent of the sixth patriarch may be represented as follows (with generation indicated in brackets).

Hui-neng
(1) Hsing-ssu
(2) Shih-t'ou
(3) T'ien-huang Tao-wu
(4) Lung-t'an Ch'ung-hsing
(5) Te-shan Hsüan-chien
(6) Hsüeh-feng I-ts'un
(7) Pao-fu Ts'ung-chan
(8) Chao-ch'ing Sheng-teng

Only branch lineages stemming from Hsüeh-feng's other students, and lineages descended from Hsüeh-feng's colleague, Yen-t'ou Ch'uan-chou, carry the transmission through eight generations. None of the other disciples of Shih-t'ou, including the illustrious lineages of Tung-shan and Ts'ao-shan, Chia-shan, and Shih-shuang Ch'ing-chu, derived through Shih-t'ou's disciple Yao-shan Wei-yen, carry the transmission this far in the *Tsu-t'ang chi*. Records for masters of these other lineages are recorded through seven generations, but not beyond. A similar situation prevails for the second main branch of lineages recorded in the *Tsu-t'ang chi*, the descendants of the sixth patriarch with lineages traced through Huai-jang and his student, the Chiang-hsi master, Ma-tsu Tao-i.

The final seven fascicles (14–20) of the *Tsu-t'ang chi* are devoted to Ma-tsu and his descendants. As numerous as Ma-tsu's students were according to the *Tsu-t'ang chi*, and as illustrious as lineages derived from Ma-tsu became, their lives are recorded through only seven generations as well (and the seventh generation is only poorly represented). Overall, the *Tsu-t'ang chi* clearly favors Ch'an lineages derived through Shih-t'ou [see accompanying Table 5.1]. Of the *Tsu-t'ang chi*'s entries, 104 are of Shih-t'ou lineage masters (including Shih-t'ou), compared to 84 for Ch'an masters in Chiang-hsi (Ma-tsu) lineages (including Ma-tsu). Even though the *Tsu-t'ang chi* clearly honors Ma-tsu's influence, it depicts the lineage's prowess as an impermanent phenomenon. Of the 84 (83 without Ma-tsu) Ma-tsu lineage records, 33 (just under 40 percent) are dedicated to Ma-tsu and his immediate disciples. From the 245 total records

TABLE 5.1. Ch'an Records in the *Tsu-t'ang chi* (Patriarch's Hall Collection)

1. Records of Ch'an Masters Prior to the Transmission to China

7	Buddhas of the past
27	Indian Ch'an patriarchs (excluding Bodhidharma)
34	Total

2. Chinese Ch'an Records Prior to Shih-t'ou and Jiangxi (Ma-tsu) Lines

14	Chinese Ch'an records through the sixth patriarch
8	Disciples of the sixth patriarch (first-generation descendants)
3	Second-generation descendants of the sixth patriarch
25	Total

3. Records of the Shih-t'ou and Chiang-hsi (Ma-tsu) Lines

7	32	Third-generation descendants
8	27	Fourth-generation descendants
8	14	Fifth-generation descendants
27	6	Sixth-generation descendants
42	4	Seventh-generation descendants
11	0	Eighth-generation descendants
103	83	Totals

in the *Tsu-t'ang chi*, 211 pertain to Chinese Ch'an masters (excluding the records for the 7 buddhas of the past and the 27 Indian Ch'an patriarchs prior to Bodhidharma). Ma-tsu and his disciples thus account for a remarkable 16 percent of the total number of the records of Chinese Ch'an masters in the *Tsu-t'ang chi*. Another 27 records (13 percent) are devoted to the students of Ma-tsu's various disciples. By contrast, the latter generations of Ma-tsu's descendants are depicted as dwindling into relative obscurity.

The depiction of Ch'an lineages derived through Shih-t'ou represent the opposite trend. From rather meager representation in the first generations, Shih-t'ou's line is depicted as blossoming in later ones. This is attributed to the activities of various masters, including Tung-shan (10 disciples), Shih-shuang (9 disciples), and Chia-shan (6 disciples). The most prominent member of the Shih-t'ou line represented in the *Tsu-t'ang chi*, however, is Te-shan's disciple Hsüeh-feng, who alone accounts for 21 disciples (10 percent), the second greatest number of disciples for a single master next to Ma-tsu. This forms the underlying criterion for the claim that Hsüeh-feng and his descendants constitute the current representatives of the Ch'an legacy championed by Ma-tsu and his disciples. The last three generations of descendants from the sixth patriarch descended through Shih-t'ou (the sixth through eighth generations) and account for 80 records in the *Tsu-t'ang chi* (38 percent of the total number of Chinese Ch'an records). In contrast, the three generations descended immediately from Ma-tsu (the third through sixth generations), the period where Ma-tsu's lineage is represented as flourishing, account for 74 records (35 percent). Viewed comprehensively, this reveals the basic intent of the compilers of the *Tsu-t'ang chi*: Hsüeh-feng, his contemporaries, and their descendants, are the true heirs of the Ch'an legacy derived from the sixth patriarch.

Although the generational representation in the *Tsu-t'ang chi* clearly shows Ma-tsu's lineage as a passing phenomena eclipsed by the wake of Hsüeh-feng's influence, some might consider it odd that the lineages that descended from Shih-t'ou (including Hsüeh-feng's) are listed before lineages that descended from Chiang-hsi (Ma-tsu). As will be seen below, the *Ch'uan-teng lu* reserved the final fascicles of its record for the lineage that its compiler, Tao-yüan, wanted most to promote. However, this pattern is not followed in all Ch'an multilineage transmission records. The *T'ien-sheng kuang-teng lu* follows the pattern of the *Tsu-t'ang chi* in including records associated with Lin-chi lineage masters, which the *T'ien-sheng kuang-teng lu* was clearly designed to promote, before those of other lineages.[51]

Because of China's political deterioration and the destructive nature of the times, the compilers of the *Tsu-t'ang chi* did not have full access to available resources. This is openly acknowledged by the compilers, when they frequently note that a particular master's record (either *hsing-lu* "record of activities," or *shih-lu* "veritable records") were unavailable for consultation.[52] This presumes the existence of such records, on the one hand, and also helps account for the great disparity in the number of Ch'an figures acknowledged in the *Tsu-t'ang chi* as compared with the more comprehensive *Ch'uan-teng lu*, which had greater access to current records.

As a result, the *Tsu-t'ang chi*, although it generously and judiciously acknowledges the contributions of numerous Ch'an lineages, may be read as ultimately representing the partisan claims of a flourishing regional phenomenon. The compilers of the *Tsu-t'ang chi* reserved special status for Sheng-teng and his contemporaries as Ch'an's true representatives, the current heirs of the "treasury of the true Dharma eye."[53] This is the image that the *Tsu-t'ang chi* consciously projects. Sheng-teng, in his preface to the *Tsu-t'ang chi*, openly affirms Ching and Yün's compilation.[54]

As noted previously, Sheng-teng viewed himself as heir to the "new style" Ch'an attributed to Ma-tsu, as evidenced in the *Ch'uan-chou Ch'ien-fo hsin-ch'u-chuo tsu-shih sung*, the Tun-huang manuscript Sheng-teng reputedly authored, in which Sheng-teng consciously links himself to Ma-tsu's legacy. According to the *Tsu-t'ang chi*, many of the masters of the Shih-t'ou branches engaged in antics and tactics, such as shouting and beating, reminiscent of those attributed to masters in Ma-tsu branches. The records of masters from these two main branches of Ch'an, as it turns out, are virtually indistinguishable in style and substance. As projected in the *Tsu-t'ang chi*, the profile of the Ch'an master supposedly developed in Ma-tsu lineages became the standard against which all Ch'an masters and their students measured themselves. This represents the underlying presumption governing the development of Ch'an identity in the *Tsu-t'ang chi*. This presumption is shared by future transmission records, including the two records compiled shortly after the *Tsu-t'ang chi* in the early Sung, the *Ch'uan-teng lu* and the *T'ien-sheng kuang-teng lu*.

Finally, one of the most important contributions of the *Tsu-t'ang chi* is the inclusion of comments on the enigmatic pronouncements and activities of the Ch'an masters that are recorded. Of the forty-eight masters to whom these comments are attributed, the vast majority are either from Hsüeh-feng's disciples and their students or from monks of other lineages (especially Tung-shan and Ts'ao-shan lineages) with whom Hsüeh-feng's disciples had close relationships.[55] Few of the comments derive from Ma-tsu's disciples. The comments are in the form of questions and answers relating to specific recorded incidents. In content, style, and substance, they are a clear forerunner to the *kung-an* collections compiled in the Sung, and may be regarded as representative of the *kung-an* tradition in action as recorded in one particular branch of the Ch'an tradition.

The *Ching-te Era Transmission of the Lamp*

Factors Associated with the Compilation of the Ch'uan-teng lu

The *Ching-te Era Record of the Transmission of the Lamp (Ching-te ch'uan-teng lu)* is regarded as the classic text in the Ch'an transmission history genre.[56] It was the first Ch'an record to be accepted in official circles, marking the acceptance of Ch'an into the Sung establishment. In defining Ch'an identity, it set standards that all other subsequent Ch'an transmission records would follow, and helped establish a number of well-known Ch'an conventions: "great awakening" *(ta-wu)*, the enlightenment experience as the culmination of Ch'an practice; confirmation of one's realization by a recognized master as the legitimate criterion for succession; the transmission verse as a poetic account of one's experience; the dialogical style of interaction between Ch'an practitioners; the witty, nonsensical remark as revelatory of the enlightened state; an appreciation of the "sacred" significance of the mundane or trivial, and so forth. Many incidents involving Ch'an masters, later memorialized in *kung-an* collections, were first recorded in the *Ch'uan-teng lu*.[57] Some of the earliest versions of Ch'an *yü-lu* (recorded sayings) texts were also first published in the *Ch'uan-teng lu*.[58] (Many of these same features are also attributable to the *Tsu-t'ang chi*, but as indicated above, because the *Tsu-t'ang chi* quickly became unavailable and forgotten in Ch'an circles, the officially acknowledged, more comprehensive, and finely edited *Ch'uan-teng lu* became the standard for future Ch'an transmission records.)

The *Ch'uan-teng lu* was compiled by Tao-yüan (fl. ca. 1000), a descendent in the Fa-yen lineage, and probably a direct disciple of T'ien-t'ai Te-shao (891–972). During the tenth century, the Fa-yen lineage flourished in the Wu-yüeh region, the most prosperous area of China at this time. The revival of Buddhism in Wu-yüeh became a defining feature of the Wu-yüeh state, and monks associated with the Fa-yen lineage headed the leading temples and monasteries in the Wu-yüeh kingdom. The *Ch'uan-teng lu* documents the spread of Ch'an in China with a comprehensiveness unknown in previous records. The 256 Ch'an figures acknowledged in the *Tsu-t'ang chi* pales in comparison to the over 1,750 names in the *Ch'uan-teng lu*. The compilers (in addition to Tao-yüan, Sung academicians reworked the *Ch'uan-teng lu* before it was issued—see below) of the *Ch'uan-teng lu* had certain advantages over their counterparts in the *Tsu-t'ang chi*. They presumably had the advantages of a stable, united empire in which to do their work. This, along with the advantage of imperial sponsorship, gave them greater access to records and information. The region of the Wu-yüeh from where Tao-yüan hailed was also the most stable and prosperous area of China throughout the turmoil that plagued China during the tenth century.

Defining Ch'an became a preoccupation of Sung government officials.

After Tao-yüan compiled the *Ch'uan-teng lu* in 1004, his work was edited by leading members of the Sung literati, headed by Yang I (974–1020), before being officially issued in 1011. Aside from the information left to us in his preface, we know little about how Yang I's editorial supervision altered the contents of Tao-yüan's work. In addition to changing confusing word order and removing coarse language to ensure that the work was of "imperial quality," and checking titles, names, and dates, Yang I stipulates that they intentionally appended material to enhance it.[59] How this affected the contents of the *Ch'uan-teng lu* remains a mystery, since we have no copy of Tao-yüan's original compilation. We do know that Tao-yüan and Yang I had different interpretations of the *Ch'uan-teng lu*. Tao-yüan's original title, *Fo-tzu t'ung-tsan chi* (Collection of the common practice of the buddhas and patriarchs), suggests harmony between Ch'an and the larger Buddhist tradition. Moreover, Tao-yüan's preface does survive, and further indicates that he understood Ch'an teaching as compatible with conventional Buddhist practice, where "myriad practices (*wan-hsing*) are employed according to differences among practitioners."[60] This stands in marked contrast to the way that Yang I interpreted the work.

According to Yang I, the record compiled by Tao-yüan went beyond the ordinary recounting of interactions and dealings of individual masters associated with monk's histories like the Biographies of Eminent Monks collections and Tsung-mi's *Ch'an-yuan chu-ch'uan chi*. Tao-yüan's work exposed the innermost meaning of abstruse wisdom and revealed the true mind, which is miraculously brilliant. By analogy, Yang I refers to it as being in tacit agreement with the transmission of the lamp (*ch'uan-teng*).[61] With this designation, Yang I marked the novel character of the work as a *Ch'uan-teng lu* (Record of the transmission of the lamp), distinguishing it from its more prosaic predecessors. In the process, Yang I was not merely championing Ch'an as the new style of Buddhism favored by the Sung establishment but also celebrating its break from conventional Buddhist approaches. This new departure was also confirmed in Yang I's exaltation of Ch'an as "a special practice outside the teaching (*chiao-wai pieh-hsing*), beyond rational comprehension."[62]

Brief Analysis of the Ch'uan-teng lu's Contents

The easiest way to survey the *Ch'uan-teng lu*'s contents is to contrast them with the *Tsu-t'ang chi*. As with the *Tsu-t'ang chi*, the *Ch'uan-teng lu* asserts that lineages descended from Nan-yüeh Huai-jang and Ma-tsu Tao-i dominated Ch'an circles in the generations immediately following the sixth patriarch. (Unlike the *Tsu-t'ang chi*, which documents descendants in generations from the sixth patriarch, the *Ch'uan-teng lu* records names of descendants in generations from Huai-jang and Ch'ing-yüan. As a result, the first-generation heirs of Huai-jang and Ch'ing-yüan in the *Ch'uan-teng lu* equal second-generation heirs of the sixth patriarch, and so on.) As with the *Tsu-t'ang chi*, the *Ch'uan-teng lu* reveals a sharp upsurge in numbers with the second generation (138 heirs). Of these, 75 are attributed to Ma-tsu, extending over three fascicles (6–8) of the *Ch'uan-teng lu*.[63] Included among these are many of the most famous names in the Ch'an tradition: Pai-chang Huai-hai, Ta-chu Hui-hai, Fen-chou Wu-yeh, Hsi-t'ang Chih-tsang, Nan-ch'uan P'u-yüan, and so on. The *Ch'uan-teng lu* claims that activity in this lineage extended over the third (117 heirs) and fourth (101 heirs) generations, before the number of representatives began to taper off. (see Table 5.2).

Among third-generation successors, Pai-chang Huai-hai is credited with 30 Dharma heirs (including Kuei-shan Ling-yü and Huang-po Hsi-yün), and Nan-ch'uan P'u-yüan is credited with 17 Dharma heirs (including Ch'ang-sha Ching-ts'en and Chao-chou Ts'ung-shen). In the fourth generation, Kuei-shan Ling-yü is claimed to have had 43 heirs (including Yang-shan Hui-chi), Chao-chou Ts'ung-shen had 13 heirs, and Huang-po Hsi-yün had 12 (most notably Lin-chi I-hsüan).

TABLE 5.2. Ch'an Records in the *Ch'uan-teng lu* (Transmission of the Lamp)

1. Ch'an Masters prior to Transmission to China

7	Buddhas of the past
27	Indian Ch'an patriarchs
34	Total

2. Chinese Ch'an Masters Excluding Shih-t'ou and Chiang-hsi (Ma-tsu) Lines

298	Chinese Ch'an records through the sixth patriarch (including collateral lineages descended from Tao-hsin and Hung-jen)
43	Disciples of the sixth patriarch (first generation)
59	Descendants of the sixth patriarch from the second generation (excluding Shih-t'ou and Chiang-hsi [Ma-tsu] lines)
400	Total

3. Ch'ing-yüan/Shih-t'ou and Huai-jang/Chiang-hsi (Ma-tsu) Lineage Masters

1	9	First generation
21	138	Second generation
23	117	Third generation
17	101	Fourth generation
112	51	Fifth generation
205	19	Sixth generation
278	11	Seventh generation
74	6	Eighth generation
75	1	Ninth generation
75	0	Tenth generation
5	0	Eleventh generation
886	453	Totals

According to the *Ch'uan-teng lu*, the numbers of heirs descended from Huai-jang began to decline somewhat in the fifth generation (51 heirs), and ceased to be much of a factor in Ch'an circles by the eighth generation (6 heirs). Although Yang-shan Hui-chi produced 10 Dharma heirs and Lin-chi I-hsüan produced 22 heirs in the fifth generation, still indicating strong vitality, only 19 heirs in total are mentioned in the sixth generation. As low as this number is, considering the vigor of previous generations, it is not matched in the next three generations combined (11 names are mentioned in connection with the seventh generation, 6 names for the eighth, and only 1 name for the ninth).

As a result, the *Ch'uan-teng lu* suggests that the lineages descended from the sixth patriarch through Huai-jang, after spectacular success, gradually lapsed into obscurity. Although beyond the scope of the current investigation, it is important to note that the main purpose of the *T'ien-sheng Era Expanded Lamp Record* (*T'ien-sheng kuang-teng lu*), issued some twenty-five years after the *Ch'uan-teng lu* in 1036, is to counter this claim in the face of the rising influence of Lin-chi Ch'an factions at the Sung court.

In contrast, lineages descended through Ch'ing-yüan and Shih-t'ou reveal an opposite trend, showing strength just at the time Huai-jang and Ma-tsu lineages begin to wane. Although Ch'ing-yüan Hsing-ssu is credited with only a single heir, Shih-t'ou Hsi-ch'ien, Shih-t'ou is credited with 21 Dharma heirs (including T'ien-huang Tao-wu and Yao-shan Wei-yen). Among third-generation descendants, Yao-shan is credited with 10 Dharma heirs. The fourth-generation heirs (17) are spread over several masters, with the most (five) credited to Ts'ui-wei Wu-hsüeh. According to the *Ch'uan-teng lu*, it is only in the fifth generation (112 heirs) that the fortunes of the Ch'ing-yüan/Shih-t'ou line begin to take a dramatic turn for the better. T'ou-tzu Ta-t'ung is credited with 13 heirs. Te-shan Hsüan-chien is credited with 9, including, most notably in this context, Hsüeh-feng I-ts'un. In addition, Shih-shuang Ch'ing-chu is said to have 41 Dharma heirs, Chia-shan Shan-hui 22 heirs, and Tung-shan Liang-chieh 26 heirs. In large part, this change in fortune is attributable to the end of the T'ang dynasty. With the decline and collapse of T'ang authority toward the end of the ninth and beginning of the tenth centuries, the future of Buddhism in China fell into the hands of southern military commissioners. The refuge and support they provided for monks at this time within a context of relative peace and prosperity formed the context for the rising popularity of new Ch'an factions that traced their lineages through Ch'ing-yüan Hsing-ssu and Shih-t'ou Hsi-ch'ien.

According to the *Ch'uan-teng lu*, the spread of Ch'ing-yüan/Shih-t'ou line influence advanced even further in the next (sixth) generation (205 heirs). Yen-t'ou Ch'uan-huo is credited with 9 heirs, Ta-kuang Chu-hui with 13 heirs, Chiu-feng Tao-ch'ien with 10 heirs, Yün-chu Tao-ying with 28 heirs, Ts'ao-shan Pen-chi with 14 heirs, Shu-shan K'uang-jen with 20 heirs, and Lo-p'u Yüan-an with 10 heirs. Most remarkable, however, is the number of heirs (56) attributed to Hsüeh-feng I-ts'un, ranking him among the most influential masters in the Ch'an tradition. This parallels the significance afforded him in the *Tsu-t'ang chi* (previously treated in this work) where half of the 42 seventh-generation descendants of the sixth patriarch through the Shih-t'ou line were deemed to be students of Hsüeh-feng.

According to the *Ch'uan-teng lu*, the most prominent Ch'an master of the next (seventh) generation (278 heirs) was Hsüeh-feng's disciple Yün-men Wen-yen (864–949), who is credited with 61 Dharma-heirs, 51 of whom have records included.[64] This stands in contrast to the *Tsu-t'ang chi*, which included the record of Yün-men, but no heirs. Since the *Tsu-t'ang chi* was initially compiled only three years after Yün-men's death, the absence of any mention of heirs there is not surprising. According to the *Ch'uan-teng lu*, Yün-men Wen-yen hailed from Chia-hsing (Zhejiang), and studied Buddhism initially under Mu-chou Tao-tsung (a.k.a. Ch'en Tsun-su, 780–877), a disciple of Huang-po Hsi-yün, before receiving the Dharma from Hsüeh-feng I-ts'un.[65] He studied the *Tsu-t'ang chi* notes as a novice at the Emptiness King Monastery (K'ung-wang ssu) in Chia-hsing under Vinaya Ch'an master (*lu-ch'an-shih*) Chih-ch'eng, and then studied the Vinaya in four divisions and the texts of the three vehicles after receiving full ordination at age twenty. Afterwards, Yün-men assumed his Ch'an studies leading to inheriting the Dharma from Hsüeh-feng.[66]

The *Ch'uan-teng lu* version, excising all non-Ch'an-related content relating to Yün-men, tells of how Yün-men concealed his talent after receiving Hsüeh-feng's Dharma, mingling unnoticed among the assembly, a claim that parallels the legendary account of the sixth patriarch, who concealed his identity after receiving affirmation as the fifth patriarch Hung-jen's heir. After leaving Hsüeh-feng, Yün-men traveled widely, visiting numerous Ch'an masters. He paid a visit to the sixth patriarch's stupa in Ts'ao-hsi (Kuang-tung), then assumed the top position in the assembly of Ling-shu Ju-min (date unknown).[67] Just before Ling-shu Ju-min passed away in 918, he sent a letter to Kuang-chou regional head Liu Yen, requesting Yün-men be made his successor. The *Ch'uan-teng lu* is quick to point out that Yün-men did not forget that Hsüeh-feng was his true teacher, a statement obviously intended to keep Yün-men's genealogical record clear.[68] In spite of this, one cannot help but look at Yün-men as an example of the arbitrariness in which genealogical affiliations were sometimes assigned in an attempt to establish a preferred lineal pattern.

Liu Yen was the younger brother of Liu Yin, a loyalist who distinguished himself during the rebellion of Huang Chao toward the end of the T'ang. As a reward, Liu Yin was made overlord of the Kuang-chou region, which he ruled with increasing autonomy through the waning years of the T'ang and the beginning of the Five Dynasties period. His younger brother Liu Yen Hsi assumed his role when he died in 911. By 915, Liu Yen dispensed with all former pretenses, and officially named himself as Emperor Kao-tsu of Southern Han (initially known as Ta Yüeh, or Great Yüeh). Yün-men's success in the region was fostered through Liu Yen's support. Liu Yen (as Emperor Kao-tsu) be-stowed a purple robe on Yün-men and an honorific title "Great Master of Correct Truth" (*Kuang-chen ta-shih*). Five years later, in 923, construction was begun on Liu Yen's orders for a Ch'an temple on Mount Yün-men. In 927, it was given the honorific title Ch'an Monastery of Enlightened Tranquility (*Kuang-t'ai ch'an-yüan*). This temple became Yün-men's teaching center for the remainder of his life, attracting a large congregation of monks.[69]

In addition to Yün-men, other prominent masters of this generation in-cluded Hsüan-sha Shih-pei (credited with 13 heirs), Chang-ch'ing Hui-leng (26 heirs), Ku-shan Shen-yen (11 heirs), Pao-fu Ts'ung-chan (25 heirs), Le-shan Tao-hsien (19 heirs), and Pai-chao Chih-yüan (13 heirs).

Although Ch'ing-yüan/Shih-t'ou lineages continued to flourish in the eighth generation (74 heirs), the number of Dharma heirs dropped precipi-tously from the previous generation, and no master dominated in the number of Dharma heirs produced. In terms of maintaining the lineage to Fa-yen Wen-i, Hsüan-sha Shih-pei (835–908) and his disciple Chang-chou Lo-han Kuei-ch'en (867–928) assume important positions in the *Ch'uan-teng lu*. Hsüan-sha Shih-pei was the Dharma heir of Hsüeh-feng I-ts'un, whose importance as the teacher of Pao-fu Ts'ung-chan (from whom Chao-ch'ing Sheng-teng inherited the Dharma), was noted in connection with the compilation of the *Tsu-t'ang chi*. The connection between the compilers of the *Tsu-t'ang chi* and the *Ch'uan-teng lu* may be thus represented by tracing their lineal filiation as in the accom-panying chart.

LINEAL FILIATION OF COMPILERS OF THE *TSU-T'ANG CHI* and *CH'UAN-TENG LU*

Hui-neng (sixth Patriarch)
(1) Ch'ing-yüan Hsing-ssu
(2) Shih-t'ou Hsi-ch'ien
(3) T'ien-huang Tao-wu
(4) Lung-t'an Ch'ung-hsing
(5) Te-shan Hsüan-chien
(6) Hsüeh-feng I-ts'un

(7) Pao-fu Ts'ung-chan	(7) Hsüan-sha Shih-pei
(8) Chao-ch'ing Sheng-teng	(8) Chang-chou Kuei-ch'en
	(9) Fa-yen Wen-i
Monks Ching and Yün	(10) T'ien-t'ai Te-shao
Tsu-t'ang chi (comp. 952)	
	Tao-yüan
	Ch'uan-teng lu (comp. 1004)

According to the *Sung kao-seng chuan*, over 700 students obtained Hsüan-sha Shih-pei's Dharma, but Lo-han Kuei-ch'en (867–928) of Chang-chou (a.k.a. T'an-chou Kuei-ch'en) was his spiritual heir.[70] The *Ch'uan-teng lu* lists 13 Dharma heirs of Hsüan-sha; the first one mentioned is Kuei-ch'en.[71] Both Tsan-ning, compiler of the *Sung kao-seng chuan*, and Tao-yüan, compiler of the *Ch'uan-teng lu*, spent their careers in the Wu-yüeh kingdom under the influence of Fa-yen faction dominance. It was easy for them to find favor in Fa-yen's teacher Kuei-ch'en.

According to the *Ch'uan-teng lu*, of the 74 eighth-generation heirs in the line from Ch'ing-yüan Hsing-ssu, only 7 were students of Kuei-ch'en. However, no master dominated this generation in terms of number of Dharma heirs produced, and Kuei-ch'en, at the head of the list in the *Ch'uan-teng lu*, definitely assumes the position of importance among them.[72] The most prominent of Kuei-ch'en's disciples, according to the *Ch'uan-teng lu*, was Fa-yen Wen-i (885–958), whose name tops the list. In addition, Fa-yen's students dominated the next (ninth) generation (75 heirs) in the line descended from Ch'ing-yüan Hsing-ssu. Of the 75 names listed, Fa-yen's disciples account for 63 heirs, projecting him as one of the most important and influential masters of the Ch'an tradition.

Fa-yen Wen-i hailed from Yü-hang (Chekiang). He entered the Buddhist order at the age of seven, studying under Ch'an master Ch'uan-wei of the Chih-t'ung (Wisdom-comprehensive) Monastery in Hsin-ting.[73] He received full ordination at a young age, at the K'ai-yüan Temple in Yüeh-chou (Chekiang). According to the *Ch'uan-teng lu*, Fa-yen was a diligent student. He frequently went to hear Vinaya expert Master Hsi-chüeh, who taught at the Aśoka (Yü-wang) Temple on Mount Mei in Ming-chou, and investigated thoroughly the intricacies of his teaching. In addition to Vinaya teaching, Fa-yen studied Confucian writings and frequented literary circles, to the extent that Master Hsi-chüeh styled Fa-yen as the equivalent of Tzu-yü and Tzu-hsia, prominent disciples of Confucius known for their learning.[74] As such, the *Ch'uan-teng lu* identifies Fa-yen as a key figure in the spread of an alternate style of Ch'an, one that favors the study of both Buddhism and Confucianism, and the cultivation of literary refinement. Fa-yen stands as a predecessor to the so-called "Confucian monks," Buddhist monks who were experts in Confucian teachings and were well-known for their literary skills.[75]

Up until this point in Fa-yen's career, his Ch'an proclivities were not strong. Other than his initiation to the Buddhist order as a child under Ch'an master Ch'uan-wei, no mention is made of Ch'an associations. But both the *Ch'uan-teng lu* and the *Sung kao-seng chuan* assert that at some unidentified point, Fa-yen developed a deep spiritual affinity with Ch'an.[76] He dispensed with all of his endeavors and went wandering south, landing in the assembly of Chang-ch'ing Hui-leng (854–932), the disciple of Hsüeh-feng I-ts'un (see above), in Fu-chou. Everyone in the congregation is said to have thought highly of him, even though he had yet to put an end to mental entanglements (*yüan-hsin*). Eventually, Fa-yen decided to set out again, heading off with a group of fellow monks. Before making much progress, they encountered a heavy rainstorm that made travel impossible. As a result, they were detained awhile at the Ti-ts'ang (Earth store [bodhisattva]) Temple to the west of Fu-chou, where Fa-yen had the opportunity to visit Kuei-ch'en. Fa-yen suddenly achieved awakening during the course of a conversation about "traveling on foot," the itinerant wandering of Ch'an monks in search of the Dharma. When asked what "traveling on foot" is, Fa-yen responded that he did not know. To this, Kuei-ch'en said, "Not knowing most closely approaches the truth." According to the *Ch'uan-teng lu*, the awakening that Kuei-ch'en's response sparked in Fa-yen led to "a thorough, tacit understanding," and a prediction of future buddhahood for Fa-yen.[77]

After attaining enlightenment and receiving transmission from Kuei-ch'en, Fa-yen wanted to erect a hermitage on Kan-che Island, but was persuaded by his traveling companions to continue on with their original plan to visit the famous monasteries south of the Yangtze River instead. When they arrived in Lin-chuan (Jiangxi), the prefectural governor invited Fa-yen to take up residence at Ch'ung-shou (Respect longevity) Monastery. According to the *Ch'uan-teng lu*, this marked Fa-yen's beginning as a Ch'an teacher. From this point on, the record of his teaching displays the jocular style of the Ch'an master. At his opening sermon at Ch'ung-shou Monastery, Fa-yen refuses to say much of anything or answer any questions, likening it the expedient methods used by his Ch'an predecessors. This marks a shift in approach from the way Fa-yen was depicted in his early career as a studious monk interested in Confucianism and literary refinements. There is no way of telling how accurate a depiction this is of Fa-yen and his teaching. The treatise attributed to Fa-yen, the *Tsung-men shih-kuei lun* (Treatise on the ten guidelines for the gateway to the source), suggests a conventional approach to Buddhist teaching, contrasting sharply with the more radical Ch'an style of his teaching in the *Ch'uan-teng lu*.[78] This dichotomy is also apparent between the writings of Yung-ming Yen-shou, a descendant of T'ien-t'ai Te-shao and heir to the Fa-yen lineage, and the way he is depicted in the *Ch'uan-teng lu* (see below).

As a result of Fa-yen's success as a teacher, monks from various areas flocked to study with him, and his assembly of students regularly numbered a thousand.[79] Fa-yen's fame eventually reached the ears of Li Ching, the leader of the kingdom of Southern T'ang. Li Ching is said to have held Fa-yen in high esteem, installing him in the Pao-en (Repaying gratitude) Ch'an Cloister outside of Chin-ling (Nanking), and granting him the honorific title Pure and Wise Ch'an Master (*Ching-hui ch'an-shih*).[80] He was later transferred to Ch'ing-liang Monastery, where he preached his message from morning to night. His influence was such that the monasteries of various regions followed Fa-yen's style of instruction, and monks traveled great distances to be near him. As a result of Fa-yen's efforts, the *Ch'uan-teng lu* asserts that the correct lineage (*cheng-tsung*) of Hsüan-sha flourished south of the Yang-tse River.[81] When he became ill, the ruler of the Southern T'ang kingdom came personally to visit him. When he passed away, the representatives from the temples and monasteries pulled his casket through the city, and officials and ministers from mentor of the heir apparent Li Chien-hsun on down donned mourning clothes to accompany Fa-yen to his tomb. He was granted the posthumous title Ch'an Master of the Great Dharma Eye (*Ta Fa-yen ch'an-shih*); his tomb was named Freedom from Form (*wu-hsiang*).[82]

According to the *Ch'uan-teng lu*, the influence of Fa-yen Wen-i spread far and wide through the efforts of his immediate disciples. Fourteen were said to have achieved great prominence, and were honored and esteemed by rulers and nobles. Three are listed by name: T'ien-t'ai Te-shao (891–972), the national preceptor (*kuo-shih*) of the kingdom of Wu-yüeh; Pao-tz'u Wen-sui (dates unknown), the national guiding preceptor (*kuo-tao-shih*) [of the Southern T'ang kingdom]; and Tao-feng Hui-chu (dates unknown), the national preceptor of Korea.[83] In addition, another forty-nine disciples of Fa-yen are claimed to have had influence in their respective locales. Of these forty-nine, only two are mentioned by name: Lung-kuang (dates unknown) and Ch'ing-liang T'ai-ch'in (d. 974).[84] The total number of nationally and regionally prominent disciples here (sixty-three) presumably refers to the same number of names of Fa-yen's disciples listed in fascicles 25 and 26 of the *Ch'uan-teng lu*.[85] The *Ch'uan-teng lu* also maintains that, owing to the practices and teachings of Fa-yen promulgated by his disciples, Fa-yen was awarded two posthumous titles: Master Who Guides Others to Profound Enlightenment (*Hsüan-chüeh tao-shih*) and Great Guiding Master through the Canon/Storehouse of Great Wisdom (*Ta-chih-tsang ta-tao-shih*). It also specifies that students collected and copied the sermons given by Fa-yen, as well as hymns, eulogies, inscriptions, annotations, etc., written by him, and disseminated them throughout the empire.[86]

The extent of influence achieved by Fa-yen's disciples is unquestionable. In addition to T'ien-t'ai Te-shao (see below), named national preceptor of Wu-yüeh in 948, many of Fa-yen's disciples assumed prominent positions in Wu-yüeh. During the *ch'ien-yu* era (948–950) of the Latter Han dynasty, the Wu-yüeh ruler Chung-i, the same ruler who appointed Te-shao national preceptor, commissioned Pao-en Hui-ming (884/9–954/9) to take up residence at Chi-ch'ung (Assisting reverance) Monastery. Later on, Chung-i erected Pao-en (Returning gratitude) Temple and appointed Hui-ming to head it, granting him the honorific title Perfectly Penetrating, Universally Brilliant Ch'an Master (*Yüan-t'ung p'u-chao ch'an-shih*).[87] Chung-i commissioned another prominent disciple of Fa-yen, Yung-ming Tao-ch'ien (d. 961), to the capital in order to administer the bodhisattva precepts; Chung-i subsequently built a large monastic complex, Yung-ming (Eternal brilliance) Temple for Tao-ch'ien to head, honoring him as Merciful Transformer, Meditation and Wisdom Ch'an

Master (*Tz'u-hua ting-hui ch'an-shih*).[88] Similarly feted was Fa-yen's disciple Ling-yin Ch'ing-sung (dates unknown), whom Chung-i commissioned to preach at two unspecified places in Lin-an (Hang-chou). He later resided at Ling-yin (Concealed souls) Temple outside the city, and was granted the title Knowing and Enlightened Ch'an Master (*Liao-hui ch'an-shih*).[89] In addition, there was Pao-t'a Shao-yen (899–971), who was also commissioned by Chung-i to preach in Wu-yüeh, and who was honored by him as Emptiness Comprehending, Great Wisdom, Permanently Illuminating Ch'an Master (*Liao-k'ung ta-chih ch'ang-chao ch'an-shih*).[90] These examples are representative of the way Wu-yüeh rulers patronized Fa-yen's disciples, and the influence they had in the region.[91]

Besides the Wu-yüeh region, Fa-yen's disciples were influential in the kingdom of Southern T'ang, the region where Fa-yen himself had risen to prominence through the patronage of the ruling Li family. As mentioned above, the *Ch'uan-teng lu* record of Fa-yen makes specific note of Pao-tz'u Wen-sui (dates unknown) in this regard.[92] After the Southern T'ang ruler Li Yü (r. 961–975) took control of the region of Chi-chou (Jiangxi), where Wen-sui lived in 964, Wen-sui was appointed to a series of prestigious temples: the Chang-ch'ing temple (Fujian), "the Ch'ing-liang temple in Chin-ling (Nanking) which Fa-yen Wen-i and Ch'ing-liang T'ai-ch'in had previously headed," and finally, the Pao-tz'u temple in Chin-ling. He was also granted the honorific title Great Guiding Master, Sound of Thunder, Sea of Enlightenment (*Lei-yin chüeh-hai ta-tao-shih*).[93] In 965, Li Yü also extended an invitation for Fa-yen's disciple Ch'ing-te Chih-yün (906–969) to preach in Southern T'ang, erecting a large practice hall called Pure Virtue (*ching-te*) in the north garden of the palace for Chih-yün to inhabit.[94] The Southern T'ang ruler also commissioned a disciple of Fa-yen, Pao-en K'uang-i (dates unknown), to the Upper Cloister (*shang-yüan*) of the Pao-en Temple (?) outside of Chin-ling, and granted the honorific title Ch'an Master Who Determines Esoteric [Meanings] (*Ning-mi ch'an-shih*).[95] Another of Fa-yen's disciples, Fa-an (d. 968/76), was also invited to head the Pao-en Temple by the ruler of Southern T'ang, marking it as an institution with strong Fa-yen lineage associations.[96]

According to the *Ch'uan-teng lu*, of the seventy-five tenth-generation heirs descended through Ch'ing-yüan Hsing-ssu and Shih-t'ou Hsi-ch'ien, forty-nine were disciples of T'ien-t'ai Te-shao (891–972). As we have noted, Te-shao became the national preceptor of the Wu-yüeh kingdom, and the prominence of the Fa-yen lineage reached new heights there through the efforts of Te-shao and his disciples.

When Fa-yen was informed of Te-shao's enlightenment, Fa-yen reportedly predicted, "Later on you will become preceptor for the ruler of a kingdom, and achieve even greater glory for the way of the patriarchs than I have."[97] The statement serves as a perfect example of why these records cannot be taken literally. It is unfathomable that Fa-yen himself would make such a grandiose and self-serving remark, even should we grant him the power of foreknowledge. It is perfectly understandable how such a remark could be placed in Fa-yen's mouth by his (and Te-shao's) self-serving descendants, as an attempt to justify Fa-yen faction Ch'an interpretation as politically supported orthodoxy. As such, the statement is best read as revealing the motives of Tao-yüan and Fa-yen faction supporters in the early Sung when the *Ch'uan-teng lu* was compiled.

The *Ch'uan-teng lu* proceeds to document how Fa-yen's prediction for Te-shao came about. It claims that after leaving Fa-yen, Te-shao won extraordinary renown in various (unspecified) regions for his enlightened activity. Eventually, Te-shao made his way to Mount T'ien-t'ai, where he received inspiration from gazing upon the remains of T'ien-t'ai master (but here identified as Ch'an master) Chih-i. Because Te-shao had the same surname as Chih-i (Ch'en), he was referred to as Chih-i's incarnation. Initially, Te-shao stayed at Pai-sha (White sands) Temple. At the time, a prince of Wu-yüeh, the future ruler Chung-i, took command of T'ai-chou, the prefecture where Mount T'ien-t'ai is located. When the prince heard of Te-shao's reputation, he extended an invitation to Te-shao to question him about his teaching. No details of their conversation are given, other than the prediction that Te-shao reportedly made of Chung-I, "In the future, you will become ruler. Do not forget the gratitude [you owe] to Buddhism."[98]

Lying behind this "prediction" are crucial political events in the course of Wu-yüeh history. Shortly after the prediction was supposedly made, the ruler of Wu-yüeh, Chung-hsien (r. 941–947), passed away at the young age of nineteen. Uncertainty surrounded the designation of a successor. The position was initially filled by Chung-hsien's brother Chung-hsun (r. 947–948), but he lasted less than a year on the throne. In 948, nineteen-year-old Chung-i (r. 948–978) lay claim to rulership of Wu-yüeh, supported by Te-shao, his fifty-seven-year-old advisor. Chung-i's successful acquisition marked the beginning of a thirty-year reign and the flowering of culture in the region. After Chung-i assumed power, he sent an emissary to fetch Te-shao and appointed him as preceptor of the Wu-yüeh state (*kuo-shih*), the position Te-shao served in for the rest of his life. Given this background, how should we interpret Te-shao's "prediction" regarding Chung-i, while the latter was commander of T'ai-chou? To take it literally would confuse *Ch'uan-teng lu* anecdotes for historical detail without taking into account the role played by subsequent parties in shaping Te-shao's biographical image.

Implicit in Te-shao's statement to Chung-i is a guarantee of support for Chung-i's claim to the throne. Considering the related prediction Fa-yen is said to have made concerning Te-shao, it is safe to assume that Te-shao was esteemed as a key figure behind the success of Chung-i's claim. This developed into the "prediction motif" that became a key feature of the way in which Te-shao was remembered. What is interesting about it here is the way it functions

as a substitute for the enlightenment prediction motifs, common in biographies of Buddhist monks, and a supplement to the enlightenment experience
motif common in records of Ch'an practitioners. In both cases, what is unique
about the Te-shao prediction episodes is their political orientation. What really
transpired between Te-shao and Chung-i in T'ai-chou remains hidden from
the historical record; it is clear that a relationship developed between them that
helped inspire Chung-i to stake his claim as Wu-yüeh leader. The relationship
between Te-shao and Chung-i would serve as the basis, in both practical and
symbolic terms, for the relationship between Buddhism and government in
Wu-yüeh. The Wu-yüeh Buddhist model of religious and government partner-
ship was eventually championed at the Sung court in a tempered form by the
Wu-yüeh scholar-monk Tsan-ning (919–1001).[99]

The only record of Te-shao's teaching are the fragments contained in the
Ch'uan-teng lu. This record is longer than most, hardly surprising given Te-
shao's influence on the compilation of the work. Like other records of monks
in the *Ch'uan-teng lu*, the record of Te-shao is composed of excerpts from his
lectures and anecdotes of exchanges that consist of questions by students and
Te-shao's responses, all framed within a biographical outline of his life. Given
Te-shao's influence over Wu-yüeh Ch'an and the compilation of the *Ch'uan-
teng lu*, and given that the *Ch'uan-teng lu* account of his teachings is the only
one we possess, the record of Te-shao it contains assumes great significance.
In addition to the "biographical" material relating to Te-shao's life, his birth,
early career as a Buddhist, major Ch'an influences, enlightenment experience,
and so on (reviewed above), the *Ch'uan-teng lu* record of Te-shao provides a
series of statements and conversations reportedly taken from Te-shao's lectures
and reports to his congregation. This material may be divided roughly into two
sections. The first includes a (relatively longer) sermon and three brief statements to the congregation at unspecified locations. The last of the three brief
statements consists simply of a four-line poem delivered to the congregation,
without any accompanying comment. The second section comprises excerpts
from a series of twelve sermons, individually identified, delivered at the opening of the Prajñā temple (on Mount T'ien-t'ai). The first recorded sermon ex-
tract in the *Ch'uan-teng lu* serves as a suitable introduction to the teaching
attributed to Te-shao.

> The expedient means of the sacred ones of old were as numerous of
> the sands of a river. When the patriarch said, "It is not the wind or
> the banner that moves; it is your mind that moves," it was nothing
> more than a Dharma-method of the unsurpassable mind-seal. My
> colleagues who are students of the disciple of this patriarch, how
> should we understand what the patriarch meant [when he said this]?
> You know that the wind and the banner do not move, the error is
> that your mind moves. You know that without fanning the wind and

the banner [with the mind], the wind and the banner move freely. Do you know what moves the wind and the banner? Some say that mind is revealed through concrete things, but you must not concede things [as real]. Some say that forms themselves are empty. Some say that [to know the meaning of] "it is not the wind or the banner that moves" requires miraculous understanding. What connection does this have with the meaning that the patriarch intended? You should not understand it in this way. You senior monks must know that when one gets to the bottom of the matter here and experiences awakening, what Dharma-method is there that does not enlighten? The expedient means of the hundred thousand buddhas are completely understood in an instant. What expedient means are you uncertain about? That is why the ancients said, "when one thing is understood, everything is clear; when confused about one thing, everything is muddled." Senior monks, how can a principle understood today not also be understood tomorrow? Does it not make sense that what is hard for those of superior abilities to understand is not understood by average people of inferior abilities? Even if you pass through innumerable aeons understanding [the patriarch's meaning] in this way, you will simple exhaust your spirit and not fully fathom it, but not know what [moves the wind and the banner].[100]

The words attributed to Te-shao here take the form of a commentary on a famous exchange reported between the sixth patriarch and two monks debating over whether the wind or a banner was moving.[101] The episode was later memorialized in the *Wu-men kuan*, the kōan collection compiled by Wu-men Hui-k'ai (1183–1260) in 1229.[102] Rather than using the episode to illustrate the ineffability of Ch'an truth, Te-shao uses it as a pretext for discussing the Dharma-method of expedient means. To more "radical" Ch'an practitioners, following the lead of the Hang-chou and Lin-chi factions, an emphasis on expedient means was anathema, an unconscionable compromise of Ch'an truth, a "slippery slope" leading to rationalized explanations of truth, doctrinal formulations, liturgical practices, patterned rituals, and so forth. The first question following Te-shao's reported sermon raises precisely this issue.

> A monk asked: "The physical characteristics (*hsiang*) of dharmas, quiescent and extinct, cannot be explained with words. What can you do for others?"
>
> Te-shao responded: "No matter the circumstance, you always ask the same question."
>
> The monk said: "This is how I completely eliminate words and phrases."

Te-shao: "This is awakening experienced in a dream (i.e., it has no relationship with reality)."[103]

In other words, the questioner asks Te-shao what can he do to help others realize enlightenment. Te-shao's answer is not just directed at the specific question but at the whole species of similarly phrased critiques. The experience of awakening that does not partake of verbal explanations, and so on, is a dream-like phantom. The "enlightened" mute lives an unreal existence, deluded by his own fantasy.

The emphasis on expedient means is developed further in Te-shao's chief heir according to the *Ch'uan-teng lu*, Yung-ming Yen-shou (904–975). It is beyond the scope of the current study to enter into the intricacies of Yen-shou's Ch'an teaching. He represents the pinnacle of Ch'an teaching and Buddhist scholarship in Wu-yüeh, and became one of the enduring figures of Chinese Buddhism.

The record of Yen-shou's life also served as inspiration to a wide variety of Buddhist practitioners.[104] According to the *Ch'uan-teng lu*, Yen-shou hailed from Yü-hang (Zhejiang), just west of present day Hangchou. He was reportedly a devout Buddhist in his youth. By the time he reached adulthood, he restricted himself to one meal a day, the strict dietary regimen of a *śramana*. He reportedly was particularly devoted to the *Lotus Sutra*, reading it seven lines at a time, and was able to recite it from memory after only sixty days. His recitation is reported to have inspired a flock of sheep to kneel down and listen.[105]

By the time the *Ch'uan-teng lu* was compiled, roughly a quarter century after Yen-shou's death in 975, Yen-shou was already being cast as a major figure of devotional Buddhism. Yen-shou's purported ability to pacify creatures of the natural order indicates a belief in his supernatural abilities. Like a Chinese St. Francis, the sanctity of Yen-shou's personage extended to an ability to defy the regular norms of the natural order. Legendary materials had long played a major role in the creation of the image of figures central to the Ch'an tradition, but the image of Yen-shou as a devotional, *Lotus Sutra*-chanting Buddhist marks a sharp departure from the Ch'an norm. Yen-shou's reputed devotional proclivities would propel him to the center of controversy in Ch'an circles long after his death.[106]

After Yen-shou had spend time on Mount Hsüeh-t'ou in Ming-chou, where he is said to have attracted a large following, Chung-i requested him to take up residence at one of the main Buddhist institutions in Wu-yüeh, the rebuilt temple on Mount Ling-yin located outside the capital. The following year (961), Chung-i requested Yen-shou to move to the recently completed Yung-ming Temple to succeed Fa-yen's disciple Tao-ch'ien as second-generation abbot.[107] Yen-shou spent the rest of his career at this prominent Wu-yüeh temple. It is clear that his activities extended beyond the range of the "typical" Ch'an monk.

In his role as a leader of the Wu-yüeh Buddhist establishment, Yen-shou participated in an array of liturgical rites aimed at ministering to the Buddhist faithful.

The *Ch'uan-teng lu* maintains that Yen-shou ordained seventeen hundred disciples over the course of his fifteen years at Yung-ming temple, and that he regularly administered the bodhisattva precepts, rites typically aimed at lay practitioners, to the Buddhist faithful. In addition, he is reported to have offered food to ghosts and spirits, spread flowers as part of a daily ritual exercise, and chanted the *Lotus Sutra* constantly, for an estimated total of thirteen thousand times throughout his life. In what must have been a massive promotion of Buddhism in Wu-yüeh, Yen-shou is said to have administered precept rites to over ten thousand people on Mount T'ien-t'ai in 974. Besides the *Tsung-ching lu* (Records of the source-mirror), he is said to have written numerous poems and *gatha*, songs and hymns of praise. From his position in Wu-yüeh, Yen-shou's influence spread far. The king of Korea, upon reading Yen-shou's works, despatched an envoy bearing gifts, and thirty-six monks from Korea were provided with stamped documentation by Yen-shou verifying their realization. Each of them, it is said, returned to Korea to spread Yen-shou's teaching in their respective homelands.[108] As a result, Yen-shou's teaching has continued to have great influence on Korean Son.[109]

The *Ch'uan-teng lu* record of Ch'an transmission in the Ch'ing-yüan Hsing-ssu lineage effectively ends with the tenth-generation descendants. Only five names are listed in the eleventh generation, two of which (Ch'an Master Fu-yang Tzu-meng and Ch'an Master Ts'e of Chao-ming Cloister) are reputed disciples of Yung-ming Yen-shou. Only one of the five, Ch'ang-shou Fa-ch'i (912–1000), has a record included in the *Ch'uan-teng lu*.[110]

The *Ch'uan-teng lu* reflected the complex array of forces that contributed to Ch'an identity through the tenth century. From its inception, Ch'an was driven by regionally based movements. These movements depended on local support. The circumstances of this support not only contributed to the movements economically but also helped determine the shape of Ch'an teaching in their respective regions. In general, Ch'an ideology swung between two poles in relation to the larger Buddhist tradition that spawned it, alternately characterized as radical and conventional, independent and harmonious, subitist and gradualistic, antinomian and ethical, and so on. In style and substance, Ch'an transmission records came to epitomize the principles associated with Ch'an as a radical, independent force within Chinese Buddhism, and to typify a uniquely Ch'an identity. The *Ch'uan-teng lu* is often hailed, with justification, as exemplifying "classical" Ch'an, with its records of the unconventional behavior and antics of famous Ch'an masters and patriarchs. Rather than historical accounts, the entries in the *Ch'uan-teng lu* are best read as fictionalized projections that conform to the model of Ch'an supposedly pioneered by Ma-tsu and his descendants. In effect, the *Ch'uan-teng lu* sanctions the principles espoused in Ch'an rhetoric as "a special transmission outside the scriptures," even while promoting the interests of the Ch'an faction initiated by Fa-yen which championed a decidedly conventional and accommodating approach to the Buddhist tradition.

As a product of the Wu-yüeh Buddhist revival and the retrospective, conservative orientation of the Fa-yen lineage masters, Te-shao, Yen-shou, and so on, who dominated the region, the *Ch'uan-teng lu* was compiled against the background of a more conservative and conventional approach to Ch'an as harmonious with Buddhist teachings, reminiscent of Tsung-mi's attempt to characterize the Ch'an in similar terms.[111] The style and substance of the *Ch'uan-teng lu*, however, clearly favors the interpretation of Ch'an forged through Ma-tsu and his descendants. Although it is unclear where Tao-yüan's compilation ends and Yang I's editing begins, it is clear that something of both tendencies remains in the *Ch'uan-teng lu* in spite of the preference accorded to the Ch'an style associated with the Ma-tsu faction. In this regard, the *Ch'uan-teng lu* might be compared with Tsung-mi's attempt to categorize the disparate regional Ch'an movements of his own day. Tsung-mi reserved the highest place in his schema for the interpretation of Ch'an provided by his own Ho-tse faction, placing the Ma-tsu, Hung-chou Ch'an interpretation just beneath it. In like manner, Tao-yüan appears to have reserved the highest place for Fa-yen Ch'an, while also reserving high regard for other Ch'an factions, especially one identifying with Ma-tsu's descendant, Lin-chi I-hsüan.

Conclusion

No understanding of Ch'an is complete without assessing the contributions of the *Tsu-t'ang chi* and the *Ch'uan-teng lu* to Ch'an identity. Knowledge of these contributions is essential to any understanding of Ch'an, how it came to be defined, the principles that guided it, and so on. While their role is generally acknowledged in determining Ch'an's religious self-definition, less attention has been paid toward the social and political factors that contributed to their compilation.

Unmistakably, Ch'an transmission records were manufactured to illustrate Ch'an orthodoxy. Above all, it was necessary to substantiate a lineal connection through Dharma transmission, even (or especially) when such connections were lacking. In addition, considerable emphasis was placed on exhibiting a Ch'an persona, a unique Ch'an style characterized by enigmatic dialogue and unconventional behavior, to the extent that masters who otherwise displayed a conventional approach to Buddhist teachings in their own writings were made to conform to a standardized Ch'an image. The increasingly powerful government officials who came to champion it illustrate the success of the Ch'an drive for orthodoxy. With the support of government leaders in Min, Nan T'ang, and Wu-yüeh, we saw how different factions of Ch'an aspired to orthodox status in their own regions and beyond.

Records like the *Tsu-t'ang chi* and the *Ch'uan-teng lu*, rather than presenting unbiased accounts of the Ch'an movement in its diversity, attempted to codify views of Ch'an orthodoxy predicated on factional biases. The claims of Sheng-teng and his disciples in the *Tsu-t'ang chi* went unheeded and were forgotten. The claims of Te-shao and his disciples for the prominence of the Fa-yen faction were mitigated by the rising tide of support for the Lin-chi faction at the Sung court. Lin-chi faction supremacy was officially acknowledged in the next transmission of the lamp record, the *T'ien-sheng kuang-teng lu*. With this, official interpretation turned in a decidedly Lin-chi faction direction; this interpretation dominated Ch'an circles throughout the Sung, and beyond.

Among the points to be considered when evaluating the *Tsu-t'ang chi* and *Ch'uan-teng lu* are the following:

- The *Tsu-t'ang chi* and the *Ch'uan-teng lu* both reflect circumstances prevailing throughout China with the decentralizing forces that accompanied the decline of the T'ang and the emergence of the Five Dynasties. Both texts champion lineages descended from a single master, Hsüeh-feng I-ts'un, who became a major figure in the southern kingdom of Min, a refuge for Buddhists escaping the travails of the north.
- The claims of the *Tsu-t'ang chi* and *Ch'uan-teng lu* are predicated on the patronage of local rulers. In the absence of effective central administration, local authorities in many regions had complete autonomy over the affairs within their domains, including religion. The temples they built and supported, and the Ch'an monks they appointed to head them, provided the institutional framework through which local Ch'an factions thrived.
- The *Tsu-t'ang chi* and the *Ch'uan-teng lu* were compiled to promote the claims for legitimacy of two regionally based Ch'an movements: in the case of the *Tsu-t'ang chi*, Chao-ch'ing Sheng-teng and his disciples (first in Min, and then Southern T'ang); in the case of the *Ch'uan-teng lu*, T'ien-t'ai Te-shao and his disciples (Wu-yüeh).
- In both texts, legitimacy is substantiated through master-disciple transmissions, manufactured and enhanced where necessary, in order to maintain the credibility of factional claims to orthodoxy.
- Both texts provide for a "typical" Ch'an style through recorded dialogues and activities, and so on. All masters with records included in the *Tsu-t'ang chi* and *Ch'uan-teng lu* conform to this stylistic prerequisite. As this style served as a defining feature of a unique Ch'an identity, distinguishing Ch'an from other forms of Buddhism, it should be

read primarily as a literary device confirming a master's Ch'an identity, and not a reflection of actual behavior. This style became the new face of Ch'an orthodoxy.

NOTES

1. Following the *Ching-te ch'uan-teng lu*, 30 fasc. (1004), the Ch'an records organized and styled after it in the Sung dynasty were: the *T'ien-sheng kuang-teng lu*, 30 fasc. (1036); the *Chien-chung Ch-ing-kuo hsü-teng lu*, 30 fasc. (1101); the *Tsung-men lien-teng hui-yao*, 30 fasc. (1183); the *Chia-t'ai p'u-teng lu*, 30 fasc. (1202); and the *Wu-teng hui-yuan*, 20 fasc. (1252).

2. Examples of the effect that Tun-huang manuscripts have had over understanding early Ch'an are represented in such works as Philip Yampolsky, *The Platform Sutra of the Sixth Patriarch* (New York: Columbia University Press, 1967); John R. McRae, *The Northern School and the Formation of Early Ch'an Buddhism* (Honolulu: University of Hawai'i Press, Kuroda Institute Studies in East Asian Buddhism, 1986); and Bernard Faure, *The Will to Orthodoxy: A Critical Genealogy of Northern Chan Buddhism* (Stanford: Stanford University Press, 1997 (translated by Phyllis Brooks, from *La volonté d'orthodoxie dans le bouddhisme chinois* [Éditions du CNRS, 1988], and *Le bouddhisme Ch'an en mal d'histoire* [École Française d' Extrême-Orient, 1989]). Among works in Japanese, too numerous to list, are the works of Yanagida Seizan, especially *Shoki zenshū shisō no kenkyū* (Kyoto: Hōzōkan, 1967), and Tanaka Ryōshō, *Tonkō zenshū bunken no kenkyū* (Tokyo: Daitō shuppansha, 1983). In Chinese (and English), there are the works of Hu Shih.

3. The most famous of these Ch'an struggles involved Shen-hui's claims, recorded in the *Ting shih-fei lun* (Treatise determining the true and the false), contained in Hu Shih, *Shen-hui ho-shang i-chi* ([1930] Taipei: Hu Shih chi-nien kuan, 1970), pp. 258–319, that his master, Hui-neng, was the true recipient of sixth patriarch's mantle, not P'u-chi's master, Shen-hsiu. These claims were later dramatically restated in the *Platform Sutra*; see Yampolsky, *The Platform Sutra of the Sixth Patriarch*. However, struggles between competing Ch'an factions are implicit in all early Ch'an transmission records: the *Leng-chia shih-tzu-chi* (Record of the masters and students of the *Laṅkāvatāra*), *Ch'uan fa-pao chi* (Annals of the transmission of the Dharma treasure), *Li-tai fa-pao chi* (Records of the Dharma treasure through the ages), and *Pao-lin chuan* (Transmission of the Pao-lin [Temple]). Regarding these records, see Bernard Faure, *The Will to Orthodoxy*, and John R. McRae, *The Northern School and the Formation of Early Ch'an Buddhism*.

4. The "five houses" refer to the Lin-chi (Rinzai), Ts'ao-tung (Sōtō), Fa-yen (Hōgen), Kuei-yang (Igyō), and Yün-men (Unmon) lineages.

5. T 48.293c; Hirata Takashi, ed. *Mumonkan, Zen no goroku* 18 (Tokyo: Chikuma shobō, 1969), pp. 37–41.

6. The development of the Śākyamuni-Mahākāśyapa story and the context surrounding its invention have been investigated in the author's "Mahākāśyapa's Smile: Silent Transmission and the Kung-an (Kōan) Tradition," in Steven Heine and Dale S. Wright, eds., *The Kōan: Texts and Contexts in Zen Buddhism* (Oxford: Oxford University Press, 2000), pp. 75–109.

7. Yanagida Seizan, ed., *Tsu-t'ang chi, Sōdōshū sakuin* 3 (Kyoto: Kyoto daigaku jinbun kagaku kenkyūjō, Meibun Shain, 1984) (cited hereafter as TTC), I:24.1–5; and *Ching-te ch'uan-teng lu* (T 51.196b–467a) (cited hereafter as CTL), 1 (T51.205b 26–28).

8. Ishii Shūdō, "*Dai Bontennō monbutsu ketsugi kyō* wo megutte," *Komazawa daigaku bukkyō gakubu ronshu* 31 (2000): 217b–220b (n. 4), has documented the various sources containing renditions of this story. It is also discussed in connection with the *Tsu-t'ang chi*, the *Ch'uan-teng lu*, and other sources by T. Griffith Foulk, "Sung Controversies Concerning the 'Separate Transmission' of Ch'an," in Peter Gregory and Daniel Getz, eds., *Buddhism in the Sung* (Honolulu: Univeristy of Hawai'i Press, Kuroda Institute Studies in East Asian Buddhism, 1999), pp. 220–294.

9. The notion that Ch'an records should be read as fiction was proposed by Yanagida Seizan; see, for example, "Shinzoku tōshi no keifu," *Zengaku kenkyū* 59 (1978): 5.

10. Alternately rendered as "eye treasury of the true Dharma."

11. Charles O. Hucker, *A Dictionary of Official Titles in Imperial China* (Stanford: Stanford University Press, 1985), p. 144, note 777.

12. Ishikawa Rikizan, "Bassō kyōdan no tenkai to sono shijishatachi" (The development of the Ma-tsu order and its supporters), *Komazawa Daigaku bukkyōgakubu ronshu* 2 (1971): 160.

13. Regarding the situation of Buddhism during the Five Dynasties, and particularly the suppression of Buddhism mounted by Emperor Shih-tsung, see Makita Tairyō, *Godai shūkyoshi kenkyū* (Kyoto: Heiraku-ji shoten, 1971).

14. The meager evidence for knowledge about the *Tsu-t'ang chi* in Sung China is considered by Yanagida Seizan, "*Sōdōshū* kaidai," in *Sōdōshū sakuin* (*ge*) (Kyoto: Meibun shain, 1984), pp. 1591ff.

15. From a scholarly standpoint, the most important studies by Yanagida are: "*Sōdōshū* no shiryō katchi (ichi)" [under the name Yokoi Shūzan], *Zengaku kenkyū* 44 (1953); "*Sōdōshū* no honbun kenkyū (ichi)," *Zengaku kenkyū* 54 (1964); and *Sōdōshū sakuin* (*jō*) (*chū*) (*ge*) (Kyoto: Meibun shain, Kyoto daigaku jinbun kagaku kenkyūjō, 1980, 1982, and 1984). For a comprehensive review of studies on the *Tsu-t'ang chi*, see Ishii Shūdō, "Chūsen zenshisō ni taisuru kenkyū," *Kankoku bukkyōgaku Seminar* 2000, vol. 8, pp. 127–161.

16. This date is found in various places in the TTC, in connection with calculating the years that have elapsed since the passing of Śākyamuni and Chinese Ch'an patriarchs from Bodhidharma through Hui-neng (minus Tao-hsin) (see TTC I: 26.14; I: 77.2–3; I: 80.11; I: 81.12; I: 89.7–8, and I: 99.9–10). Yanagida's discussion of it is in "*Sōdōshū* no shiryō katchi," pp. 35–36.

17. TTC I: 1.8.

18. See Ishii Shūdō's review of research on the *Tsu-t'ang chi* in "Chūsen zenshisō ni taisuru kenkyū," esp. pp. 140–149. My own review here is indebted to Professor Ishii's account.

19. Ishii Mitsuō, "Zen to tenseki," in *Zen no sho* (Tokyo: Shunyōdō shoten, 1952). T'a-kuan Ch'ih-yün's record is contained in CTL 25.

20. Mizuno Kōgen, "Denpōge no seiritsu ni tsuite," *Shugaku kenkyū* 2 (1960). Ku-yin Ch'ih-ching's record is contained in CTL 23; Shih-men Yün's record is found

in *T'ien-sheng Kuang-teng lu* ZZ 76, 420a–574b; HTC 135. 595a–902b (hereafter KTL), 24.

21. Yanagida Seizan, "*Sōdōshū* no honbun kenkyū (ichi)," *Zengaku kenkyū* 54 (1964): 16.

22. Shiina Kōyū, "*Sōdōshū* no hensei," *Shūgaku kenkyū* 21 (1979): 66–72.

23. Ibid., pp. 70–71.

24. Kinugawa Kenji, "*Sōdōshū* satsuki," *Zen bunka kenkyūjō kiyō* 24 (1998): 113–128.

25. TTC I: 1.13–2.1. The second preface is discussed by Yangida, "*Sōdōshū* no honbun kenkyū," pp. 18–21.

26. TTC I: 1.13. The evidence that faulty printing is the cause for the number 10 in Chinese to be read as 1 is clearer in the *Zenbunka kenkyūjō* edition of the *Tsu-t'ang chi* (1.13). Further support for this reading comes from I: 1.18, where enumeration for the number 23 (indicated in Chinese by the combination of 2–10–3 [as in 2 × 10 + 3]) also contains a similarly faulty 10. In the latter case, there can be no other explanation than faulty printing, as the combination 2–1–3 has no meaning.

It should be noted here that the printed manuscript of the *Tsu-t'ang chi* is highly corrupt and virtually unreadable in places. Kinugawa's method involved the use of a mirror to reflect the inverted form of marred characters from the backside of the "leaves" (as Chinese folded pages are referred to) they are printed on. In this way, he was able to determine the correct form of many marred characters, the results of which are contained in the *Zenbunka kenkyūjō* edition.

27. In this regard, Kinugawa follows the lead suggested earlier by Arthur Waley, "A Sung Colloquial Story from the *Tsu-t'ang chi*," in "Two Posthumous Articles by Arthur Waley," *Asia Major* 14 no. 2 (1968), where Waley points out that the term *kuang-nan* used in the *Tsu-t'ang chi* came into use only after the Sung.

The *Tsu-t'ang chi* is currently the subject of an ongoing seminar investigation involving a number of Japanese scholars from disciplines ranging from Chinese literature, history, and Buddhism, meeting monthly at the Institute of Far Eastern Culture (Tōyō bunka) of the University of Tokyo. The group is lead by Okayama Hajime of the University of Tokyo, Ogawa Takeshi of Komazawa University, and Kinugawa Kenji of Hanazono University. As of this writing, three research reports, "*Sōdōshū kenkyūkai hōkoku no ichi (ni) (san)*," of carefully annotated translations into Japanese of sections from the *Tsu-t'ang chi* have been issued by the seminar in *Tōyō bunka kenkyūjō kiyō* 139, 140, and 141 (1999, 2000, and 2001). Successive issues will presumably continue to carry further such research reports.

28. In addition to Yanagida Seizan's articles cited above, work on Sheng-teng has been carried out by Ishii Shūdō, "Senshū fukusen Shūkei-in no Jōshu zenji Shūtū to Sōdōshū," *Komazawa daigaku bukkyō gakubu kenkyō kiyō* 44 (1986): 155–197; and "*Senshū Kaigen-ji shi* no Shūkei Shōtō no den ni tsuite," *Indogaku bukkyōgaku kenkyū* 34 (1985): 270–277. The dates for Sheng-teng's life are based on Ishii's reconstruction.

29. Chao-ch'ing Sheng-teng's record is contained in TTC 13 (IV: 21.14–29.10); there are also records in the *Ch'uan-chou K'ai-yuan ssu chih* (see Ishii articles cited in the previous note), and CTL 22 (T 51.382a20–b27). Hsüeh-feng I-ts'un's record is contained in TTC 7 (II: 99.1–115.6) and in CTL 16 (T 51.327a11–328b13).

30. Yanagida, "Sōdōshū kaidai," p. 1589.

31. The Ch'ien-fo hsin-chu-chuo tsu-shih sung is recorded in Sodōshū (Kuoto: zen bunka kenkyūjō, 1994) (hereafter SDS), 1,635, a copy of which is found in T 85.1320c–1322c; see Yanagida, "Sōdōshū kaidai," pp. 1,585–1,586.

32. TTC 14 (IV: 43.13–44.1).

33. This is particularly evident in the Li-tai fa-pao chi, where the robe, the symbol of transmission, is reputedly sent to court by Hui-neng, only to have it awarded by Empress Wu to Chih-hsien, who carts it off to Ssu-ch'uan, where it served as the pretext for orthodoxy by Chih-hsien's descendants.

34. Following the metaphor to describe the Ch'an "tradition" suggested by Bernard Faure (and others). See Faure, Ch'an Insights and Oversights (Princeton: Princeton University Press, 1993), p. 120.

35. Given Kinugawa's suggestion that the Tsu-t'ang chi was actually an early Sung compilation, it may very well prove to be that much of its contents were shaped by forces beyond Min and the Southern T'ang, and that Lin-chi influences had a more direct bearing on the shaping of its contents than previously supposed.

36. The three kao-seng chuan works are the Kao-seng chuan (T no. 2059, compiled ca. 520), the Hsü kao-seng chuan (T no. 2060, compiled 667), and the Sung kao-seng chuan (T no. 2061, compiled 988).

37. TTC 3 (I:101.2–111.8).

38. TTC 3 (I:111.9–112.4; ten lines total, two of which are a commemorative verse by Sheng-teng).

39. For the list of Hui-neng's disciples in the Platform Sutra, see Yampolsky, The Platform Sutra, p. 170.

40. Borrowing Hu Shih's characterization of Hsing-ssu and Huai-jang in "Ch'an (Zen) Buddhism in China: Its History and Method," Philosophy East and West, 3 no.1 (1953): 12.

41. Sung kao-seng chuan T 50.709a–900a (hereafter SKSC), 9 (T 50.760c1–8; appended to the entry for I-fu), where Hui-neng is referred to by the posthumous title Ta-chien (great mirror), awarded by Emperor Hsien-tsung.

42. TTC 3 (I:112.2–4).

43. CTL 5 (T 51.240c).

44. SKSC 9 (T 50.760c7–8).

45. TTC 3 (I:142.2–145.7). There are also records in SKSC 9 (T 50.761a–b), CTL 5 (T 51.240c7–241a26), and KTL 8 (ZZ 78, 447c6–448b19). A Ming edition of Huai-jang's "recorded sayings," the Nan-yüeh ta-hui Ch'an-shih yü-lu, is located in Ku-tsun-su yü-lu.

46. For an accessible discussion of the Pao-lin chuan, see Yampolsky, The Platform Sutra, pp. 47–55. A partial copy of the Pao-lin chuan was discovered in the 1930s. Unknown for centuries, three crucial fascicles of its ten chapters (7, 9, and 10) are still unknown, leaving many question marks regarding the exact nature of its contents. It was compiled in 801 by an otherwise unknown monk by the name of Chih (or Hui)-chü. The title of the work alone indicates some of its principal presuppositions. The name Pao-lin chuan (Transmission of the treasure grove) derives from Hui-neng's temple, the Pao-lin ssu, in Shao-chou (Kuang-tung), and indicates an acceptance of Shen-hui's depiction of Hui-neng as the sixth patriarch. There is

considerable speculation regarding the contents of chapters 9 and 10, crucial for our understanding of the work. It is generally accepted that the work reflects the rising importance of Ma-tsu and his students in Chan circles. Presumably, chapters 9 and 10 were compiled in accordance with this perspective. There is general consensus that they contained the records of Tao-hsin, Hung-jen, and Hui-neng, at the least, and possibly the record of Nan-yüeh Huai-jang, the master through whom Ma-tsu's lineage is traced to the sixth patriarch, and that of Ma-tsu Tao-i himself. Shiina Kōyū, however, speculates that chapters 9 and 10 also contained records of Hui-neng's disciples Huai-jang, Hsing-ssu, Pao-chüeh, Pen-ching, Ling-yü, Hui-chung, and Shen-hui, plus those of Ma-tsu Tao-i and Shih-t'ou Hsi-ch'ien; see his "*Hōrinden* itsubun no kenkyū," *Komazawa Daigaku Bukkyō gakubu ronshu* 11 (1981): 234–257.

47. *Heng-chou P'an-jo ssu Kuan-yin ta-shih pei-ming* Ch'uan T'ang-wen (Taipei: 1961) hereafter CTW) 619.7935–7936); Yampolsky, *The Platform Sutra*, p. 53 n. 190. This interpretation is confirmed by the mention of Ma-tsu's disciples (*Tao-i zhi men-jen*) in the opening lines of the inscription.

48. These are the realms of possible transmigration: rebirth in hell, as a hungry spirit, animal, *asura*, human, or in heaven.

49. TTC 3 (I:142.2–5).

50. On the characterization of early Ch'an records according to these two types, see Faure, *The Will to Orthodoxy*.

51. See the table of Contents of the KTL (ZZ 78, 420a–425c), also contained in HTC 135.595a–606a.

52. As expected, where notation is made that information was unavailable, the master's record is generally short; see, for example, the records of T'ien-huang Tao-wu TTC 5 (I:156.2–14) and Chien-yüan Ch'ung-t'ien TTC 6 (II:71.11–72.6). It would be interesting to compare the TTC records where this notation is made against the records of the same masters in the CTL to see what kind of differences emerge, but I have not had time to undertake this task for the present study.

53. Among Sheng-teng's contemporaries, special note should be reserved for Chao-ch'ing Tao-k'uang (dates unknown), the disciple of Chang-ch'ing Hui-leng. According to the *Tsu-t'ang chi* TTC 13 (IV:1.3–4), after his enlightenment, Tao-k'uang was invited by Army Chief(?) (*t'ai-i*) Wang of Ch'uan-chou to preach at the Chao-ch'ing yüan. The Min ruler subsequently granted him a purple robe the honorific title "Great Master upon Whom the Dharma Depends" (*Fa-yin ta-shih*).

54. TTC preface (I:1.8–12). A treatment of Hsüeh-feng and his descendants, leading to the compilation of the *Tsu-t'ang chi*, is included in a manuscript, "Ch'an Transmission and Factional Motives in the *Patriarch's Hall Collection*," which I hope to publish in the future.

55. Shūzan Yokoi (a.k.a. Yanagida Seizan), "*Sōdōshū* no shiryō kachi (ichi)" (Value, as research material, of the *Tsu-t'ang chi*), *Zengaku kenkyū* 44 (1953): 31–80 (esp. pp. 67–72).

56. The position of the *Ch'uan-teng lu* among Ch'an transmission records is universally acknowledged; see, for example, Jan Yün-hua's entry, "Ch'an yü-lu" in William H. Nienhauser, ed., *The Indiana Companion to Traditional Chinese Literature* (Bloomington: Indiana University Press, 1986), p. 202.

57. Of the forty-eight cases in the *Wu-men kuan*, for example, twenty-five are

found in the *Ch'uan-teng lu*; see the chart by Ishii Shūdō in his review of Nishimura Eshin's translation of the *Mumonkan* in *Hanazono Daigaku bungakubu kiyō* 28 (1996): 125–135.

58. Collected in CTL 28 (T 51.437c–449a).

59. Yang I's preface is found in T 51.196b–197a. I have used the version reproduced in Ishii Shūdō, *Sōdai zenshūshi no kenkyō* (Tokyo: Daitō shuppansha, 1987), pp. 21–23; see especially p. 23b, lines 2–5 and line 10.

60. Tao-yüan's preface to the *Fo-tzu t'ung-tsan chi* is found in the collected works of Yang I, the *Wu-i hsin-chi* (Literary collection of Yang I), contained in *Ssu-k'u ch'uan-shu chen-pen* 8, vol. 7.24a–26b; reference here is to Ishii Shūdō's reproduction of the preface in *Sōdai zenshūshi no kenkyū*, pp. 21–23. For the line is question see p. 22a.

61. Ishii 23b5–7; Japanese translation on p. 10.

62. Ishii 21b4. I have explored Yang I and Tao-yüan's prefaces more thoroughly in a manuscript being prepared for publication, "The Role of Secular Officials in Lin-chi Faction Ascendancy at the Sung Court."

63. T 51.246c–263c.

64. T 51.384b–391b.

65. T 51.356b. Mu-chou Tao-tsung's record is contained in CTL 12 (T 51.291a–292b), under the name of Ch'en Tsun-su. There is also a record of his teachings in *Ku-tsun-su yü-lu* 6.

66. TTC 11 (III:92.1–5).

67. Ling-shu Ju-min's record is contained in CTL 11 (T 51.286b–c) and TTC 19 (V:107.12–108.7).

68. T 51.356b29–c2.

69. Urs App, *Master Yunmen: From the Record of the Chan Master "Gate of the Clouds"* (Tokyo: Koda usha International, 1994), pp. 24–26, based on information contained in two inscriptions composed about Yün-men shortly after his death: *Ta-han shao-chou Yün-men shan ta-chüeh ch'an-ssu ta-tz'u-yün k'uang-shen hung-ming ta-shih pei-ming* (964) by Ch'en Shou-chung, and *Ta-han shao-chou Yün-men shan kuang-t'ai ch'an-yüan k'uang-chen ta-shih shih-hsing-pei* (959) by Lei Yüeh, both contained in Tokiwa Daijō, *Shina bukkyō shiseki kinenshō* (Tokyo: Bukkyō shiseki kenkūkai, 1931), pp. 110–121.

70. T 50.786a4–5.

71. CTL 21 (T 51.371a–374a; for Kuei-ch'en's record, see 371a–372a.

72. See CTL 24 (T 51.398b–407a).

73. Located in the western part of Sui-an Prefecture, Zhejiang Province.

74. CTL 24 (T 51.398b4–6).

75. The term "Confucian monk" (*ju-seng*) is used by Makita Tairyō in connection with Tsan-ning in "Sannei to sono jidai," *Chūgoku kinsei bukkyō kenkyū* (Kyoto: Heira-kuji shoten, 1957). In this connection, also see my chapter, "A Buddhist Response to the Confucian Revival: Tsan-ning's Notion of *Wen* in the Early Sung," in Gregory and Getz, eds., *Buddhism in the Sung*, pp. 21–61; and Peter K. Bol, *"This Culture of Ours": Intellectual Transitions in T'ang and Sung China* (Stanford: Stanford University Press, 1992), pp. 148–175.

76. CTL 24 (T 51.398b7); SKSC 13 (T 50.788a25).

77. CTL 24 (T 51.398b8–13).

78. The *Tsung-men shih-kuei lun* is contained in ZZ 110, 877–882. Note, for example, the stipulation given in Fa-yen's preface: "Thus, even though Ch'an truth (*li*) consists in sudden awakening (*tun-ming*), in fact (*shih*) it must be gradually realized (*chien-cheng*). While numerous techniques have been established in each individual Ch'an lineage (*men-t'ing*), . . . they are all based in (*kuei*) the same source. In cases where one has no experience with doctrinal teachings (*chiao-lun*), it is difficult to destroy deluded understanding (*shih-ch'ing*)" (877a17–877b1).

79. T 51.398c1. The numbers of students given in records such as these should not be taken literally, but simply as an indication that a master had many students.

80. T 51.398c26–27.

81. T 51.399c24–27.

82. T 51.399c29–400a6.

83. For their records, see CTL 25 (T 51.407b6–410b12, 411c6–412a9, and 414b26–c3, respectively).

84. Lung-kuang is otherwise unknown; for the record of Ch'ing-liang T'ai-ch'in, see CTL 25 (T 51.414c4–415b18). The *Leng-chia shih-tzu chi*, citing the *Leng-chia jen-fa chih*, distinguished between nationally and regionally prominent disciples of the fifth patriarch (T 85.1289c).

85. T 51.407b6–420c11. This assumption is questionable, however, given the absence of Lung-kuang's name from the list here. In the CTL record of Fa-yen, Lung-kuang is mentioned as one of Fa-yen's regionally prominent disciples (T 51.4007–4008).

86. T 51.400a8–11.

87. T 51.410c1–2 and SKSC 23 (T 50.859c4–6).

88. T 51.412b29–c1 and SKSC 13 (T 50.788c24–26).

89. T 51.413a14–15.

90. T 51.415b23–24; according to SKSC 23 (T 50.860b22–23), a special cloister, the Shang-fang ching yüan, was erected for Shao-yen at P'an-t'a Temple.

91. For a look at the broader influence of Buddhism in Wu-yüeh, see Abe Chō-ichi, *Chūgoku Zenshūshi no kenkyū*, revised edition (Tokyo: Kenbun shuppan, 1986), pp. 123–210. For a more recent assessment, see Ishii Shūdō, "Senshū Fukusen Shūkei-in no Jōshu zenji Shōtō to Sōdōshū," *Komazawa daigaku bukkyō gakubu kenkyū kiyō* 44 1986: 183b–190b.

92. T 51.400a6.

93. T 51.411c15–17.

94. T 51.414b6–7.

95. T 51.411b16.

96. T 51.415c28–29.

97. T 51.407b26–27.

98. T 51.407b27–c4. The term for "ruler" (*bazhu*) implies a "hegemon" (*ba*) in contrast to a "true king" (*wang*), an important distinction in Chinese history between rulers considered legitimate by Heaven and the people for their commitment to peace and benevolent rule, and those who usurped power illegitimately through force. The designation here probably reflects the perspective of the *Ch'uan-teng lu*'s Sung compilers, who officially looked upon nonimperial claims to authority as illegitimate.

99. On Tsan-ning and his promotion of Buddhism at the Song court, see my

previous work on Tsan-ning, "A Buddhist Response to the Confucian Revival," and "Tsan-ning and Chan: The Changing Nature of Buddhism in Early Song China," *Journal of Chinese Religions* 23 (1995): 105–140; see also Makita Tairyō, "Sannei to sono jidai."

100. T 51.407c10–23.

101. Recorded in CTL 5 (T 51.235c3–7).

102. Case 29; T 48.296c17–26.

103. T 51.407c23–25.

104. The study of the records of Yen-shou's life were a principal aim of my doctoral research on Yen-shou, published as *The Meaning of Myriad Good Deeds: A Study of Yung-ming Yen-shou and the "Wan-shan t'ung-kuei chi"* (New York: Peter Lang, 1993); esp. pp. 39–99. A translation of select records is found in pp. 193–203. Shih Heng-ching accepts the more conventional interpretation of Yen-shou in her *The Ch'an-Pure Land Synthesis in China: With Special Reference to Yung-ming Yen-shou* (New York: Peter Lang, 1992).

105. T 51.421c8–11.

106. See *The Meaning of Myriad Good Deeds*.

107. T 51.421c19–25.

108. T 51.422a9–17.

109. See Robert E. Buswell, *The Korean Approach to Zen: The Collected Works of Chinul* (Honolulu: University of Hawai'i Press, 1983).

110. T 51.429b–c.

111. On Tsung-mi, see Peter N. Gregory, *Tsung-mi and the Sinification of Buddhism*, and Jan Yün-hua, "Tsung-mi: His Analysis of Ch'an Buddhism," *T'oung Pao* 58 (1972): 1–54.

6

The *Record of Hongzhi* and the Recorded Sayings Literature of Song-Dynasty Chan

Morten Schlütter

A wealth of Chinese Buddhist writing appeared in the Song dynasty (960–1279). As private and commercial printers increasingly prolif- erated throughout the Song era, printed texts of different kinds came into circulation and prices dropped, enabling printed works to be available to a large segment of the educated elite. This gave rise to an unprecedented book culture, where members of the educated elite became enthusiastic readers and book collectors, and even pub- lished writers themselves.[1] Printing had begun its development in China centuries earlier under Buddhist patronage, and it should be no surprise that the Buddhist elite in the Song were active and pro- lific participants in this new culture of books and printed texts.

The Chan school was, by far, the most prolific school of Song Buddhism, and part of the considerable body of texts it created is still extant.[2] The volume of literature produced by the Chan school far outweighs anything produced by any other groups of Buddhism in the Song. The irony of the Song Chan school's claim to embody "a separate transmission outside the teachings, not setting up words" (*jiaowa biechuan, bu li wenzi*) was not lost on less than sym- pathetic contemporaries such as the bibliophile Chen Zhensun (ca. 1190–after 1249) who in his catalogue of his book collection in- cluded a section on Buddhist works.[3] Here he points out that four of the Chan transmission of the lamp histories altogether consist of 120 fascicles comprising several tens of millions of characters, and he mockingly twists the Chan school's self-description of "not setting up words" (bu li wenzi) to read as its homophonic "never separated from words."[4]

However, the Chan slogan of a "separate transmission not setting up words" was not just empty rhetoric but rather a deeply felt sentiment at the very foundation of Chan self-identity. Nevertheless, Chan masters were very much aware that the publication and spread of its literature was essential for the success and survival of the Song Chan school and for their own careers; Chan literature cannot be fully understood without an appreciation of this context.

Several different literary genres were created within the Song-dynasty Chan school.[5] The transmission of the lamp histories that Chen Zhensun referred to were especially important in establishing the orthodox lineages and teachings, and in illustrating the Chan school's claim to stem directly from the historical Buddha himself. Although the transmission of the lamp histories elucidated lineage relationships and emphasized the unity of the Chan school, individual Chan masters could express themselves, and gain personal reputations, through the production and publication of texts in several other well-established genres. The most important, and most well known, of these genres is the yulu or "recorded saying," as the term is usually rendered in English, which became emblematic for the Song Chan school. However, as will be discussed in the following, yulu is a complex term that denotes both a very specific genre and a very broad "metagenre" that could include almost all genres of Chan literature.

The Chan yulu

Although the yulu of Tang-dynasty (618–907) Chan masters such as Linji (d. 866) and Mazu (709–788) are the most famous examples of recorded sayings texts, the term yulu in a Chan context is actually not attested to until the Song dynasty (960–1279), and extant Tang-Chan yulu only exist in editions compiled in the Song and later.

The Song gaoseng zhuan from 988 is commonly cited as the earliest work to use the word yulu in the sense of "recorded sayings."[6] But it is in fact doubtful whether the occurrences here can be taken as evidence of the existence of actual yulu works at the time.[7] The earliest evidence of the term as referring to individual texts is probably in the preface to the transmission of the lamp history, the Jingde chuandeng lu, from 1004, where it is said that the compiler selected from the yulu of various quarters to put his work together.[8]

Beginning in the eleventh century, however, a number of Chan yulu texts started to circulate, many in printed editions; by the end of the Song several hundred had appeared. Since the Song, hundreds more yulu have been created in China, Japan, and Korea, and they continue to be produced by modern Chan/

Zen masters. In the Song, the *yulu* genre was also picked up by the neo-Confucian tradition, which produced a number of texts that were considered *yulu*.[9]

Of course, the origin of the *yulu* can be traced back to the Tang, and perhaps even further.[10] The *yulu* of the famous Tang Chan masters that were published in the Song were very possibly based on materials originating in the Tang.[11] Whatever the early history of the *yulu*, it was only in the Song that it came into is own as a reasonably well-defined and very popular genre. It was in the Song that the *yulu* became a critical component in the Chan school's construction of self-identity and autonomy, and an essential element in the success of this school of Buddhism.

There has been considerable confusion in modern scholarship as to what *yulu* really is, and the term has often been used very broadly and loosely.[12] The most literal meaning of *yulu* in our context is something like a "record of utterances." It refers to sermons and talks given by a master, and sometimes addresses encounters and dialogues he had with others, which purport to have been recorded and written down by someone who was present at the occasion. A large number of such "*yulu* proper" texts exist, but rarely in independent editions. When surveying independent works with *yulu* in their title, we find that they are usually compilations of a number of different texts, many of which are not records at all but were composed and written down by the Chan master himself. However, self-defined *yulu* all contain at least some recorded sermons or conversations in the material they include, that is, what I here refer to as "*yulu* proper." Thus, it seems by synecdoche, the *yulu* proper contained in a broader collection of Sōtō texts came to name the whole work. Furthermore, texts titled "*xx-yulu*" are all works centered on a single Chan master or are parts of compilations with other Chan masters' *yulu*, where the emphasis on a particular individual is retained.[13]

On the basis of this, I will here distinguish between "*yulu* proper" and "*yulu* collections," the latter being a kind of meta-*yulu*, or compilations that always include one or more *yulu* proper but that also include a number of other types of text. It should be noted that a *yulu* collection does not always have *yulu* in its title; other common terms used are *guanglu* (broad or expanded record"), *bielu* (separate record), or just *lu* (record). Or, it could possibly have a completely different title, since there was little consistency in the use of these designations.

The two distinctive features of independent works with *yulu* in their title, that is, the inclusion of a *yulu* proper and the focus on a single Chan master, can serve as a useful definition for Chan *yulu*. This category excludes the transmission of the lamp histories, because, although they may have been partly based on individual *yulu*, their emphasis is not on individual Chan masters but rather on Chan lineages. The definition also excludes any single-authored Chan work; although such texts cannot be considered *yulu* by themselves, however, they can still be part of a work that is a *yulu* (referred to here as a "*yulu* collection").

Hongzhi Zhengjue and the *Hongzhi lu*

The work that I will focus on to exemplify a Song-dynasty *yulu* is the *yulu* collection of the Caodong school Chan master Hongzhi Zhengjue (1091–1157), which is entitled simply *Hongzhi lu,* or the *Record of Hongzhi.*[14] There are several reasons why the *Hongzhi lu* makes a good case study. Hongzhi was an important Song Chan master, and the *Hongzhi lu* is one of the largest collections still extant, demonstrating well the broad range of texts that could be included in a *yulu* collection. But perhaps most important, the *Hongzhi lu* has been preserved in Japan in a unique Song edition, which includes several original prefaces and postfaces, along with some publication notes; this makes it possible to examine how and when its different parts were first published, and how it was later put together.[15] Most Song-dynasty *yulu* that are currently accessible have not retained this kind of material. In most cases, sometime after a Chan master's death an authoritative *yulu* collection that drew on whatever materials were available and deemed suitable would be compiled; new prefaces and publication information would be added, leading to the loss of the original publication data.[16] Fortuitously, the Song edition of the *Hongzhi lu* is in a sort of unhomogenized state and appears as a rather loose collection of various texts. In China, a much shorter and very neatly organized text, which contains none of the original divisions and publication information, was the only version of Hongzhi's *yulu* that survived.[17] This text does contain all the material that is included in the *Hongzhi lu,* however, which serves to remind us that the material in extant *yulu* collections, in probably all cases, is only a subset of what once was in circulation.

The *Hongzhi lu* did not escape Japanese attempts to bring the format of the text in line with other *yulu* collections; it became the source for several Japanese versions, which again were the basis for the edition presently found in the Taishō canon.[18] Although the Taishō edition preserves most of the text of the Song edition, it completely rearranges it. The Song edition is therefore crucial in trying to reconstruct how Hongzhi's recorded sayings came into being.[19]

Hongzhi Zhengjue was one of the most illustrious Chan masters of the Song dynasty. In his own time, and in later history, he was seen as the most prominent representative of the revived Song-dynasty Caodong tradition of Chan. The Caodong tradition had started to decline only a few generations after it was "founded" by Dongshan Liangjie (807–869), and it had almost disappeared by the eleventh century. But beginning with Furong Daokai (1043–1118), the Caodong tradition underwent a remarkable renaissance, and by the second generation after Furong (to which Hongzhi belonged) it had become one of the most powerful groups of elite Buddhism.

I have argued elsewhere that one key to the Caodong tradition's success was its strong emphasis on the doctrine that all beings are inherently endowed with the Buddha-nature and a certain deemphasis on the need for a shattering moment of enlightenment, an approach that has come to be known as "Silent Illumination," after a famous poem by Hongzhi.[20] Although this particular understanding of practice and enlightenment can be discerned throughout the whole twelfth-century Caodong tradition, Hongzhi was especially eloquent in his presentation of it. The "Silent Illumination" approach sparked a strong reaction from the Linji tradition of Chan, especially as represented by Hongzhi's famous contemporary, Dahui Zonggao (1089–1163), who denounced it as heterodox and, I believe, developed his strictly enlightenment-focused *kanhua* Chan (also known as Kōan Introspection Chan) to counter it.[21]

Hongzhi was from a family of literati that had a strong interest in Chan; he was ordained as a Buddhist novice at the age of eleven.[22] Later, after visiting several Chan masters, he had a decisive enlightenment experience under the Caodong master Danxia Zichun (1064–1117), at the young age of twenty-three. During the following decade, Hongzhi served in various administrative offices at a number of different monasteries, although always under the abbacy of Caodong masters. Finally, in 1124, while Hongzhi was serving as the head monk under his older Dharma-brother Zhenxie Qingliao (1088–1151) at Mount Changlu (in Zhenzhou, north of present-day Nanking), he was appointed to the abbacy of Puzhao Monastery in Sizhou (in modern northern Anhui). This was at the recommendation of the official Xiang Zijin (1085/6–1152/3), who later wrote a postface for one of Hongzhi's publications. In 1127, Hongzhi moved to the abbacy at Taiping Xingguo Monastery in Shuzhou at the Yangzi River in southern Anhui. But by the tenth month of the same year, through the agency of Zhao Lingcheng (dates unknown), Hongzhi moved to the Yuantong Monastery at Mount Lu. The scholar-officials Feng Wenshu (dates unknown) and Fan Zongyin (1098–1136), who both wrote prefaces to collections of Hongzhi's recorded sayings, first met Hongzhi at Yuantong.

The next year (1128), in the sixth month, Hongzhi moved to Nengren Monastery, north of Mount Lu, at the Yangzi River. After a few months at Nengren, under circumstances that are not recorded, Hongzhi excused himself from his official capacities and traveled to Mount Yunju, where the famous Linji master Yuanwu Keqin (1063–1135) was the abbot. Together with Zhao Lingjin (d. 1158), who later authored a biography of Hongzhi, he compelled Hongzhi to take up the abbacy at the now vacant Mount Changlu, where Hongzhi had previously served as the head monk.

The following year Hongzhi left Changlu, probably to evade the incursions of the Jurchen army that were common in the area in years after the fall of Kaifeng. In the autumn of 1129 he arrived in the Zhejiang area. Here he happened to pass by the Jingde Monastery at Mount Tiantong, which at the time was without an abbot. The congregation and local officials prevailed upon Hongzhi to take up the post. For the rest of his life, Hongzhi continued in the abbacy at Tiantong. It was unusual for a high-profile Chan master to stay in one position for so long, nearly thirty years, but it would seem that Hongzhi managed to fend off attempts to move him. Once, in 1138, Hongzhi was by imperial order transferred as abbot to the Lingying Monastery at the Southern Song capital in Hangzhou, which was a highly prestigious position. But Hongzhi only served there for a couple of months before he returned to his previous position at Tiantong.

From then until his death on October 31, 1157, Hongzhi remained as the abbot at Tiantong, and became so strongly associated with the monastery that even today his tenure is one of the first things mentioned to visitors.

None of the biographers mentions the existence of editions of Hongzhi's recorded sayings, although they must have known of them. Perhaps this information was considered too well known to warrant discussion.

Contents and Structure of the *Hongzhi lu*

Hongzhi had a long career and was a prolific sermonizer. He also wrote many poems and other texts. It appears that a great deal of material associated with him circulated at one time in China. The Song edition of the *Hongzhi lu* that survived in Japan preserves much of this material. It is bound in six volumes, but is not divided into fascicles, and although the volumes are numbered on the outside it is not clear that they originally were in a specific order. No title is given for the text as a whole, but on the box in which it is kept, the inscription *Hongzhi lu* (J. *Wanshi roku*) appears with the added words "Brought over by Kōso," a reference to the founder of Sōtō Zen, Dōgen (1200–1253), who returned to Japan from a four-year pilgrimage to China in 1227.

The Song text consists of printings from several different sets of wood blocks, evidenced by the different number of lines and characters per line. However, it appears that except for volume five, the volumes were carved by one team of carvers. These volumes contain several dates from sixty-year cycles; the earliest years signify 1197, 1198, and 1201.[23] Volume five stands alone as clearly from an earlier edition, which gives a precise dynastic date for its publication, 1157.[24] It seems clear that the Song text is a conglomerate of several different printings done mostly after Hongzhi's lifetime, but reports in Japan of other similar texts also indicate that it was at one time published as a single edition.[25] The following discusses the individual texts found in the six volumes of the *Hongzhi lu*.

Changlu Jue heshang yulu *(Recorded sayings of the venerable Jue of Changlu)*

The whole first volume of the *Hongzhi lu* consists of a *yulu* collection, as I have defined it above.[26] It was obviously printed as a unit, since the page numbering is consecutive (except for the last two pages). No title is given for the collection but attached to it is a preface by Fu Zhirou (d. 1156), dated October 23, 1131, titled *Changlu Jue heshang yulu xu*. The volume contains *yulu* proper from Hongzhi's first five appointments, each with individual headings, as well as a collection of "informal talks," and several poems and other writings by Hongzhi.

The preface must have been written at a time when the collection was about to be published, very possibly in printed form. Fu says in his text that "someone recorded [Hongzhi's] subtle words, and came to me asking for a preface."[27] Other than this, the preface does not say anything about the contents of the *yulu*. It begins by introducing Hongzhi and explaining his lineage, indicating the writer's assumption that Hongzhi might not be well known to the reader. It seems clear that this is one of the earliest publications of Hongzhi's words that was directed toward a larger audience.

It is, of course, impossible to determine whether the collection for which Fu's preface was originally written was the same as that found in volume one of the *Hongzhi lu*. However, since the preface was written after Hongzhi had left the last of the five monasteries for which *yulu* are included, it seems likely that the original compilation contained at least these five, and very possibly the other parts too. This early edition of Hongzhi's *yulu* may have circulated quite widely. The *Changlu Jue yulu* that is listed in the *Suichutang shumu*, a catalogue by the well-known Song scholar You Mao (1124–1193), is almost certainly a reference to this *yulu* collection.[28]

Each of the five *yulu* proper in this collection follows a format quite typical of a Song-dynasty *yulu*; an unusual amount of detail regarding the occasions for the sermons that were given are recorded, which in interesting ways reflect the life of a Chan master and the daily schedule in a public monastery. We here find many of the regulations described in the important 1103 rule book for Chan monasteries, the *Chanyuan qinggui*, to be corroborated and supplemented.[29]

For example, the *yulu* from Hongzhi's first appointment at Puzhao contains several sermons by Hongzhi, given after he had accepted the appointment but before he had left his position as head monk at Changlu.[30] The *Chanyuan qinggui* tells us that when a person was invited to take up an abbacy he should, after having accepted, ascend the Dharma seat in his old monastery and give a Dharma talk, and here we can see that this also applied to someone who had not previously held abbacy.[31] Hongzhi's *yulu* from Taiping Xingguo and Yuantong also contain such leavetaking sermons.[32] The *Qingyan qinggui* also tells us that if the person invited to the abbacy has never held a position as abbot before then he is to be given a robe that is proper for his new position.[33] Hongzhi's receipt of such a robe is recorded in the *yulu* from Puzhao.

Hongzhi's *yulu* from Puzhao further contains a report from the inaugural ceremony held to install Hongzhi as the abbot at Puzhao, a ceremony referred to as *kaitang*, "opening the hall." This was an elaborate affair, with the prefect, who was the highest official in the prefecture, participating in the ceremony, and no doubt several other secular officials, as well. Hongzhi here offers incense for the long life of the emperor and for the well-being of the military and civil officials; he declares himself the Dharma heir of Danxia Zichun. This is followed by a lengthy sermon.[34]

Hongzhi's *yulu* from Yuantong also contains a report from the *kaitang* ceremony, and it contains most of the elements of the earlier one, showing that this was a regular procedure when someone was installed as an abbot.[35] The other *yulu* in this collection do not contain details from the inaugural ceremonies, but they all include excerpts from Hongzhi's first sermons, which are dated precisely and thus are helpful in reconstructing Hongzhi's biography.

Almost all the material in the five *yulu* proper in this collection is from *shangtang* (ascending the hall) sermons. Such sermons were formal occasions that were strictly regulated. Here the Chan master would take the high seat in the Dharma hall in full regalia, underscoring his role as the resident Buddha. Everyone in the monastery was expected to attend. But despite the formality of the occasion, the monks were allowed, or even required, to ask questions. The *Chanyuan qinggui* sternly advises its readers that there should be no laughter or even smiling if someone asks an amusing or stupid question at these occasions.[36]

Most of the *shangtang* sermons in this *yulu* collection are introduced by the words "[Hongzhi] ascended the hall and said," which is followed by a general sermon, or by "[Hongzhi] ascended the hall and raised [a kōan]," which then is followed by a brief summary of a kōan story with Hongzhi's commentary on it. Sometimes Hongzhi's initial remarks are skipped and the section starts with a question from a monk in the audience. According to the *Chanyuan qinggui*, *shantang* sermons were to be given every five days, but from Hongzhi's *yulu* here it is clear that *shangtang* sermons were given at a number of other occasions too.[37] *Shangtang* sermons were mandatory, it seems, at such occasions as the beginning and end of the summer retreat, on various days that mark a change in season, and on all Buddhist feast days. Hongzhi also gave them impromptu when someone important came to visit, when he promoted someone to a monastic office, when he bestowed an inheritance certificate on someone, or when a monk passed away.[38]

There seem to have been few, if any, rules for what a *shangtang* sermon could contain. In his sermons, Hongzhi comments on many kōans and touches upon a number of different topics, but in the end his main point always seems to be that all beings are already endowed with perfect Buddha-nature; he eloquently exhorts his audience to awaken to that fact.

Another type of sermon commonly included in *yulu* proper together with *shangtang* sermons, but almost absent from Hongzhi's five *yulu*, is the *xiaocan* or "informal" sermon. However, in the *Changlu Jue heshang yulu* a collection of *xiaocan* sermons is appended to the *yulu* proper from his first five appointments.[39] The collection of *xiaocan* sermons must also be considered a *yulu* proper, but no title or any other information is given, and no clues in the text point to where or when these sermons were held. It is impossible to tell whether the collection was part of the original edition of Hongzhi's *yulu*, but it is clear that it was part of the printing of volume one of the *Hongzhi lu*, since its pages are numbered consecutively.

The *xiaocan* was given in the evening, inside the abbot's quarters. It seems that there were no set days for this kind of sermon. In its discussion of the *xiaocan* sermon, the *Chanyuan qinggui* is not entirely clear, and the text could be interpreted to say that *xiaocan* sermons were to be held in the evenings on the days when prayers to thank the dragons and spirits were held (the 3rd, 8th, 13th, 18th, 23rd, and 28th days of the month). However, the *Zuting shiyuan* from 1108 states explicitly that *xiaocan* sermons were to be held in the evenings but otherwise had no fixed time.[40]

Interestingly, the *Chanyuan qinggui* notes that *xiaocan* sermons were occasions for expounding the teachings of the abbot's particular Chan affiliation, as well as discussing matters of discipline and any inappropriate behavior that had occurred in the monastery.[41] However, I have found no *xiaocan* sermon that records such discussion of disciplinary matters, and the topics for *xiaocan* sermons do not, in general, seem to differ in any systematic way from those of *shangtang* sermons.

Hongzhi's *xiaocan* sermons never note a particular occasion for which they were held, although the *xiaocan* of other Song Chan masters indicate that they could be held on many of the same occasions as *shangtang* sermons.[42] In Hongzhi's case, his *xiaocan* sermons are as a rule longer than his *shantang* sermons, but this does not seem typical of the genre in general. Another interesting difference between Hongzhi's *shangtang* and *xiaocan* sermons, which may be due to chance, is that we find only one instance of a monk asking a question at a *xiaocan* sermon, whereas it is a fairly common occurrence in the *shangtang* sermons. This fact and the length of the sermons seem to indicate that Hongzhi's *xiaocan* sermons were hardly relaxed chatting sessions with the master but, rather, strict and formal occasions.

Also part of volume one, and probably included in the original *Changlu Jue heshang yulu*, is a short collection of religious poems by Hongzhi (C. *jiesong*, Skt. *gatha*).[43] Here Hongzhi offers short verses on the "five ranks" of the Caodong tradition and the "four relationships between guest and host," among other similar topics. Also found in this section is Hongzhi's famous long poem, the *Mozhao ming*, or *Inscription on Silent Illumination*, which can be seen as a kind of manifesto of Silent Illumination. This is significant because it shows that this important text was considered by the compilers of the *Hongzhi lu* to belong to the early period of Hongzhi's career. In the Taishō edition it is placed at the end of fascicle eight.[44] Again, it is not clear whether this was part of the original 1131 publication, but it might well have been.

The final text that is included in volume one of the *Hongzhi lu* is the *Sengtang ji*. It was written by Hongzhi at the occasion of the completion of a new residence hall for the monks at Tiantong and internally dated to the spring of 1134. It cannot have been part of the original publication of Hongzhi's *yulu*, since the preface is dated 1131. It seems that it may not originally have been part of volume one of the *Hongzhi lu* either, since it is carved on separate plates with a different number of lines and characters.

Changlu Jue heshang songgu niangu ji *(Collection of songgu and niangu by the venerable Jue of Changlu)*

Although it seems likely that the individual *yulu* proper of the *Changlu Jue heshang yulu* must have circulated before they were brought together in the 1131 edition, the earliest text by Hongzhi, which was formally published, quite possibly in a printed edition, appears to have been a collection of two sets of commentaries on one hundred kōans each; judging by its preface, it was published in 1129. It is found in the second volume of the *Hongzhi lu*.[45] The first set of kōan commentaries is in verse, which was a genre known as *songgu*, "eulogizing the old," and is entitled *Sizhou Puzhao Jue heshang songgu*; the second set is in prose, a genre known as *niangu*, "picking up the old," here entitled *Zhenzhou Changlu Jue heshang niangu*. Thus the *songgu* commentary is from Hongzhi's time at Puzhao, whereas the *niangu* commentary is from his time at Changlu. No title is given for the whole collection, but a title can be surmised from the title of its preface, *Changlu Jue heshang songgu niangu ji xu*, which was written by Hongzhi's prominent disciple, Xuedou Sizong (1085–1153), and dated August 2, 1129.

The preface does not say much about the circumstances of the publication, but does mention that there were two hundred pieces altogether. With this information, it is clear that the two collections were published together. Hongzhi was still the abbot at Changlu when the preface was written, although he must have left Changlu shortly after word. Sizong became the abbot at Puzhao after Hongzhi left in 1127, and he probably was still there when he wrote the preface.

Hongzhi's kōan commentaries here follow a well-established format. Each kōan is retold, followed by a short poem in the free-form *zi* style, or a short prose commentary. The kōans that Hongzhi uses here come from the whole spectrum of Chan lore, and there is no discernible sectarian bias in his selections. This is perhaps a reflection of how well established the new Caodong tradition had become at Hongzhi's time. A similar collection attributed to Hongzhi's master Danxia Zichun only has kōans involving masters in the Caodong lineage, or "neutral" monks descending from Qingyuan Xingsi (d. 740).[46]

It is not surprising that Hongzhi's first real publication should be *songgu* and *niangu* kōan commentaries. Such commentaries had become very popular in the Song, initially spurred, it seems, by Xuedou Mingjue's (980–1052) creation of *songgu* and *niangu* collections in the Tianxi era (1017–1021), which Sizong refers to in his preface.[47] The brief and often enigmatic comments on famous kōans that were typical of the genre were highly prized for both their elegance and startling qualities by literati and monastics alike.

Although many Song masters have *songgu* or *niangu* collections included in their *yulu*, not many separate editions exist. Both the ancestor to the twelfth-century Caodong tradition, Touzi Yiqing (1032–1083) and Hongzhi's master, Danxia Zichun, had *songgu* collections published separately.[48] However, masters in the Linji lineage were also prolific producers of *songgu* and *niangu*, and many are included in their *yulu*; aside from Xuedou, Foyan Qinggui (1067–1120), Yuanwu Keqin, and Dahui Zonggao, they all have *songgu* or *niangu* collections in their *yulu*.[49] Even lay people tried their hands at this genre, such as the famous Zhang Shangyin (1043–1121) and the scholar Feng Ji (d. 1153).[50]

As it turned out, Hongzhi's first publication also became his most enduring written legacy. Most of the *Hongzhi lu* as we know it from the Song edition preserved in Japan was lost in China. However, Hongzhi's kōan commentary collection was preserved in several ways. Most important, the Caodong monk Wansong Xingxiu (1166–1246) created a work entitled the *Congrong lu* by adding another layer of commentary to Hongzhi's one hundred *songgu* pieces, in a manner similar to the famous *Biyan lu*, Yuanwu Keqin's commentary on kōan verses by Xuedou.[51] This text was published in 1224 and came to be considered one of the most important texts in the Caodong tradition. In addition, Wansong also compiled a commentary on Hongzhi's *niangu* entitled *Qingyi lu*.[52] Hongzhi's *songgu* collection also became part of a text known as the *Sijia lu* from 1342. This work contained *songgu* collections by four Chan masters, that is, Hongzhi, Xuedou, Touzi Yiqing, and Danxia Zichun.[53]

Hongzhi's *songgu* and *niangu* collection also seems to have been successful in his own time. The version in the *Hongzhi lu* is followed by a postscript by Xiang Zijin dated 1134, which probably indicates that the collection was reprinted in that year, four years after its initial publication.

Mingzhou Tiantongshan Jue heshang yulu *(Recorded sayings of the venerable Jue of Mount Tiantong in Mingzhou)*

The next publication of Hongzhi for which there is evidence is found in volume three of the *Hongzhi lu*.⁵⁴ The whole volume consists of just the one lengthy *yulu* proper. A preface by Fan Zongyin (1098–1136) dated September 8, 1132, is attached.

The *yulu* begins with a sermon by Hongzhi given on the occasion of receiving the invitation to become the abbot at Tiantong on December 14, 1129. Since his biography states that Hongzhi was traveling at the time, it seems the sermon must have been given at Tiantong. Based on the date of the preface, the *yulu* should contain material from Hongzhi's first three years or so at Tiantong. However, the *yulu* clearly covers a period much longer than that. There are five sermons given on New Year's, five sermons given to mark the peak season of winter, and five sermons each for opening and closing the summer retreat. Furthermore, if we assume that all items in the *yulu* are in chronological order, the last sermon for which a time is given must be the one from the first day of the year (February 12) of 1138.⁵⁵

Since Hongzhi left Tiantong in October of 1138 to move briefly to the Lingyin Monastery in Hangzhou, it seems very possible that the *yulu* as we have it here was edited around this time. In any case, the *yulu* cannot cover fewer than five years and must extend at least into 1134. The preface therefore cannot have been written for this version of *yulu*, so we must assume that there were at least two different versions of the *yulu*, the one we have here and the one for which the 1132 preface was written. It is interesting that in the Song edition of the *Hongzhi lu*, the preface is on a separate plate, carved in a different style and with a different number of lines from the rest of the volume. Thus the preface probably came from another edition of Hongzhi's *yulu*, perhaps similar to the first part of the text in volume three.

As was the case of the *yulu* proper from Hongzhi's first five appointments, the *Mingzhou Tiantongshan Jue heshang yulu* consists almost exclusively of *shangtang* sermons. They tend to be somewhat longer than the sermons recorded in the earlier collection, and the fact that his audience now was given a more complete record of his sermons, perhaps, can be seen as a sign of the fame Hongzhi had achieved.

Mingzhou Tiantong Jue heshang xiaocan yulu *(Recorded xiaocan sermons by the venerable Jue of Mount Tiantong in Mingzhou)*

This text is found in volume four of the *Hongzhi lu*, and is also a *yulu* proper.⁵⁶ It is a collection of Hongzhi's recorded *xiaocan* sermons, which as we saw earlier were recorded separately from his *shangtang* sermons. A preface by Feng

Wenshu (dates unknown) dated February 11, 1138, is attached. Feng Wenshu mentions that disciples of Hongzhi recorded his sermons, and ends by asking "How could these be empty words?" He also has an interesting comment about Hongzhi's emphasis on meditation when he writes, "The master instructs the congregation to practice stillness and to sit erect like withered trees."[57]

As was the case of the *xiaocan* in the *Changlu Jue heshang yulu*, there is nothing that dates any of the *xiaocan* sermons internally, and they are never noted to have been given on a particular occasion. Again, Hongzhi's *xiaocan* sermons here are quite long, considerably longer than his *shangtang* sermons in the collection discussed above. But unlike the earlier *xiaocan* sermons, the sermons here record much interaction with students who ask questions. In fact, almost all the sermons begin with a question from a monk in the audience. This seems to reflect a change in Hongzhi's sermon style, or at least a change in how he preferred to have his teachings presented to the wider audience. We might speculate that an older, more mature Hongzhi came to be more comfortable with student interactions than he had been in the early part of his career.

Tiantong Jue heshang fayu *(Dharma lectures by the venerable Tiantong Jue)*

This text is also contained in volume four of the *Hongzhi lu*.[58] A preface is attached to this collection, but unfortunately it is not dated, and there is no internal evidence that can be used to date it. The preface is by the Chan monk Puchong (dates unknown), who for a while studied with Hongzhi but later became the Dharma heir of the Linji master Caotang Shanqing (1057–1142). It seems unlikely that he could have written the preface as a student of Hongzhi, who was not even sanctioned as a Dharma heir. It appears he must have done so after having become the abbot at Ayuwang near Tiantong. It is not clear when Puchong held this position, but it was probably in the late 1140s; the *fayu* here are probably from the later part of Hongzhi's career.[59]

In Song Chan recorded sayings literature, *fayu* refer to written sermons or homilies usually produced at someone's request. Puchong's preface describes how both interested lay people and clergy would come and request them from Hongzhi.[60] Unlike his recorded sermons, Hongzhi's *fayu* have very few references to Chan lore, and they are never constructed as a commentary to a kōan story. Instead they are lyrical celebrations of the inherent Buddha-nature of all existence, and are exhortations to the reader to lay down preconceived notions and experience the purity of this reality.[61] Unfortunately, no information is given regarding for whom the individual *fayu* were written. This information is commonly recorded in the case of other Chan masters' *fayu*, such as those by Keqin and Dahui.[62] One wonders if this was a decision on the part of the editors of this text, or if Hongzhi himself may have felt that it was preferable not to include the names of those for whom the *fayu* were directed.

Chishi Hongzhi chanshi xingye ji *(Biography of the Chan master Hongzhi, posthumously titled by imperial order)*

To the end of volume four there is attached a biography of Hongzhi by Wang Boxiang (1106–1173) dated to July 1166.[63] This is the most complete biography of Hongzhi available, and is an important resource for the study of Hongzhi. Such biographies are very common additions to *yulu* collections, and almost every *yulu* collection that is extant as an independent work contains one.

Wang's biography is printed from plates that are different from the rest of volume four of the *Hongzhi lu*. It is impossible to tell when and with what texts it was first published. As it appears here, a publication note dated 1198 is attached to it.

Tiantong Jue heshang zhenti *(Portrait inscriptions by the venerable Tiantong Jue)*

This is the only text contained in volume five of the *Hongzhi lu*.[64] It is a collection of portrait inscriptions by Hongzhi with a preface by Hongzhi himself, dated May 26, 1157, just months before his death. In the text the date 1143 is found, and it seems clear that the collection is from the last part of Hongzhi's career, and that is was published in the form we have it here while he was still alive or shortly after his death.[65]

Hongzhi's preface is here signed in Hongzhi's calligraphic style (possible because of the use of woodblock print, where each page was carved on separate plates). Hongzhi's signature adds an interesting personal touch, which seems an efficient and powerful way for Hongzhi to connect to his readers.

Inscribed portraits were themselves an extremely important venue for keeping good and close relations with both monastic and lay supporters.[66] The great majority of portrait inscriptions that Hongzhi produced were written on portraits of himself. It was common that monastic officers, disciples, other abbots, and important lay people would approach a Chan master such as Hongzhi with a portrait of him that they had drawn (or probably, in many cases, commissioned) and ask him for an inscription. Such inscribed portraits of the master were held in great esteem. His likeness, animated by his own calligraphy, turned the portrait into something like a holy icon and an object of great power. A strong connection was created between Hongzhi and the owner of his inscribed portrait.

Hongzhi's self-inscribed portraits were also used for fund-raising. Many of the inscriptions recorded here were for traveling fund-raisers (*huazhu*), who would prepare portraits of Hongzhi and have him inscribe them before setting out to raise funds for the monastery. No doubt, the fund-raiser would then give these inscribed portraits to generous donors, important officials, and other people with whom good relations were important.

Hongzhi's collection of portrait inscriptions also contains inscriptions that he had written, usually at someone's request, on the portraits of past Chan masters. These are many fewer, but clearly functioned in a way similar to his own inscribed portrait. These works were like icons animated by Hongzhi's inscription.

Although the majority of inscriptions do not identify the person who requested them, some do, and they give important clues as to the clergy and lay people with whom Hongzhi interacted. But again, there seems to be a certain reticence here in naming the people for whom the texts were written. Other Chan masters around Hongzhi's time also had collections of portrait inscriptions included in their *yulu*. It is here that we commonly learn the name of the recipient.[67] However, Hongzhi has many more portrait inscriptions than any other Song Chan master.

The *Tiantong Jue heshang zhenti*, as it is found in the *Hongzhi lu*, is especially interesting because it appears to be in the actual printing from 1157. Furthermore, a publication note at the end, dated May 26, 1157, has an appended list of donors who supported the publication. The donors listed comprised two laymen, three monks, and two laywomen. The note gives an interesting glimpse of patterns of publication patronage in the Song, and indicates that women could be supporters and donors in their own right.

Mingzhou Tiantongshan Jue heshang zhenti jisong *(Portrait inscriptions and gatha by the venerable Jue of Mt. Tiantong in Mingzhou)*

This text is found in volume six of the *Hongzhi lu*.[68] It contains a smaller selection of portrait inscriptions very similar to what we saw above. One of its pieces is internally dated to 1136, but it has no preface nor any indication of when it was edited or published.[69]

No poem that would normally be classified as a *gatha* is included in the text, and it is possible that the title was meant for the whole volume six, encompassing the two texts below. In the Song edition of the *Hongzhi lu* all the pages in volume six are consecutively numbered with the same number of lines per page and characters per line; it seems clear that it was published as a unit.

Xia huo *(Cremation/funerary verses)*

This short section contains verses composed by Hongzhi that were chanted at the ritual lighting of a funeral pyre.[70] In a few cases the names of the monks being cremated are included, generally someone who held high monastic office. In most cases, nothing is noted. Several times it is simply stated that the verse was for the funeral of two, or sometimes three monks, to show that ordinary monks were often not given individual funeral ceremonies, but were cremated in groups of two or three. (It was not unusual in the Song that bodies would be stored for a long time before cremation or burial.) The last verses in this section were written for the occasion of entering the ashes of a cremated monk into a stupa. It is very possible that this section was originally published as a part of the previous section, since there is no separate colophon for it in the *Hongzhi lu.*

Jisong (Gatha)

Finally, in volume six of the *Hongzhi lu*, there is a section of *gatha*, or religious verses.[71] In actuality, however, this is a long section of various kinds of poems by Hongzhi, not just religious verse. Many of the poems are dedicated to a named person; the majority of those are for members of the clergy, but some are for laypersons. Some items in this section are dated internally, one in 1120 and two in 1124.[72]

Volume six of the *Hongzhi lu* seems in general to contain material from various stages of Hongzhi's career, and it seems likely that its parts were published together, sometime after his death.

Although the *Hongzhi lu* includes examples of most of the major genres of Chan literature in the Song, there are a few that it does not include. First of all, Hongzhi has no *pushuo* (general preaching) sermons. This seems to have been a form of sermon for which there were no specific rules, and which could be held whenever the abbot so chose. *Pushuo* sermons may not have been in common use at Hongzhi's time, but the form was made famous and popular by Dahui, who often used it to address laity.[73]

Also, the *Hongzhi lu* does not include any of Hongzhi's letters to disciples or lay supporters. Few Song Chan masters actually have letters included in their *yulu*, but many of Dahui's letters, especially those addressed to literati, have been preserved.[74] After Dahui, it became more common for Chan *yulu* to include letters.

The Production of Texts and the Success of the Chan School

As should be clear from the above examination on the *Hongzhi lu*, *yulu* as metagenre, what I here have called a *"yulu* collection," could encompass a number of very different genres or subgenres, several of which consisted of written compositions. In the *Hongzhi lu*, about half of the material consists of recorded sermons, while the other half are texts directly authored by Hongzhi. Other Song Chan masters also have substantial sections of directly authored material in their *yulu* collections.[75]

Nevertheless, the *yulu* proper remained emblematic and synecdochic of the metagenre, clearly indicating that the *yulu* proper was understood both to be central to the Chan school's self-definition and to be the genre that was the most suitable vehicle for the teachings of a Chan master. The *yulu* proper does seem a perfect medium for a tradition that tried to distance itself from reliance on the written word. It was ostensibly a product of students surreptitiously taking down the master's spontaneous, implicit, reluctantly delivered sermons and encounters with disciples. Although he knows words to be ultimately useless, the master nevertheless compassionately utters them in the hope that they might help someone in the audience see his own Buddha-mind. Written down and offered to the public in a *yulu*, the master is left without any responsibility for his own words, and the *yulu* becomes an authored text without any author at all.

Even in the case of genres of text that were directly written by the master, attempts to maintain a similar distance can be discerned. In Hongzhi's 1157 preface to his own collection of portrait eulogies that he had directly authored, he states, "The monk Shiyan (who edited the collection) asked me for a preface," thus subtly shifting the responsibility for the collection on to his disciple Shiyan.[76] Likewise, Puchong's preface to Hongzhi's collection of *fayu*, again, directly authored texts, describes how both interested laypersons and clergy would come and request *fayu* from Hongzhi. Puchong then states that Hongzhi responded however the occasion required, much like a mirror that reflects whatever is put before it.[77] Again the author is depicted as not really an agent. This sort of distancing is even reflected in Fu Zhirou's preface to Hongzhi's first *yulu* collection, when he says "someone recorded [Hongzhi's] subtle words, and came to me asking for a preface." This remark shifted the responsibility for his preface onto the unnamed disciple whose request he could not turn down.[78]

But the idealized and romantic image of a Chan teaching setting, where students secretly wrote down the words of the master in spite of his stern warnings not to cling to them, is hardly supported by the evidence. As is obvious from an examination of the contents of the *Hongzhi lu*, the Chan master here is not an unwilling and unwitting accomplice. First of all, the sermons that were recorded were given at specific occasions mandated by rules agreed upon within the Chan school. Most Chan masters probably spoke from carefully prepared notes, and it seems extremely likely that certain students were formally given the task of recording sermons, and that the master let them have access to his written notes.

Given social mores in premodern China, it is inconceivable that Hongzhi's students could have requested prefaces from specific persons for publications of his *yulu* without Hongzhi's prior approval. Hongzhi himself may very well have suggested what persons to approach. As we have seen, *yulu* proper by Hongzhi appear to have been published in 1131, 1132, 1137, and probably 1138. We must dismiss the notion that this was simply the work of his disciples and that Hongzhi had little or nothing to do with these publications. On the contrary, Hongzhi must have been very aware that when he was giving sermons he was addressing an audience that was far larger than the congregation he was facing. The success and popularity of his published *yulu* proper would have a decisive effect on his career.

Of course, there is abundant evidence that Hongzhi and other Chan masters at his time were not averse to putting their teachings down in writing themselves. Texts directly authored by Hongzhi seem to have been published in 1129, 1134, in the late 1140s, and in 1157. It is quite likely there were other publications too, of which the *Hongzhi lu* does not give evidence. This prolific publication schedule must be understood as a kind of ongoing communication and conversation that was extremely important for Hongzhi's relations with the wider monastic Chan community as well as with interested literati, and thus crucial for his own reputation and career.

In part, Hongzhi's publications must be seen in the context of the sectarian climate at his time. In 1134, the famous Linji master Dahui had started his attacks on Silent Illumination and, as I have discussed elsewhere, his target was the entire Caodong tradition of his day, including Hongzhi, a fact of which his contemporaries must have been very much aware.[79] Although Hongzhi is not on record as having defended himself directly, his published words eloquently reiterate his position. Evidence points to Hongzhi's older Dharma brother Zhenxie Qingliao as the impetus for Dahui's attacks on Silent Illumination, but it seems possible that Hongzhi's *yulu* published in 1131 and 1132 might also have fueled Dahui's ire. After all, the term "Silent Illumination" is not found in any of Qingliao's surviving record or writings; it was prominently used in Hongzhi's *Inscription on Silent Illumination*, which was probably included in the 1131 *yulu* collection.

However, Hongzhi's stream of publications was not, as one might suppose, produced primarily in debate with fellow Chan masters, or for the benefit of Buddhist monks undergoing Chan training. Certainly, monks and nuns studying Chan were eagerly perusing this literature. In fact, they were probably expected to be familiar with it, and most likely had access to early versions of *yulu* and other materials circulating in manuscript form. I argue, however, that the real audience for Song-dynasty Chan literature was the educated elite, many members of which enjoyed reading Chan works for entertainment and edification.

Hongzhi's successful early career moving from monastery to monastery, continuously being appointed to ever more prestigious abbacies, probably has much to do with the success of his circulated recorded sayings and writings. Through printed and hand-copied texts, Hongzhi was reaching a large audience and was able to build a reputation for his eloquent and accessible teaching that emphasized the perfect essence of human nature. The reputation he developed enabled him to garner considerable support from members of the educated elite. The important role of literati in Hongzhi's publication program is evident from the prefaces and postfaces that they wrote on several of his works. Such contributions from members of the educated elite implied an important endorsement and recommendation to fellow literati.

Hongzhi was not unique in using his published *yulu* and other texts as a means of communication with interested literati. Although we do not have nearly as extensive evidence of different publications during the lifetimes of other Chan masters, there are many indications that a number of them also had works published throughout their careers.[80] However reluctant producers of texts Chan masters might have presented themselves to be, they were very much aware that the publications associated with their names were absolutely crucial to their careers, and that the whole body of Chan literature was necessary for the success and survival of the Chan school.

In the Song, as in other periods of Chinese history, the secular elite and the imperial court had decisive power over appointments to abbacies, and controlled such things as the bestowal of honorific titles and purple robes (a prized emblem of clerical prominence). It was of supreme importance for a Chan master to be appointed to an abbacy at a public Chan monastery; in fact, only as an abbot at such a monastery could a person be considered a Chan master at all. At a public monastery, the Chan master would have an audience not only of talented and promising students but also of interested literati, who would often visit and even stay for longer periods. Perhaps even more important, only in the position of an abbot could a Chan master give transmission to his students and have his lineage continue. So although someone had received a transmission from a Chan master, he or she was not recognized as a true member of a transmission lineage and could not pass on the transmission until having received an appointment to the abbacy at a public monastery.[81]

So in the Song, the success of a Chan master was, to a large degree, dependent on his ability and willingness to participate in literati culture. The abbots who were in charge of the monasteries needed to maintain good connections with changing, powerful bureaucrats in order to insure the continued official recognition of their monastery. Good relations with high-ranking officials were also crucial for the personal ambitions of a Chan master, who may well have felt that as the abbot of a well-known monastery he would be able to spread his teachings more efficiently. But the less illustrious members of the literati also held great importance. Many were quite wealthy and could donate land, serfs, or money to the monastery. They would visit Chan masters for short stays at their temple compounds, and the presence of literati lent legitimacy and fame to the master with whom they were associating. Connections with well-known and even not so well-known literati were often pointed out in biographies of Chan masters, as a measure of their fame and great virtue. Song Chan masters usually had a classical education, could write poetry and elegant prose, and participated as equals in gatherings of literati.[82] Most Chan masters seem to have come from the same social group, as did the literati, of course; it is not surprising that they should have felt quite comfortable in this setting.

In Song book culture, Chan literature became part of the broad range of texts that were available to literati for study and enjoyment. Any Chan master who hoped to spread his Dharma successfully, facilitate the awakening of as many people as possible, as well as secure the continuation of his lineage, would do well to participate in this culture of published texts.

Although the literary production of individual masters was crucial for their own careers and lineages, the body of Chan literature was crucial for the success of the Chan school. It was very much due to the existence and authority of this literature that the Chan school became the school of Buddhism most favored by the elite in the Song. The *yulu* of famous Chan masters of the past became an important source of legitimacy and authority for the Chan school, and such works became kinds of holy literary shrines that entombed famous masters in their own words.

A word of caution is perhaps due here. Chan monks of the Chinese past are usually depicted as lofty individuals who sought the tranquillity of the mountains in faraway places, unconcerned with the dusty secular world. But although this was an image the Chan school itself perpetuated, the reality was probably always very different. We must not yield to the temptation of pronouncing Song Chan a faint, degenerate version of the great Chan of the Tang, and must remember that the picture of Tang Chan that today is available to us is largely a creation produced by the Song Chan school itself.

In conclusion, as was the case of all Song *yulu*, Hongzhi's words in the *Hongzhi lu* are multivalent and multilayered in their intention and meaning. When Hongzhi gave his sermons, he was addressing the monastics in front of him, some of whom were destined to become his heirs and one day have their own congregations; the educated lay people who might also be present; also the much larger audience of other Chan masters and Chan students, especially literati, who would eventually become readers of his publications. Hongzhi must also have known that people in a time distant from his might some day also read his words, although he probably could not have imagined the contemporary Western audience that is likely to buy a book of his translated works.

Then as now, the audience for a Chan master's recorded words was not primarily the dedicated practitioner, but rather those of us who derive enjoyment, edification, and respite from busy and demanding lives by spending few leisurely hours in the company of an enlightened master.

NOTES

1. See Susan Cherniack, "Book-culture and the Dynamics of Textual Transmission in Late Medieval China," *Harvard Journal of Asiatic Studies* 54 (1994): 5–126 (part 1). It should be noted that manuscript copies continued to be used, and more books existed in manuscripts than in printed form throughout the Song. Printed texts could reach a much larger audience, of course, and were far more likely to survive than manuscripts.

2. For information on both extant and lost Chan texts, see the monumental work by Shiina Kōyū, *Sō-Gen han zenseki no kenkyū* (Tokyo: Daitō, shuppansha, 1993).

3. This is best known in a four-phrase formula, in which the last two lines include "directly pointing at the human mind, seeing one's own nature Buddhahood is achieved." See the *Zuting shiyuan*, by Mu'an Shanqing, compiled in 1108, XZJ 113 66c.

4. See the *Zhizhai shulu jieti*, 12.13b, *Siku quanshu* (Taibei: Taiwan shangwu yinshu guan, 1983–), vol. 674. This note is repeated in Ma Duanlin's more famous *Wenxian tongkao*, 227. 15a, *Siku quanshu*, vol. 614; cited in Guo Peng, *Song Yuan fojiao* (Fuzhou: Fujian renmin chubanshe, 1981), p. 29.

5. I am using the work "genre" to denote a category of written text that is recognized as distinct from other categories of text by their creators and (at least most) readers. See Bob Hodge and Gunther R. Kress, *Social Semiotics* (Ithaca: Cornell University Press, 1988), p. 7: "[Genres] control the behaviour of producers of such texts, and the expectations of potential consumers." Cited in Daniel Chandler (1997), "An Introduction to Genre Theory," (online document) http://www.aber.ac.uk/media/Documents/intgenre/intgenre.html.

6. See the entries on the Chan masters Zhaozhou, Tiantai Deshao, and Huangbo, T 50.775c, 789b, 842c.

7. See the linguistic analysis and discussion of the occurrences in Christian Wittern, *Das Yulu des Chan-Buddhismus: die Entwicklung vom 8.–11. Jahrhundert am Beispiel des 28. Kapitels des "Jingde chuandenglu" (1004)*. Schweizer asiatische Studien, Monographien 31 (Bern: Peter Lang, 1998), pp. 53–55.

8. See T 51.196c2.

9. See the discussion in Daniel K. Gardner, "Modes of Thinking and Modes of Discourse in the Sung: Some Thoughts on the *Yü-lu* (Recorded Conversations) Texts," *Journal of Asian Studies* 50 no. 3 (1991): 574–603.

10. The most famous of all Chinese works, the *Lunyu*, can be said to be a *yulu*, since it purports to be a record of the words of Confucius.

11. There exists a relatively large amount of scholarship on the development of the *yulu*, which I will not attempt to summarize here. See the monumental Yanagida Seizan, "Goroku no rekishi: Zen bunken no seiritsu shiteki kenkyū," *Tōhō gakuhō* 57 (1985): 211–663; Yanagida, "The 'Recorded Sayings' Texts of Chinese Ch'an Buddhism," in Whalen Lai and Lewis Lancaster, eds., *Early Ch'an in China and Tibet*

(Berkeley: University of California Press, 1983), pp. 185–205; and the thoughtful discussion in Wittern, *Das Yulu des Chan-Buddhismus*.

12. See, for example, Ishii Shūdō, *Daijō butten, Chūgoku Nihon hen*, Zen no go-roku 12 (Tokyo: Chūōkōronsha, 1992), pp. 403–409, which ultimately concludes that any Chan text can be called *yulu*.

13. Wittern, *Das Yulu des Chan-Buddhismus*, pp. 77–85.

14. Hongzhi was his posthumous title. In his own time he was known mostly as Tiantong Zhengjue, or Tiantong Jue, but since he is now best known as Hongzhi I will use this name as a general term of reference.

15. Held at the Senpuku Temple in Oita prefecture. The text is reproduced in Ishii Shūdō, ed., *Wanshi roku* (Tokyo: Meisho fukyūkai, 1988), vol. 1.

16. A number of Song editions, and Japanese *gozan* editions (usually copies of Song editions) of various *yulu* collections are still extant, however. A comprehensive study of their publication data may yield interesting information.

17. It is in four fascicles and entitled *Mingzhou Tiantong Jingde chansi Hongzhi Jue Chanshi yulu*, in the *Ming you xuzangjing*, box 7. This edition is reproduced in Ishii, *Wanshi roku*, pp. 46–516.

18. See T 48.1–121. It was retitled *Wanshi zenji kōroku* (Ch. *Hongzhi chanshi guanglu*). For a discussion of different Japanese editions of the *Hongzhi lu*, see Ishii Shūdō, "*Wanshi kōroku kō*," *Komazawa daigaku bukkyōgakubu kenkyū kiyō* 30 (1972): 107–140.

19. Ishii Shūdō has done extensive research on the *Hongzhi lu*. See his "*Wanshi kōroku kō*" and *Wanshi roku*, which in addition to a reproduction of the Senpukuji text and several Japanese editions and commentaries on the *Hongzhi lu*, also contains an article by him. In the following I will refer to the Song text of the *Hongzhi lu* as found in Ishii's edition with corresponding page numbers. For ease of reference I will also include the page numbers of the Taishō edition of Hongzhi's recorded sayings.

20. See Morten Schlütter, "Silent Illumination, Kung-an Introspection, and the Competition for Lay Patronage in Sung-Dynasty Ch'an," in Peter N. Gregory and Daniel Getz, eds., *Buddhism in the Sung* (Honolulu: University of Hawai'i Press, 1999), pp. 109–147.

21. See ibid., and Morten Schlütter, "The Twelfth-Century Caodong Tradition as the Target of Dahui's Attacks on Silent Illumination," *Komazawa Daigaku zengaku kenkyūjo nenpō* 5 (1995): 53–114. For a discussion of Dahui's notion of *kanhua* Chan, see Robert E. Buswell, Jr., "The 'Short-cut' Approach of *K'an-hua* Meditation: The Evolution of a Practical Subitism in Chinese Ch'an Buddhism," Peter N. Gregory, ed., in *Sudden and Gradual Approaches to Enlightenment in Chinese Thought* (Honolulu: University of Hawai'i Press, 1987), pp. 321–377.

22. In the following I draw on three Song-dynasty biographies of Hongzhi: Wang Boxiang, *Chishi Hongzhi chanshi xingye ji* in *Hongzhi lu*, pp. 316–318 and T 48.119b–121a; Zhou Kui, *Hongzhi Chanshi Miaoguang taming* in *Liangzhe jinshi zhi* 9.5a–8b, in *Shike shiliao xinbian*, 14.10,392–10,393; and Zhao Lingjin, *Chishi Hongzhi chanshi houlu xu*, in *Tiantong si zhi*, 1851 edition, 8.1a–2b.

23. See, respectively, the *Hongzhi lu*, p. 119 (the date here is actually not readable

in the reproduction, but is reported by Ishii in the table on p. 530), p. 322, and pp. 202 and 238.

24. *Hongzhi lu*, p. 391. See also the table comparing various editions on pp. 530–531.

25. See Ishii, "*Wanshi kōroku kō.*"

26. *Hongzhi lu*, pp. 1–80 and T 48.1.1–18, and 8.99–101.

27. *Hongzhi lu*, p. 1. This preface is not included in the Taishō edition.

28. *Suichutang shumu*, p. 55a, in *Siku quanshu* vol. 674. Quoted in Shiina Kōyū, "Sō-Gendai no shomoku ni okeru zenseki shiryō (ni)," *Sōtōshū kenkyū kiyō* 8 (1976): 76. Unfortunately, it is not known when the catalog was written.

29. See the Chinese text in Kagamishima Genryū, et al., *Yakuchū zennen shingi* (Tokyo: Sōtōshū shūmuchō, 1972). It is expertly translated into English in Yifa, *The Origins of Buddhist Monastic Codes in China: An Annotated Translation and Study of the Chanyuan Qinggui* (Honolulu: University of Hawai'i Press, 2002).

30. See *Hongzhi lu*, pp. 5–7. 2–4 and T 48. 1b8–2a2.

31. See the text in Kagamishima, *Zennen shingi*, p. 253, translated in Yifa, *The Origins of Buddhist Monastic Codes.*

32. See *Hongzhi lu*, p. 31.91, p. 39.114 and T 48.8a25 and 10b08.

33. See the *Chanyuan qinggui* in Kagamishima, *Zennen shingi*, p. 253, translated in Yifa, *The Origins of Buddhist Monastic Codes*, p. 214 and *Hongzhi lu*, p. 5.2; *Hongzhi guanglu*, p. 1b11. However, the *Chanyuan qinggui* states that the envoys inviting the new abbot bring the robe, whereas in the *yulu* from Puzhao it seems to be Qingliao who gives Hongzhi the robe.

34. See *Hongzhi lu*, pp. 2–3.1; this part is not included in the Taishō edition. The *kaitang* ceremony is mentioned, but not described, in the *Chanyuan qinggui*; see Kagamishima, *Zennen shingi*, p. 256.

35. See *Hongzhi lu*, pp. 32–34.91 and T 48.8b08.

36. See the *Chanyuan qinggui* in Kagamishima, *Zennen shingi*, p. 75, translated in Yifa, *The Origins of Buddhist Monastic Codes*, p. 136.

37. See the *Chanyuan qinggui* in Kagamishima, *Zennen shingi*, p. 71, translated in Yifa, *The Origins of Buddhist Monastic Codes*, p. 135.

38. See the exhaustive list and discussion in Ishii, *Wanshi roku*, pp. 537–540.

39. *Hongzhi lu*, pp. 50–63 and T 48.14–18.

40. See XZJ 113.236 b. Cited in Yifa, *The Origins of Buddhist Monastic Codes*, p. 138.

41. See the *Chanyuan qinggui* in Kagamishima, *Zennen shingi*, pp. 79–80, translated in Yifa, *The Origins of Buddhist Monastic Codes*, p. 140.

42. See, for example, the many examples in Xutang Zhiyu's (1185–1269) *yulu* collection, T 47.984b–1057c.

43. *Hongzhi lu*, pp. 72–80 and T 48.99–101.

44. T 48.100a–b.

45. *Hongzhi lu*, pp. 81–149 and T 48.2.18–27, and 3.27–35.

46. XZJ 124.249d–257b.

47. See *Chanlin baoxuan* 1036b–c, where Dahui's disciple, Wan'an Daoyan (1094–1164), is cited stating that the practice of *songgu* began with Fenyang Shanzhao

(947–1024) (who is credited with having revived a moribund Linji school) and shortly after was popularized by Xuedou. Xuedou's epitaph from 1065 mentions that separate editions of both his *songgu* and his *niangu* were in circulation at the time. See T 47.713a01.

48. See XZJ 124.232b–238a and XZJ 124.249d–257b.

49. See, respectively, XZJ, 118.591, T 47.798, T 47.850c. Dahui was also the co-author of an unusual "double commentary" *songgu* that still exists as a separate work; see the *Donglin heshang Yunmen anzhu songgu*, XZJ 118.795–822.

50. Both collections are now lost. See Shiina, *Sō-Gen han zenseki*, pp. 633 and 617.

51. See the *Congrong lu* in T 48.226–292, and the *Biyan lu* in T 48.139–225. Both collections have been translated; see Thomas Cleary, *Book of Serenity* (Hudson: Lindisfarne, 1990), and J. C. Cleary and Thomas Cleary, *The Blue Cliff Record* (Boston: Shambhala, 1977).

52. See XZJ 117.321–391.

53. This work was recently rediscovered. See Shiina Kōyū, "Genhan 'Shikeroku' to sono shiryō," *Komazawa daigaku bukkyōgakubu ronshū* 10 (1979): 227–256.

54. *Hongzhi lu*, pp. 151–235 and T 48.4.35–57, although the preface has been moved to the front of the Taishō edition, p. 1.

55. See the table in Ishii, *Wanshi roku*, pp. 530–531.

56. *Hongzhi lu*, pp. 237–296 and T 48. 5. 57–73.

57. *Hongzhi lu*, p. 237a7 and T 48. 57b18.

58. *Hongzhi lu*, pp. 297–315 and T 48. 6. 73–78.

59. See the discussion in Ishii, *Wanshi roku*, p. 534.

60. *Hongzhi lu*, p. 297 and T 48. 73.

61. For an English translation of this collection, see Taigen Daniel Leighton with Yi Wu, *Cultivating the Empty Field: The Silent Illumination of Zen Master Hongzhi* (San Francisco: North Point, 1991).

62. See T 47. 775–788 and T 47. 890–916.

63. *Hongzhi lu*, pp. 316–322 and T 48. 9. 119–121.

64. *Hongzhi lu*, pp. 323–391 and T 48. 9. 101–119.

65. *Hongzhi lu*, p. 326 and T 48. 101c.

66. For a thorough discussion of the nature and function of portrait inscriptions to which I am here indebted, see T. Griffith Foulk and Robert H. Sharf, "On the Ritual Use of Ch'an Portraiture in Medieval China," *Cahiers d'Extrême-Asie* 7 (1993–1994): 149–219.

67. See, for example, the *yulu* of Foyan Qingyuan (1067–1120), XZJ 118. 554a–555a, and Dahui's *yulu*, T 48. 860b–863a.

68. *Hongzhi lu*, pp. 393–406 and T 48. 7. 78–82.

69. *Hongzhi lu*, p. 393 and T 48. 79a.

70. *Hongzhi lu*, pp. 407–412 and T 48. 7. 82–84.

71. *Hongzhi lu*, pp. 414–467 and T 48. 8, 84–99.

72. *Hongzhi lu*, p. 427 and T 48. 88a; *Hongzhi lu*, pp. 424 and 445, and T 48. 86c and 92c.

73. T 47. 890–916, Ishii, *Daijō butten, Chūgoku Nihon hen*, Zen goroku 12, pp. 91–242; Ishii Shūdō, "Yakuchū "Daie Fukaku Zenji hōgo (zoku) (jō)," *Komazawa*

daigaku Zenkenkyūjo nenpō 4 (1993): 20–62; and Ishii Shūdō, "Yakuchū "Daie Fukaku Zenji hōgo (zoku) (ka)," *Komazawa daigaku Zenkenkyūjo nenpō* 5 (1994): 84–127. See also the discussion in Miriam Levering, "Ta-hui and Lay Buddhists: Ch'an Sermons on Death," in David W. Chappell, ed., *Buddhist and Taoist Practice in Medieval Chinese Society*. Buddhist and Taoist Studies 2, (Honolulu: University of Hawai'i Press, 1987), pp. 181–206.

74. T 47. 916–943, and Araki Kengo, *Daie sho* (Tokyo: Chikuma shobō, 1969).

75. See, for example, Yuanwu Keqin's *yulu* in T 47, where pp. 714–775 contain *yulu* proper, and pp. 775–810 is authored material; and Dahui's *yulu*, where pp. 811–889 is *yulu* proper and pp. 890–956 is authored materials.

76. *Hongzhi lu*, p. 323 and T 48. 101a–b.

77. *Hongzhi lu*, p. 297 and T 48. 73b–c.

78. *Hongzhi lu*, p. 1 (not included in the Taishō edition).

79. See Schlütter, "The Twelfth-Century Caodong Tradition."

80. For example, among Chan masters around Hongzhi's time we have evidence that Qingliao (1088–1151) had a work published in 1134; see Schlütter, "The Twelfth-Century Caodong Tradition." Also, Dahui had a *yulu* published in 1147; see Ishii Shūdō, "Daie goroku no kisoteki kenkyū (jō)," *Komazawa Daigaku bukkyōgakubu kenkyū kiyō* 31 (1973): 283–292. Wuzu Fayan (1024?–1104) had a *yulu* published in 1098; see *Zengaku daijiten*, p. 349. Finally, Yuanwu Keqin (1063–1135) had *yulu* published in 1133; see *Zengaku daijiten*, p. 1081. It is also common that funerary inscriptions written shortly after a master's death will note that *yulu* and others writings by the master were in circulation.

81. See Schlütter, "The Functions and Meanings of Lineage in Song-Dynasty Buddhism," unpublished paper.

82. For a discussion see Robert M. Gimello, "Marga and Culture: Learning, Letters and Liberation in Northern Sung Ch'an," in Robert E. Buswell, Jr., and Robert M. Gimello, eds., *Paths to Liberation: The Marga and Its Transformations in Buddhist Thought*. Studies in East Asian Buddhism 7 (Honolulu: University of Hawai'i Press, 1992), pp. 371–437.

7

The *Wu-men kuan* (J. *Mumonkan*): The Formation, Propagation, and Characteristics of a Classic Zen Kōan Text

Ishii Shūdō

Translated by Albert Welter

Motivations for Researching the *Wu-men kuan*

The *Wu-men kuan* text is a record of the lectures from the Sung dynasty Lin-chi (J. Rinzai) Ch'an monk, Wu-men Hui-k'ai.[1] It is a kōan collection containing forty-eight "cases." In the monastic halls of Japan's Rinzai sect, one often sees a prominently displayed notice announcing a "Lecture on the *Wu-men kuan*," the *Wu-men kuan* being one of the most widely read texts in the Rinzai sect. Nor is it the case that the *Wu-men kuan* has no bearing on the Sōtō (C. Ts'ao-t'ung) sect in Japan. According to the recently published work of Ishikawa Rikizan, *Zenshūsōden shiryō no kenkyū* (Research on materials concerning transmission inheritance in the Zen school), the *Wu-men kuan* was deeply implicated in the so-called "heresy incident."[2]

Two incidents occurred during the Edo period, the first in 1649 and the second in 1653. The first involved the expulsion of monks responsible for undermining Sōtō doctrine connected to the three major Sōtō temples in the Kantō region.[3] The second involved a similar expulsion of monks associated with Kasuisaiji, Sōjiji, and Eiheiji temples. Both incidents involved the impermissible study of heretical doctrines from outside the teachings established by the

Sōtō school. This study of heretical doctrines undermined Sōtō teaching and violated the system for determining the relationship between head and branch temples, and the rules of etiquette. As a result of the violation, numerous monks, beginning with Bannan Eishū (1591–1654), were expelled. The *Wu-men kuan* was one of the texts singled out as an object of criticism during the "heresy incident"; Bannan Eishū was expelled for authoring the *Mumonkan shū*, a commentary on the *Wu-men kuan*, at this time.[4] Bannan was the person who revived Kōshōji Temple, originally founded by Dōgen and located in Fukakusa, by relocating it to its present site at Uji. Bannan passed away in 1654. After his passing, Manzan Dōhaku (1636–1715) carried out a full-scale revival of the Sōtō school. Manzan issued the *Mumon ekai goroku* (The recorded sayings of Wu-men Hui-k'ai), where he commented as follows: "After the *Pi-yen ji* (or *Pi-yen lu*, Blue cliff anthology), a great number of works praised kōan. Yet, the only one who resides on the path of liberation and reveals the fundamental source of their teaching is Wu-men Hui-k'ai. I know this from reading the forty-eight-case *Wu-men kuan*."[5]

As indicated here, Manzan, who is also known as the patriarch who revived the Sōtō school, held out extraordinarily high praise for the *Wu-men kuan*. The aforementioned work by Ishikawa Rikizan discusses in detail the important status that kōan in the *Wu-men kuan* held in the Sōtō school during the Edo period. Knowing that Sōtō school doctrine during the Edo period was like this, it seems clear that the "heresy incident" was not simply a matter concerning a rejection of the *Wu-men kuan* text, but must be viewed from other perspectives.

Although the *Wu-men kuan* was, on occasion, the object of criticism in the history of the Sōtō school, it was a frequently read text in the Rinzai school along with the sacred scripture, the *Pi-yen lu*. In the Sōtō school the *Ts'ung-jung lu* is referred to along with the *Pi-yen lu*. Because Wan-sung Hsing-hsiu (1166–1246) praised such things as the one hundred cases in Hung-chih Cheng-chüeh's (1091–1157) *Hung-chih sung-ku*, it was referred to as a fundamental sacred text in the Sōtō school. Although he was the founder of Sōtō, Dōgen never denied the role of the kōan, which was used to instruct Zen practitioners in the history of the Sōtō school. With the continued influence of the Rinzai school, the *Wu-men kuan* was a frequently read text in the Sōtō school as well.

In recent years, studies on the vernacular use of language have flourished in Chinese studies, and new problems have emerged concerning the traditional reading of Ch'an "recorded sayings" (*yü-lu*, J. *goroku*) texts. As an example of this, there is Iriya Yoshitaka's three-volume annotated translation of the *Pi-yen lu*.[6] Iriya's reading is completely different from the Japanese rendering of the Chinese (*kundoku*) by Asahina Sōgen, former administrative director of Engaku Temple.[7] There is also an annotated translation of the *Wu-men kuan* based on a new Japanese rendering of the Chinese by Hirata Takashi.[8] Building on the results of this previous work, Nishimura Eshin recently published an annotated translation of the *Wu-men kuan*.[9] In a review that I wrote on Nishimura's translation, I made a strong case for research into the hitherto completely unindicated sources for the *Wu-men kuan*'s contents.[10] I noted for the first time that the *Tsung-men t'ung-yao chi* was a source for the *Wu-men kuan*'s contents, and indicated the need for a reevaluation of previous explanations that failed to take this into account. The *Tsung-men t'ung-yao chi* had a huge influence over Ch'an in the Sung dynasty, and is a text whose importance cannot be disregarded.[11] The results of my studies showed that references to the *Tsung-men t'ung-yao chi* appear throughout the *Wu-men kuan*, and I am of the opinion that the *Tsung-men t'ung-yao chi* also exerted a large influence on the way the *Wu-men kuan* should be read.

The following list indicates the place occupied by the *Tsung-men t'ung-yao chi* among the important Ch'an texts of the Sung dynasty.

1004	Ch'eng-t'ien Tao-yüan compiles the *Ching-te ch'uan-teng lu*.
1036	Li Tsun-hsü compiles the *T'ien-sheng kuang-teng lu*.
1038	Yuan-ch'en compiles the *Hsüeh-tou hsien ho-shang ming-chüeh ta-shih sung-ku ku-chi*.
1052	Hsüeh-tou Ch'ung-hsien passes away at age seventy-three.
1093	Layman Mao-shan, also known as Yao Tzu, writes a preface for the *Tsung-men t'ung-yao chi* (contained in Eizan Library and the National Diet Library).
1100	Chien-ch'i Tsung-yung writes the *Tsung-men t'ung-yao chi chi* (contained in Eizan Library and the National Diet Library). [Did Yü Chang-li issue the first publication of the *Tsung-men t'ung-yao chi* at this time?]
1101	Fo-kuo Wei-po compiles the *Chien-chung ching-kuo hsü-teng lu*.
1111	Yuan-Wu K'o-ch'in, living at the Ling-ch'üan Cloister on Mount Chia in Li-chou, lectures on the *Pi-yen lu*.
1125	Hung-chih Cheng-chüeh, after having lived at the Ta-sheng p'u-chao Temple in Szu-chou, writes the *Hung-chih sung-ku*.
1133	Hui-tse of the T'ien-ning Temple in Fu-t'ien reissues the *Tsung-men t'ung-yao chi*. Keng Yen-hsi writes the *Fu-t'ien hsin-k'ai tsung-men t'ung-yao hsü* (Tōyō bunko).
1135	Szu-ming Szu-chien republishes the *Tsung-men t'ung-yao chi*. Layman Pen-jan, also known as Cheng Ch'en, writes a preface for the *Tsung-men t'ung-yao chi*.
1146	Layman I-an of Mount Lu, also known as Liu, republishes the *Tsung-men t'ung-yao chi*.
1157	Layman Ta-yin, also known as Ch'en Shih, compiles the *Ta-tsang i-lan chi*.
1179	The Szu-ming edition is reissued. The imperial prince, Wei Wang, writes a postscript for the *Tsung-men t'ung-yao chi*.
1183	Hui-weng Wu-ming compiles the *Tsung-men lien-teng hui-yao*.
1202	Cheng-shou of Thunder Hermitage compiles the *Chia-t'ai p'u-teng lu*.

1224   Layman Shen Jan writes the preface for the *Ts'ung-jung lu*.

1228   Wu-men Hui-k'ai compiles the *Wu-men kuan*.

1229   The *Wu-men kuan* is published.

1230   Wu-men Hui-k'ai lectures on the *Wu-men kuan* at Jui-yen Temple in Ming-chou at the invitation of Wu-liang Tsung-shou.

1245   Meng Kung writes a postscript for the republication of the *Wu-men kuan*.

1246   Layman An-wan (Cheng Ch'ing-chih) writes the *Ti ssu-shih-chiu yu*.

1252   Hui-ming compiles the *Wu-teng hui-yuan*.

As related in a previous study, I encountered the connection between the *Tsung-men t'ung-yao chi* and *Wu-men kuan* on three noteworthy occasions.[12] The first time was around thirty years ago, when I wrote an article on the Sung edition of the *Tsung-men t'ung-yao chi* contained in the library of the Tōyō bunko.[13] The second time occurred over a two year period between 1981 and 1982, when I studied under Yanagida Seizan at Kyoto University's Humanities Research Institute. The importance of the *Tsung-men t'ung-yao chi* as a source for Dōgen's *Mana Shōbōgenzō* (*Shōbōgenzō*), written in Chinese, generally referred to as *Sanbyakusoku* [three hundred cases]) became clear to me at that time.[14] The third time occurred during my aforementioned investigation of the sources for the *Wu-men kuan*, when it emerged that the *Tsung-men t'ung-yao chi* was the source.

Previously, the text of the *Tsung-men t'ung-yao chi* that I used was contained in the library of the Tōyō bunko, a Sung edition issued in the third year of the *shao-hsing* era (1133). Shiina Kōyū introduced a different Sung edition, the *Tsung-men t'ung-yao hsü-chi* contained in the National Diet Library and an edition of the *Tsung-men t'ung-yao chi* contained in the library of Eizan bunko.[15] To my surprise, these editions were published in 1093, forty years before the Sung edition that I had been using. The five lamp history texts (*Wu-teng*) of Ch'an Buddhism were formed in order, starting with the *Ching-te ch'uan-teng lu* (1004), and continuing with the *T'ien-sheng kuang-teng lu* (1036), *Chien-chung ching-kuo hsü-teng lu* (1101), *Tsung-men lien-teng hui-yao* (1183), and the *Chia-t'ai p'u-teng lu* (1202). As a result, the *Tsung-men t'ung-yao chi* had already been issued when the *Chien-chung ch'ing-kuo hsü-teng lu* was published in 1101. This makes the *Tsung-men t'ung-yao chi* the first important Ch'an text after the *Ching-te ch'uan-teng lu* and its successor, the *T'ien-sheng kuang-teng lu*.

A special feature of the *T'ien-sheng kuang-teng lu* is its inclusion of numerous materials relating to the Lin-chi faction. Although this represented a departure from the *Ching-te ch'uan-teng lu*'s emphasis on the Fa-yen faction, there is hardly any difference in characteristics between the two records. Nor is there a great time difference between the publication of the two records. The most conspicuous difference between the two works is the abundant inclusion of "recorded sayings" contents in the *T'ien-sheng kuang-teng lu* for Ma-tsu Tao-i, Pai-chang Huai-hai, Huang-po Hsi-yun, and Lin-chi I-hsüan, later compiled into a separate text, the *Ssu-chia yu-lu*. The Sung transmission of the lamp history (*teng-shih*) text that follows the *T'ien-sheng kuang-teng lu* is the *Chien-chung ching-kuo hsü-teng lu*, but because the *Tsung-men t'ung-yao chi* was formed prior to it, we must recognize even more than before, the *Tsung-men t'ung-yao chi*'s fundamental importance for understanding this formative period in the development of Ch'an.

When the Northern Sung ended in 1127 and the era of the Southern Sung dawned, Ch'an made the Southern Sung capital Hang-chou (Lin-an) its center. It came to flourish there, and the institution of the Five Mountains (designations for the five leading Ch'an monasteries) was established. The Ch'an school developed around the Five Mountains in present-day Che-chiang prefecture. As indicated in my previous article, the *Ching-te ch'uan-teng lu* and the *Tsung-men t'ung-yao chi* were continually published in the Che-chiang region as two works representative of Ch'an.[16]

The fact that they were issued together in this way is extremely interesting. It is clear that Ch'an monks at that time read these two texts with very great frequency. There are further matters surrounding the circumstances of their publication. Concerning the *Pi-yen lu*, when Yü'an-Wu K'o-ch'in lectured on it while living on Mount Chia in 1111, he offered critical acclaim for the one hundred-case *Hsüeh-tou sung-ku*. In fact, in a portion of this critical acclaim, the *Tsung-men t'ung-yao chi* is quoted.[17] As indicated previously, the *Tsung-men t'ung-yao chi* was also quoted in the *Wu-teng hui-yuan*, compiled in 1252.[18] Disregarding the *Tsung-men t'ung-yao chi* renders impossible the study of tendencies in Ch'an from the period of the latter half of the eleventh through the thirteenth centuries.

It is interesting to note that the *Wu-men kuan* has not been read in China to the extent that it has in Japan. My own interest in the *Wu-men kuan* is to learn the reason why such an overwhelming concern for this work has existed throughout Japanese Zen history. This is one of the concerns addressed in the present study.

The Formation Process of the *Wu-men kuan*

Among the publication and compilation of Ch'an works in the Sung dynasty, the *Wu-men kuan* was compiled in the first year of the *shao-ting* era (1228). The *Wu-men kuan* was compiled the year after Dōgen returned from China. As stated above, both Dōgen and the *Wu-men kuan* are cited in the *Tsung-men t'ung-yao chi*. I have already considered the degree of correspondence between the *Tsung-men t'ung-yao chi* and *Wu-men kuan* in my review of Nishimura's translation of the *Wu-men kuan* mentioned above, and will summarize the details here.

Let us begin by looking at the activities of Wu-men Hui-k'ai, the compiler of the *Wu-men kuan*, in relation to the compilation of the *Wu-men kuan*. The primary source for the biography of Wu-men Hui-k'ai is the six-chapter *Tseng-chi hsü ch'uan-teng lu*, compiled by Nan-shih Wen-hsiu in the Ming dynasty.[19] Wu-men's Dharma lineage is as follows:

> Fen-yang Shan-chao (947–1024) → Tz'u-ming Ch'u-yuan (986–1039) → Yang-ch'i Fang-hui (992–1049) → Pai-yün Shou-jui (1025–1072) → Wu-tsu Fa-yen (?–1104) → K'ai-fu Tao-ning (1053–1113) → Yueh-an Shan-kuo (1079–1152) → Ta-hung Tsu-cheng (dates unknown) → Yueh-lin Shih-kuan (1143–1217) → Wu-men Hui-k'ai (1183–1260) → Hsin-ti Chüeh-hsin (1207–1298).

This is the Dharma lineage of the Yang-ch'i branch of the Lin-chi faction. Among the members of the Yang-ch'i branch, Yang-ch'i's "grandson" Wu-tsu Fa-yen had a particularly large influence on later developments.[20] Among Wu-tsu's disciples, three achieved fame: Fo-kuo K'o-ch'in (1063–1135), the compiler of the *Pi-yen lu*; Fo-chien Hui-ch'in (1059–1117); and Fo-yen Ch'ing-yuan (1067–1120). Since they all shared the honorific name "Fo" (Buddha), they were commonly referred to as the "three buddhas." Wu-men Hui-k'ai is in the lineage descended from K'ai-fu Tao-ning, a fellow practitioner of these "three buddhas."

Hui-k'ai was born in Liang-chu, in Hang-chou (Che-chiang Prefecture). His family name was Liu. His mother had the family name Sung. He inherited the Dharma of Yueh-lin Shih-kuan. Hui-k'ai's activities at this time are described in the *Tseng-chi hsü ch'uan-teng lu* as follows.

> [Hui-k'ai] paid respects to Monk Kung of T'ien-lung, and accepted Monk Kung as his teacher. He practiced with Yüeh-lin at Wan-shou [Temple] in Su[-chou]. Yüeh-lin had him read the account of [Chao-chou's] *Wu* (J. *Mumonkan*). Even after six years, [Hui-k'ai] was far from penetrating its meaning. Thereupon, he summoned his will and resolved to sever his doubts, saying "I will give up sleeping even if it destroys me." Whenever he felt perplexed, he walked down the corridor and struck his head against a pillar. One day, while standing near the lecturer's seat [in the Dharma hall], he was suddenly awakened when he heard the sound of the drum [calling the monks] for the recitation of the monastic rules (*chai*). He composed a verse, which said:
>
> With the sun shining and the sky blue, the sound of thunder peels open the eyeballs of the earth's living beings.
> The myriad phenomena existing between heaven and earth all prostrate themselves;

Mount Sumeru leaps to his feet and dances the dance "three
stages."[21]

The following day, he entered the master's room seeking confirmation for his attainment. Yueh-lin said in an off-hand manner,
"Whenever I look at kindred spirits (*shen*), I see nothing but demons
(*kuei*)." Hui-k'ai then shouted. Yueh-lin also shouted. Hui-k'ai then
shouted again. In this way, his awakening was confirmed.[22]

When we look at the process whereby Wu-men practices meditation, experiences awakening, and inherits the Dharma, we can understand why his
teacher Yüeh-lin Shih-kuan plays such a large role in the *Wu-men kuan*. The
episode involving Chao-chou's *Wu* that Yüeh-lin gave to Wu-men is one of the
most famous kōans, well-known to virtually everyone. When a monk asked
Chao-chou Ts'ung-shen: "Does a dog also have the Buddha-nature?" Chao-chou
responded: "*Wu!* (No)" In the *Wu-men kuan*, this *Wu* does not indicate the
relative *wu* in contrast to *yu*, but refers to absolute *Wu* transcending these
relative distinctions. In this way, the episode involving Chao-chou's *Wu* serves
as the stereotypical kōan case. In another version of this experience of enlightenment, Wu-men was given this kōan by his teacher Yüeh-lin. For six years,
he grappled with it. His reported actions during this period have counterparts
in other sources, involving other masters. The action of "striking one's head
against a pillar" is also attributed to Chung-feng Ming-pen (1263–1323) in
Hsüeh-lou Chu-hung's *Ch'an-kuan tse-chin*. This episode brings to mind the
action of "picking up a chisel and jabbing oneself" attributed to Tz'u-ming
Ch'u-yuan (986–1039) in the same source. This is an example of the behavior
prior to Wu-men.[23] The great formulator of the Edo-period Rinzai sect, Hakuin
(1685–1768), was inspired upon reading this account of "picking up a chisel
and jabbing oneself." It is said that he became devoted to his practice, jabbing
himself with a chisel, to awaken himself whenever he felt drowsy. Not to be
outdone by the account of "jabbing oneself with a chisel," Wu-men struck his
head against a pillar to keep awake as he grappled with the episode involving
Chao-chou's *Wu*. Then, one day he heard the sound of the drum and achieved
great awakening, commemorating the occasion with a four-line verse reflecting
his awakened state. On the day following his great awakening, he entered the
master's room and was told by the master, "Where have I met such an idiot?"
Wu-men then let out an angry shout. Yüeh-lin also responded with an angry
shout. In response to this, Wu-men retorted with another angry shout. The
master and disciple formed a single entity here. Wu-men's awakening was
acknowledged, and he inherited the Dharma.

There is a "recorded sayings" (*yü-lu*) text for Wu-men's teacher, Yüeh-lin
Shih-kuan.[24] At the end of it, there is a record of Yüeh-lin's tomb inscrip-

tion, where it states the following: "When [students] went to [the master's] room, [Yüeh-lin] kept them off guard with his extraordinarily sharp verbal attacks, so they would not go near him."[25] We know from this that Yüeh-lin was especially hard on his students and very strict with lazy practitioners, to the extent of being unapproachable. Wu-men was thus nurtured by this master, Yüeh-lin.

Afterward, in the eleventh year of *chia-ting* (1218), Wu-men succeeded the founding abbot Yüeh-lin at the Pao-yin yu-tz'u Ch'an Temple in Hu-chou. Wu-men's first appointment was serving after Yüeh-lin, as the second abbot. From there he succeeded the denoted as abbot at the following locations. T'ien-ning Ch'an Temple and Huang-lung ch'ung-en Ch'an Temple in Lung-hsing District; Ling-yen hsien-ch'in ch'ung-pao Ch'an Temple in P'ing River District; the Ts'ui-yen kuang-hua Ch'an Temple in Lung-hsing District; again at the Huang-lung ch'ung-en Ch'an Temple; P'u-ji Ch'an Temple on Mount Chiao in Chen River District; K'ai-yuan Ch'an Temple in P'ing River District; Pao-ning Ch'an Temple in Chien-k'ang District, until he became abbot of Hu-kuo jen-wang Ch'an Temple in Hang-chou, in the sixth year of *ch'un-yu* (1246).[26] Wu-men instructed Ch'an practitioners at these important Ch'an temples successively, and in his final years is said to have lived at a hermitage on the shores of West Lake (in Hang-chou).

On one occasion, Wu-men was invited by Emperor Li-tsung (r. 1224–1264) to lecture at the Hsuan-te Pavilion in the imperial palace. Whenever he was called on to pray for rain, it is said that rain suddenly fell. As a result of these achievements, Wu-men was awarded a gold-threaded Dharma-robe and the honorific title Fo-yen (Buddha-eye) Ch'an Master. It is recorded that he forecast his own death on the seventh day of the fourth month of the first year of *ching-ting* (1260) with the parting verse: "With emptiness, there is no birth; with emptiness, there is no death. If one realizes emptiness, one is no different from emptiness." He was seventy-eight years of age. Among disciples who inherited his Dharma are Hsi-an Tsung, Patriarch Wu-ch'uan, Hsia-lü Wu-chien, and Layman Fang-niu Yu, who are well known, and Shinichi Kakushin, who is famous in Japan.

The *Wu-men kuan* makes it clear, however, that Wu-men became accomplished prior to his first appointment as an abbot of temple practitioners. Wu-men's own preface to the *Wu-men kuan* states as follows:

The mind the Buddha spoke of is the fundamental source (*tsung*); gatelessness (*Wu-men*) is the Dharma-gate. If it is gateless, how do you pass through it? Have you not heard it said that "nothing entering through the gate is valued by the family; whatever is obtained through circumstance will not last." In the summer of the first year of *chao-ting* (1228), I, Hui-k'ai, headed the congregation at Lung-hsiang Temple in Tung-chia. Because of the frequent requests of the monks [for instruction], I proceeded to take cases (*kung-an*) [involving] past masters, using them as brickbats to batter the gate, guiding the students in accordance with their capabilities. Eventually they were recorded, inadvertently becoming an anthology. They have not been arranged according to any particular order, altogether there are forty-eight cases. It is generally referred to as the *Wu-men kuan* (Gateless gate).[27]

As stated here, Wu-men completed a compilation of forty-eight ancient cases while chief meditator (*shou-tso*) at the Lung-hsiang Temple. He relates that the forty-eight cases should not be considered in order. In an announcement offered to the current emperor Li-tsung, Wu-men also stated: "The fifth day of the first month of the second year of *shao-ting* (1229) graciously corresponds to the emperor's birthday. I, the humble monk Hui-k'ai, previously, on the fifth day of the twelfth month of the first year [of *shao-ting*] (1228), selected forty-eight cases regarding the awakening opportunities of buddha-patriarchs for publication [in your honor]," and it is added that the forty-eight cases were published on the fifth day of the twelfth month of the same year (1229).[28] In this way, the *Wu-men kuan* was compiled and published in a short time span.

Concerning the term *Wu-men* used in the title of the work, we should consider the following lecture recorded at the beginning of the *Yüeh-lin yu-lu*, delivered at Mount Tao-ch'ang. "[Yueh-lin] pointed to the saying on the monastery gate: 'The mind which the Buddha spoke of is the fundamental source; gatelessness is the Dharma-gate. Enter here with your whole self, and you become specially joined with the entire universe.'"[29]

Regarding the use of the term *Wu-men* by Wu-men Hui-k'ai, Furuta Shōkin proposes that it was adopted from Yüeh-lin.[30] Given that we can ascertain Yüeh-lin's use of the term, I agree with Furuta's proposition. By acknowledging this, it becomes clear that the term *Wu-men* in the *Wu-men kuan* is deeply connected with its author, Wu-men Hui-k'ai.

The *Wu-men kuan* that Wu-men compiled contains forty-eight kōans. The four character titles of these kōans are listed as follows:[31]

1. Chao-chou's "Wu!"
2. Pai-chang and the Fox
3. Chu-chih Raises a Finger
4. The Western Barbarian with No Beard
5. Huang-yen's "Map up in a Tree"
6. The World Honored One Holds up a Flower
7. Chao-chou's "Wash Your Bowl"
8. Hsi-chung the Wheelmaker
9. Ta-t'ung Chih-sheng
10. Ch'ing-shui Is Utterly Destitute

11. Chao-chou Sees the Hermits
12. Jui-yen Calls His Master
13. Te-shan Holds His Bowls
14. Nan-ch'üan Kills the Cat
15. T'ung-shan's Sixty Blows
16. When the Bell Sounds, a Seven-Piece Robe
17. The National Preceptor Calls out Three Times
18. T'ung-shan's "Three Pounds of Flax"
19. "Ordinary Mind Is the Way"
20. The Man of Great Strength
21. Yun-men's "Shit-Stick"
22. Mahakasyapa's "Knock down the Flagpole"
23. Think neither Good nor Evil
24. Feng-hsüeh's Parting Words
25. The One in the Third Seat Preaches the Dharma
26. Two Monks Roll up the Blinds
27. "It Is Neither Mind nor Buddha"
28. Long Admired Lung-t'an
29. Neither the Wind nor the Flag
30. "Mind Itself Is Buddha"
31. Chao-chou Investigates an Old Woman
32. A Non-Buddhist Questions the Buddha
33. "No Mind, No Buddha"
34. "Wisdom Is Not the Way"
35. Ch'ien-nü's Soul Separated
36. Meeting a Man of the Tao on the Road
37. The Oak Tree in the Front of the Garden
38. A Buffalo Passes through the Window
39. Yün-men Says "You Missed It"
40. Kicking over the Water Pitcher
41. Bodhidharma Pacifies the Mind
42. A Woman Comes out of Meditation
43. Shou-shan's Staff
44. Pa-chiao's Staff
45. "Who Is He?"
46. Step Forward from the Top of the Pole
47. Tou-lu's Three Barriers
48. Ch'ien-feng's One Road

The Ch'an lineages of the people appearing in these kōan are provided in the essay at the end of Hirata Takashi's translation of the *Wu-men kuan*. [32]

The Special Circumstances Associated with the Propagation of
the *Wu-men kuan* in Japan

The individual who brought the *Wu-men kuan* to Japan was Shinichi Kakushin
(1207–1298). He inherited the Dharma from the *Wu-men kuan*'s author, Wu-
men Hui-k'ai.[33] There is an interesting story regarding Shinichi Kakushin's
awakening experience and his transmission of the *Wu-men kuan* to Japan. It
is said that when he was fifteen, Kakushin studied scriptures in Konobeakata.
He received full ordination at Tōdai-ji when he was twenty-nine. Subsequently,
he studied esoteric doctrine with Kakubutsu at the Denbō-in and practiced
under Gyōiu (Eisai's Dharma heir) at the Kongō zanmai-in, and studied with
Dōgen at Fukakusa Gokuraku-ji. After this, he practiced with a number of
teachers, and then Kakushin went to Sung China at the age of forty-three,
studying with Ch'ih-chüeh Tao-ch'ung (Dharma heir of Ts'ao-yüan Tao-sheng)
on Mount Ching and Ching-sou Ju-ch'ueh (Dharma heir of Ch'ih-tun Chih-
ying) on Mount Tao-ch'ang, before experiencing awakening under Wu-men
Hui-k'ai. The entry for the first year of *pao-yu* (1253) in Kakushin's *Chronological
History* states as follows.

> The master [Shinichi Kakushin] was forty-seven years old. On the
> twenty-eighth day of the second month, he climbed Mount Ta-mei
> and paid respects at the tomb of Ch'an master [Fa-]ch'ang. He met
> someone from Japan, Genshin. Because they had practiced together
> in the past, Kakushin asked him, "I have not practiced here for a
> long time. Have you met anyone yet with the wisdom of the enlight-
> ened eye?" Genshin replied, "The monk Wu-men is an enlightened
> master [encountered rarely] in an entire generation. You should go
> and meet with him." He then proceeded to go to Hu-kuo Temple in
> Hang[-chou]. As soon as he met Wu-men, Wu-men grabbed him
> and said: "I have no gate [for practitioners] here. Where have you
> come from?" The master (Kakushin) answered: "I've come from Wu-
> men's place." Wu-men then asked: "What is your name?" The mas-
> ter replied: "Kakushin." Wu-men then composed a verse that said:

> > Mind is Buddha;
> > Buddha is mind.
> > Mind and Buddha being in a state of suchness,
> > They extend through the past and the present.

The fact that Wu-men's response was four lines of verse indicated that his
awakening had been certified. Wu-men called further to Kakushin, "You arrived
here quite late." He then stood his fly whisk up and said: "Look!" Kakushin

experienced awakening as soon as Wu-men had uttered this word. It was the twenty-eighth day of the ninth month. Kakushin then asked, "When you have renounced everything, what do you use to instruct people with?" Wu-men replied, "I look for the essence seen in each individual thing." Kakushin bowed in respect, and departed. Wu-men presented Kakushin with [a copy of] the *Tui-yü lu* in two volumes and a monk's robe.³⁴

Shinichi Kakushin met Wu-men Hui-k'ai at Hu-kuo Temple and experienced awakening there under him. Kakushin visited him once more after he departed, and before returning to Japan. The leading entry for the following year, the second year of *pao-yu* (1254), in Kakushin's *Chronological History* states as follows:

> The master was forty-eight years old. On the twenty-seventh day of the third month, he again visited [Wu-men Hui-k'ai at] Hu-kuo Temple. When he related his intention to return to Japan, Wu-men presented him with three pictures painted on silk of the Ch'an heroes Bodhidharma, Han-shan, and Shih-te. On the twenty-ninth day, Kakushin called on Wu-men to bid farewell. Wu-men said: "This brings the matter to an end." Kakushin then lit incense and bowed in respect. Wu-men further presented Kakushin with [copies of] the *Yüeh-lin [yü-]lu* and the *Wu-men kuan*.³⁵

Accordingly, Shinichi Kakushin brought copies of the *Yüeh-lin yü-lu*, the record of Wu-men Hui-k'ai's teacher, and the *Wu-men kuan* to Japan. He arrived in Hakata in the sixth month of that year (1254). He visited Gyōiu at the Zenjō-in on Mount Kōya, and on the following day was promoted to chief meditator. There is evidence of correspondence between Kakushin and Wu-men Hui-k'ai under entries in the *Chronological History* for ages fifty and fifty-one. Subsequently, Kakushin was invited by Ganjō to become founding abbot of Saihō-ji on Mount Juhō in Yura in 1258. In the fourth year of kōan (1281), he was invited by the retired emperor Kameyama to live at Shōrin-ji in the capital. The same year, he was asked by Emperor Gouda to become the founding abbot of Zenrin-ji, but he declined and returned to Saihō-ji. In 1285, he was invited by Prime Minister Fujiwara Morotsugu and his son Moronobu to live at Myōkō-ji in the capital. Kakushin was seventy-nine years old at the time. Kakushin announced his passing at Saihō-ji on the thirteenth day of the tenth month, 1298. He was ninety-two years old, and had been a monk for sixty-four years. He was granted the honorific title Hottō Zenji (Zen master Dharma lamp) from retired emperor Kameyama, and received the posthumous title Hottō enmyō kokushi (Perfectly awakened national preceptor of the Dharma lamp) from Emperor Godaigo.

Concerning the *Wu-men kuan* text that Kakushin brought to Japan, it seems that the text went through several publications early on, and these are the sources for existing versions of the text. In fact, the *Wu-men kuan* known to us at present contains forty-nine rather than forty-eight cases, with the story of "Huang-lung's three barriers" added at the end. As a result, this presently known text of the *Wu-men kuan* would not appear to be the originally published text, but a republished version. According to Kawase Kazuma, the first publication of the *Wu-men kuan* in Japan was in 1291, but none of the editions derived from this printing is known to us.[36] The basis for Kawase's explanation is the following notice in an edition contained in the library of Daichō-in at Kennen-ji:

> This volume (i.e., the *Wu-men kuan*) exposes the marrow of the buddha-patriarchs, and is the hammer for pounding open monk's eyes. Moreover, it has yet to be published in Japan. Accordingly, it displays their great talent, and I will have a printer carve printing blocks to publish it. At present, an edition of this text is located at Saihō zen-in on Mount Juhō. With an expanded printing, it could be transmitted endlessly. If there is some gentleman who has the insight to take it upon himself, it will be said that even my efforts will not have been fruitless. Signed by Shamon (Monk) Sōshin, on a rising tide in the middle of Spring in the Shōbō era.

Kawase understands the date to be 1291. The name of the Saihō zen-in, which appears in the notice is also connected with Shinichi Kakushin, as noted above. The versions of the *Wu-men kuan* that are in wide circulation at present are from an edition first published in 1405. It is clear that this was not the first publication. Moreover, since it states that the old edition had disappeared, we can tell that the 1405 edition was the basis for those that were widely circulated.

At this point, I would like to change subjects and talk briefly about Shinichi Kakushin and the Sōtō sect. Shinichi Kakushin, as the Dharma heir of Wumen Hui-k'ai, undeniably belonged to the Rinzai sect. His Dharma lineage is referred to as the Hōttō faction. This faction has very deep connections with the Sōtō sect.[37] First of all, Keizan Jōkin (1264–1325), who created the basis for the development of the Sōtō sect by founding Sōji-ji, studied with Kakushin. In addition, Kakushin's Dharma heir, Kohō Kakumyō (1271–1361), studied with Keizan and received the bodhisattva precepts from him. Moreover, there was intimate communication between Keizan and the Hōttō faction.

What is of further interest is the fact that Shinichi Kakushin also had a large influence on and connection with Dōgen. As indicated in the chronological history, Eihei-ji was actually erected for the enlightenment of Hōjō Masako and the third Shōgun Sanetomo. This letter is not from an old record. It was transmitted as an indication of the connection that both Kōkoku-ji and Eihei-ji had to Sanetomo and Hōjō Masako. Sanetomo had wanted to visit the King Asoka (A-yü wang) temple in China. He even constructed a boat to go to China for that purpose. He had the Sung artisan Ch'en Ho-ch'ing build the boat, and intended to moor it at Yuiga beach in Kamakura, but regrettably the boat did not stay afloat. Consequently, Sanetomo's plans for going to China were dashed. According to the *Chronological History*, the one who fulfilled Sanetomo's dream of going to China was Shinichi Kakushin, but Sugio Genyū suggests that Dōgen might also have fulfilled it.[38] Regarding the strange affinity between Sanetomo and Dōgen, it is clear that there is an important connection between them that cannot be ignored. However, in the absence of older substantiating documentation, one problematic point remains. The end of the aforementioned entry for the third year of Karoku in the *Chronological History* speaks of a connection between Dōgen and Kōkoku-ji. In the year 1227 when this occurred, Dōgen was twenty-seven years old, and had just returned from China. The entry claims that before returning to Kyoto, Dōgen stopped at Kōkoku-ji (at the time named Saihō-ji) in Yura in Wakayama Prefecture, and inscribed the nameplate for the temple. Because the presently existing Kōkoku-ji no longer reflects the state of the temple at that time, the nameplate regrettably no longer exists.

In addition, there is another entry concerning Dōgen in the *Chronological History* for the third year on *ninji* (1242): "The master (Shinchi Kakushin) was thirty-six years old. He studied with Dōgen at the Gokuraku-ji in Fukakusa, to the south of the city, and received the bodhisattva precepts [from him]. When Dōgen was in China, he personally received transmission [of these bodhisattva precepts] from T'ien-t'ung Ju-ching. Dōgen subsequently became an expert in the Buddha-Dharma who founded Eihei-ji."[39]

It is a historical fact that Shinichi Kakushin visited Dōgen prior to going to China and received the bodhisattva precepts from him. Moreover, Dōgen personally received these bodhisattva precepts from T'ien-t'ung Ju-ching when he was in China. In Sugio Genyū's study referred to above, a connection was noted between Sanetomo, Kōkoku-ji, and Dōgen. Recently, Sugiō has maintained that the starting point of Dōgen Zen, Dōgen's enlightenment experience of "dropping off of body and mind" (*shinjin datsuraku*), stands between Dōgen's experiences on Mount A-yü-wang and his connection with Sanetomo.[40] This is a large issue in Dōgen studies. Here, I can do nothing more than point it out.

As indicated in the chart above outlining publications of Zen texts in the Sung dynasty, the *Wu-men kuan* was frequently read during Wu-men's lifetime, but there is little evidence that it was read in China after this.[41] However, the *Wu-men kuan* was read with very great frequency in Japan. Of course, it was naturally read in the Rinzai sect, but it was regarded with importance in the Sōtō sect as well. According to research by Yanagida Seiji, the number of translations of the *Wu-men kuan* in Japan is extremely high.[42] What of the situation of Zen in Korea? Many old Ch'an works were published in Korea, but the *Wu-men kuan*, or its translations, do not appear among them.[43]

The popularity of the *Wu-men kuan* was unique to Japan, and created an extraordinary sensation there. The initiation of this phenomenon was created when Dharma Lamp National Preceptor Shinichi Kakushin (1207–1298), the traveler to Sung China and inheritor of Wu-men Hui-k'ai's Dharma, brought the *Wu-men kuan* to Japan.

New Perspectives on the Material Cited in the *Wu-men kuan*

Regarding the content of the text, I will investigate problems connected to the citation of the sixth kōan in the *Wu-men kuan*, the story entitled "The World-Honored One Holds up a Flower." At the same time, I would like to consider the special circumstances associated with the adoption of the *Wu-men kuan* by the Japanese people, especially their understanding of the "flower" (or "blossom") in this case.

The story "The World-Honored One Holds up a Flower" is one of the best known Zen kōans.[44] It relates how the World-Honored One (Śākyumuni Buddha), on one occasion, faced a large group of assembled practitioners. Just as he was about to begin to preach, Brahma offered him a flower. The World-Honored One took the flower and held it up, while remaining silent. The practitioners wondered what he was doing, and thinking it strange, did not understand it at all. Only Mahākāśyapa broke into a smile. The passage of the original text in the *Wu-men kuan*, along with the commentary by Wu-men Hui-k'ai, reads as follows:

> The World-Honored One long ago instructed the assembly on Vulture Peak by holding up a flower. At that time, everyone in the assembly remained silent; only Mahākāśyapa broke into a smile. The World-Honored One stated, "I possess the treasury of the true Dharma-eye, the wondrous mind of nirvana, the subtle Dharma-gate born of the formlessness of true form, not established on words and letters, a special transmission outside the teaching. I bequeath it to Mahākāśyapa."
> Wu-men's comment:
> Yellow-faced Gautama really mocked his listeners. He denigrated good people as despicable sorts who sold dog's meat labeled as sheep's head. He thought that this was somehow ingenious [but in fact it was not]. But if everyone in the assembly had smiled at that moment, how would the treasury of the true Dharma-eye been transmitted? Or, suppose that Mahākāśyapa had not smiled, how would the treasury of the true Dharma-eye been transmitted? If you say that the treasury of the true Dharma-eye is transmitted, the yellow-faced geriatric is a bumpkin-cheating city-slicker. If you say it is not transmitted, then why did he approve of Mahākāśyapa?
> [Wu-men's] verse:

Holding up a flower,
[the Buddha] revealed his tail.
When Mahākāśyapa broke into a smile;
Humans and gods were all bewildered.[45]

There is not even the slightest trace that this story "The World-Honored One Holds up a Flower" existed in India. It is generally believed to have first appeared in the *Ta fan-t'ien wen-fo chüeh-i ching* (The scripture in which Brahman asks Buddha to resolve his doubts), a scripture fabricated in China. The story is connected to portions of the text in the two versions of the *Ta fan-t'ien wen-fo chüeh-i ching* contained in the *Zokuōkyō* edition, to one passage in the two-chapter version, and to two passages in the one-chapter version.[46] Any of these passages from the *Ta fan-t'ien wen-fo chüeh-i ching* could be the source for "The World-Honored One Holds up a Flower" story recorded in the *Wu-men kuan*. For example, this is the allegation made in the earliest surviving translation of the *Wu-men kuan* in Japan, the *Mumonkan jiunshō*, by Kihaku Genbō of the Genjō branch of the Rinzai sect, and has been explained in recent years in the works by Hirata Takashi and Nishmura Eshin.

In addition, another well-read work in Japan, the *Tsung-men tsa-lu* [Miscellaneous records of the Ch'an school], contained in chapter five of the *Jen-t'ien yen-mu* [The eyes of humans and gods] (compiled in 1188), provides the following verification for the source of the *Wu-men kuan* story, "The World-Honored One Holds up a Flower":

Wang, the duke of Ching, asked Ch'an master Fo-hui Ch'üan: "What source is [the story] The World-Honored One Holds up a Flower related by members of the Ch'an lineage (*ch'an-chia*) based on?"

[Ch'an master] Ch'üan replied, "It is not contained at all in the scriptures of the [Buddhist] canon."

The duke said: "The other day in the Han-lin Academy, I happened to read the three-chapter *Scripture in Which [Brahma Asks] Buddha to Resolve His Doubts* (*Wen-fo chüeh-i ching*). Based on what I read there, a passage from this scripture unequivocally contains the story. [It states that] when the Brahma king lived on Vulture Peak, he presented to the Buddha a gold-colored *po-lo* flower. He withdrew to take up his seat, asking the Buddha to preach the Dharma for the sake of sentient beings. The World-Honored One got up from his seat and communicated to the assembly by holding up the flower. None of the hundreds of myriads of humans and gods grasped [the meaning of this]. Only one among them, the gold-colored ascetic, broke into a smile. The World-Honored One stated: "I possess the treasury of the true Dharma eye, the wondrous mind of nirvana, the formlessness of true form. I now bequeath it to Mahākāśyapa." This scripture discusses frequently how Indra served the Buddha and asked him questions. As a consequence, it contains secrets which the world has yet to hear."[47]

Wang, the duke of Ching, referred to here is Wang An-shih. Based on the information presented here, the *Ta fan-t'ien wang wen-fo chüeh-i ching* already existed in China at this time. However, there is a persuasive argument by a member of the Sōtō sect that the version of the scripture contained in *Zokuōkyō* was created in Japan during the Edo period.[48] Nukariya Kaiten successfully adopted this argument in his own research.[49] I have also adopted the argument that it was compiled in Japan, concurring with the argument made by Nukariya.

Based on this, kōan number six in the *Wu-men kuan*, "The World-Honored One Holds up a Flower," is not based on an apocryphal scripture, even though the same story appears in the *Ta fan-t'ien wang wen-fo chüeh-i ching*. Among Ch'an "transmission records" (*teng-lu*), the story "The World-Honored One Holds up a Flower" first appears in chapter 2 of the *T'ien-sheng kuang-teng lu* [T'ien-sheng era supplementary transmission record], in the entry for Mahākāśyapa.[50] Prior to this, we know that members of the Lin-chi lineage transmitted the story "The World-Honored One Holds up a Flower"; it is contained in sources such as the *Recorded Sayings* (*yü-lu*) of Tz'u-ming (a.k.a. Shih-shuang) Ch'u-yüan (986–1039), for which there is a preface dated 1027.[51] The fact that the *Wu-men kuan* developed the story "The World-Honored One Holds up a Flower" based on the *Tsung-men t'ung-yao chi* is readily apparent from a comparison of case number six in the *Wu-men kuan* and the following entry on Sakyamuni from chapter 1 of the *Tsung-men t'ung-yao chi*.

> The World-Honored One long ago instructed the assembly on Vulture Peak by holding up a flower. At that time, everyone in the assembly remained silent; only Mahākāśyapa broke into a smile. The World-Honored One stated, "I possess the treasury of the true Dharma-eye, the wondrous mind of nirvana, the subtle Dharma-gate born of the formlessness of true form, not established on words and letters, a special transmission outside the teaching. I bequeath it to Mahākāśyapa."[52]

The wording of the two versions is exactly the same. Following the *Tsung-men t'ung-yao chi* version are comments by Lin-chi masters Hai-hui Tuan and Huang-lung Hsin. Even though the *Ta fan-t'ien wen-fo chüeh-i ching* is understood to be the source for "The World-Honored One Holds up a Flower" story in translations of the *Wu-men kuan* into Japanese, the fact that the *Tsung-men t'ung-yao chi* was actually the source means that the story was already functioning as a kōan. This is known from the comments of Lin-chi masters appended to the end of the story in the *Tsung-men t'ung-yao chi*, where the meaning of the story is discussed in kōan-like fashion.

Next, I turn to the question of the flower. What kind of flower was it that the World-Honored One held up? What is the "gold-colored *po-lo* flower" mentioned in the *Ta fan-t'ien wen-fo chüeh-i ching*? Because Dōgen referred to the flower in this story as the *udonge* or "*udon* flower" in the *Shōbōgenzō*, it is postulated to be *udumbara* in Sanskrit, but it probably refers to the image of a lotus blossom (Skt. *utpala*) generally acknowledged as the representative flower of Indian Buddhism. Let us next consider the problem of the flower presented in case number nineteen in the *Wu-men kuan*, the story "Ordinary Mind Is the Way."

> Nan-ch'üan, in passing, was asked by Chao-chou: "What Is the Way?" Nan-ch'üan replied, "Ordinary mind is the Way." Chao-chou asked: "Then should I direct myself toward it, or not?" Nan-ch'üan answered, "When you try to direct yourself toward it, you go away from it." Chao-chou persisted, "How will I know it is the Way unless I try for it?" Nan-ch'üan responded, "The Way is not something one knows or does not know. Knowing is an illusion; not knowing is blankness. If you truly attain the Way without effort, it is vast and boundless like the great void. How can you insist on [categorizing it in terms of] right and wrong?" With these words, Chao-chou was suddenly awakened.
> Wu-men's comment:
> Questioned by Chao-chou, Nan-ch'üan straight away made the tile disintegrate and the ice melt, and [showed that] explanations were impossible, even though Chao-chou experienced awakening, he must practice for another thirty years before he will begin to get it.
> [Wu-men's] verse:
>> A hundred flowers in spring, the moon in autumn;
>> A cool breeze in summer, snow in winter.
>> If trivial matters do not clutter your mind,
>> It is a good season for such a person.[53]

"Ordinary mind is the Way" means that our normal mind is the Way, just as it is. "The Way" (*tao*) is one of the ancient translations for the Sanskrit term *bodhi*. The Chinese considered "the Way" to be the same as "awakening" (*satori*). Given this meaning, the phrase "Ordinary mind is the Way" can be said to represent the zenith of Chinese Ch'an.

However, when we read Wu-men's commemorative verse for this kōan, we are reminded of Dōgen's poem *Honrai menmoku* (Poem: The original face).[54]

Haru wa hana, natsu totogisu, aki wa tsuki, fuyu wa kiete suzushikari-
keri.[55]

Although this verse was originally famous among Dōgen's poetic works,
what attracted even more attention was the citation of it by Kawabata Yasunari
at the beginning of his commemorative presentation in Stockholm when he
was awarded the Nobel Prize for Literature, in 1968.[56] Seidensticker translated
the verse as follows.

> In the spring, cherry blossoms; in the summer, the cuckoo.
> In the autumn, the moon; in the winter, snow, clear, cold.

It is unclear whether Dōgen was thinking of "cherry blossoms" (*sakura no
hana*) when he mentioned *hana* (flower) in his verse. Prior to considering this,
let's look at the problem concerning the *Sanshōdōeishū*, which contains this
verse. According to the explanation of Funazu Yōko, Dōgen did not write all
of the verses in the *Sanshōdōeishū*. A verse with the same title, *Honrai no
menmoku* (The original face) is contained in the *Hekigan hyaku kattō* (A hundred entanglements on the blue cliff by Kyōkai): *Haru wa hana, natsu totogisu,
aki wa tsuki, fuyu wa takane ni yuki zo furikeri* [translation (following Seidensticker): In the spring, cherry blossoms; in the summer, the cuckoo; in the
autumn, the moon; in the winter, without amassing, snow continues to fall].
Funazu considers this as follows: "A similar poem appears in the *Hekigan
hyaku kattō*, a work by Kyokai Tōryū (?–1852) which commits the *Hekigan roku*
(*Pi-yen lu*, Blue cliff record) to verse. Considering the time that it was written,
it would seem that Kyōkai's verse is an adaptation of the one from Dōgen's
Sanshōdōeishū. But it is also possible that it is based on a verse by an unknown
author transmitted by Zen monks since ancient times as representative of the
circumstances of Zen monks' lives."[57]

Funazu simply pointed out that the authorship of the original verse is
unclear. However, it is possible to consider that the verse by Wu-men Hui-k'ai
in his commentary to the kōan "Ordinary Mind Is the Way" was the source,
especially given that it was popular in Japan and had been transmitted over a
long period of time.

Concerning the issue of the "flower" (*hana*), one is reminded of Dōgen's
use of the term in *Genjōkōan*: "Moreover, whatever one says, it is regrettable
when blossoms (*hana*) scatter; it is sorrowful when weeds flourish."[58]

Because it states that when they scatter it is regrettable, it seems that in
this case the "flowers" referred to are cherry blossoms. However, in the case
of Wu-men Hui-k'ai's verse "In the spring, a hundred flowers," I doubt if we
can think of the "hundred flowers" as cherry blossoms. Wu-men, who was
Chinese, would not have been thinking of cherry blossoms. It is more likely
that Wu-men would have been thinking of peach blossoms. The Zen poem,
"The willow is green, the blossoms (*hana*) are red," is well known, but in

chapter 2 of the *Wu-tsu fa-yen yu-lu* [The recorded sayings of Wu-tsu Fa-yen], there is the verse, "The willow is green, the peaches are red."⁵⁹ When one speaks of "flowers" in the Chinese context, peach blossoms are representative. In the Ch'an school, the story of Kuei-shan Ling-yu's disciple Ling-yün Chih-ch'in experiencing awakening upon seeing a peach blossom is famous, as is the story of Hsiang-yen Ch'ih-hsien experiencing awakening upon hearing the sound of bamboo striking a rock. If Dōgen had said, "In the spring, flowers (*hana*)," he probably would have been referring to plum blossoms, which bloom in early spring. There is a work entitled *Cheng-fa yen-tsang mei-hua* (*Shōbōgenzō Baika*, The plum blossoms of the eye treasury of the true Dharma), connected with the fact that Dōgen's teacher, T'ien-t'ung Ju-ching, was very fond of plum trees. As a result, the cultural traditions passed down among Chinese and Japanese are not necessarily the same when it comes to flowers, which are representative of the respective cultures. Moreover, among Japanese there are various seasonal considerations as well. Dōgen did not simply say, "In the spring, flowers." Given that his poem reads, "it is regrettable when blossoms (*hana*) scatter; it is sorrowful when weeds flourish," it is likely that the text was conceived in response to nature.

However, in addition to the famous words of Dōgen in *Genjokōan*, there survives an exchange connected with the figure known as Niu-t'ou Ching, a Dharma-heir of the Kuei-yang lineage master, Pa-chiao Hui-ch'ing, recorded in chapter 25 of the *T'ien-sheng kuang-teng lu*.

> Someone asked: "What is your teaching style, master?"
> The master (Niu-t'ou Ching) replied: "It is regrettable when blossoms fall; it is sorrowful when weeds flourish."⁶⁰

No one who considers this famous poem by Dōgen would think that it was not Dōgen's own composition, but the words uttered here by Niu-t'ou Ching suggests otherwise.⁶¹ What kind of "blossoms" was Niu-t'ou Ching referring to? Because he was Chinese, and a member of the Kuei-yang lineage, he was probably referring to peach blossoms. From the use of the verb "fall" (*ochi*), it is possible to imagine that he was referring to the *mu-tan* or *shao-yao* flower. All that we can say for sure is that the "flower" he referred to was not the cherry blossom.

Since there is such a large difference between Japanese and Chinese people's understandings of "flower," this raises the question of differences of perception between Chinese and Japanese regarding the expression "Ordinary mind is the Way." The verses from the *Wu-men kuan*, hugely popular among Japanese as mentioned previously, were understood differently in the Japanese context from the way they were intended in China. As a result, I would suggest that in the adaptation of the *Wu-men kuan* to the Japanese context, there was a tendency to affix meanings that were unintended by the Chinese.

The Nature of the *Wu-men kuan*

The most prominent feature of the *Wu-men kuan* is displayed in its first kōan, known either as "Chao-chou's Dog" or "Chao-chou's Word *Wu* (No)." We can investigate the way that this *kōan* was originally understood by looking to Wu-tsu Fa-yen.[62] The last chapter of the *Wu-tsu Fa-yen yu-lu* states as follows.

> [Chao-chou] entered the hall [to address the assembly]. A monk asked Chao-chou: "Does a dog have the Buddha-nature, or not?" Chao-chou replied: "*Wu* (Not)" The monk asked: "All sentient beings, without exception, have the Buddha-nature. How is it that a dog does not?" Chao-chou replied: "Because it remains in a state of kar-mic consciousness."
> Master [Wu-tsu] commented: "How do you members of the great as-sembly understand the quest for permanence? If I seek permanence by simply uttering the word *Wu!* my search is over. If you penetrate this one word, no one in the world will be able to question you. How will you penetrate it? Have you penetrated it thoroughly and gotten to the bottom of it? If you have, come forward and say it for me. I do not need you to say that you have done it, nor do I need you to say that you haven't, nor do I need you to say that you have neither done it nor have not done it. What will you say? Please take care.[63]

Originally, the question "Does a dog have the Buddha-nature" and Chao-chou's reply "*Wu!* (No)" appeared in the *Chao-chou lu* (Record of Chao-chou). When the questioner supposed that the dog did not have the Buddha-nature, Chao-chou replied that it did have it. In this way, in spite of the fact that two responses are recorded in the *Chao-chou lu*, the positive response was elimi-nated and only the negative response *Wu!* continued to be recorded in the kōan version of the exchange. The clue to this transformation can be inferred from the above cited *Recorded Sayings of Wu-tsu Fa-yen*. One of Wu-tsu Fa-yen's de-scendants was Ta-hui Tsung-kao, the formulator of the style of Ch'an known as *k'an-hua ch'an* (J. *kanna zen*, the Ch'an/Zen of kōan introspection phrases). Ta-hui referred frequently to the kōan involving Chao-chou's *Wu!* He explains the structure of this kōan in the "Lecture given at the request of a noblewoman from the principality of Ch'in," the mother of Prime Minister Chang Chun, contained in chapter 14 of the *Ta-hui P'u-chüeh Ch'an-shih yu-lu* (The recorded sayings of Chan Master Ta-hui P'u-chüeh). The noblewoman from the prin-cipality of Ch'in was the best of Ta-hui's female students and a powerful donor of Ta-hui's.

One time, the noblewoman made a request to Ta-hui's disciple, K'ai-shan Tao-ch'ien, "Please explain to me how Monk Ching-shan [Ta-

hui] normally instructs practitioners?" Tao-ch'ien replied, "Monk Ta-
hui simply presents the story "A Dog Has No Buddha-nature" or
"Shou-shan's Bamboo Comb" to practitioners. On such occasions,
no matter what the practitioner says or thinks, the Master criticizes
it; as soon as they try to do anything, as soon as they try to say anything, the Master responds with criticism. [The solution to these]
cannot be grasped at all through [the use of] distinctions or
words."[Tao-ch'ien] explained it by simply relating [the lines] "Does a
dog have the Buddha-nature? *Wu* (No)*!*" Listening to this, the noblewoman put her faith in it and both day and night grappled with the
word *Wu* (No). The noblewoman had regarded reading scriptures
and performing offerings to the buddhas as normal Buddhist practice. However, Tao-ch'ien told her: "If you consider how Monk Ta-
hui sought awakening through ordinary daily activities, you will refrain from planned activities, reading scriptures, performing
offerings to the buddhas, chanting invocations, and so on, and just
grapple with the kōan word *Wu!* If you concentrate on reading scriptures, performing offerings to the buddhas, and become attached to
seeking blessings through these activities, on the contrary, they become obstacles to seeking awakening. However, after you have attained awakening, [Ta-hui] teaches that it is possible to read scriptures, make offerings to the buddhas, offer flowers and burn incense,
and to perform the confession ritual and engage in all of the superb
activities of the buddhas, as is natural."

When the Noblewoman heard what Tao-ch'ien said, she divested
herself from reading scriptures and performing offerings to the
Buddhas, and concentrated on sitting in meditation and the kōan
word *Wu!* One year, during the winter, she suddenly experienced
awakening. Excitedly, she stood up, and was able to experience a
world of sudden joy, realizing this kōan word *Wu!* as if sitting in
mediation in the meditation hall.[64]

Here we have Ta-hui's method of seated meditation (C. *tso-ch'an*, J. *zazen*),
and his method of grappling with the "critical phrase" (C. *hua-t'ou*, J. *watō*)
during seated meditation, his so-called *k'an-hua ch'an* (J. *kanna zen*) method
simply explained for us.[65] Moreover, we can easily understand from this that
Ta-hui recommended the use of the *Wu* kōan.

Wu-men Hui-k'ai developed the first *kōan* in the *Wu-men kuan*, the story
of "Chao-chou's Dog," through the tradition conveyed by Wu-tsu Fa-yen and
Ta-hui Tsung-kao. Although I introduced the following material in the previous
volume in this series, *The Kōan: Texts and Contexts in Zen Buddhism*, it is
indispensable for understanding the *Wu-men kuan* as well.

A monk asked Chao-chou: "Does a dog have the Buddha-nature?"
Chao-chou answered: "*Wu!*"

Wu-men's comment:

"In studying Ch'an, one must pass through the barrier set up by the
patriarchs. To attain inconceivable enlightenment (*miao-Wu*), one
must completely eliminate mental activity. Those who have not
passed through the barrier of the patriarchs and eliminated mental
activity are all ghosts inhabiting plants and trees. Now, tell me, what
is the barrier of the patriarchs? It is none other than the one word
"*Wu!*" spoken by Chao-chou here. This is the first barrier of the
Ch'an school (*tsung-men*). As a result, I have titled this work "The
Gateless Barrier of the Ch'an School" (*Ch'an-tsung Wu-men kuan*).
Those who are able to pass through this barrier not only meet with
Chao-chou as a close friend, they will further be able to walk hand
in hand with the patriarchs of history, intimately linked eyebrow to
eyebrow. They will see with the same eyes as the patriarchs and hear
with the same ears. What a wonderful thing this is!

Now, is there anyone who wants to pass through this barrier? If
so, then with your 360 bones and 84,000 pores, you will produce
one irresolvable doubt throughout your entire body—concentrate on
what this word *Wu* is, and absorb yourself day and night with this
problem. Do not misunderstand the word *Wu* either in terms of
Taoist "nihilism" (*hsü-wu*) or as "nonexistence" (*yu-wu*) conceived
dualistically in terms of "existence" and "nonexistence" (*yu-wu*). It is
like swallowing a red-hot ball of iron and trying to spit it out, but
without success. If you wash away completely the depraved knowledge and perverse theories studied previously, applying yourself ear-
nestly over a long period, distinctions like "inner" and "outer" will
naturally be fused together. Your experience is like a deaf-mute who
has a dream. You yourself are the only one who knows about it. You
cannot communicate it to anyone else. When suddenly the doubt is
resolved (that is, you break through the barrier), this event will
astonish the heavens and shake the earth. It is as if you have
snatched the great sword away from General Kuan-yü, met the Buddha and killed the Buddha, met the patriarchs and killed the patriarchs. Living in the world of birth and death (*saṃsāra*) you have attained complete freedom. Continually experiencing life according to
the four modes of life on the six transmigratory paths, you wander
joyfully in *samādhi*.

What then should one do to exert oneself with this word *Wu*?
Exhausting all your spiritual energy in this constant pursuit, you
must absorb this word *Wu*. If you succeed without wavering for a

moment, it will seem as if the light of the Dharma suddenly ignited in your mind.
[Wu-men's verse:]

> Does a dog have the Buddha-nature?
> The Buddhas and patriarchs have completely resolved this doubt.
> Whether you answer "yes" or "no,"
> Your fate is sealed.[66]

In this way, the story "Chao-chou's Dog" is the story of how to grapple with the one word *Wu!* by focusing one's whole body and entire spirit on it. The way to concentrate on the one word *Wu!* is explained relatively clearly by Wu-men Hui-k'ai, the author of the *Wu-men kuan*, in the final chapter of the *Wu-men Hui-k'ai yü-lu* (The recorded sayings of Wu-men Hui-k'ai), as follows.

And, [a student] raised the point that revered masters throughout history have presented verses on the story "A Dog Has No Buddha-Nature." The master [Wu-men] said: "I too have a verse. It is similar to those presented by others. I dare not employ reason. If I believe in it completely, I will attain perfect freedom while standing on the shore of birth and death."
[Wu-men's verse:]

> No! No! No! No! No! No! No! No! No! No!
> No! No! No! No! No! No! No! No! No! No![67]

According to Wu-men's *Recorded Sayings*, many Ch'an teachers throughout history composed verses for the "Dog Has No Buddha-nature" story, and Wu-men himself also composed one. The verse composed by Wu-men repeats the word *Wu* (No) twenty times. At the same time that the verse relates the special feature of Wu-men's teaching, one feels that there is something unusual about it. Iriya Yoshitaka makes the following comment regarding this.

I have held doubts for some time even with regard to the way the so-called "Chao-chou's Word No" has been previously dealt with. To the question "Does a dog have the Buddha-nature?", on the one hand Monk Chao-chou replied affirmatively, but on the other hand he replied negatively. However, Zen adherents in Japan have rendered the kōan exclusively in terms of his negative response, and completely ignored the affirmative one. Moreover, it has been the custom from the outset to reject the affirmative response as superficial compared to the negative one. It seems that the *Wu-men kuan* is responsible for this peculiarity.[68]

With regard to this, case number 18 in chapter 2 of the *Hung-chih lu* (Record of Hung-chih) (equals case number 18 in the *Ts'ung-jung lu*) states the following.

A kōan was introduced. A monk asked Chao-chou: "Does a dog have the Buddha-nature?" Chao-chou replied: "Yes." The monk asked: "If it already has it, why is it thrust into this bag of skin?" Chao-chou replied: "To purposely assault your assumptions."

On another occasion, a monk asked: "Does a dog have the Buddha-nature?" Chao-chou replied: "No." The monk asked: "All sentient beings, without exception, have the Buddha-nature. How is it that a dog does not?" Chao-chou replied: "Because it remains in a state of karmic consciousness."[69]

Dōgen's *Shōbōgenzō* "Busshō" [*Shōbōgenzō*, "Buddha Nature" fascicle] was developed from this kōan. Hung-chih Cheng-chüeh dealt with the kōan by combining both the affirmative and negative responses. The *Wu-men kuan* systemized the Lin-chi (J. Rinzai) *k'an-hua ch'an* (J. *kanna zen*) tradition, distinguishing itself from Hung-chih by focusing exclusively on the negative response.[70]

Yet, as previously stated, in the Lin-chi (Rinzai) school the *Wu-men kuan* is a collection of kōan cases with which one must grapple all costs. However, Hirata Takashi is critical toward the traditional way of dealing with the *Wu-men kuan* in the Japanese Rinzai school. In the "Explanation" section of Hirata's previously mentioned translation of the *Wu-men kuan*, he states the following: "As is the case within our own house (that is, the Rinzai school), there are masters without vision who make us labor over the *Wu-men kuan*, investigating each case in order, one after another, from the first to the forty-eighth. They are fools who know nothing at all of Wu-men Hui-k'ai's intention when he stated, 'Do not treat them in order, from first to last.'"[71]

According to this perspective, it is unnecessary to treat all of the forty-eight cases in order. Which of the forty-eight cases, then, have traditionally been regarded as important in the Japanese Rinzai school? Hirata employs a traditional scheme in classifying the kōan into three types: *li-chih* (J. *richi*), *chi-k'an* (J. *kikan*), and *hsiang-shang* (J. *kōjō*).[72] *Li-chi* refers to cases in which the Zen instructor guides practitioners by teaching them to focus on the general assumption and idea of the kōan. *Chi-k'an* refers to the method whereby the instructor guides practitioners by providing individually directed hints and suggestions one way or another. *Hsiang-shang*, because it means "above," refers to when the teacher breaks beyond the former two methods of instruction and indicates to the practitioner to go beyond (that is, literally, "above") them. The type that appears first in the *Wu-men kuan* is the *li-chih*, which is found in the first kōan, "Chao-chou's Dog." As examples of the *chi-k'an* type, there is kōan number 14, "Nan-ch'üan Kills the Cat," as well as number 43, "Shou-shan's Bamboo Comb." An example of the *hsiang-shang* type is found in kōan number

13, "Te-shan's Begging Bowl." Kōan number 38, "A Buffalo Passes through the Window," is regarded as an important kōan that proceeds through all three types. Being outside of the Rinzai Zen tradition, the above is simply my personal understanding of the characteristics of the *Wu-men kuan*.

Case 14, "Nan-ch'üan Kills the Cat" is also a well-known kōan. When Nan-ch'üan P'u-yuan saw practitioners from the eastern and western monks' halls arguing about a cat, he grabbed the animal and posed a question to them, "If you can utter one enlightened word, I will spare the cat. If you cannot, I will kill it." None of them could respond to this, so Nan-ch'üan killed the cat. In the evening, Chao-chou returned to the temple. Nan-ch'üan told him of the day's incident. When Chao-chou heard about it, he removed his sandals, put them on his head, and walked away. Seeing this, Nan-ch'üan said: "Had you been there, the cat could have been saved." Wu-men commented in his verse, "Had Chao-chou been there, he would have taken action. Had he snatched the sword away, Nan-ch'üan would have begged for his life."[73]

The next case, 43 is also a typical kōan. It is often referred to by Ta-hui Tsung-kao along with his comments on Chao-chou's *Wu!* kōan. Shou-shan Sheng-nien held up his staff and said: "If you monks call this a "staff," you are complicit in the restrictions imposed on it by others (that is, affirm its existence). If you don't call it a "staff," you invalidate what others assume (that is, deny its existence). So, what do you call it?" In his verse, Wu-men stated, "Holding up a staff, he is carrying out the orders to let live and to kill. If complicity in restricting it (that is, affirming its existence) and invalidating assumptions (that is, denying its existence) are both advanced, even the buddhas and patriarchs will beg for their lives."[74]

Case 13, "Te-shan's Begging Bowl," is a kōan that combines comic and serious aspects. One day, Te-shan Hsüan-chien was on his way to the dining hall with his bowl. His disciple Hsüeh-feng I-ts'un asked him: "Venerable master, the bell and the drum signaling meal time have not been sounded. Where are you going with your bowl?" Te-shan immediately returned to his room. When Hsüeh-feng related what had happened to his fellow disciple Yen-t'ou Ch'uan-huo, Yen-t'ou commented, "As great as Te-shan is, he has yet to grasp the final word." Upon learning what had been said, Te-shan sent an attendant to summon Yen-t'ou and asked him, "Do you not approve of me?" Yen-t'ou whispered to Te-shan what he had intended with his remark. Te-shan remained silent. The following day, when Te-shan took the rostrum in the lecture hall to preach the Dharma, his topic varied from his normal ones. Yen-t'ou went to the front of the monk's hall, clapped his hands, laughed heartily, and proclaimed: "Shouldn't he be congratulated? Te-shan has grasped the final word. From now on, no one will be able to outdo him." Wu-men's perspective is stated clearly in his opening comment: "Even if there were a final word, neither Yen-t'ou nor Te-shan have seen it even in a dream."[75]

Case 38, "A Buffalo Passes through the Window," is conveyed in the Rinzai tradition as an example that provides the three types of kōan together in a single story. This kōan is based on a lecture given by Wu-tsu Fa-yen. Wu-tsu said: "Suppose that you dreamed a water buffalo walked through the frame of a window. Although the water buffalo's head, horns, and four legs all pass through, why does only the tail not?" In his verse, Wu-men states: "If the water buffalo passes through, it falls into a ditch. If it turns back, it destroys the window-frame. So, this tail is truly marvelous."[76]

The subject of this kōan is unique, and said to be difficult. Because the reviver of the Rinzai school in Japan, Hakuin Ekaku, counted it among the eight most difficult kōan to penetrate, the great representative instructors of the Rinzai school from the Meiji period down to the present also consider it as one of the traditionally difficult kōan. The source for this episode involving Wu-tsu comes from a story in chapter 22 of the *Ta-p'an nieh-p'an ching*, translated by Dharmaraksa: "It is like a water buffalo that ravages a grain field when someone has not protected it well. Ordinary people do not regulate the five sense organs, are constantly involved with them, and endure many afflictions. Good sons! Whenever bodhisattva-mahasattvas cultivate nirvana and practice the way of the Sage (that is, Buddha), they are always well ordered, guarding and regulating the five sense organs."[77]

It was Inoue Shūten who first pointed out the source for the *Wu-men kuan* episode.[78] According to Inoue, it is based on a dream episode of King Ai-min (Ch'i-li-chih), contained in the final chapter of the *Fo-shuo chi ku-chang-che nü te-tu yin-yüan ching*, translated by Dinapala in the Northern Sung: "At that time, King Ai-min unexpectedly had ten dreams during the night. In the first, he dreamed that a large elephant passed through a window lattice; even though the body [of the elephant] could get through, its tail could not."[79]

Although there is definitely a difference in the story between the water buffalo referred to by Wu-tsu and the elephant mentioned here, the basic content can be acknowledged as the same. As a result, other interpretations of the kōan become possible. Inoue interprets this dream by King Ai-min in terms of a problem for the Buddha, as supported by the following explanation from the *Fo-shuo chi ku-chang-che nü te-tu yin-yüan ching*: "Even as the king dreamed that a great elephant passed through a window lattice, its body passing through but its tail not, after the Buddha enters nirvana, those he has bequeathed the Dharma to, be they Brahmin, elders, laypeople, male or female, will discard their relatives to leave home and study the Way (that is, Buddhism). It is as if they were unable to liberate their minds from covetous attachment to fame and wealth and customary habits, even though they have left home."[80]

Acknowledging this as the source for the *Wu-men kuan* episode changes the interpretation of Wu-tsu's "tail." When Wu-tsu refers to the "tail" remaining, if it is meant to indicate that leaving home is not complete, since the mind is covetously attached to fame and wealth and customary habits, the kōan may be explained in terms of the impossibility of attaining true liberation. Based on the Rinzai tradition, which counts this as one of its difficult kōan, "this tail is a truly strange thing," as stated by Wu-men, but if it is explained as Wu-tsu's admonishment of those who leave home without doing it thoroughly, is it necessarily so difficult a kōan to penetrate?

I have introduced the three types of kōan in the *Wu-men kuan* according to the Rinzai school. Because they are among the kōan used relatively often in training practitioners and appear very challenging on the surface, they were categorized by the tradition as intrinsically difficult to penetrate. However, it seems to me that it is possible to question the compulsory way they have been understood, based on new interpretations.

Special Features of the *Wu-men kuan* in the Context of Sung Ch'an Textual History

In conclusion, I would like to consider the special features of the *Wu-men kuan* within the context of the textual history of Sung Ch'an. My purpose here is to explain the special features of the *Wu-men kuan* as compared to the *Wu-teng hui-yüan* (The five lamps meeting at the source), a text compiled slightly later than the *Wu-men kuan*. These two Ch'an texts belong to the two following streams, A and B, based on their respective tendencies.

A. (*Tsu-t'ang chi*, chapter 20; 952) → *Ching-te ch'uan-teng lu*, 30 fascicles (1004) → compilation of "ancient cases," or kōan → *Tsung-men t'ung-yao chi*, 10 fascicles (1093) → *Wu-men kuan* (1228)

B. *Ching-te ch'uan-teng lu*, 30 fascicles (1004) → *T'ien-sheng kuang-teng lu*, 30 fascicles (1036) → *Chien-chung Ch-ing-kuo hsü-teng lu*, 30 fascicles (1101) → *Tsung-men lien-teng hui-yao*, 30 fascicles (1183) → *Chia-t'ai p'u-teng lu*, 30 fascicles (1202) → *Wu-teng hui-yuan*, 20 fascicles (1252)

Stream B is generally referred to as leading to the compilation of the *Wu-teng hui-yuan*. This is affirmed in the preface by Wang Yung, written in the first year of k'ai-yu (1253):

> During the ching-te era, the *Ching-te ch'uan-teng lu* was publicly circulated. Following it were the *T'ien-sheng kuang-teng lu*, *Tsung-men lien-teng hui-yao*, *Chien-chung Ch-ing-kuo hsü-teng lu*, and *Chia-t'ai p'u-teng lu*. Transmission of the lamp records appeared in succession; separated by sect and divided by lineage, they originated based on the same principals. Those who know these lamp records understand their method as the means to destroy ignorance. Now, for convenience, the elder monk Hui-ming has collected five of the lamp records into a single collection, calling it the *Wu-teng hui-yuan*.[81]

Regarding stream A, the reference to the *Ching-te ch'uan-teng lu* is not to all thirty fascicles but only to the latter half of fascicle 27.[82] All the portions of the *Ching-te ch'uan-teng lu* other than the latter half of fascicle 27 belong in stream B. Although it might be better to include the *Tsu-t'ang chi* in stream B, it contains the genesis of the kōan genre in comments attributed to members of the Hsüeh-feng faction.[83] Moreover, since the *Tsu-t'ang chi* exerted hardly any influence over the transmission of the lamp genre that continued following the compilation of the *Ching-te ch'uang-teng lu*, we can consider that stream B began with the compilation of the *Ching-te ch'uan-teng lu* in 1004. As a result, stream B can be said to have considerable significance for the investigation of Sung dynasty Ch'an sources.

As an example of the *Ching-te ch'uan-teng lu* contents, let us look at Ma-tsu Tao-i's record in fascicle 6. In the first place, it relates his record of activities (*hsing-ch'uang*), and dialogues (*wen-t'a*), and ends by describing the events of his passing. In contrast to this type of material, we find examples of comments by Ch'an masters to kōan cases raised in various places at that time, recorded in the latter half of fascicle 27. The story of "A Non-Buddhist Questions the Buddha," kōan number 32 in the *Wu-men kuan*, appears in the latter half of fascicle 27. This section of fascicle 27 in due course established the styles of "commemorating the ancients" (*sung-ku*) and "selections from the ancients" (*nien-ku*), which are crucial methods of commentary in the evolution of the kōan genre. Among the works in which these so-called kōans were collected is the *Tsung-men t'ung-yao chi*. Many of the "ancient cases" (*ku-tse*) selected for inclusion among the forty-eight cases in the *Wu-men kuan* are taken from kōan collected in the *Tsung-men t'ung-yao chi*.

On the other hand, how should we consider the *Wu-teng hui-yüan* in stream B? As stated above, the *Wu-teng hui-yüan* indicates the five lamp records, the *Ching-te ch'uan-teng lu*, *T'ien-sheng kuang-teng lu*, *Chien-chung Ch'ing-kuo hsü-teng lu*, *Tsung-men lien-teng hui-yao*, and *Chia-t'ai p'u-teng lu*, were compiled into one extensive lamp record. As a result, the two streams of Ch'an texts in the Sung dynasty, not to mention the special features of Sung Ch'an itself, are found in the different characteristics of the *Wu-teng hui-yüan* and the *Wu-men kuan*, two Ch'an texts compiled at roughly the same time. In other words, the *Wu-men kuan* is a kōan collection, and the *Wu-teng hui-yüan* may be referred to for the most part as a historical work of the Ch'an school, tra-ditionally called a "transmission of the lamp history" (*teng-shih*). Even among the five lamp records, the *Chien-chung Ch-ing-kuo hsü-teng lu* is divided into five sections, "orthodox lineage" (*cheng-tsung men*), "responses in accordance with practitioners' abilities" (*tui-ch'i men*), "selecting the ancients" (*nien-ku men*), "commemorating the ancients" (*sung-ku men*), and "gathas and verses" (*chieh-sung men*), suggesting the appearance of stream A material in stream B documents. The tendency reflected here in the *Chien-chung Ch-ing-kuo hsü-teng lu* emerged in the Northern Sung period, around the year 1100. In other words, we can say that this tendency in the *Chien-chung Ch-ing-kuo hsü-teng lu* reflects the influences exerted on Ch'an in the period when the *Tsung-men t'ung-yao chi* was compiled (1093).

The *Wu-men kuan* clearly possesses the features of a kōan collection in the style of stream A. Moreover, it is possible to read a different intention for the work into Wu-men Hui-k'ai's comments in the story "Jui-yen Calls His Master," case number 12 in the *Wu-men kuan*, than what has been understood as the special feature of the work up to now from looking at the first kōan, "Chao-chou's Dog." Monk Jui-yen every day called out to himself "Master," and responded, "yes." Then he would say, "Stay wide awake?" and answer, "Yes, I will." "From now on, never be deceived by others." "No, I will not."

> Wu-men's comment:
> "Old Jui-yen buys and sells himself. He plays around by displaying a
> lot of spirit disguises and demon masks. Why? Take a look! One
> calling out and one answering; one wide awake and one never to be
> deceived. If you acknowledge any of these guises as real, you are
> mistaken. If, on the other hand, you imitate Jui-yen, you have mas-
> tered the perspective of the wild fox.
> [Wu-men's] verse:
>
>> Students of the Way do not understand the truth,
>> Clinging only to their former discriminating consciousness.
>> The basis for birth and death through endless eons,
>> Idiots refer to as their original self.[84]

In other words, the special feature of Ch'an is here regarded, on the one hand, as a transformation engendered by "irrational dialogue" (*muriewa*), the tendency to deny discrimination and rational understanding as harmful. But on the other hand, doesn't a religious aspect emerge embedded in this story? As understood from Wu-men's own record of activities, Wu-men achieved "a thorough understanding of my one great event" (*chi-shih yen-ming*) through the strict instruction of his master, Yüeh-lin. There is a religious aspect contained in this, which involves the perilous nature of attaining spritual transformation through "irrational dialogue." Although the special character possessed by the *Wu-men kuan* highlights the perilous nature of irrationality, when the text was transmitted to Japan it seems to have matched squarely the dispositions of the Japanese people, and has been read with very great frequency down to the present day, mainly for its emphasis on irrationality.

If we understand the situation in this way, the special characteristics associated with the *Wu-men kuan* suggest very different qualities from those associated with Dōgen's style of Zen. The fact that either a yes or no response was acceptable even in the one word *Wu!* is already contained in the *Hung-*

chih sung-ku. Dōgen adopted this approach in his *Mana Shōbōgenzō*, and eventually developed the position that either response was acceptable in detail in the "Busshō" fascicle of the *Shōbōgenzō*. When compared to Dōgen's Zen style, the unique features of the *Wu-men kuan* seem rather distinct.

Why was the *Wu-men kuan* not read or published in China to the extent that it was in Japan? Although there are uncertainties regarding the answer to this question, it appears that texts other than the *Wu-men kuan* were sought by Chinese students and practitioners, such the *Tsung-men t'ung-yao chi*, from stream A, or from stream B the *Tsung-men lien-teng hui-yao*. Because the actual compilation of the *Tsung-men lien-teng hui-yao* is close to that of the *Tsung-men t'ung-yao chi*, it may be preferable to place it in stream A.[85] It seems that the *Wu-teng hui-yuan* established stream B retrospectively by collecting five works comprising 30 fascicles, and since the Ta-hui branch of Ch'an was the most prominent movement, their main kōan collection, the *Tsung-men lien-teng hui-yao*, was included. Moreover, the *Ching-te ch'uan-teng lu*, *T'ien-sheng kuang-teng lu*, *Chien-chung Ch-ing-kuo hsü-teng lu*, and *Chia-t'ai p'u-teng lu* are connected as supplements to one another. The Ch'an adherents who compiled each of these works formed them without duplicating what had been recorded previously. The fact that the *Tsung-men lien-teng hui-yao* has characteristics closely connected to kōan collections, which select materials from the *Ching-te ch'uan-teng lu*, *T'ien-sheng kuang-teng lu*, and *Chien-chung Ch-ing-kuo hsü-teng lu*, has already been pointed out. This makes it significantly different from the other four transmission of the lamp records. As a result, even though the *Tsung-men lien-teng hui-yao* was selected as one of the five lamp records in the *Wu-teng hui-yuan* and included in stream B, it should be noted that in terms of each characteristics as a Ch'an text, the *Tsung-men lien-teng hui-yao* follows the *Tsung-men t'ung-yao chi* in stream A.

REFERENCE CHART OF THE CH'AN TRANSMISSION LINEAGE

Numbers indicate the kōan number where individuals in question appear in the *Wu-men kuan*

Śākyamuni (6, 22, 32, 42)
Mahākāśyapa (6, 22)
Ānanda (22, 32)
twenty-five Indian patriarchs
Bodhidharma (41)
Hui-k'o (41)
Seng-ts'an
Tao-hsin
Hung-jen
Hui-neng (23, 29)

Nan-yang Hui-ch'ung	Ch'ing-yuan Hsing-ssu	Nan-yüeh Huai-jang
(17)	(see Lineage A)	(see Lineage B)

Lineage A
(Ch'ing-yuan Hsing-ssu)
Shih-t'ou Hsi-ch'ien
1. Yao-shan Wei-yen

Tao-Wu Yuan-chih	Yun-yen	
Shih-hsuang Ch'ing-chu	Tung-shan Liang-chieh	
Ch'ang-chuo Hsiu-tsai (39)	Yüeh-chou Ch'i-feng (48)	Ts'ao-shan Pen-chi (10) Ch'ing-shui (10)

2. T'ien-huang Tao-Wu
Lung-t'an Ch'ung-hsin (28)
Te-shan Hsüan-chien (13, 28)

Yen-t'ou Ch'uan-huo (13)	Hsüeh-feng I-ts'un (13)	
Jui-yen Shih-yen (12)	Hsüan-sha Shih-pei	Yun-men Wen-yen (15, 16. 21, 39, 48)
	Ti-tsang Kuei-shen	Tung-shan Shou-ch'u (15, 18)
	Fa-yen Wen-i (26)	

Lineage B
(Nan-yüeh Huai-jang)
Ma-tsu Tao-i (30, 33)
1. Ta-mei Fa-ch'ang (30)
T'ien-lung (3)
Chu-chih (3)
2. Pai-chang Huai-hai (2, 40)

Huang-po Hsi-yün (2)	Kuei-shan Ling-yu (40)	
Lin-chi I-hsüan	Hsiang-yen Chih-hsien (5)	Yang-shan Hui-chi (25)
Hsing-hua Tsun-chiang		Nan-t'a Kuang-yung
Nan-yuan Hui-yung		Pa-shao Hui-ch'ing (44)
Feng-hsüeh Yen-shao (24)		Hsing-yang Ch'ing-jang (9)

Shou-shan Hsing-nien (43)
Fen-yang Shan-chao
Shih-hsuang Ch'u-yuan

Huang-lung Hui-nan		Yang-chi Fang-hui
Pao-feng K'o-wen	Hui-t'ang Tsu-hsin	Pai-yün Shou-jui
Ts'ung-yüeh (47)	Shih-hsin Wu-hsin (39)	

Wu-tsu Fa-yen (35, 36, 38, 45)

Yuan-Wu K'o-ch'in   K'ai-fu Tao-ning

Hu-kuo Ching-yuan	Hu-chiu Shao-lung	Yueh-an Shan-huo (8)
Huo-an Shih-t'i (4)	Ying-an T'an-hua	Ta-hung Tsu-cheng
	Mi-an Hsien-chieh	Yueh-lin Shih-kuan
	Sung-yuan Ch'ung-yen (20)	Wu-men Hui-k'ai
		Shinchi Kaku-shin (Japan)

3. Nan-ch'uan P'u-yuan (14, 19, 27, 34)

Ch'ang-sha Ching-sui (46)   Chao-chou Ts'ung-shen (1, 7, 11, 14, 19, 31, 37)

NOTES

1. Translator's note: The *Wu-men kuan* (J. *Mumonkan*) may be translated into English as *The Gateless Barrier*. For the sake of consistency, I have referred to the text using the Chinese pronunciation, even in the Japanese context.

2. Ishikawa Rikizan, *Zenshūsōden shiryō no kenkyū* (Kyoto: Hōzōkan, 2001). Initially, Ishikawa reported on the "heresy incident" in "Zatsugaku jiken to kinsei bukkyō no seikaku" (The Heresy Incident and the Characteristics of Modern Buddhism), *Indogaku bukkyōgaku kenkyū* 37 no. 1 (1988): 246–252; and "Bannan eishu to zatsugaku jiken," *Sōtōshū kyōgi hōwa taikei* 7 (1991): 378–384. Prior to this, there were studies of the "heresy incident" by Nakayama Jyōji, "Daigo kōroku jiken kō" (A consideration of the *Daigo kōroku* incident), *Sōtōshū kenkyū kiyō* 11 (1979): 133–156; and by Yoshida Dōkō, "Bannan eishu to zatsugaku jiken" (Bannan Eishu and the heresy incident), *Eiheiji shi*, vol. 2 (1982), pp. 723–738.

3. Translator's note: This refers to the so-called *kansansetsu*, the term used by Ishii here: Sōneiji in Chiba prefecture, Daichōji in Tochigi prefecture, and Ryōonji in Saitama prefecture.

4. Other works, which were criticized included such texts for the study of kōan cases as *Daiendai*, *Ryōshūdai*, *Kenkokudai*, and *Zenrin ruiju*.

5. ZZ 120.264c.

6. Iriya Yoshitaka, trans., *Hekiganroku*, 3 vols. (Tokyo: Iwanami shoten, 1992, 1994, 1996).

7. Asahina Sōgen, trans., *Hekiganroku*, 3 vols. (Tokyo: Iwanami bunko, 1937).

8. Hirata Takashi, trans., *Mumonkan* (Tokyo: Chikuma shobō, 1969).

9. Nishimura Eshin, trans., *Mumonkan* (Tokyo: Iwanami bunko, 1994).

10. Ishii Shūdō, "Shohyō: Nishimura Eshin yakuchū *Mumonkan*," *Hanazono Daigaku bungakubu kiyō* 28 (1996): 113–136.

11. Concerning *Tsung-men t'ung-yao chi*, see Ishii Shūdō, "Kung-an Ch'an and the *Tsung-men t'ung-yao chi*," in Steven Heine and Dale S. Wright, eds., *The Kōan:*

Texts and Contexts in Zen Buddhism (New York: Oxford University Press, 2000), pp. 110–136. Here, I am particularly focusing on *Tsung-men t'ung-yao chi* in relation to the *Wu-men kuan.*

12. Ibid., pp. 118–120. The *Tsung-men t'ung-yao chi*, previously difficult to obtain, has been published along with the Yuan-dynasty text *Hsü-chi tsung-men t'ung-yao*, by Yanagida Seizan and Shiina Kōyū in *Zengaku tenseki sōkan* (Tokyo: Rinsen shoten, 1999).

13. Ishii Shūdō, "*Shūmon tōyōshū* ni tsuite (jō) (ge)," *Komazawa Daigaku bukkyō-gakubu ronshū* 4 (1972): 43–58, and 5 (1974): 37–63.

14. Even though Kagamishima Genryū's *Dōgen zenji to inyō kyōten, goroku no kenkyū* (Tokyo: Mokujisha, 1965), was a groundbreaking work in the study of the sources that Dōgen relied on, the *Tsung-men t'ung-yao chi* was not mentioned.

15. Shiina Kōyū, "*Shūmon tōyōshū* no shoshiteki kenkyū," *Komazawa Daigaku bukkyōgakubu ronshū* 18 (1987): 299–336.

16. Ishii, "Kung-an Ch'an and the *Tsung-men t'ung-yao chi*."

17. Ishii Shūdō, "*Shūmon tōyōshū* to *Hekiganroku*," *Indogaku bukkyōgaku kenkyū* 46 no. 1 (1997): 215–221.

18. Ishii, "Kung-an Ch'an and the *Tsung-men t'ung-yao chi*."

19. The *Tseng-chi hsü ch'uan-teng lu* is contained in ZZ 142. The preface by Wen-hsiu is dated the fifteenth year of *yung-lo* (1417). Wu-men Hui-k'ai's biography is also contained in *Chien-chung ching-kuo hsü-teng lu*, fasc. 35; *Wu-teng hui-yuan hsü-lueh*, fasc. 2; *Wu-teng yen-teng*, fasc. 22; and *Wu-teng ch'uan-shu*, fasc. 53, among others.

20. Although Wu-tsu Fa-yen was an important figure in the history of Ch'an during the Northern Sung, basic research regarding him remains to be carried out. Regarding his biography, see Ishii Shūdō, "Goso Hōen no kenkyū no oboegaki," (*Komazawa Daigaku*) *Chūgoku busseki kenmon ki* 8 (1987): 27–34.

21. Although *san-t'ai* is usually read as referring to a place, "on three stages." I take it here to be referring to the name of a song called "three stages."

22. ZZ 142.390c.

23. Fujiyoshi Jikai, trans., *Zenkan sokushin* (Tokyo: Chikuma shobō, 1970), p. 173.

24. The *Yueh-lin Shih-kuan ch'an-shih yu-lu* in one chapter, compiled by his attendant, Fa-pao, etc. (ZZ 120).

25. ZZ 120.249Lb (left-sided leaf of pp. 249, column b).

26. The record of Wu-men Hui-k'ai's career was written down by his attendants P'u-ch'ing, P'u-t'ung, Liao-hsin, P'u-li, Fa-tzu, P'u-yen, P'u-chüeh, Kuang-tsu, and Yi-chien in the *Wu-men Hui-k'ai Ch'an-shih yu-lu*, fasc. 2 (ZZ 120).

27. T 48.292b.

28. T 48.292b.

29. ZZ 120.242b.

30. Furuta Shōkin, trans., *Mumonkan* (Tokyo: Kadokawa shoten, 1959), p. 141.

31. Translator's note: In rendering the titles of the kōan here, I have consulted the English translations of Katsuki Sekida, *Two Zen Classics: Mumonkan and Hekigan-roku* ([1977]; New York: Weatherhill, 1996).

32. Hirata Takashi, trans. *Wu-men kuan* (Tokyo: Chikuma shobō, 1969).

33. The basic record for Shinichi Kakushin's life is the *Juhō kaisan hottō enmyō kokushi gyōjitsu nenpu*, compiled by Seikun, contained in *Zokugunshoruijū* 9A. Accord-

ing to the explanation of Chijiwa Minoru, there are records of Kakushin's life re-corded in the *Juhō kaisan hottō enmyō kokushi tōmei* by Seikan, and the *Kōkoku kaisan hottō enmyō kokushi tōmei* by Unrin Shikei, and so on, housed in the National Diet Library.

34. *Zokugun shoruijū* 9, pt. 1, pp. 351b–352a.

35. Ibid., p. 352a.

36. Kawase Kazuma, *Gozanban no kenkyū* (Nihon koshoseki shōkyōkai (Tokyo: Antiquarian Booksellers Association of Japan, 1970).

37. Research clarifying the relation between the Hōttō faction and circumstances in the Sōtō sect surrounding Keizan has been very active in recent years. There is a series of studies on this topic by Satō Shūkō, "Kohō Kakumyō to Koken Chitotsu: Rinzaishū Hōttō ha to Sōtōshū no hazama de," *Shūgaku kenkyū* 37 (1995): 245–250; and "Kyō Unryū to Kaga Daijō-ji: Keizan Jōkin to no kakawari wo megutte," *Shūgaku kenkyū* 39 (1997): 174–179.

38. Sugiō Genyū, "Minamoto Sanetomo no nyōssō kikaku to Dōgen zenji," *Shūgaku kenkyū* 18 (1976): 41–46.

39. *Zokugun shoruijū* 9, pt. 1, p. 350a.

40. Sugio Genyū, "Dōgen zenji no Banshōkokkoku issai shūmetsu no shinjin datsuraku to Asoka; amoji saihō: Shōgun Sanetomo no nōkotsu junbi kara staato suru Dōgen Zen to *Shōbōgenzō*," *Shūgaku kenkyū* 38 (1996): 7–12; and Sugio, "Aso-kaōji 'Useki ou' hakken no igi: genzō kaishaku wa konponteki ni dou kawaruka," *Shūgaku kenkyū* 39 (1997): 19–24.

41. The *Ch'an-tsung sung-ku lien-chu chi* is a collection of kōan and verses (325 kōan and 2,100 verses) compiled by Fa-ying Pao-chien in the second year of *ch'un-hsi* (1175). Later, in the Yuan dynasty, Lu-an P'u-hui added to it to form the *Ch'an-tsung sung-ku lien-chu t'ung-chi*, a 40-fascicle work with 493 kōan and 3,050 verses. The fact that the added portions included the *Wu-men kuan* indicates that it was one of the influences. This expanded version is contained in vol. 115 of the Ming edition of the supplementary canon, the *Zokuzōkyō*. Yanagida Seizan, in the "Kakukan shuroku sho-moku kaisetsu" chapter of his *Mumonkan shōsho shūsei*, Zengaku tenseki sōkan 9 (To-kyo: Rinsen shobō, 1999), indicates, "Translations [of the *Wu-men kuan*] have all been done in Japan. The original text of the *Wu-men kuan* was transmitted to Japan early on, owing to the fact that our own Shinchi Kakushin went to China and studied with Wu-men. There is no evidence that it was read in China." Moreover, according to the comprehensive research on Chinese Zen sources by Shiina Kōyū in the *Sōgenban Zenseki no kenkyū* (Tokyo: Daitō shuppansha, 1993), there is no information whatso-ever on Chinese editions of the *Wu-men kuan*.

42. Yanagida Seiji, *Muromachi jidaigo shiryō toshite no shōmotsu kenkyū*, 2 vols. (Mushashino shoin, 1998), counts seventeen works on the *Wu-men kuan* compiled by monks connected to the Sōtō sect. And, according to Yanagida's "Kōzan-ji zō *mumon-kan shū* ni tsuite" (included in the research report volume *Kōzan-ji shozō no tenseki bunsho no kenkyū narabi ni Kōzan-ji shiryō sōsho no henshū* [Tokyo: Monbushō Kagaku-kenkyūhi sōgo kenkyū, 1983], pp. 110–129), there have been 121 works on the *Wu-men kuan* in Japan. The number of works by monks connected to the Sōtō sect would thus seem to be fairly substantial.

43. Neither Kuroda Ryō, *Chosen kyōsho kō* (Tokyo: Iwanami shoten, 1940) or Shi-

ina Kōyū, *Sōgenban Zenseki no kenkyū* contains any information on editions of the *Wu-men kuan* published on the Korean peninsula. The thirty-fascicle *Ch'an-men nien-sung* (contained in *Kao-li ta-tsang-ching* 46) was compiled by the Dharma heir of P'u-chao Chih-ne, Yung-i Hui-ch'en (1178–1234), and his disciples, Chen-hsun, and so on, in the fourteenth year of *chen-yu* (1226), two years prior to the *Wu-men kuan*. This work selected 1,125 kōan for inclusion. Since it popularized the selected stories and verses of Ch'an masters, it is conceivable that it rendered the reception of the *Wu-men kuan* on the Korean peninsula unnecessary.

44. I have investigated this problem in detail in Ishii Shūdō, "Nenge mishō no wa no seiritsu wo megutte" (Hirai Shun'ei hakushi koki kinen ronbun shu *Sanron kyōgaku to Bukkyō shoshisō* (Tokyo: Shunjusha, 2000), pp. 411–430; and "Daibon tennō monbutsu ketsugi kyō wo megutte," *Komazawa daigaku Bukkyō gakubu ronshū* 31 (2000): 187–224. In addition, there is an article by Sugio Genyū, "Dōgen, Zeami, Bashō, and Heidegger," *Yamaguchi Daigaku Kyōiku gakubu kenkyū ronsū* 16 no. 1 (1967): 1–146, which considers the flower in terms of the world of beauty developed in the Noh theater of Zeami. There is also a study by Onishi Ryōhō, "Zeami no hana to Zenshisō," *Komazawa Tanki Daigaku bukkyō ronshu* 6 (2000): 177–190, which points to the story of the World-Honored One holding up a flower, and Mahākāśyapa breaking into a smile, in terms of the ultimate meaning that the flower has.

45. T 48.293c.

46. See ZZ 1–87–4:303c, 326c, and 327b–c. Translator's note: Ishii's original manuscript contained copies of the actual passages in question, following in the main body of the text. These have been omitted in the translation, as being primarily the concern of philological specialists. Those interested may consult the passages contained in ZZ referred to above.

47. T 48.325b.

48. The argument that it was created by a Japanese person during the Edo period was made by the Sōtō sect member Menzan Zuihō (1683–1769), in fascicle 1 of his *Daichi zenji geju monge* (*Zoku Sōtōshū zensho*, "Explanatory Note 2," pp. 242–243). The same argument is made in two places by the Vinaya master of Tainin, Myōryō (1705–1785), in *Kōge zuihitsu*, pt. 1 (32b–33a and 33a), as well as in the "apocryphal scripture" (*gikyō*) entry in chapter 3 of *Kōge dansū* (*Dai nihon zensho hon*, p. 210).

49. Nukariya Kaiten, "*Daibon tennō monbutsu ketsugi kyō* ni tsuite" (contained in *Zengaku hihanron*, Tokyo: Kōmeisha, 1905).

50. Contained in Yanagida Seizan, editor in chief, *Zengaku sōsho no go* (Tokyo: Chūmon shuppansha, 1975), p. 369.

51. *T'an-chou Hsing-hua yuan yu-lu*, contained in *Tz'u-ming Ch'an-shih Wu-hui chu-ch'ih yu-lu* compiled by Huang-lung Hui-nan (ZZ 120.88d). The *Recorded Saying* (*yü-lu*) has a preface dated the fifth year of T'ien-sheng (1027).

52. Sung edition, 16b–17a. On the close connection between the *Wu-men kuan* and the *Tsung-men t'ung-yao chi*, see the references to works by Ishii in notes 10 and 11.

53. T 48.295b. Translator's note: Zenkei Shibayama, *Zen Comments on the Mumonkan*, (translated by Sumiko Kudo) (New York: Mentor, 1974), p. 145, and Sekida, *Two Zen Classics: Mumonkan and Hekiganroku*, p. 73, were consulted for the translation.

54. Translator's note: In addition to the meaning of "poem," or "verse," the word *ei* in the title of the work can be translated as "looking at," or "studying," in which case the title of the poem could be rendered "Looking at the original face."

55. Kawamura Kōdō, ed., *Shohon taikō: Eihei kaisan Dōgen zenji gyōjū-Kenzeiki* (Tokyo: Daishūkan shoten, 1975), p. 88. Translator's note: I have taken the liberty of omitting the technical, philological discussion of issues related to understanding Dōgen's poem cited here, as being of little interest to the English reader.]

56. Kawabata Yasunari, *Utsukushii Nihon no Watakushi*, translated by Edward G. Seidensticker, in Seidensticker, *Japan, The Beautiful, and Myself* (Tokyo: Kōdansha, 1969).

57. Funazu Yōko, "*Sanshōdōeishū* no meishū, seiritsu, seikaku," *Otsuma kokubun* 5 (1974): 24–44.

58. *Dōgen zenji zenshū* (Tokyo: Shunjūsha, 1999), vol., p. 2

59. *Wu-tsu fa-yen yu-lu* (T 47.656b).

60. Yanagida, ed., *Zengaku sōsho no go*, p. 591.

61. There is also a citation of these words by Niu-t'ou Ching by Dōgen in his fifty-first lecture in chapter 1 of the *Eihei kōroku*, in Ōkubo Dōshū, ed., *Dōgen zenji zenshū*, (Tokyo: Chikuma shobō, 1971) vol. 2, p. 18. This lecture was delivered when Dōgen was forty-two years old.

62. Regarding Wu-tsu Fa-yen, see note 20.

63. T 47.665b–c.

64. T 47.869c.

65. Ta-hui's Ch'an style is very different from the style of *zazen* encouraged by Dōgen. See Ishii Shūdō, "*Zazenshin kō*," *Komazawa Daigaku Zen kenkyūjō nenpō* 8 (1997): 37–72; and "Dai'e Sōkō no kanna zen to 'Masen sakyō' no wa," *Komazawa Daigaku Zen kenkyūjō nenpō* 9 (1998): 39–76.

66. T 48.292c–293a.

67. ZZ 120.260d.

68. Iriya Yoshitaka, "Zengo tsurezure," contained in *Gudō to etsuraku: Chūgoku no Zen to shi* (Tokyo: Iwanami shoten, 1983).

69. Meichō fukyōkai, ed. *Wanshi roku* (Tokyo: 1988), p. 88.

70. Yanagida Seizan, "Muji no atosaki: sono tekisuto wo sakanoboru," contained in *Zen to Nihon bunka* (Tokyo: Kōdansha gakushū bunko, 1985); and Hirano Sōjō, "Kusu mu Busshō no wa wo megutte" *Zengaku kenkyū* 62 (1983): 9–25.

71. Hirata, trans., *Mumonkan*.

72. Regarding the meaning of these three, see Iriya Yoshitaka and Koga Hidehiko, eds., *Zengo jiten* (Tokyo: Shibunkaku shuppan, 1991).

73. T 48.294c.

74. T 48.298b.

75. T 48.294b–c.

76. T 48.297c.

77. T 12.496a.

78. Inoue Shōten, *Mumonkan no shin kenkyū*, vol 2 (Tokyo: Hōbunkan, 1925).

79. T 2.852c.

80. T 2.853b.

81. Chung-hua shu-chu ed., p. 2.

82. See Ishii Shūdō, "*Keitoku dentōroku* maki 27 no tokushoku," in *Sōdai Zen-shūshi no kenkyū* (Tokyo: Daitō shuppansha, 1987).

83. This is analyzed in detail in Yanagida Seizan, "*Sodōshu* no shiryō katchi," *Zengaku kenkyū* 44 (1953): 31–80.

84. T 48.294b. Translator's note: Shibayama, *Zen Comments on the Mumonkan*, p. 93, and Sekida, *Two Zen Classics: Mumonkan and Hekiganroku*, pp. 53, were consulted in the translation.]

85. See Ishii Shūdō, "Daie sōkō to sono deshitachi (1): *Gotō egen* no seiritsu katei to kanren shite" (*Indogaku bukkyōgaku kenkyū* 18/no. 2 [1970]: 332–333; "*Shōmon rentō eyō* no rekishiteki seikaku," ibid., 19 no. 2, (1971); and "*Shōmon toyōshu* ni tsuite (jō) (ge)," *Komazawa Daigaku bukkyō gakubu ronshu* 4 and 5, 1973 and 1974. Translator's note: For a discussion in English, see Ishii's "Kung-an Ch'an and the *Tsung-men t'ung-yao chi*," in Heine and Wright, eds., *The Kōan*, especially pp. 121–126.

8

The *Eihei kōroku*: The Record of Dōgen's Later Period at Eihei-ji Temple

Steven Heine

This chapter examines the textual history, structure, and function of the *Eihei kōroku* (Extensive records of the Eihei-ji first patriarch). This is one of the two main texts produced by Dōgen (1200–1253), the founder of the Sōtō Zen sect in thirteenth-century Japan, and the primary work representing the later period of Dōgen's career. The later period covered the last decade of his life (1244–1253), when Dōgen served as abbot of Eihei-ji temple in the remote Echizen mountains, far removed from the capital and the center of Japanese Buddhism in Kyoto. The *Eihei kōroku* is a collection of various kinds of verses and sermons, especially formal sermons composed in Chinese (*kanbun*) that are contained in the first seven of ten volumes. It was compiled by Dōgen's disciples according to the model of the "recorded sayings" (*yü-lu* or *kuang-lu*; J. *goroku* or *kōroku*) genre, or collected records of the great Chinese Ch'an masters of the Sung dynasty. The *Eihei kōroku* is probably the first main example of this genre produced in Japan.

After discussing a general overview of the formation of the text and its various sections and subsections, I will examine the historical and theoretical significance of the work by analyzing a number of passages representing different styles and time periods of composition. In particular, I will show the original and innovative approach of Dōgen, who cited from or alluded to a vast repertoire of Chinese Ch'an writings with which he was intimately familiar and which he almost singlehandedly was responsible for introducing to Japan. At the same time, Dōgen critiqued or rewrote numerous Chinese sayings, including those of his mentor during the time of his pilgrimage to China, Ju-ching (1163–1227), and one of Ju-ching's main predecessors in the Ts'ao-tung (J. Sōtō) sect lineage, Hung-chih (1091–1157).

Overview: Structure and Function of the Text

Until recently, the *Eihei kōroku* has received far less attention in Dōgen studies than his other main text, the *Shōbōgenzō* (Treasury of the true Dharma-eye).[1] The *Shōbōgenzō*, a collection of informal sermons, is generally considered the first writing on Buddhism in the Japanese vernacular; it was the primary work of Dōgen's earlier period, the ten years (1233–1243) he spent as abbot of Kōshō-ji temple in the town of Fukakusa on the outskirts of Kyoto. The composition of the *Shōbōgenzō* was almost entirely completed by the time of the move to Echizen (currently Fukui) Province. Therefore, this work does not reveal Dōgen's teachings or training style from the later period, although Dōgen apparently continued to edit some of the *Shōbōgenzō* fascicles. During this period he also composed additional fascicles that are included in a special edition known as the 12-fascicle *Shōbōgenzō*, in contrast to the better known collection from the earlier period known as the 75-fascicle *Shōbōgenzō*.

Some portions of the *Eihei kōroku* were completed prior to the Eihei-ji period, especially the first fascicle, which contains formal sermons delivered at Kōshō-ji temple in Kyoto, the ninth fascicle, which contains verse comments on kōans composed in 1236, and some of the Chinese verses contained in the last volume, which are from his travels to China in the mid-1220s. But the vast majority of material in the other volumes reflects Dōgen's teachings in the role of abbot of Eihei-ji temple.

Both the *Shōbōgenzō* and the *Eihei kōroku* consist primarily of collections of sermons delivered by Dōgen to his assembly of disciples. However, they represent two very different styles of sermonizing, as shown in Table 8.1. The *Shōbōgenzō*, composed in Japanese, contains *jishu*-style or informal sermons

TABLE 8.1. The Two Different Styles of Sermons Collected in the *Eihei kōroku* and the *Shōbōgenzō*, respectively

	Jōdō	*Jishu*
Text	*Eihei kōroku*, vols. 1–7	*Shōbōgenzō*, up to 95 fascicles
Where	*hattō*	*hōjō*
When	day	evening
Style	formal	informal
Expression	demonstrative	rhetorical
Length	brief and allusive	extended, with details and citations
Audience	monks, with general guests	diverse, those requesting instruction
Atmosphere	public, communal	private, individual

with lengthy discussions of specific doctrines and citations of passages from Mahāyāna sutras in addition to many different examples of Zen kōans. The *jishu* sermons were delivered at different times of the day, as well as late at night, mainly as a special instruction for those who requested or required it in the abbot's quarters (*hōjō*) or some other setting in the monastic compound. They were often written out prior to delivery, and then recorded and subsequently edited by Dōgen's main disciple, Ejō. Several of these sermons were delivered on more than one occasion or were apparently rewritten and reedited several times over the years.

The *Eihei kōroku*, composed in Chinese, contains records of *jōdō* (C. *shang-t'ang*) style of formal sermons, which were delivered exclusively in the Dharma hall (*hattō*), generally according to a set schedule and at a fixed time of the day, often for a ceremonial or memorial occasion. Although this style is considered formal, the *jōdō* was an oral manner of teaching recorded by disciples that contains many examples of spontaneous gestures and utterances.[2] Like the *Shōbōgenzō*, the *jōdō* sermons often cite kōan cases, and also cite or allude to a multitude of passages from the recorded sayings of Zen masters as well as the transmission of the lamp histories of the various schools that were collected during the time when Zen was the dominant form of Buddhism in Sung China during the eleventh and twelfth centuries. Both texts are therefore characterized by a remarkably extensive intertextuality, in that they achieve a great degree of originality and creativity through the process of citing and commenting on a wide variety of earlier Ch'an/Zen texts.

Editions

There are two main editions of the *Eihei kōroku* text. One is the 1598 edition attributed to the monk Monkaku, which is generally considered the authentic version that is used in the main modern edition of the collected writings of Dōgen, the *Dōgen zenji zenshū*.[3] There is an edition believed to be older than the Monkaku known as the Sozan edition, but this is undated and not verified. The Sozan edition seems to be almost wholly consistent with the Monkaku edition, so that most scholars feel that it was the model used by Monkaku and they now generally refer to the texts interchangeably. The other edition is the 1672 version edited by Manzan Dōhaku, one of the leaders of the eighteenth-century revival of Sōtō scholarly studies. This is also known as the *rufubon*, or popular edition.

The Monkaku edition is considered questionable, partly because it seems to have been based on a prominent but controversial abbreviated version of the text known as the *Eihei goroku*. The *Eihei goroku* was apparently created in China in the 1260s, about a decade after Dōgen's death, when one of his leading disciples, Giin, went to China to show Dōgen's Dharma brothers samples of the master's works. This makes it the earliest edition of at least some of *Eihei kōroku* material in circulation, but it is not truly representative of the source text.⁴

The *Eihei goroku*, which consists of selections of about 20 percent of the longer text, became one of the most frequently cited works (much more so than either the *Eihei kōroku* or the *Shōbōgenzō*) in the Sōtō sect's scholastic and esoteric, hermeneutic traditions of the medieval Kamakura and Muromachi eras. This tradition produced a body of literature known as *shōmono* writings, with several important subgenres representing different styles and levels of commentary on the original materials. An emphasis on the *Eihei goroku* persisted until there was a renewed interest in studying the original texts of the sect's founder during the Tokugawa era, which was spearheaded by Manzan and one of his main followers, Menzan, among others. During this revival, the *Shōbōgenzō*, as well as the *Eihei kōroku*, started to receive greater attention. This development helped pave the way for modern textual studies, although scholars today, who are also helped considerably by the legacy of Tokugawa-era studies, must struggle to ascertain and overcome the inaccuracies and intrasectarian biases evidenced in some of the seminal Tokugawa editions and commentaries.

Despite numerous and at times significant discrepancies between the Monkaku/Sozan and Manzan/*rufubon* editions, especially in the numbering of the passages, particularly in volume 1, and in the exact wording of numerous passages, particularly in volume 10, the contents of all *Eihei kōroku* editions follow the same basic structure.⁵

1. *Kōshō-ji goroku* (*jōdō* sermons, no. 1–126, dated 1236–1243, rec. Senne)—two-year hiatus during transition from Fukakusa to Echizen with no Dharma hall
2. *Daibutsu-ji goroku* (nos. 127–84, dated 1245–1246, rec. Ejō)
3. *Eihei-ji goroku* (nos. 185–257, dated 1246–1248, rec. Ejō)
4. *Eihei-ji goroku* (nos. 258–345, dated 1248–1249, rec. Ejō)
5. *Eihei-ji goroku* (nos. 346–413, dated 1249–1251, rec. Gien)
6. *Eihei-ji goroku* (nos. 414–470, dated 1251, rec. Gien)
7. *Eihei-ji goroku* (nos. 471–531, dated 1251–1252, rec. Gien)
8. Miscellaneous (20 *shōsan* from Daibutsu-ji/Eihei-ji, 14 *hōgo* from Kōshō-ji, *Fukanzazengi*, rec. Ejō and others)
9. *Kōshō-ji* collection (90 kōan cases with *juko* comments from 1236, rec. Senne and others)
10. Kanbun poetry collections (5 *shinsan*; 20 *jisan*; 125 *geju*, dated 1223–1253, rec. Senne and others)

A key feature is that the *Eihei kōroku* contains a variety of materials that generally include sermons which often incorporate verse comments or poems that usually have a didactic function. Both the sermons and poetry evoke, allude to, or comment directly on a vast storehouse of Chinese Ch'an kōans and other kinds of records.

Sermons

The first seven volumes of the *Eihei kōroku* consist of 531 *jōdō* sermons collected over a fifteen-year period. These begin with the opening of the Dharma hall at Kōshō-ji (1236–1243), as contained in volume 1. But most of the sermons stem from the time of Dōgen's abbacy at Daibutsu-ji/Eihei-ji, as contained in the other six volumes that continued to be collected until 1252, a year before the end of Dōgen's life, when he fell ill and apparently stopped delivering sermons. The other volumes contain a variety of genres that are typical of Zen Buddhist recorded sayings texts. These include two other kinds of informal, vernacular sermons in volume 8, including 20 *shōsan* for smaller meetings from the Kōshō-ji period, and 14 *hōgo* or Dharma discourses from the Eihei-ji period. Both the *shōsan* and *hōgo* styles are somewhat different from the *jishu*-style of the *Shōbōgenzō*. In general, they are less filled with philosophical depth and rhetorical flourish and more concerned with concrete, practical affairs in the life of the monastery. The brief meditation manual, the *Fukanzanzengi*, which was probably composed in 1233, is also included at the end of volume 8.

The ninth volume contains verse commentaries (*juko*) on 90 kōan cases composed in 1236, a year after the compiling of the *Mana Shōbōgenzō* collection of 300 kōans, which is a listing of cases with no commentary. Therefore, volume 9 represents an early attempt by Dōgen to find an appropriate style for providing commentary on kōans. Dōgen's collection of 150 poems in volume 10 were composed in three styles in Chinese script (*kanshi*) and stem from different periods ranging throughout his entire career. The composition of these poems began with Dōgen's travels to China, and the poems are among the only known writings from this very early period. The poetry collection also includes works that range from the period of transition to Echizen, when Dōgen stayed in mountain hermitages for nearly a year, to the later days at Eihei-ji as he approached his demise. It is clear that the majority of poems was composed during the Echizen years.

The first seven volumes can be further subdivided in two ways. One way is by the three locations for the sermons, including the Dharma Halls at Kōshō-ji temple (vol. 1), Daibutsu-ji temple, the original name of Eihei-ji when Dōgen first moved to Echizen in 1244 until it was changed in 1246 (vol. 2), and Eihei-ji temple proper (vols. 3–7). The other way of subdividing the text is by the three prominent assistants (*jisha*) to Dōgen who served as recorders or editors of the sermons. These include Senne (recorder of vol. 1, in addition to vols. 9 and 10), the primary early commentator on the *Shōbōgenzō* who remained in Kyoto with his main disciple Kyōgō after Dōgen and the rest of the community left for Echizen in 1243; Ejō (vols. 2–4 and 8), who became the second patriarch of Eihei-ji after Dōgen's death and was the primary editor of the *Shōbōgenzō* fascicles; and Gien (vols. 5–7), a disciple of Ejō who became the fourth Eihei-ji patriarch.

The transition from Ejō's editorship to Gien's that occurred around the ninth month/first day of 1249 is a significant turning point, according to some scholars, particularly Ishii Shūdō. This is because this period also marked another important shift for Dōgen, who had completed work on the 75-fascicle *Shōbōgenzō* several years before and now began writing and collecting the new collection known as the the 12-fascicle *Shōbōgenzō*. It is particularly notable that there are some basic correspondences between the sermons of the Gien volumes and the 12-fascicle *Shōbōgenzō*, particularly in an emphasis on the doctrines of karmic causality and moral retribution. This seems to mark an important and dramatic intellectual shift or "change" (*henka*) in Dōgen's approach to Buddhist doctrine.[6]

On the one hand, there is a basic consistency of style and content that runs throughout the seven volumes of *jōdō* sermons. For example, as illustrated in Table 8.2, which shows the numbers of all the sermons that can be dated conclusively based on the identifying introductory material contained in the passages themselves, many of the sermons were delivered for ceremonial occasions. These range from Buddhist events, such as memorials for the birth and enlightenment anniversaries of the Buddha, to seasonal and secular festivities. Also, a majority of sermons were based on the citations of kōans and other earlier Zen writings from China, as well as the demonstrative use of staffs and fly whisks as symbols of the master's authority and transcendent power.

There are some basic themes and approaches that are consistently employed throughout the text. These include the frequent use of the imagery of plum blossoms as a symbol of renewal and awakening; an emphasis on the role of the continuous practice of *zazen* as an essential component of the religious quest; the demonstrative use of the Zen staff and fly whisk as indicators of the master's authority; and Dōgen's eagerness to critique the eminent Chinese Ch'an predecessors whose records he frequently cites. For example, *jōdō* no. 2.135, a sermon for the winter solstice at Daibutsu-ji temple that appears near the beginning of volume 2, evokes a combination of these images, symbols, and attitudes in citing and revising a passage from the record of Hung-chih:

> When the ancient buddha Hung-chih was residing at Mount T'ien-t'ung, during a winter solstice sermon he said, "Yin reaches its fullness and yang arises, as their power is exhausted conditions change. A green dragon runs away when his bones are exposed. A black panther looks different when it is covered in mist. Take the skulls of all the buddhas of the triple world, and thread them onto a single rosary. Do not speak of bright heads and dark heads, as truly they are sun face, moon face. Even if your measuring cup is full and the balance scale is level, in transactions I sell at a high price and buy

when the price is low. Zen worthies, do you understand this? In a bowl the bright pearl rolls on its own without being pushed.

"Here is a story," [Hung-chih continued].

"Hsüeh-feng asked a monk, 'Where are you going?'"

"The monk said, 'I'm going to do my communal labor.'"

"Hsüeh-feng said, 'Go ahead.'"

"Yün-men said [of this dialogue], 'Hsüeh-feng judges people based on their words.'"

Hung-chih said, "Do not make a move. If you move I'll give you thirty blows. Why is this so? Take a luminous jewel without any flaw, and if you carve a pattern on it its virtue is lost."

The teacher [Dōgen] then said: Although these three venerable ones [Hung-chih, Hsüeh-feng, Yün-men] spoke this way, old man Daibutsu [Dōgen] does not agree. Great assembly, listen carefully and consider this well. For a luminous jewel without flaw, if polished its glow increases. . . .

With his fly-whisk [Dōgen] drew a circle and said: Look!

After a pause [Dōgen] said, Although the plum blossoms are colorful in the freshly fallen snow, you must look into it further to understand the first arrival of yang [with the solstice].

Here, Dōgen is indebted to Hung-chih's original passage, which cites Ma-tsu's famous saying, "Sun face [or eternal] buddha, moon face [or temporal] buddha" in *Book of Serenity* (C. *Ts'ung-jung lu*, J. *Shōyōroku*) case 36, and also includes a saying about the bright pearl that appears in the fourth line of Hung-chih's verse comment on this case. But Dōgen challenges all the masters. After making a dramatic, well-timed demonstration with the fly whisk as a symbol of authority, Dōgen then evokes the image of plum blossoms in the snow to highlight the need for continually practicing *zazen* meditation. This reinforces his rewriting of the jewel metaphor to put an emphasis on the process of polishing.

At the same time, there seem to be some key differences in the materials collected by the three recorders of the *Eihei kōroku* sermons. First, in volume 1 there are numerous short and concise sermons (about 15 percent of the total), which consist of only one or two sentences.[7] For example, no. 1.34 queries simply, "If this greatest cold does not penetrate into our bones, how will the fragrance of the plum blossoms pervade the entire universe?" and no. 1.23 states, "Deeply see the blue mountains constantly walking. By yourself know the white stone woman gives birth to a child at night." Both sermons conclude with a reference to the fact that following the brief verbal utterance "Dōgen descended from his seat."

In the second main section (vols. 2–4, recorded by Ejō), we find that a new pattern emerges, as seen above, in which Dōgen cites eminent predecessors

TABLE 8.2. Chronology of Eihei Koroku Construction

YEAR	1/1 New Year	1/10 10th Day	1/15 Full Moon	2/15 Buddha Death	3/1 Open Hearth	3/14 Return Kamakura	3/20 20th Day	4/8 Buddha Birth	4/15 Summer Retreat	4/25 25th Day	5/1 New Moon	5/5 Boys' Fest	5/27 Memor Butsuju[a]	6/1 New Moon	6/10 10th Day	6/10 Emperor Birthday	6/15 Temple Name[b]
1236	X	X	X	X	X	X	X	X	X	X	X	X	X	X	X	X	X
1240																	
1241	32							42	44								
1242	90h							98									
1243	116			121	122			75	118								
1244	X	X	X	X	X	X	X	X	X	X	X	X	X	X	X	X	X
1245	X	X	X		X	X		X	127		X	X					
1246	142H			146			152h	155h	158h			169	171				177
1247	216H		219	225				236H	238			242H			247		
1248	X	X	X	X	X	251		256H	257H	259	261H	X					
1249	303H	305		311				320H	322H	324	325	326H					
1250				367												379	
1251			412	418				427				435					
1252			481	486	489			495					504	505			
Total	6	1	3	7	2	1	1	9	7	2	2	4	2	1	1	1	1

YEAR	7/5 Memor. Eisai[c]	7/15 Close Retreat	7/17 Memor. Ju-ching	8/1 Tenchū Fest.	8/1 New Moon	8/6 Ju-ching Record	8/15 Harvest Moon	9/1 New Moon	9/2 Memor. Minamoto	10/1 Open[d] Temple	10/15 Open Hearth	11 mo. Winter Solstice	12/8 Rohatsu	12/10 Tenth Day	12 mo. Memor. Mother	12/25 Year End	Total
1236	X	X	X	X	X	X	X	X	X	(1)	X	X	X	X	X	X	1–31 = 31
1240		X	X	X	X	X	13H	X	X		14H	25		X	X		32–65
1241							77H						88				76–89 = 48
1242		102	X	104	X	105	106				109	115	X	X	X		90–115 = 26
1243			X	X	X	X	X		X	X	X	X	X	X	X	X	66–75
1244	X	X	X	X	X	X	X	X	X	X	X	X	X			X	116–126 = 21
																	0
1245		130										135H	136				127–141 = 15
1246		183h	184				189	193			199	206H	213				142–215 = 74
1247		248	249		250	X	X	X	X	X	X	X	X	X	X	X	216–250 = 35
1248			274				277	279			288	296H	297			302	251–275 / 277–302 = 51
1249		341	342				344H	347			353		360				303–345 / 346–360 = 58
1250			384				413	389	363		396		406	392	409		361–411 / 413 = 52
1251	441	442	276				448	451			462		475		478		276, 412 / 414–480 = 69
1252	512	514h	515				521	523	524		528		506				481–531 = 51
TOTAL	2	7	7	1	1	1	9	6	2	8	8	5	8	1	2	1	531

H = direct influence of Hung-chih, h = indirect influence

LINE = beginning of Gien's editing of the EK, and Dōgen's focus on the composition of the 12-fascicle *Shōbōgenzō*.

[a] 1184–1221, disciple of Eisai and teacher of Dōgen.

[b] Change name from Daibutsu-ji to Eihei-ji.

[c] 1141–1225, a.k.a. Myōan Senkō.

[d] The opening of Kōshōji Temple in 1236 was marked by record in the Manzan edition only.

of Chinese Ch'an but also is willing to challenge, critique, revise, and rewrite their sayings to express his own unique understanding and appropriation of Buddhist teaching. For example, in no. 3.207 Dōgen criticizes Yün-men, as well as the whole notion of the autonomy of a "Zen school" (*Zen-shū*) that may take priority over the universal Buddha Dharma.

> [Dōgen] said: Practitioners of Zen should know wrong from right. It is said that after [the ancestor] Upagupta, there were five sects of Buddha Dharma during its decline in India. After Ch'ing-yüan and Nan-yüeh, people took it upon themselves to establish the various styles of the five houses, which was an error made in China. Moreover, in the time of the ancient buddhas and founding ancestors, it was never possible to see or hear the Buddha Dharma designated as the "Zen school," which has never actually existed. What is presently called the Zen school is not truly the Buddha Dharma.
>
> I remember that a monk once asked Yün-men, "I heard that an ancient said that although the [patriarch of the Ox Head school] expounded horizontally and vertically, he did not know the key to the workings of going beyond. What is that key to the workings of going beyond?"
>
> Yün-men said, "The eastern mountain and the western peak are green."
>
> If someone were to ask Eihei [Dōgen], "What is that key to the workings of going beyond?" I would simply reply to him, "Indra's nose is three feet long."

Note the way Dōgen rewrites Yün-men's response. Neither expression addresses the question directly, and it could be argued that each has its merits as a manifestation of Zen wisdom. Yet Dōgen seems to suggest that Yün-men's phrasing is deficient and that his own saying is on the mark, perhaps because it is at once more indirect and absurd yet more concrete and down-to-earth.

The third section of *jōdō* sermons (vols. 5–7, recorded by Gien) is characterized by numerous very lengthy passages, many of which stress the doctrine of karmic causality and moral retribution experienced throughout the three tenses of time, often by citing the texts of pre-Mahāyāna Buddhism, as in *jōdō* nos. 5.381, 6.437, 7.485, and 7.517. For example, no. 6.437 from 1251 makes it clear that those who advocate the inescapable efficacy of karmic retribution alone are the true Buddhists, whereas those who reject this doctrine in favor of a metaphysical principle beyond morality and considered free from karma must be considered heretics. The passages have a close affinity with the "Jin-shin inga" and "Sanjigo" fascicles of the 12-fascicle *Shōbōgenzō*, which were also composed in the early 1250s. They stress the significance of causality as crucial for appropriating the Buddha Dharma and severely criticize those who dismiss or ignore this outlook. At the same time, there are passages in this section of sermons that reflect an emphasis on supernaturalism, which is also in accord with some elements in the 12-fascicle *Shōbōgenzō*. For example, *jōdō* no. 5.388 tells a story of repentance involving demons and celestial spirits.

The differences between the three sections of the *jōdō* sermons may reflect an evolution or transition in Dōgen's own approach and attitudes. Or, they may be based on the diverging skills and perspectives of the recorders, although it is impossible to determine how much input the editors may have actually had in the formation of the text. In any case, it is crucial to see that Dōgen's style and approach were by no means static, but shifted significantly throughout the periods during which the records were collected.

Historical and Theoretical Levels of Significance

The levels of significance of the various kinds of records collected in the *Eihei kōroku* encompass diverse aspects. There is a historical dimension, which includes the importance of monastic rituals as well as issues in Dōgen's biography, such as his changing attitudes toward the development of Zen in China and Japan. There is also a theoretical dimension, which includes Dōgen's use of diverse literary styles and citations of Zen and other kinds of Buddhist texts, in addition to his approach to various doctrines in Chinese and Japanese Buddhism.

Monastic Routine

The passages in this category reveal the role of liturgy and ritual in Dōgen's approach to Zen monasticism, especially in the main sermons that were delivered in a rather mechanical fashion for ceremonial occasions and memorials, although they still often express a sense of spontaneity, especially through the use of verse commentary or demonstrative gestures near the conclusion of the discourse. According to the pattern prescribed in the *Ch'an-yüan ching-kuei* (J. *Zen'en shingi*) of 1103, the seminal text containing Chinese Ch'an monastic rules, the *jōdō* sermons were to be delivered at least five or six times a month, on the first, fifth, tenth, fifteenth, twentieth, and twenty-fifth days of the month, in addition to other special occasions.[8] Dōgen apparently adjusted the prescribed schedule that was implemented in China to fit the needs of his development of Zen monasticism at Eihei-ji temple in Japan. Based on the numbers of sermons in Table 8.2 it is clear that the Buddha's birth (4/8), death (2/15), and enlightenment (12/8) anniversaries, in addition to memorials for his Japanese teacher Eisai and Chinese mentor Juching, were favorite events in the yearly cycle. Dōgen also consistently presented sermons for seasonal celebrations, especially in the fall (new and full moons in the eighth, ninth, and tenth months).

A prime example of a ceremonial sermon is *jōdō* no. 1.90, delivered on New Year's day in 1242 at Kōshō-ji temple, which concludes with a seasonal verse on blossoms blooming in spring as a symbol of renewal and personal awakening.

> As the heavenly sky is clear, each and every thing purifies each and
> every other thing. The earth is covered with nourishing moisture,
> penetrating a thousand things and soaking ten thousand things.
> How is it at such a time as this?
>   After a pause [Dōgen] said:
>
> The harmonious expression of spring makes the whole world fragrant,
> The deity of spring sits impassively in the Cloud [monks'] hall,
> On every branch their flowers blooming of coral color,
> The opening of blossoms throughout the world open makes this is a
>   celestial realm.

Similarly, *jōdō* no. 4.297, a sermon delivered in 1248 for the Buddha's Enlightenment Day (traditionally celebrated in Japan on 12/8), evokes the image of plum blossoms, which are beginning to come to the fruition of their growth cycle even when they are still far from visible in the midst of the winter snow, that starts with an exclamation cited from the verse comment to a story about Layman Pang playing in the snow in the *Blue Cliff Record* (C. *Pi-yen lu*, J. *Hekiganroku*), case 42.

> The snowball hits! The snowball hits! It hits as the cold plum blossoms in the snow. On this eighth day of the twelfth month, the
> bright star in heaven and a wooden ladle on the earth appear before
> the spring.

In many of the ceremonial sermons, Dōgen cites through either praise or criticism—or some playful, ironic combination—the teachings of his predecessors in Sung Chinese Ch'an, especially Ju-ching and Hung-chih. In *jōdō* no. 3.249, Dōgen uses a memorial for the anniversary of Ju-ching's death as an opportunity to eulogize the master's transcendence of secularism and corruption.

> Today Ju-ching frolics among the spirits and fans the clouds with
> the traditions of buddhas and patriarchs. He is resented by the
> crowds of the corrupt secular world, whose ignorant karmic con-
> sciousness continues to affect future generations.

No. 2.184 was delivered on a memorial day for Ju-ching in a different year, when Dōgen said, "When I entered China I studied walking to be like someone from Handan.[9] I worked very hard carrying water and hauling firewood. Don't say that my late teacher deceived his disciple. Rather, T'ien-t'ung Ju-ching was deceived by Dōgen." In no. 2.167 Dōgen continues the self-deprecating tone by saying, "I would simply say, I cannot avoid deceiving my late teacher." There are many other examples, some of which will be discussed in following sections, in which Dōgen eulogizes his teacher.[10] There are examples, however, such as no. 2.179, also cited below, in which Dōgen criticizes Ju-ching along with other Chinese Ch'an predecessors. Furthermore, in no. 5.390, Dōgen revises Ju-ching's view of meditation, and also criticizes and revises Pai-chang's view of monastic regulations in Zen.

Dōgen attitude toward Hung-chih is particularly interesting in that he seems to rely heavily on the Chinese master's recorded sayings as a model for some of his ceremonial sermons, and yet in citing Hung-chih he rarely loses the opportunity to critique or one-up him, as he also does in the *Shōbōgenzō* "Zazenshin" fascicle. For example, in *jōdō* no. 3.236 for "Bathing [the baby] Buddha," a celebration of the Buddha's birthday in 1247, Dōgen tells that when Hung-chih was abbot at Mount T'ien-t'ung, in a sermon delivered on the same occasion, he had cited an anecdote in which Yün-men performed the bathing ritual and had apologized to the Buddha for using "impure water." However, Dōgen criticizes Hung-chih's interpretation by suggesting:

> Although the ancient buddha Hung-chih said it like this, how
> should Eihei speak of the true meaning of the Buddha's birthday?
> Casting off the body within the ten thousand forms, the conditions
> for his birth naturally arose. In a single form after manifesting as a
> human body, he discovered anew the path to enlightenment. What
> is the true meaning of our bathing the Buddha?
> After a pause [Dōgen] said, Holding in our own hands the bro-
> ken wooden ladle, we pour water on his head to bathe the body of
> the Tathāgata.

It is notable that according to Table 8.2 Dōgen cited Hung-chih three or four times on the occasion of the Buddha's birthday between 1246 and 1249, and also on other occasions such as New Years during these years, the beginning of the summer retreat, the Boys' Festival, and the winter solstice, often employing the same strategy of combining citation with criticism. These passages are from the section of the *Eihei kōroku jōdō* sermons edited by Ejō, and this trend of a reliance on the Hung-chih text for the most part did not continue in the later sections edited by Gien.

Dōgen's Life and Attitudes

The passages in this category focus on biographical and historical issues reflecting or surrounding events in the life of Dōgen and how his attitudes toward key people, texts, and ideas developed and in some cases may have changed markedly during the course of his teaching career. The passages in the *Eihei kōroku* are particularly notable for revealing key features and facts of Dōgen's life about which little else is known and for which there are few, if any, available sources. Some of the events revealed in the *Eihei kōroku* include Dōgen's pilgrimage to China and his relation to Ju-ching and Ch'an Buddhist teaching styles; his life at Kōshō-ji temple and his move to Echizen and establishment of Eihei-ji; and his return from a trip to visit the new shogun, Hōjō Tokiyori, in Kamakura in 1247–1248.

Dōgen's poems in *kanbun* contained in volume 10 are one of the main sources of information about his trip to China. For example, verse 10.32c shows that as part of his practice he visited a pious layman, who was mourning the death of his son. He tried to comfort the bereaved father; this is an interesting function of Ch'an monks in relation to mainstream society:

> When he opens his true eyes, the pupils are clear;
> Looking at his face, he seems steady,
> Tears having already been shed,
> Though his son has entered the realm of the dead.
> Lord Yama!
> You won't catch him crying.

Apparently Dōgen also participated in several "verse contests," during which Ju-ching challenged his disciples to change and revise his own poem on a particular topic, such as the harvest moon or a Buddhist symbol. Verse 9.58 is a rewriting of Ju-ching's verse on the symbolism of the ringing of the Buddhist bell that Dōgen also cites in *Hōkyōki* and the *Shōbōgenzō* fascicles "Makahannyaharamitsu" and "Kokū." According to Ju-ching's original poem:

> The bell looks like a mouth, gaping,
> Indifferent to the wind blowing in the four directions;
> If you ask it about the meaning of wisdom,
> It only answers with a jingling, tinkling sound.

Dōgen's verse uses tautology and onomatopoeia to make the conclusion more concrete and practical:

> The bell is a voice articulating emptiness,
> Playing host to the wind blowing in the four directions,
> Expressing in its own elegantly crafted language
> The tintinnabulation: the ringing of the ringing . . .

Whereas the verses show some aspects of what Dōgen was doing and thinking in China, there are numerous *jōdō* sermons that reveal his approach to inheriting and transmitting the teachings to Japan. For example, in no. 1.48, which appears as 1.1 in the Manzan edition (and is also the first sermon in the *Eihei goroku*), Dōgen reflects on Ju-ching in the self-deprecating language he uses elsewhere, and also offers a couple of brief yet frequently noted verses that highlight the teaching that he brought back from China:

> [Dōgen] said, This mountain monk [Dōgen] has not passed through many monasteries. Somehow I just met my late teacher Ju-ching. However, I was not deceived by T'ien-t'ung. But T'ien-t'ung was deceived by this mountain monk. Recently, I returned to my homeland "empty handed" (*kūshū genkyō*). And so this mountain monk has no Buddha Dharma. Trusting fate, I just spend my time.
>
> > Every morning, the sun rises in the east.
> > Every evening, the moon sets in the west,
> > Clouds gathering over the foggy peaks,
> > Rain passes through the surrounding hills and plains.
> > [Also:]
> > A leap year comes every fourth year,
> > A rooster crows at dawn.

Jōdō no. 1.105 is notable because it indicates that text of the recorded sayings of Dōgen's mentor, the *Ju-ching yü-lu* (J. *Nyojō goroku*), was delivered to Japan in 1242, and this marked a renewed interest in citing Ju-ching's works, as evidenced by numerous *Shōbōgenzō* fascicles from this period dealing with Ju-ching. No. 2.128, which appears at the beginning of volume 2, is particularly significant for the insight it offers into Dōgen's view of Ju-ching's role in Zen monastic life, particularly regarding the delivery of sermons at evening meetings (*bansan*), as well as Dōgen's general approach to language and the meaning of "words and phrases" in Zen discourse. According to Dōgen, the merit of a monastery is not found in the size of the congregation, for having one great sage as a master is sufficient. Dōgen points out that eminent masters such as Fen-yang, Chao-chou, and Yao-shan had only a relative handful of followers.

Rather, the key to the master's ability to lead and instruct is the evening sermons, which are meant to be spontaneous and intense spiritual experiences. Dōgen asserts that contemporary abbots did not have the ability demonstrated by the early T'ang patriarchs to deliver compelling sermons, and that is why the practice of evening meetings died out. As in many other passages in his writings, Dōgen is highly critical of the practice of the Ch'an school in China, and in no. 4.301 he says, "Throughout the entire world, there is nobody who understands Buddha Dharma," and he agrees with Huang-po that practitioners "are just gobblers of dregs." This saying is a paraphrase of Huang-po's comment recorded in *Blue Cliff Record* case 11 and *Book of Serenity* case 53.

The one main exception is Ju-ching, the kind of leader who only appears "once in a thousand years." In no. 2.128, an evening sermon, which echoes what is said about Ju-ching in *Shōbōgenzō* "Shohō jissō," Dōgen describes the excitement that is so unusual in his teacher's approach:

> Regardless of what the regulations in monastic rules manuals actually prescribed, at midnight, during the early evenings, or at any time after the noonday meal, generally without regard to the time, Ju-ching either had someone beat the drum for entering the abbot's quarters (*nyūshitsu*) to give a general talk (*fusetsu*) or he had someone beat the drum for small meetings (*shōsan*) and then for entering the abbot's quarters. Or sometimes he himself hit the wooden clapper in the Monks hall three times and gave a general talk in the Illuminated hall. After the general talk the monks entered the abbot's quarters. Sometimes he hit the hanging wooden block in front of the head monk's quarters, and gave a general talk in the head monk's room. Again, following the general talk the monks entered the abbot's quarters.
>
> These were extraordinary, truly exceptional experiences! Because Daibustu [Dōgen] is a disciple of Ju-ching, I am also conducting evening meetings, which is happening for the very first time in our country.[11]

Also, in the same sermon, Dōgen expresses his own view of the role of language in relation to silence in Zen discourse. He mentions Tan-hsia (Hung-chih's teacher), who once reported that Te-shan said, "There are no words and phrases (*goku*) in my school," but Tan-hsia said, "In my school, there are words and phrases." Dōgen adds, "I would not have spoken like this. Great assembly, do you want to hear what I have to say. In my school *there are only words and phrases (yui-goku)*" [emphasis added].

Numerous passages in the *Eihei kōroku* are important because they show some key features of Dōgen's monastic leadership, once he was finally established in Japan. For example, *jōdō* no. 1.41 indicates that there were thirty-one followers at Kōshō-ji temple, and several of the *hōgo* sermons, especially nos. 8.2h and 8.3h, reveal something about the disciples Dōgen taught there, which included nuns as well as Confucianists, and the ways he instructed them, including the use of kōans. The preface to volume 2 indicates that Dōgen moved to the mountain in Echizen on 7/18 of 1244, and that in the following year, "many disciples from the four directions flocked like clouds to practice with him." No. 2.177 concerns the renaming of the temple on 6/15 in 1246, and after that Dōgen referred to himself as "Eihei" (rather than Daibutsu).

One of the most important *jōdō* sermons is no. 3.251, delivered on 3/15 in 1248 upon Dōgen's return to Eihei-ji after spending eight months in Kamakura at the behest of the shogun. Apparently disturbed by the emergence of "Warrior Zen" in evidence in the temporary capital, Dōgen declined the offer to lead a temple that was being built in Kamakura and went home with a new emphasis on the doctrine of karmic causality as well as a greater appreciation for his monk disciples. Yet it is not clear that Dōgen's effort to reassure his worried followers was fully successful:

> [Dōgen] said, On the third day of the eighth month of last year, this mountain monk departed from this mountain and went to the Kamakura District of Sagami Prefecture to expound the Dharma for patrons and lay disciples. In the third month of this year, just last night, I came home to this temple, and this morning I have ascended this seat. Some people may be wondering about the reasons for my travels. After crossing over many mountains and rivers, I did expound the Dharma for the sake of lay students, which may sound like I value worldly people and take monks lightly.
>
> Moreover, some may ask whether I presented some Dharma that I never before expounded, and that they have not heard. However, I did not preach a Dharma there that was different from what I have previously expounded to you here. I merely explained to them that people who do good for others and renounce all evil action will reap the rewards of cause-and-effect. So cast away tiles and pick up jewels. This is the one matter I, Eihei, clarify, explain, believe, and practice. Followers, you must learn this truth!
>
> After a pause, [Dōgen] said, You may laugh to hear my tongue speaking of causality so casually. How many follies I have committed in my effort to cultivate the way. Today it is pitiful that I have become a water buffalo. This is the phrase for expounding Dharma. How shall I utter a phrase for returning home to the mountains? This mountain monk has been gone for more than half a year. I was like a solitary wheel placed in vast space. Today, I have returned to the mountains, and the clouds [that is, monks] are feeling joyful. My great love for this mountain is greater than it has ever been.

In addition to his reaction to the quality of Zen in Kamakura, another major turning point in Dōgen's later career was the reception of a complete copy of the *Tripitaka* (J. *Agonkyō*) at Eihei-ji near the end of 1249 from his patron, Hatano Yoshishige. This is commemorated in no. 5.361, which acknowledges the receipt, no. 5.362, which gives thanks, and no. 5.366, which describes the embroidered cover that was made for the texts. Once he had the *Tripitaka* in his possession, Dōgen then began to focus on drawing his citations from early Buddhist texts rather than strictly from the Zen canon. This tendency reinforced the emphasis on the basic doctrine of karmic causality and retribution, which seemed to begin with no. 3.251 and was also expressed extensively in the 12-fascicle *Shōbōgenzō* composed during this period of Dōgen's career.

There were other doctrines emphasized by Dōgen in the later, post-

Kamakura period, which will be discussed below. At the same time, Dōgen seemed to be influenced by another approach to the issues of karma, retribution, and penance, that is, the supernatural early Buddhist *jātaka* tales that were often translated or integrated into East Asian morality tale literature (*setsuwa bungaku*). *Jōdō* no. 5.379, for example, delivered on 6/10 in 1250, deals with the use of a master's supranormal spiritual power in fertility rites. Dōgen states that his intention is to invoke a clear sky, and says that "last year rain fell ceaselessly but now I wish for clear weather like my master at Mount Ching-liang Temple [a temple where Ju-ching was abbot before serving at Mount T'ien-t'ung], who went to the Dharma hall to wish for fine weather. When he did not go to the Dharma hall, the buddhas and patriarchs did not either. Today I am in the Dharma hall, just like my former teacher." Yet, Dōgen concludes with an ironic, iconoclastic commentary by pausing, sneezing, and saying "Once I sneeze, clouds break, and the sun appears." Then, he raised the fly whisk, saying, "Monks! Look at this. The cloudless sky swallows the eight directions."

Literary and Rhetorical Significance

This category covers two main topics, one with an internal significance, and the other with an external reference. The internal level includes passages that demonstrate the way that Dōgen uses a variety of prose and poetic literary styles in the sermons and other records. His heavy reliance on verse is such that even his prose sermons often reflect a sense of rhyme and rhythm. The external reference involves the high degree of intertextuality in Dōgen's selection and citation of earlier Zen texts, especially the records of Hung-chih, the single main patriarch who influenced his approach to delivering *jōdō* sermons.

Several examples of poetry used as a kind of commentary on the main part of the sermon have been discussed above, including 1.42 and 1.48. Another example of a verse providing lyrical commentary in the first seven volumes includes no. 4.279, delivered on 9/1 in 1248, traditionally a day when the relaxed post-*ango* retreat summer period gave way to more intensive training:

> Sit on your cushions and think beyond thinking; play vividly and energetically, and don't be fooled by any demonic spirits. The old monk abiding on this mountain swallows buddhas and living beings with one gulp. The crouching lion catches rabbits and enraged elephants with one swipe of his paw. Smashing the polished tile of trying to become a buddha by sitting as a buddha, laugh and destroy the net of doubts of the three vehicles and five vehicles.

> > After a pause [Dōgen] said,
> > The opening of the petals plum blossoms,
> > Heralds the beginning of spring.

In the sky at dawn,
There is only the round, full moon.

Another example is no. 4.327, on how buddhas transmit their teaching without attachment:

In the dead of the night.
The moon low in the sky,
As Śākyamuni enters *parinirvāṇa,*
The jade forest, turning white,
Cannot play host to
A thousand-year-old crane,
Whose glistening feathers
Fly right by the empty nest.

At the same time, several examples contained in the poetry collection in volume 10 are notable for their philosophical significance. For example, no. 10.10b, which accompanies a portrait of Dōgen painted at Kōshō-ji temple, makes an interesting statement on the issue of illusion and reality:

If you take this portrait of me to be real,
Then what am I, really?
But why hang it there,
If not to anticipate people getting to know me?
Looking at this portrait,
Can you say that what is hanging there
Is really me?
  In that case your mind will never be
  Fully united with the wall [as in Bodhidharma's wall-gazing
    meditation].

Similarly, 10.63c deals with the paradoxical sayings of Ma-tsu, who early in his career taught that "Mind Itself Is Buddha" (*sokushin zebustsu*), but later changed to the opposite view, "No mind, no Buddha" (*hishin hibutsu*).

"Mind itself is buddha"—difficult to practice, but easy to explain;
"No mind, no buddha"—difficult to explain, but easy to practice.

Another aspect of the internal literary significance is the way that even the prose sections of the *jōdō* sermons integrate poetry as well as other lyrical and literary elements by orchestrating a variety of subgenres to establish patterns of rhythm and rhyme. For example, Andō Yoshinori provides an innovative analysis of several *jōdō* sermons, which could easily be read merely as straight-forward prose narratives but actually consist of multiple prose and poetic sections. Both examples cited below culminate in the linguistic device of the "turning word" (*ittengo*) which is used in numerous kōan collections and recorded sayings texts as an expression of the power of brief, allusive words used as an indirect communication to transform the mind.

The first example, no. 1.68, opens with a formal comment, and the remaining prose and verse passages can be seen as further commentary on this.[12]

> When we exhaust our strength to express it,
> Even half a word is like a pillar holding us up,
> Training the mind and confirming enlightenment,
> We use a wooden ladle to scoop up a mouthful.   *Formal comment*

For a person with the ability to hear and with the ability to practice—

> Before emotions are born
> And forms have appeared.   *Short verse*
> All voices resounding,
> Each and every thing clearly revealed.   *Short verse*
> Without awakening,
> Advancing each step we stumble over our feet,
> Making seven or eight mistakes.
> Not yet resting,
> Taking a step backward we stumble over our exposed legs,
> Arriving here and arriving there.   *Low Comment*
> Jumping up and kicking over Mount Sumeru,
> Raising it up and placing it within everyone's eyeballs.
> Stumbling and overturning the great ocean,
> Pick it up and place it within everyone's nostrils.   *High Comment*
> Why does everyone not awaken and not understand?   *Mediation*
> After a pause:
> Last night a flower blossomed and the world became fragrant,
> This morning a fruit ripened and bodhi matured.   *Turning Word*

The next example, no. 3.243, opens with a dialogue (*mondō*) on the differences between Mahāyāna and Hinayāna teachings, which followed with indirect commentary highlighting natural imagery that emphasizes nonattachment:

> Someone asked, "What is Buddha?"
> Dōgen replied, "In the end, future births will no longer be necessarily based on the attainment of a special kind of cessation that is not caused by analysis [but rather by original nature—*Abhidharmakośa*].
> The monk said, "Master, don't instruct people by referring to the Dharma of the Lesser Vehicle."
> Dōgen said, "I am not teaching people using the Dharma of the Lesser Vehicle."
> The monk asked again, "What is Buddha?"
> Dōgen said, "In the end, future births will no longer be neces-

sary based on the attainment of a special kind of cessation that is
not caused by analysis."   *Dialogue*

> Then Dōgen said,
> Heaven is not high,
> The earth is not dense.   *Low Comment*
> Mountains, and rivers, and the sun and moon, are not obstructed,
> The radiant light of each and every place penetrates
>   each and every other place.   *Response*
> A Persian riding on a white elephant enters the Buddha hall,
> People from Handan with bare feet circumambulate
>   the Monks hall.   *Response*
> What kind of principle can we hold on to?   *Mediation*

After a pause Dōgen said: The bright moon follows someone as
if there were a reason. White clouds provide rain, originally with no
mind.   *Turning Word*

Another key aspect of the literary significance of the *Eihei kōroku* is intertextuality in terms of the remarkably extensive citations of kōans as well as
citations and allusions from other genres of texts dealing with Zen masters.
The following list shows the main transmission of the lamp and recorded
sayings texts cited by Dōgen.[13]

SOURCES CITED IN THE *EIHEI KŌROKU*

TEXT	NO. OF CITATIONS
1. Ching-te ch'uan-teng lu	68
2. Hung-chih lu	43
3. Tsung-men t'ung-yao chi	25
4. Tsung-men lien-t'ung hui-yao	24
5. Ju-ching lu	10
6. Chia-t'ai p'u-teng lu	7
7. Yüan-wu lu/sung-ku	9
8. T'ien-sheng kuang-teng lu	9
9. Ta-hui lu	2
10. Huang-po lu	2
11. Hsü ch'uan-teng lu	2
TOTAL	211

The single main Ch'an master from China who influenced Dōgen's text
is Hung-chih, who is cited forty-three times, with the majority of these stemming from the period of sermons edited by Ejō, when Dōgen was first in
Echizen and establishing Eihei-ji temple. The following is a list of *Eihei kōroku*
passages that are based on Hung-chih citations:

No. 1.6, 10, 20, 21, 23, 77, 90
No. 2.135, 142, 152, 155, 158, 180, 183
No. 3.186, 187, 203, 206, 216, 220, 222, 223, 226, 227, 236, 242, 246, 256, 257
No. 4.261, 266, 269, 296, 303, 330, 320, 322, 326, 341, 344
No. 5.400, 403
No. 7.514

Doctrinal Themes

Many *Eihei kōroku* passages are notable for expressing various specific key doctrines that are also addressed in *Shōbōgenzō* fascicles, especially in volumes 1 and 9, as well as more general doctrines concerning Zen practice, especially in volumes 2–4, and also doctrines that are characteristic of the late Dōgen's view of causality and antisyncretism, as in volumes 5–7. Throughout the text there is a consistent emphasis on *zazen* training and the attainment of the crucial enlightenment experience of the casting off of body-mind (*shinjin dat-suraku*). Despite apparent variations in substance accompanied by shifts in the style of preaching, it seems that Dōgen never wavered from the core principles of his approach to religious practice.

Some of the doctrines dealt with extensively in *Shōbōgenzō* fascicles also are treated more briefly or elliptically in *jōdō* sermons include "Zenki" (no. 1.52), "Genjōkōan" (1.51), "Immo" (1.38), "Kattō" (1.46), "Ikkya myōjū" (1.107), "Kūge" (2.162), "Ōsakusendaba" (3.254), and "Udonge" (4.308). No. 3.205 comments ironically on the "Pai-chang and the wild fox" kōan that is the main theme of the "Daishugyō" and "Jinshin inga" fascicles, and is also discussed in 1.62 and 9.77, among other passages. The kōan concerns the relation between two views of casuality, one affirming and the other denying the role of karma:[14]

> After relating the story of Pai-chang and the wild fox, [Dōgen] asked the great assembly: Because of the former Pai-chang's saying, "not falling into cause and effect," why was he transformed into a wild fox body? As to the current Pai-chang's saying, "not obscuring cause and effect," how did this cause the release from the wild fox body?
>
> The teacher [Dōgen] himself said: Look at this wild fox spirit shaking his head and wagging his tail. Stop, stop!

No 3.195 makes iconoclastic or demythological remarks on the topic of supranormal powers that is also the subject of the "Jinzū" fascicle and is discussed in nos. 1.17, 2.196, and 9.27.

> [Dōgen] said, An accomplished master must be endowed with the six spiritual powers. The first is the power over physical limita-

tions; the second is the power to hear everything; the third is the power to know others' minds; the fourth is the power to know previous lives; the fifth is the power to see everywhere; and the sixth is the power to extinguish outflows [attachments].

Everyone, do you want to see the power to go anywhere? The teacher [Dōgen] raised his fist.

Do you want to see the power to know others' minds? [Dōgen] let one of his legs hang down from his seat.

Do you want to see the power of hearing everywhere? [Dōgen] snapped his fingers once.

Do you want to see the power of knowing previous lives? [Dōgen] raised his fly-whisk.

Do you want to see the power of seeing everywhere? [Dōgen] drew a circle in the air with his fly-whisk.

Do you want to see the power of extinguishing outflows? [Dōgen] drew a single horizontal line [the character for "one"] with his whisk and said, Although this is so, ultimately, six times six is thirty-six.

Other sermons deal with various general Buddhist doctrines, such as no. 4.310, which gives a concrete, down-to-earth, demythological interpretation of the notion of mindfulness:

[Dōgen] said, Our Buddha [Śakyamuni] said to his disciples, "There are four foundations of mindfulness on which people should depend. These four foundations of mindfulness refer to contemplating the body as impure; contemplating sensation as suffering; contemplating mind as impermanent; and contemplating phenomena as nonsubstantial."

Eihei also has four foundations of mindfulness: contemplating the body as a skin bag; contemplating sensation as eating bowls; contemplating mind as fences, walls, tiles, and pebbles; and contemplating phenomena as old man Zhang drinking wine, old man Li getting drunk.

Great assembly, are my four foundations of mindfulness the same or different from the ancient Buddha's four foundations of mindfulness? If you say they are the same, your eyebrows will fall out [from lying]. If you say they are different, you will lose your body and life.

The phrase about mind as fences, walls, tiles, and pebbles suggests the concrete manifestations of phenomenal reality, and the connection to Zhang and Li, also used in no. 1.32, alludes to a passage in the recorded sayings of Yün-men that refers to new year's festivities and implies interconnectedness and the pervasiveness of the Dharma. Also, no. 4.307 uses deceptively simple white-and-black imagery to depict the state of nonduality:

> After a pause [Dōgen] said: A white heron perches in a snowy nest; in sameness there is difference. A crow alights on a black horse; within difference there is sameness.

In the final sections of the *Eihei kōroku* (vols. 5–7, ed. Gien), there are numerous passages that deal explicitly with doctrines that generally assert the doctrine of karmic causality or refute syncretic or assimilative tendencies in Zen Buddhism. These passages have a striking resonance and consistency with the outlook of the 12-fascicle *Shōbōgenzō*. For example, in nos. 5.381, 6.437, 7.485, and 7.517, among others, Dōgen argues for a strict adherence of karma (*inga*) and moral retribution in the three moments of time (*sanjigo*). Also, in nos. 4.383 and 5.412 he criticizes the notion of the "unity of three teachings" (Buddhism, Confucianism, Taoism) (*sankyō itchi*); in 5.390 he dismisses syncretism; in 5.402 and 7.472 he refutes the "naturalism heresy" (*jinen gedō*) that equates or identifies the identification of absolute reality with all of or particular parts of nature, or advocates an anthropomorphic view; and in 6.447 and 7.509 he rejects spiritism (*reichi*). At the same time, in no. 7.491 he rejects the view of a distinctive, autonomous Zen sect (Zen-shū), and in 4.335 he criticizes the distinction between different approaches to the actualization of Zen enlightenment, including Tathāgata Zen based on the sutras and Patriarchal Zen based on the special transmission outside words and letters:

> *Tathāgata* Zen (*nyorai Zen*) and Patriarchal Zen (*sōshi Zen*) were not transmitted by the ancients, but only transmitted falsely in the Eastern Land (China). For several hundred years some have been clinging with delusion to this vain name. How pitiful is the inferior condition of this age of decline.

Through the *jōdō* sermons collected in *Eihei kōroku*, despite other kinds of variations and disputations, Dōgen asserts the priority of *zazen* practice, as in no. 3.191, which refers to a story from *Ching-te ch'uan-teng lu*, volume 15:

> [Dōgen] said: I remember, a monk asked Tou-tsi [Ta-t'ung], "What are the causes and conditions of this single great matter?"
>
> Tou-tsi said, "Minister Yin asked me to open the hall and give a sermon."
>
> The teacher [Dōgen] said, If it had been Eihei, I would not have spoken like this. If someone asks me, "What are the causes and conditions of this single great matter?" I would just say to him, "In the early morning I eat gruel and at noon I eat rice. Feeling strong, I practice *zazen*; when tired I sleep."

He also continually emphasizes the experience of casting off body-mind, as in nos. 18 and 4.318.

> My late teacher [Ju-ching] instructed the assembly, "Practicing Zen with a teacher (*sanzen*) is dropping off body and mind."
>
> Great assembly, do you want to understand thoroughly the meaning of this?
>
> After a pause [Dōgen] said, Sitting upright and casting off body and mind, the ancestral teachers' nostrils are flowers of emptiness.

The two doctrines of *zazen* and casting off body-mind are presented as a single experience in no. 4.337:

> Great assembly, do you want to hear the reality of just sitting, which is the Zen practice that is casting off of body and mind?

Conclusions: The Rhetoric of Criticism

The *Eihei kōroku* is extremely important for understanding the history of Dō-gen's approach to monasticism and Zen thought and is remarkably rich in literary and rhetorical devices. Throughout the *Eihei kōroku*, especially the *jōdō* sermons, Dōgen expresses great respect and admiration for Zen Buddhism as practiced in China, particularly a reverence for Ma-tsu's saying "sun-face, moon-face," as well as for Sōtō predecessors Hung-chih and Ju-ching, whose sayings are often quoted or cited or alluded to. Yet Dōgen also relishes his role as a critical commentator and revisionist of many of the leading Chinese masters, including the leading figures of his lineage. A common refrain in many of the sermons is, "Other patriarchs have said it this way, but Eihei says it this way."

In the first volume of *Eihei kōroku*, Dōgen shows a tendency to revise and rewrite and even reverse the sayings of Chinese masters, as in no. 1.10 on Tung-shan and others, and no. 1.12, in which Dōgen argues that his predecessors were only partially correct in their interpretation. No. 2.131 takes up a dialogue from the *Ching-te ch'uan-teng lu* that was also cited in the *Mana Shō-bōgenzō* (no. 2), in which Pai-chang contends with his disciple Huang-po, who he referred to as a tiger, and he concludes by saying "I thought you were that person [to continue the lineage]":

> These two old men could only speak of a tiger's stripes, they could not speak of a person's stripes. Moreover, they could not speak of a tiger without stripes, a person without stripes, a phoenix without markings, or a dragon without markings. . . . The question is not complete, the answer is not complete.

Dōgen goes on to gloss each line of the Pai-chang–Huang-po dialogue and suggest alternative renderings at every step. He is also especially critical of Chao-chou, as in nos. 1.140, 4.331, and 4.339, in addition to no. 2.154, in which he first appears to be defending the Chinese master in citing a passage from Chao-chou's recorded sayings against a critique by a disciple, but concludes by overturning Chao-chou's standpoint:

> Consider this. A monk asked Chao-chou, "What is the path without mistakes?"
>
> Chao-chou said, "Clarifying mind and seeing one's own nature is the path without mistakes."
>
> Later someone said, "Chao-chou only expressed 80 or 90 percent. I am not like this. If someone asks, 'What is the path without mistakes?' I would tell him, 'The inner gate of every house extends to Chang'an [the capital, lit. "long peace"].' "
>
> The teacher [Dōgen] said: Although this was how it was said this is not worth considering. The ancient buddha Chao-chou's expression is correct. Do you want to know the clear mind of which Chao-chou spoke?
>
> [Dōgen] cleared his throat, then said, Just this is it.
>
> Do you want to know about the seeing into one's own nature that Chao-chou mentioned?
>
> [Dōgen] laughed, then said, Just this is it.
>
> Although this is so, the ancient buddha Chao-chou's eyes could behold east and west, and his mind abided south and north. If someone asked Daibutsu, "What is the path without mistakes?" I would say to him, "You must not go anywhere else."
>
> Suppose someone says to me, "Master, isn't this tuning the string by gluing the fret?" I would say to him, "Do you fully understand tuning the string by gluing the fret?"

The phrases about not going anywhere else and "gluing the fret" allude to concrete manifestations of phenomenal reality rather than conceptual abstractions that may impede an appropriation of enlightenment experience.

In no. 4.296 on the winter solstice in 1248, Dōgen cites Hung-chih, as he had on several other occasions, including nos. 135 and 206. Dōgen says, " 'My measuring cup is full and the balance scale is level,' but in the marketplace I buy what is precious and sell it for a low price," thereby reversing the statement in Hung-chih's sermon, "Even if your measuring cup is full and the balance scale is level, in transactions I sell at a high price and buy when the price is low." Perhaps Dōgen is demonstrating a bodhisattva-like generosity or showing the nondual nature of all phenomena that only appear to have different values.

Of course, Dōgen's mentor Ju-ching is not immune to this treatment, as in no. 3.194:

> [Dōgen] said, I remember, a monk asked an ancient worthy, "Is there Buddha Dharma or not on a steep cliff in the deep mountains?"
>
> The worthy responded, "A large rock is large; a small one is small."
>
> My late teacher T'ien-t'ung [Ju-ching] said, "The question about the steep cliff in the deep mountains was answered in terms of large and small rocks. The cliff collapsed, the rocks split, and the empty sky filled with a noisy clamor."
>
> The teacher [Dōgen] said, Although these two venerable masters said it this way, Eihei [Dōgen] has another utterance to convey. If someone were to ask, "Is there Buddha Dharma or not on a steep cliff in the deep mountains?" I would simply say to him, "The lifeless rocks nod their heads again and again. The empty sky vanishes completely. This is something that exists within the realm of the buddhas and patriarchs. What is this thing on a steep cliff in the deep mountains?"
>
> [Dōgen] pounded his staff one time, and descended from his seat.

The phrase, "The lifeless rocks nod their heads again and again," is a reference to Tao-sheng, Kumārajiva's great disciple and early Chinese Buddhist scholar, who, based on a passage in the *Mahāparinirvāṇa Sūtra* that all beings can become buddha, went to the mountain and preached the Dharma to the rocks, which nodded in response.

Finally, in no. 2.179 Dōgen critiques five prominent figures, Śākyamuni and four Chinese masters, who respond to a statement of the Buddha in the *Śūraṅgama Sūtra*, chapter nine, as also cited and discussed with the same conclusion in *Shōbōgenzō* "Tenbōrin":

> [Dōgen] said, The World-Honored One said, "When one person opens up reality and returns to the source, all space in the ten directions self-destructs."
>
> Teacher Wu-tsu of Mount Fa-yen said, "When one person opens up reality and returns to the source, all space in the ten directions crashes together resounding everywhere."
>
> Zen Master Yüan-wu of Mount Jia-shan said, "When one person opens up reality and returns to the source, in all space in the ten directions flowers are added on to brocade."
>
> Teacher Fo-hsing Fa-t'ai said, "When one person opens up real-

ity and returns to the source, all space in the ten directions is nothing other than all space in the ten directions."

My late teacher T'ien-t'ung [Ju-ching] said, "Although the World-Honored One made the statement, 'When one person opens up reality and returns to the source, all space in the ten directions disappears,' this utterance cannot avoid becoming an extraordinary assessment. T'ien-t'ung is not like this. When one person opens up reality and returns to the source, a mendicant breaks his rice bowl."

The teacher [Dōgen] said, The previous five venerable teachers said it like this, but Eihei has a saying that is not like theirs. When one person opens up reality and returns to the source, all space in the ten directions opens up reality and returns to the source.

Frequently Dōgen defeats the tendency in Zen toward abstraction and aloofness with interpretations based on concrete phenomena, perhaps influenced by Japanese Tendai thought, while also stressing the role of continuing practice as a corrective to Tendai esoteric (mikkyō) and mixed or assimilative practices. In this instance, however, Wu-tsu, Yüan-wu, and Ju-ching each suggest a concretization, especially the latter's rice-bowl comment, so Dōgen adapts a different strategy by declaring a tautology based on another Tendai strategy of equalizing the microcosm and macrocosm.

NOTES

1. From the Kamakura period until the revival of Sōtō scholarship in the seventeenth century, both texts were largely ignored, although an abbreviated version of the *Eihei kōroku* known as the *Eihei goroku* received much attention. During and since the Tokugawa era, the *Shōbōgenzō* has been seen as Dōgen's magnum opus.

2. Dōgen may have written some of the sermons out first, as they reveal a subtle use of rhyme and rhythmic patterns. An interesting question is the extent to which Dōgen's disciples knew enough Chinese to be able to follow the sermons at the time of their delivery.

3. Kagamishima Genryū, ed., *Dōgen zenji zenshū*, vols. 3 and 4 (Tokyo: Shunjūsha, 1988). Also, Ōtani Teppū has edited editions of both the Monkaku and Manzan versions. In writing this paper, all translations are from the Monkaku edition in the Kagamishima edited volumes. I have also consulted the new English translation currently being prepared for Wisdom Publications (tentative publication date 2005) by Taigen Dan Leighton and Shohaku Okumura, and I greatly appreciate their showing me the manuscript draft.

4. See Ishii Shūdō, "*Eihei Ryaku Roku* kangae: Jūnikanbon *Shōbōgenzō* to Kanren shite," *Matsugaoka Bunko Kenkyū Nempō* 11 (1997): 73–128. The *Eihei goroku* contains about one-seventh of the material in the *Eihei kōroku*.

5. In the following list of the contents and dates of composition for the *Eihei kōroku*, the first seven volumes are collections of *jōdō* sermons from Kōshō-ji, Daibutsu-ji and Eihei-ji, and the last three volumes collect various kinds of lectures and poetry.

6. The notion of change in the late Dōgen is crucial to the theory of Critical Buddhism (*Hihan Bukkyō*). See Steven Heine, "Critical Buddhism and Dōgen's *Shōbōgenzō*: The Debate over the 75–Fascicle and 12–Fascicle Texts," in Jamie Hubbard and Paul L. Swanson, eds., *Pruning the Bodhi Tree: The Storm over Critical Buddhism* (Honolulu: University of Hawai'i Press, 1997), pp. 251–285.

7. Other examples include 1.65, 1.66, 1.67, 1.71, 1.75, 1.76, 1.81, 1.83, 1.85, 1.86, 1.87, 1.95, 1.103, 1.104, 1.108, 1.109, and 1.112–1.122.

8. See Yifa, *The Origins of Buddhist Monastic Codes in China* (Honolulu: University of Hawai'i Press, 2002).

9. According to Okumura and Leighton, " 'Studying walking to be like someone from Handan' is a reference to a story by Chuang-tzu in the chapter on 'Autumn Water.' In this story someone from the countryside went to the city of Handan and imitated the fashionable walking of the townspeople. But before he had succeeded in mastering their walking, he had forgotten his own country walking, and had to crawl home on his hands and knees; see Sam Hamill and J. P. Seaton, trans., *The Essential Chuang Tzu* (Boston: Shambhala, 1999), p. 92."

10. See also 1.48, 2.171, and 2.184.

11. For other comments on the role of giving sermons and related topics in introducing Zen monasticism to Japan, see also no. 2.128 on the first first evening discourse (*bansan*) in Japan; 2.138 on Dōgen's being the first to transmit the role of the chief cook (*tenzo*) to Japan; no. 3.244 in which Dōgen says, "I am expounding Zen discourse all over the country"; no. 4.319 on dedicating the monks' hall on Mount Kichijō in Echizen; no. 5.358 on Japanese "listening to the name of *jōdō* for the first time since I transmitted it"; no. 5.378 about Dōgen's delivery of sermons being "the most extraordinary thing"; no. 5.406 on ceremonies in Japan to celebrate birth of Śākyamuni Buddha, in which Dōgen says, "I, Eihei, imported [this ritual] twenty years ago and held it. It must be transmitted in the future."

12. Andō Yoshinori, *Chūsei Zenshū bunseki no kenkyū* (Tokyo: Kokusho kankōkai, 2000), pp. 144–164. See also Hata Eigyoku, *"Eihei Kōroku—sono sodoku to chūkai,"* *Sanshō* (1975–1977).

13. Dōgen also often cites non-Zen or pre-Zen writings, including Pali texts and Mahāyāna sutras, especially during this period.

14. See Steven Heine, *Shifting Shape, Shaping Text: Philosophy and Folklore in the Fox Kōan* (Honolulu: University of Hawai'i Press, 1999).

9

Chanyuan qinggui and Other "Rules of Purity" in Chinese Buddhism

T. Griffith Foulk

The *Chanyuan qinggui* (Rules of purity for Chan monasteries) was compiled in the second year of the Chongning era (1103) by Changlu Zongze (1107?), abbot of the Hongji Chan Cloister, a public monastery in Zhending Prefecture. In the world of Song-dynasty Chinese Buddhism, abbots had considerable leeway and authority to establish or change the organizational principles and ritual procedures used within their own monasteries. Zongze's stated intent in compiling the *Chanyuan qinggui*, however, was not simply to regulate his own cloister but also to provide a set of shared guidelines that would help to standardize the organization and operation of all Chan monasteries. From our standpoint today, almost exactly nine centuries later, we can say that Zongze's project was successful beyond anything that he himself could have imagined or hoped for. In the first hundred years after its initial publication, the *Chanyuan qinggui* circulated widely and did indeed become a standard not only for Chan monasteries but also for all public monasteries in China.[1]

The *Chanyuan qinggui* represents an important milestone in the history of Chinese Buddhism, for it was the first indigenous set of monastic rules to attain a status roughly equivalent to that of the Vinaya, which had been translated into Chinese (in various recensions) from Indic languages, and was traditionally regarded as the word of Śākyamuni Buddha. It is also the oldest text we have that bears the phrase "rules of purity" (*qinggui*) in its title, a phrase that subsequently came to refer to an entire class of Chan and Zen monastic rules.

When Japanese monks such as Eisai (1141–1215), Dōgen (1200–

1253), and Enni (1202–1280) made pilgrimages to major Chinese Buddhist monastic centers in the first half of the thirteenth century, they all encountered the *Chanyuan qinggui*, recognized it as an authoritative source, and used it upon their return as a standard for establishing Zen monastic institutions in Japan. The text has remained a classic within the Japanese schools of Zen from the thirteenth century to the present, being the subject of numerous reprintings, commentaries, and citations. The *Chanyuan qinggui* also played an important role in the history of Buddhist monasticism in Korea, where an edition of the text was first published in 1254.

This essay will focus on the historical setting, authorship, and contents of the *Chanyuan qinggui*, as well as the origins of the text, and the role that it subsequently played in establishing the "rules of purity" genre in Chinese Buddhism.

Historical Setting of the *Chanyuan qinggui*

When the *Chanyuan qinggui* was first published in 1103, Buddhism had already been a vital presence in Chinese culture for roughly a millennium. During that period there had been many and sundry efforts not only to translate Indian Vinaya texts but also to interpret and adapt them for use in China. Among the various schools of Vinaya exegesis that competed in Sui (589–618) and Tang (618–906) dynasty China, the one that eventually asssumed the mantle of orthodoxy for all Buddhists was the Nanshan school (*Nanshan zong*), which was based on commentaries by Daoxuan (596–667).[2] As influential as his writings were, however, their authority was ultimately grounded in the Vinaya proper and the sacred person of Śākyamuni Buddha.

The authority of the Vinaya in the first millennium of Chinese Buddhism was also enhanced by the state, which made various efforts to regulate and control the saṅgha by taking certain provisions of the Vinaya and giving them imperial sanction as official "saṅgha regulations" (*sengzhi*).[3] A basic tool of governmental control was to require all monks and nuns to go through proper (as defined by the Vinaya) ordination rites at state-approved monasteries, and then obtain official ordination certificates as proof that they had done so. This provided a vehicle for taking censuses of the Buddhist saṅgha, restricting its size by limiting the number of certificates issued in a given year.

Neither the Vinaya proper, the commentarial tradition associated with it, nor governmental regulations based on it, however, covered all the aspects of monastic administration and practice that gradually evolved in Chinese Buddhism. From early on, countless monks worked to supplement Vinaya-related rules by developing new architectural arrangements, bureaucratic structures, and ritual procedures that came to be sanctioned by custom, but had no clear precedent in the received teachings of the Indian Buddha. A few eminent prelates, such as Daoan (312–385) and Zhiyi (538–597), became famous enough that the rules and regulations they wrote entered into the historical record and collective consciousness of the Buddhist saṅgha, and exerted considerable influence on subsequent generations of Buddhist leaders.[4] Prior to Zongze's *Chanyuan qinggui*, however, no set of indigenous Chinese monastic rules ever came close to matching the universal acceptance and unquestioned authority of the Vinaya.

At the time when the *Chanyuan qinggui* was compiled, Buddhism was flourishing in China.[5] Buddhist monasteries of every size and description were a ubiquitous feature of the landscape, and their numbers were increasing. With estate lands, mills, oil presses, fleets of canal boats, and moneylending operations, the larger monasteries played a vital role in their local and regional economies. Buddhism had been embraced by the rulers of the Song dynasty as a means of revering their ancestors and increasing the security and prosperity of the regime. It had found numerous supporters (and some opponents) among the landed gentry and the closely related cadre of educated bureaucrats known as the literati. The former sometimes sponsored monasteries called "merit cloisters" (*gongde yuan*) that were dedicated to the care of their familial ancestral spirits and (not incidentally) served to take productive land off the tax rolls by nominally rendering it property of the Buddhist saṅgha. The latter, when sent to regional and local posts as governors and magistrates, frequently befriended the abbots and leading monk officials (often men of similar social and educational backgrounds) in their districts, eliciting their assistance in maintaining order and imperial authority and lending political and financial support to their monasteries in return. It was not uncommon in the Song for wealthy and influential lay men and women to become the disciples of Buddhist prelates, embrace Buddhist teachings as a matter of personal belief and salvation, and engage in specialized modes of study and practice that had been handed down within the monastic tradition.

Belief in the saving powers of Buddhist dieties such as Amituo (Amitābha) and Guanyin (Avalokiteśvara) was widespread, and their cults cut across every stratum of society, including monks and laity, educated elites and illiterate peasants. Buddhist associations, especially ones organized around Pure Land beliefs and practices, gained followers. Buddhist sites, including sacred mountains and great stupa towers containing relics, were famous across the land as pilgrimage destinations. Buddhist images (paintings and sculpture) were produced on a grand scale, and great publication projects printed and distributed the Buddhist canon, a massive and growing collection of sacred texts. At the local level, among the peasantry and ordinary townsfolk, countless unofficial temples and shrines were maintained, festivals thrived, and some religiously inclined or economically motivated people illegally set themselves up as monks and nuns, by avoiding the state-sanctioned processes of postulancy, novice ordination, and full ordination.

There were basically two classes of Buddhist monasteries in the Song: public and private. The former were known as "ten directions monasteries" (*shifang cha*) because they were supposed to be the property of the Buddhist order at large, the so-called "saṅgha of the ten directions" (*shifang seng*). Those monasteries were public in the sense that any properly ordained Buddhist monk or nun could take up residence in them without regard for ordination lineage or Dharma lineage. They were also referred to as "ten directions abbacy cloisters" (*shifang zhuchi yuan*) because their abbacies, too, were in theory open to all eminent members of the "saṅgha of the ten directions," not restricted to disciples of previous abbots. Private monasteries, known as "disciple-lineage cloisters" (*jiayi tudi yuan*), were distinguished by the fact that the abbacy was passed down directly from master to disciple within a single teaching line. Unlike their public counterparts, the communities of monks or nuns in residence in private monasteries could, in principle, be limited to the followers of a particular teacher.

In general, public monasteries were the largest, most prestigious and powerful Buddhist establishments in Song China. Typical bureaucratic structures, arrangements of buildings, and religious practices are important details.[6] It is sufficient to quote one summarizing passage from a work that discusses this:

> They [public monasteries] had spacious compounds encompassing over fifty major and minor structures, facilities for a rich variety of religious practices and ceremonies, and sometimes more than a thousand persons in residence, including monastic officers, ordinary monks and nuns, lay postulants and laborers. In addition, they were well endowed with estate lands and were the proprietors of other income-producing property, such as mills and oil presses. They were granted official monastery name plaques to be displayed over their main gates and were often called upon to dedicate merit produced in various religious rituals to the well being of the emperor and the prosperity and defense of the state.[7]

The patronage (and control) of Buddhism by the imperial court and most powerful officials among the literati tended to focus on the great public monasteries. Not surprisingly, those same institutions were the arena in which the most influential leaders of the Buddhist saṅgha got their training and pursued their careers as monastic officers and abbots.

From early in the Song, two elite movements within the Buddhist saṅgha competed for imperial patronage and recognition as conveyers of orthodoxy: proponents of the Chan lineage and the Tiantai tradition, respectively.[8] Although the public monasteries were in theory open to all Buddhist monks, sometime in the late tenth century the Chan school managed to have the imperial court designate some of them as "ten directions Chan monasteries" (*shifang chanyuan*). That meant the abbacies were restricted to monks who belonged to some branch of the Chan lineage. The principle of not allowing disciples to succeed their own teachers as abbot was maintained, however, and the monasteries remained open to any properly ordained member of the Buddhist saṅgha, whether or not they were followers of the Chan school. According to annals dated 1011, proponents of the Tiantai teachings followed suit, and in 996 successfully petitioned the court for the establishment of two monasteries with "ten-directions, teachings-transmitting abbacies" (shifang chuanjiao zhu-chi).[9] By the time the Chanyuan qinggui was compiled in 1103, quite a few public monasteries had been designated by the court as "Chan" or "Teachings" establishments, and the former outnumbered the latter by a considerable margin.[10] The phrase "Chan monastery" (chanyuan) in the title of Zongze's compilation referred to those public monasteries that had abbacies restricted to the Chan lineage.

In the early Song, the designation "Vinaya monastery" (luyuan, lusi) had nothing to do with a Vinaya "school" or "lineage" (zong). It referred, rather, to the general class of private monasteries that were regulated by the Vinaya and had no state-determined policies concerning their abbacies. By the thirteenth century, however, the Nanshan school of Vinaya exegesis (nanshan luzong) had been revived, and managed to lay claim to the abbacies of a few public monasteries, which were then called "ten-directions Vinaya monasteries" (shifang luyuan). Even so, there continued to be many "disciple-lineage Vinaya monasteries" (jiayi lu-yuan), ordinary private monasteries.

The situation of the Buddhist institution in Zhejiang Province (home of the Southern Song capital) in the early thirteenth century is reflected in the Gozan jissatsu zu (Charts of the five mountains and ten monasteries).[11] A table found in that text records what was written on the name plaques that hung above various gates at some eighty-eight large public monasteries. Such plaques were often bestowed by the imperial court, and gave official notice of the lineage affiliation (if any) of the abbacy at a given establishment. In all, forty-eight of the eighty-eight monasteries mentioned were designated as Chan monasteries, nine as Teachings (Tiantai) monasteries, and four as Vinaya monasteries. The remaining twenty-seven had nothing in their names to indicate any association with a particular lineage.[12]

How did the Chan school succeed in promoting itself as the leading representative of Buddhist orthodoxy and dominating the public monasteries of the Song in this manner? In the first place, the Chan school employed an effective polemic in which it claimed to possess the Dharma of the Buddha in its purest form. Whereas other schools (Tiantai in particular) transmitted the Dharma (teachings) through the medium of written sutras and commentaries, as the argument went, the Dharma transmitted to China by Bodhidharma was nothing other than the "Buddha-mind" (foxin), or enlightenment itself. This superior Dharma was said to have been vouchsafed from person to person (master to disciple) down through the lineage of Chan patriarchs, as if it were a flame forever kept alive by being passed from one lamp to the next, in a process called "transmission of mind by means of mind" (*yixin chuanxin*). Thus, the Chan school could claim that its ancient patriarchs, and indeed its current leaders, who were heirs to Bodhidharma's lineage, were all buddhas. This conceit was played out in ritual as well as literary form. When Chan abbots took the lecture seat in a Dharma hall, they sat on the kind of high altar (*xumitan*) that was conventionally used for buddha images. Their sermons and exchanges with interlocutors were recorded, and later entered into the Buddhist canon (*dacangjing*). This is a process that mirrored the recording and collection of Śākyamuni Buddha's sutras, as traditionally understood to have occurred.[13]

In addition to providing China with its first native buddhas, the Chan tradition equipped them with a powerful new mode of rhetoric that made use of vernacular Chinese, as opposed to the rather stilted, translated Chinese of the Śākyamuni Buddha. Chan rhetoric shied away from long, discursive treatments of abstract philosophical concepts, favoring instead a kind of repartee (*wenda*, literally "question and answer") that employed down-to-earth, albeit highly metaphorical, imagery to discuss Buddhist doctrines.

Finally, the story of patriarch Baizhang Huaihai (749–814), who was said to have founded the first independent Chan monastery and who wrote the first Chan monastic rules, helped thoroughly solidify the assertions of the Chan school in the Song. It was able to both legitimize and claim as its own a long tradition of indigenous monastic rule making that lacked the imprimatur of the Indian Buddha, having been developed outside the scope of the Vinaya and its associated commentaries.

The Baizhang story had been circulating in China from the latter half of the tenth century, promoted chiefly by a short text known as the *Chanmen guishi* (Regulations of the Chan school). Some version of that text was in existence before 988, when parts of it were cited in the *Song kaoseng zhuan* (Song biographies of eminent monks).[14] The *Chanmen guishi* was subsequently quoted or paraphrased in numerous other works,[15] but the oldest complete edition, and historically most influential, was one appended to Baizhang's biography in the *Jingde chuandeng lu* (Jingde era record of the transmission of the flame), compiled in 1004.[16]

The opening passage of the *Chanmen guishi* reads as follows.

> From the origination of the Chan lineage with Xiaoshi [the first patriarch Bodhidharma] up until Caoqi [the sixth patriarch Huineng] and after, most [members of the lineage] resided in Vinaya monasteries. Even when they had separate cloisters, they did not yet have [independent] regulations pertaining to preaching the Dharma and the appointment of abbots. Chan Master Baizhang Dazhi was always filled with regret on account of this. He said, "It is my desire that the way of the patriarchs be widely propagated. . . . What we hold as

essential is not bound up in the Mahāyāna or Hinayāna, nor is it completely different from them. We should select judiciously from a broad range [of earlier rules], arrange them into a set of regulations, and adopt them as our norms." Thereupon he conceived the idea of establishing a Chan monastery (*chanju*) separately.[17]

In the early Song when this was written, the term "Vinaya monastery" (as explained above) referred to an ordinary monastery regulated by the Vinaya, as opposed to a public monastery where there were indeed "regulations pertaining to preaching the Dharma and the appointment of abbots." Baizhang himself is thus credited with originally conceiving what was, in actuality, a Song government policy! The text of the *Chanmen guishi* then goes on to summarize the features of the independent Chan monastery that Baizhang purportedly founded.

1. A spiritually perceptive and morally praiseworthy person was to be named as abbot (*zhanglao*).
2. The abbot was to use his quarters (*fangzhang*) for meeting with students, not as a private room.
3. A Dharma hall (*fatang*) was built, but not a Buddha hall (*fodian*). This was because the current abbot, representing the buddhas and patriarchs when he ascended the hall (*shangtang*) and took the high seat to lecture, was to be regarded as the "honored one" (*zun*)—a term usually applied to a monastery's central buddha image.
4. All trainees, regardless of numbers or status, had to reside on platforms in the saṅgha hall (*sengtang*), where they were placed in rows in accordance with their seniority.
5. Sleep was minimized and long periods of sitting meditation (*zuochan*) were held.
6. Proper deportment (*weiyi*) was stressed at all times. The proper posture for sleep was to lie on one's right side (like the Buddha when he entered nirvana) with one's pillow on the edge of the platform.
7. Entering the abbot's room (*rushi*) for instruction was left up to the diligence of the trainees.
8. The trainees convened in the Dharma hall (*fatang*) morning and evening to listen to the abbot's sermons and engage him in debate.
9. Meals were served but twice a day, one early in the morning and one before noon.
10. Seniors and juniors were required to do equal work during periods of communal labor (*puqing*).
11. There were ten administrative offices (*liaoshe*).
12. Troublemaking monks were expelled from the monastery by the rector (*weina*).
13. Serious offenders were beaten and, in effect, expelled from the Bud-

dhist order by having their robes, bowls, and monkish implements burned in front of the assembled community.

The primary author of the *Chanmen guishi*, himself evidently the abbot of a Chan monastery, ended the text with the following admonition: "The Chan school's (*chanmen*) independent practice followed from Baizhang's initiative. At present I have briefly summarized the essential points and proclaimed them for all future generations of practitioners, so that they will not be forgetful of our patriarch [Baizhang]. His rules should be implemented in this monastery (*shanmen*)."[18] From this it is clear that one of his primary motivations in composing the text was to promote Baizhang as a founding patriarch, worthy of praise and remembrance.

The Baizhang story was a powerful element in the self-understanding of the Chan school in the Song, one that manifested itself not only in numerous written records but in ritual performances as well. Beginning in the late eleventh and early twelfth centuries, just around the time of the compilation of the *Chanyuan qinggui*, images of Bodhidharma and Baizhang began to be enshrined in the patriarchs halls (*zutang*) of Chan monasteries, which previously had held only portraits of the succession of former abbots.[19] The images served as the focal point of routine offerings of nourishment (*gongyang*) and elaborate annual memorial services (*ji*) for the ancestral spirits. Bodhidharma was venerated as the first patriarch (*chuzu*) of the Chan lineage, and Baizhang was honored as the founder of the Chan monastic institution. In his "Preface to the Rules for the Patriarchs Hall" (*Zutang gangji xu*), an influential manual composed in 1070, Chan master Baiyun Shouduan (1025–1072) wrote: "It is thanks to the principles established by the first patriarch Bodhidharma that the way [of the Chan lineage] flourishes in this land. It is thanks to Baizhang Dazhi that the regulations for Chan monastaries have been established here. . . . It is my desire that in patriarchs halls throughout the empire, Bodhidharma and [Baizhang] Dazhi be treated as primary (*zheng*), and the founding abbots and their successors be treated as secondary (*pei*)."[20]

In his *Linjianlu* (Linjian Record), published in 1107, the Chan monk historian Huihong Juefan (1071–1128) echoed Shouduan's "Rules for the Patriarchs Hall" and wrote: "It is due to the power (*li*) of Chan Master [Baizhang] Dazhi that monasteries flourish in the land. In the patriarchs hall, an image of the first patriarch Bodhidharma should be set up in the center, an image of Chan Master Dazhi should face west, and images of the founding abbot and other venerables [i.e., former abbots] should face east. Do not set up the images of the founding abbot and venerables alone, leaving out the patriarchal line (*zuzong*)."[21] It is evident from this that in Chan circles during the Song, Baizhang was regarded not merely as a historical figure but also as an ancestral spirit whose presence was palpable and whose protection of the monastic institution could be secured through proper offerings and worship. By the same token, when Baizhang was thanked for establishing the "regulations for Chan monastaries," the reference was not to some ancient document but to the very rules and procedures that regulated Chan monasteries at the time, during the Song.

The pairing of Bodhidharma and Baizhang as "cofounders" of the Chan school was a common motif in Song Chan literature, and one that Zongze himself echoed in his preface to the *Chanyuan qinggui*.[22] What is significant about the pair is that both figures, albeit in different ways, provided Chinese Buddhists with their own native sources of legitimacy and authority, rather than looking entirely to the Indian Buddha. We have already seen how the Bodhidharma legend gave Chinese Buddhists the confidence to begin claiming that monks born in their own country were buddhas. Baizhang, Bodhidharma's "partner" in the establishment of the Chan school in China, can also be seen as a Chinese patriarch who (in the minds of Song-dynasty Buddhists) gained a status and assumed a function parallel to that of the Indian Buddha. Whatever role Baizhang actually (from the standpoint of modern, critical historiography) played in the historical development of Chinese Buddhist monastic rules, the imagined Baizhang (whose image was enshrined in Song Chan patriarchs halls) mirrored Śākyamuni's traditional role as the founder of the Buddhist monastic order (*saṅgha*) and promulgator of the Vinaya.

In short, the Chan school represented a kind of coming of age of Chinese Buddhism in the Song, providing for the first time native equivalents of the Indian Buddha, his sermons, and his rules for the monastic order: the "three jewels" of Buddha, Dharma, and Saṅgha. Those developments made Buddhism more appealing and accessible to the educated elites than it had been in earlier periods, helped to remove the stigma of cultural foreignness that had plagued it from the start, and rendered it less threatening to the imperial order. Without leaving lay life, literati could engage in repartee with Chan abbots, appreciate the wit and intellectual subtleties of Chan literature, participate in some aspects of monastic life, and even entertain aspirations for their own attainment of enlightenment. Officials who were indifferent or hostile to Buddhism, meanwhile, could take comfort in the fact that the monastic rules embodying state controls of the saṅgha were not extracanonical (as they had been in the past), but fully sanctified by their association with the Chan patriarch Baizhang.

Authorship of the *Chanyuan qinggui*

The compiler of the *Chanyuan qinggui*, Changlu Zongze, is a somewhat enigmatic figure.[23] The oldest biography we have for him is found in a collection entitled *Jianzhong jingguo xudeng lu* (Jianzhong Jingguo era supplementary record of the flame), which was completed in 1101.[24] Zongze was still alive at the time, but the text, a collection of numerous brief hagiographies, was mainly concerned with establishing individual monks as members of the Chan lineage, so for each it gave only a sketchy account of their childhood and career as a monk, and a few quotes selected from their discourse records.[25] About a century later, a proponent of the Pure Land tradition named Zongxiao (1151–1214), who was striving to construct a quasi lineage based on the highly successful Chan model, claimed Zongze as the fifth "great teacher" (*dashi*) following the Pure Land "first patriarch" Huiyuan (344–416).[26] This appropriation of Zongze was based on the fact that he wrote a great number of essays on Pure Land teachings and organized a group of Pure Land practitioners in his monastery called the "sacred assembly of the lotus" (*lianhua shenghui*). It did not go so far as to claim any direct master-to-disciple transmission of the Pure Land Dharma in the manner of the Chan lineage. In any case, none of the hagiographies of Zongze that appear in either the Chan or Pure Land collections contains much concrete biographical data beyond the brief account found in the oldest of them, the *Jianzhong jingguo xudeng lu*.

Based on the extant hagiographies, Yifa states, three important facts about Zongze emerge: "First, he was a member of the Yunmen lineage, the most influential Chan school of the time; second, he was a learned advocate of Pure Land thought and practice; third, he is remembered for his exalted sense of filial piety."[27] Yifa goes on to relate the sketchy details of Zongze's childhood, tonsure, early training, moment of enlightenment, lineage deriving from Yunmen, devotion to his mother, and patronage by the government official Yang Wei (1044–1112), through whose intercession he received the honorific title Cijue Dashi (Great Teacher Cijue) from the court.[28] The biographical records suggest that Zongze was abbot of three monasteries during his career, but they do not corroborate one another, so the details are unclear. What seems certain is that Zongze was serving as abbot of a public monastery, the Hongji Chan Cloister, at the time when he compiled the *Chanyuan qinggui*, and that he was the abbot of at least one other monastery, the Changlusi.[29]

The upshot of all this is that Zongze's approach to Buddhist thought and practice is accessible to us mainly through his extant writings. The best source we have for understanding his motivations for compiling the *Chanyuan qinggui* and the circumstances under which he did so is nothing other than the *Chanyuan qinggui* itself. Zongze's preface to the text, translated here in full, is quite revealing in this respect:

PREFACE TO THE RULES OF PURITY FOR CHAN MONASTERIES

> Compiled by Zongze, Great Teacher Chuanfa Cijue, abbot of the Ten Directions Hongji Chan Cloister in Zhending Prefecture.
> Although [in principle] there are not two kinds of Vinaya (*bini*), the Chan school standards (*chanmen shili*) are characteristic of our own

distinctive tradition (*jiafeng*) and stand apart from the general [Buddhist] norms. If those who are on the path accept these and put them into practice, they will naturally become exceptionally pure and lofty. But if they go against them, they will be at a total impasse, and to tell the truth, they will lose people's respect. Therefore, I have sought the advice of virtuous and knowledgeable monks and collected texts from all sides, wherever there were [materials] to supplement what I know from firsthand experience, and present all the details here under organized headings.

Alas, the phenomenon of Shaolin [i.e., Bodhidharma's establishment of the Chan lineage in China] was already like gouging out [healthy] flesh and developing ulcers. Baizhang's standards (*Baizhang guisheng*) can also be said to represent a willful creation of new regulations. And that is not to mention the profusive growth in monasteries,[30] so unbearable that I must avert my eyes. Moreover, with laws and ordinances (*faling*) increasingly in evidence,[31] such things are all the more numerous! Nevertheless, in order to dignify and protect the shrines and raise the Dharma flag, not a single [rule] can be omitted by those of us who follow Buddhist observances.

Now, as for the three groups [of precepts] for bodhisattvas (*pusa sanju*) and seven classes [of precepts] for śrāvakas (*shengwen qipian*), it is remarkable that a set of laws could be so complex. But that is no doubt because [the Buddha] established teachings in response to particular circumstances as they arose.

I sincerely hope that beginning trainees who come after me may consult these rules in detail, and that virtuous seniors will kindly favor me with their corroboration of them. Preface written on the 15th day of the 8th month of Chongning 2 (1103).[32]

If we analyze the formal structure of this document, we can see that it consists of a number of objections or criticisms that might be raised against a compilation such as the *Chanyuan qinggui*, each followed by a response in which Zongze defends his undertaking.

In the opening line, "although [in principle] there are not two kinds of Vinaya," Zongze acknowledges that it might seem presumptuous or sacrilegious to compile a set of monastic rules that competes with or differs from those established by the Buddha. He counters that objection with several arguments. First, it is not he alone who dares to do this: there is an established precedent in the Chan school for producing its own standards, and he has based his work on preexisting texts and the advice of knowledgeable senior monks, not simply his own experience and opinions. Moreover, Zongze argues, the Chan standards are conducive to spiritual progress, and going against them is not; and in any case, they must be followed for public relations reasons.

The second criticism raised in the preface is the rather surprising allusion to the founding of the Chan lineage in China as something akin to "gouging out [healthy] flesh and developing ulcers." This sounds like the opinion of an opponent of the Chan school who regards Bodhidharma's "separate transmission apart from the teachings (*jiaowai biechuan*)" as something superfluous and ultimately injurious to Buddhism. Zongze, interestingly, does not refute the statement; indeed, he seems to endorse it with his lament, "Alas." But this apparent criticism of Bodhidharma's lineage, coming from a monk who was heir to it, was more likely the kind of backhanded praise that is typical of Chan rhetoric, and a tacit reference, by way of apologizing for it to other Buddhists, to the dominance of the Chan school.[33]

The third objection, echoing the first one, is that "Baizhang's standards" too are like "gouging out [healthy] flesh." In other words, the Vinaya alone is sufficient, and the creation of any other rules just makes for trouble. Zongze counters this by arguing that Chinese Buddhists (following Baizhang) have already gone down the path of creating their own monastic rules, so there is no turning back. The resulting tangle of overgrown monkish and civil regulations must be brought into some kind of coherent order by yet more rule making.

Finally, Zongze tacitly raises the objection that the Vinaya itself (the three groups of precepts for bodhisattvas and seven classes of precepts for (śrāvakas) is too complex. The reason for that, he points out, is that the Buddha had to make up numerous new rules on a case-by-case basis in response to particular circumstances.[34] This is a subtle way of arguing that the Indian Vinaya is too arcane and obsolete to be followed in its entirety. The point that the Buddha himself, in the Vinaya, established a precedent for making up new rules whenever the circumstances called for it, further justifies the compilation of the *Chanyuan qinggui*.

To sum up the message of Zongze's preface, we may say that he was clearly aware of opposition within the Buddhist saṅgha of his day, both to the Chan school and to its use of the figure of Baizhang to legitimize the formulation of new monastic rules. Zongze paid due respect to those opponents, but basically took the position that the Chan school was strong enough to get its own way, whether they liked it or not. What really bothered him was not those critics so much as the confusion and lack of consistency among the many sets of monastic rules that had sprung up within the burgeoning Buddhist institution. Zongze's comment about the "profusive growth in monasteries" being "unbearable" may also have been a nod in the direction of anti-Buddhist officials who felt that the entire Buddhist institution was getting out of hand. For them, as well, he seemed to say the *Chanyuan qinggui* promised a good weeding and trimming of the "garden" (*yuan*) of Chan—the public monasteries.

Contents and Intended Functions of the *Chanyuan qinggui*

The text of the *Chanyuan qinggui* consists of ten fascicles containing seventy-seven sections or chapters, each with its own topical heading.[35] The table of contents reads as follows:

FASCICLE ONE

Receiving Precepts
Upholding Precepts
A Monk's Personal Effects
Packing Personal Effects
Staying Overnight in a Monastery
Taking up Residence in a Monastery
Attendance at Meals
Attendance at Tea Services
Requesting Abbot's Instruction
Entering Abbot's Room

FASCICLE TWO

Convocations in Dharma Hall
Recitation of Buddha Names
Small Assemblies in Abbot's Quarters
Opening Summer Retreat
Closing Summer Retreat
Winter Solstice and New Year Salutations
Inspection of Common Quarters by Abbot
Entertaining Eminent Visitors
Appointment of Stewards

FASCICLE THREE

Controller
Rector
Cook
Labor Steward
Retirement of Stewards
Appointment of Prefects
Head Seat
Scribe
Sūtra Library Prefect

FASCICLE FOUR

Guest Prefect
Prior
Bath Prefect
Solicitors of Provisions, Water Chief, Charcoal Chief, Hua-yen Preacher
Mill Chief, Garden Chief, Manager of Estate Lands, Manager of Business Cloister
Manager of Infirmary, Chief of Toilets
Buddha Hall Prefect, Chief of Bell Tower
Holy Monk's Acolyte, Chief of Hearths, Sangha Hall Monitor
Common Quarters Manager, Common Quarters Head Seat
Abbot's Acolytes

FASCICLE FIVE

Fundraising Evangelist
Retirement of Prefects
Tea Services Hosted by Abbot
Tea Services in the Sangha Hall
Tea Services Hosted by Stewards or Prefects
Tea Services in the Common Quarters Hosted by Senior Monks
Tea Services in the Common Quarters in Special Honor of a Senior Guest
Tea Services in the Common Quarters in Special Honor of Venerable Elders

FASCICLE SIX

Tea Services Hosted by Dharma Relatives and Room-Entering Disciples in Special Honor of Abbot
Procedure for Burning Incense at Tea Services for Assembly of Monks
Serving a Specially Sponsored Meal
Thanking the Sponsor of a Tea Service
Sutra Reading
Feasts Sponsored by Donors
Exit and Entrance
Signaling the Assembly
Special Delivery Letters
Sending Letters
Receiving Letters
Sick Leave and Return to Duty

FASCICLE SEVEN

Using the Toilet
Death of a Monk
Appointing Retired Officers
Inviting a Venerable to be Abbot
A Venerable's Acceptance of an Invitation to be Abbot
A Venerable's Entry into Monastery as New Abbot
A Venerable's Role as Abbot
Death of a Venerable Abbot
Retirement of an Abbot

FASCICLE EIGHT

Admonitions for Officers
Principles of Seated Meditation
Essay on Self Discipline
One Hundred and Twenty Questions
Disciplining Novices

FASCICLE NINE

Liturgy for Novice Ordinations
Regulating Postulants

FASCICLE TEN

Guiding Lay Believers
Procedure for Feasting Monks
Ode to Baizhang's Standards

The contents of the text are explained in five basic types of rules and procedures: first, standards of behavior addressed to individual monks; second, procedures for communal calendrical rites; third, guidelines for the organization and operation of public monastery bureaucracies, fourth, procedures for rituals of social interaction; and fifth, rules pertaining to the relationship between public monasteries and the outside world, in particular civil authorities and lay patrons. These five classes of rules and procedures are a product of my own analysis of the *Chanyuan qinggui*, and are not found in the text as such.

One major class of rules treated in the *Chanyuan qinggui* consists of behavioral guidelines addressed to individual monks, concerning such things as personal morality, etiquette, and belongings. Sections of the text representative of this type of rule include: Receiving Precepts (*shoujie*), Upholding Precepts (*hujie*), A Monk's Personal Effects (*biandaoju*), Packing Personal Effects (*zhuan-*

bao), Staying Overnight in a Monastery (*danguo*), Taking up Residence in a Monastery (*guada*), Attendance at Meals (*fuzhoufan*), Attendance at Tea Services (*fuchatang*), Using the Toilet (*daxiao bianli*), and Principles of Seated Meditation (*zuochanyi*).³⁶ Many of the rules for individuals treated in these sections were rooted in Chinese translations and interpretations of Indian Vinaya texts. The text clearly states that monks should be ordained with and should keep all the precepts of the traditional "Hinayāna" *pratimokṣa* outlined in the *Sifen lu* (Four-Part Vinaya), as well as the bodhisattva precepts of the Mahāyāna *Fanwang jing* (Sutra of Brahma's Net).³⁷ Other rules for individuals, however, were basically government regulations designed to control monkish ordinations, travel, and exemption from taxation. The text carefully details, for example, what legal documents a monk must obtain and carry if he wishes to enter a monastery, or travel away from a monastery where he is registered. Still other rules were adopted in imitation of ritual procedures at the imperial court and the manners of the cultured elites.

Some prime examples are the etiquette prescribed for the ubiquitous tea services and the elaborately polite phrases stipulated for use by all parties when formally negotiating the appointment of senior monastic officers.³⁸ By encouraging individual monks to understand and adhere to all religious strictures and civil laws, the *Chanyuan qinggui* served the interests of the large public monasteries, which did not want to be found harboring "impure" monks, unauthorized persons, or criminals within their walls. At the same time, the text promoted the movement of legitimate monks between those monasteries by providing a common set of procedures and behavioral norms that individuals could follow wherever they went.

A second major class of rules treated in the *Chanyuan qinggui* consists of procedural guidelines for communal rituals performed on a regular calendrical basis, including: Requesting Abbot's Instruction (*qingyinyuan*), Entering Abbot's Room (*rushi*), Convocations in Dharma Hall (*shangtang*), Recitation of Buddha Names (*niansong*), Small Assemblies in Abbot's Quarters (*xiaocan*), Opening Summer Retreats (*jiexia*), Closing Summer Retreats (*xiexia*), Winter Solstice and New Year Salutations (*dongnian renshi*), and Inspection of Common Quarters by Abbot (*xunliao*). It is interesting to speculate why Zongze treated just those rituals, and not various other calendrical rites that were commonly held in the public monasteries of his day, such as the daily and monthly sutra-chanting services (*fengjing*) in which merit was produced and dedicated to the Buddha, patriarchs, arhats, protecting deities, and so on, or the annual memorial services (*nianji*) that honored patriarchs and former abbots. It is impossible that Zongze omitted such services on the grounds that they had no proper place in the workings of public monasteries, because elsewhere in the *Chanyuan qinggui* he described the duties of the monastic officers who are in charge of the altars and ritual implements in the buildings (Buddha hall, arhats hall, patriarchs hall, etc.) where the services were held. His reason for ignoring them may have been a belief that it was not necessary to establish procedures for them that would be the same in all monasteries. Perhaps diversity in such matters was desirable or tolerable; or perhaps the rites were already so common and routinized that no further standardization was called for.

In any case, a clue to the significance of the calendrical rituals that are treated in the *Chanyuan qinggui* is the fact that the abbot plays a central role in all of them. Zongze may have felt that it was important to establish a standard set of procedures for those rites because high-ranking monks in his day frequently served as abbots in a series of different monasteries, but there was more to it than that. Abbots were not only the spiritual leaders of their communities who were supposed to "represent the Buddha in preaching and converting (*daifo yanghua*),"³⁹ they were the point men for entertaining powerful government officials and lay patrons when those came to visit. The rituals treated in detail in the *Chanyuan qinggui* do feature the abbot in his role of teacher and upholder (*zhuchi*) of moral purity, but by the same token, many of them were precisely the major public ceremonies that such officials and patrons were most likely to attend.

A key defining feature of the public monasteries in Song China was the fact that appointment to their abbacies was regulated by the state, both in terms of general eligibility and with regard to the selection of individual candidates, which was subject to approval by the civil authorities. Accordingly, the *Chanyuan qinggui* pays a great deal of attention to the bureaucratic and ritual details involved in the process of choosing, installing, and removing abbots. Relevant sections of the text include: Inviting a Venerable to be Abbot (*qing zunsu*), A Venerable's Entry Into Monastery as New Abbot (*zunsu ruyuan*), A Venerable's Role as Abbot (*zunsu zhuchi*), and Retirement of an Abbot (*tuiyuan*).

A third major concern of the *Chanyuan qinggui* is to establish guidelines for the organization and operation of public monastery bureaucracies. The text names and explains the duties of about thirty major and minor monastic offices: Controller (*kanyuan*), Rector (*weina*), Cook (*dienzuo*), Labor Steward (*zhisui*), Head Seat (*shouzuo*), Scribe *(shuzhuang)*, Sūtra Library Prefect (*cangzhu*), Guest Prefect (*zhike*), Prior (*kutou*), Bath Prefect (*yuzhu*), Solicitors of Provisions *(jiefang)*, Water Chief *(shuitou)*, Charcoal Chief *(tantou)*, Huayan Preacher *(huayantou)*, Mill Chief *(motou)*, Garden Chief (yuantou), Manager of Estate Lands (*zhuangzhu*), Manager of Business Cloister (*xieyuanzhu*), Manager of Infirmary (*yanshou tangzhu*), Chief of Toilets *(jingtou)*, Buddha Hall Prefect (*dianzhu*), Chief of Bell Tower (*zhongtou*), Holy Monk's Acolyte (*shengseng shizhe*), Chief of Hearths *(lutou)*, Saṅgha Hall Monitor (*zhitang*), Common Quarters Manager (*liaozhu*), Common Quarters Head Seat (*liao shouzuo*), Abbot's Acolytes (*tangtou shizhe*), and Fundraising Evangelist (*huazhu*). For each of those positions the text outlines the duties of the office in a general way and, in many cases, describes the personal qualities and ideal mental attitude that holders of the office should possess. A summary of the duties pertaining to the top positions in a monastery bureaucracy is given in the section entitled Admonitions for Officers (*guijingwen*).

Several sections of the text deal with transitions in a monastery bureaucracy: Appointment of Stewards (*qing zhishi*), Retirement of Stewards (*xia zhishi*), Appointment of Prefects (*qing toushou*), Retirement of Prefects (*xia toushou*), and Sick Leave and Returning to Duty (*jiangxi cantang*), the last of which pertains to both the abbot and senior monastic officers. The text stipulates exactly which polite, exaggeratedly humble phrases should be used by all parties in the formalities that mark the appointment and retirement of officers.

A fourth major class of rules appearing in the *Chanyuan qinggui*, all called "tea services" (*jiandian*), are essentially rituals of social interaction. A perusal of the topics covered in fascicles five and six will confirm that communal drinking of tea was a ubiquitous feature of life in the public monasteries of the Song. Tea services were held in several monastery buildings, including: the abbot's compound (*tangtou*); the saṅgha hall (*sengtan*), where the main body of monks in training slept, ate, and sat in meditation at their individual places (*tan*) on the platforms; and the common quarters (*zhongliao*), where the monks could do things prohibited in the saṅgha hall (reading, writing, using moxa, sewing, etc.) in a somewhat more relaxed atmosphere. Some tea services held in the abbot's compound were occasions on which the abbot received government officials or lay patrons. Most other tea services, however, were carefully orchestrated social gatherings in which individuals or groups belonging to one class within a monastery hierarchy paid their respects to those of another class by inviting them to drink tea and (on the more formal occasions) eat sweets together. Top officers in a monastery bureaucracy (the abbot, stewards, and prefects), for example, could host tea services for the ordinary monks in the saṅgha hall or common quarters, and those monks in turn could invite the officers. A few major tea services were built into the annual schedules of the public monasteries, but most seem to have been more or less spontaneous events, initiated by monks who wished to thank their juniors, ingratiate themselves to their seniors, or get together with others (both junior and senior) belonging to their own particular "Dharma families" or lineage subgroups. The hosts paid for the entertainment, the expense of which depended on the number of guests and the quality of the tea and cakes served. The *Chanyuan qinggui* pays careful attention to such details as the quality and quantity of the refreshments, the utensils used, the order of service, and the etiquette of who sits where and says what.

Tea services had no particular Buddhist meaning or content, and were in fact a common feature of elite Song culture. In Buddhist monasteries, however, at least one tutelary deity, the "Holy Monk" (usually Manjusri) enshrined in the saṅgha hall, was included in the tea service; a gesture that symbolized his membership in the assembly of monks. The serving of tea functioned to facilitate good social relations within a monastic community even as it reinforced the social hierarchy. Tea services were an especially effective way of assimilating newly arrived monks and recent appointments to monkish offices, for they amounted to public announcements of exactly where the newcomers fit in and how much respect was due to them.

Finally, in addition to the four broad classes of rules discussed above, there are a number of sections of the *Chanyuan qinggui* that can be grouped together on the grounds that they pertain to the relationship that the public monasteries had with the outside world—civil authorities and lay patrons in particular. Various sections of the text already mentioned above also meet this description, so it is obvious that the categories I have posited for the sake of analysis are not mutually exclusive. We have seen, for example, that certain rules promulgated for individual monks (especially those pertaining to documentation) were in fact a response to government regulation of the Buddhist saṅgha. Similarly, many of the guidelines for communal rituals, administrative procedures, and tea services involving the abbot were clearly formulated with the intention of fostering good relations with lay officials and patrons. The rules that aimed at standardizing monastic bureaucracies, too, include numerous provisions that explicitly state how particular officers are to deal with the authorities and other elements of the surrounding lay society.

There remain, however, a number of sections of the *Chanyuan qinggui* that have not yet been mentioned and do fall into the category of rules concerning the relationship between public monasteries and the outside world. Four that pertain specifically to interactions with lay patrons are: Sutra Reading (*kancanjing*), a rite in which sutras are chanted to produce merit that is dedicated in support of patron's prayers, in exchange for a cash donation; Feasts Sponsored by Donors (*zhongyanzhai*); Exit and Entrance (*churu*), which explains the manner in which the assembly of monks is to go out from a monastery temporarily to attend a feast sponsored by a donor; and Guiding Lay Believers (*quan tanxin*). Two other sections of the text, Sending Letters (*fashu*) and Receiving Letters (*shoushu*), also address the question of how to deal courteously and effectively with lay people in positions of political and economic power.

The typology of rules that I have introduced here does not entirely exhaust the contents of the *Chanyuan qinggui*. Fascicle seven treats two kinds of funerals, which may be classified as occasional rituals, or rites of passage: Death of a Venerable Abbot (*zunsu qian hua*), and Death of a Monk (*wangseng*). Fascicle eight includes two separate texts by Zongze that are better described as Buddhist homilies than as rules or procedural guidelines: "Essay on Self-Discipline" (*zijingwen*) and "One Hundred and Twenty Questions" (*yibai ershi wen*) are two examples. The latter is a list of Buddhist ideals framed as questions for monks to test their own state of moral and spiritual development. It is known to have also circulated as an independent text, apart from the *Chanyuan qinggui*.[40]

The very last section of the *Chanyuan qinggui*, etitled "Ode to Baizhang's

Standards" (*Baizhang guisheng song*), also stands as a separate piece, different in form from any other section of the text. On the surface, it appears to consist of a set of forty-one prose passages, each pertaining to some aspect of monastic organization and discipline, each with a laudatory verse (song) attached to it. Both the formal structure and the title of the text signal that the prose passages are "Baizhang's standards" (*Baizhang guisheng*), and that the verses are Zongze's comments on them. A similar form of commentary, called "verses on old cases" (*songgu*), was a standard feature of kōan (*gongan*) collections found in the discourse records (*yulu*) of Chan masters from about the middle of the eleventh century.[41] Zongze, of course, commenting on a set of rules attributed to Baizhang, not on the dialogues or "root cases" (*benze*) that were attributed to famous Chan patriarchs of the Tang, but the basic literary dynamics are the same. That is to say, the commenter's verses "extol" or "laud" (song) the root text as something worthy of great respect, while at the same time assuming the stance of a judge who is qualified to evaluate it and elaborate on its meaning.

A closer examination of the "Ode to Baizhang's Standards," however, reveals an interesting sleight of hand on Zongze's part. The first eleven sections of the root text are nothing other than the edition of the *Chanmen guishi* (Regulations of the Chan school) that was appended to Baizhang's biography in the *Jingde chuandeng lu*, compiled in 1004. The remaining thirty sections of the root text that also have laudatory verses attached to them are referred to by Zongze as "Baizhang's extant principles" (*Baizhang cun ganglin*); they did not circulate with the *Chanmen guishi* and indeed are found nowhere but in this section of the *Chanyuan qinggui*. The eleven sections that together comprise the widely circulated *Chanmen guishi* are descriptions of Baizhang's principles of monastery organization; they do not speak in the imperative voice that is characteristic of monastic rules proper. The thirty additional sections, however, are in the imperative voice. The rules they establish are more detailed and specific than any that appear in the *Chanmen guishi*, and the system of monastic training they pertain to is none other than that layed out in the main body of the *Chanyuan qinggui* itself. The obvious conclusion is that the thirty additional sections were written by Zongze himself as a kind of synopsis of the *Chanyuan qinggui*. By combining them with the *Chanmen guishi* and attaching laudatory verses to both alike, Zongze gave the impression that they were written by Baizhang. For anyone taken in by this strategy, it would appear the main body of the *Chanyuan qinggui* was a kind of elaborated version of Baizhang's original standards, which Zongze had in hand.

It is clear from the overall contents of the *Chanyuan qinggui* that Zongze did not intend the text to stand alone as a complete set of guidelines for any particular monastery. For one thing, he explicitly stated that the receiving and keeping of traditional Buddhist precepts was to be carried out in accordance with the Vinaya. Moreover, the *Chanyuan qinggui* is conspicuously lacking in two types of materials that all monasteries needed to function: first, a calendar of daily, monthly, and annual administrative and ritual activities, and second, a set of liturgical texts for use in communal religious services. Nor, as noted above, do we find procedural instructions for all of the major ceremonies and rituals that the *Chanyuan qinggui* presumes were performed in the monasteries it was meant to regulate. The topics that Zongze dealt with, rather, were matters of fundamental institutional organization and operation, and things that pertained to the state sanction and regulation of the Buddhist monastic institution at large. Judging from the contents, it would seem that the *Chanyuan qinggui* was written with the aims of: first, standardizing the bureaucratic structures of the great public monasteries; second, facilitating the interchange of personnel, including ordinary monks and high-ranking officers, between those monasteries; and third, insuring that the class of public monasteries remained beyond reproach in the eyes of governmental authorities and lay patrons.

Origins of the *Chanyuan qinggui*

We have seen that within a century of the publication of the *Chanyuan qinggui* followers of the Chan school (and many other Buddhists as well) had come to regard the text as the direct descendant, if not the actual embodiment, of rules for Chan monasteries that were first compiled by Baizhang. Modern research on the text, dominated by scholars affiliated with the Sōtō school of Zen in Japan, has never seriously challenged that traditional point of view. Although Japanese scholars disagree on various details, most have taken the position that Baizhang did author a "rules of purity" text that was subsequently lost.[42] As for the contents of those rules, virtually all accept the account given in the *Chanmen guishi* (summarized above). As I have argued elsewhere, that account has gained credence with modern scholars because it is congruent with their preconceived belief that Chan arose in the Tang dynasty as an iconoclastic, sectarian movement that rejected the Vinaya and traditional Buddhist practices such as scriptural study, prayers, repentances, and rituals for producing and dedicating merit in exchange for patronage.[43] The *Chanyuan qinggui*, according to this point of view, was a later product of the same independent, sectarian Chan movement, which had survived the persecutions of Buddhism that took place during the Huichang era (841–846) of the Tang and emerged as the dominant school of Buddhism in the Song.

However, a serious problem with this interpretation is the disjunction between the early Chan school's putative sectarianism, iconoclasm, and economic self-sufficiency, and what is known about the actual organization and operation of Chan monasteries in the Song. The *Chanyuan qinggui* refers to numerous bureaucratic arrangements and religious rituals that are not mentioned in the *Chanmen guishi*, and it clearly pertains to a monastic institution that was regulated by the state and supported on a grand scale by patronage, landholdings, and various commercial ventures. Modern Japanese scholars have thus been at pains to explain the great difference between the arrangement of the prototypical Chan monastery that they imagine existed in the Tang and that of the large public Chan monasteries that undeniably existed in the Song. To state the same problem differently, they have struggled to explain the disjunction between the simplicity of Baizhang's "original" rules as reflected in the *Chanmen guishi* and the complexity of the *Chanyuan qinggui*.

The most common solution to this problem has been to claim the Chan institution "degenerated" between the ninth and the twelfth centuries, gradually absorbing many elements of religious and social practice that were extraneous to "pure Chan" (*junsui zen*) and thereby succumbing to "syncretism" (*kenshūka*). According to this scenario, the Chan monastic institution fell victim to its own success in the early Song and suffered from increasing formalization and secularization, a growing reliance on state support and lay patronage, a corresponding increase in prayer services aimed at currying favor with patrons and the imperial court, and a heavier involvement in the management of estate lands and commercial ventures, such as oil presses and grain milling operations.[44] The appearance of a Buddha hall (*fodian*) in the *Chanyuan qinggui*, for example, is said to evince "a loss of independence and dilution of meditation, as Chan monasteries, in return for patronage, became vehicles for the satisfaction of secular intentions."[45] Similarly, the text's account of funeral services for ordinary monks is said to betray an admixture of Pure Land beliefs and practices.

I first became suspicious of this paradigm of "purity" and "degeneration" in Tang and Song Chan monastic institutions when, in the course of researching my doctoral dissertation years ago, I found that the basic claims of the *Chanmen guishi* were demonstrably false. Virtually all the features of Chan monastery organization attributed to Baizhang in that text, I discovered, were neither invented by him nor unique to the Chan school: all had clear precedents in the Indian Vinaya, or in monastic practices established in China prior to and apart from the Chan tradition.[46] The *Chanyuan qinggui* too, I found, had numerous elements that derived from the Vinaya and indigenous Chinese tradition of Vinaya exegesis.[47] Modern Japanese scholarship, I argued, was so captivated by the idea of an independent, sectarian Chan institution in the Tang and Song that it could not even conceive the possibility of links to the Vinaya tradition, let alone engage in comparative research of Chan and non-Chan monastic rules. I did pursue that line of research, however, and the conclusion I reached was that the claims of the *Chanmen guishi* concerning Baizhang were an element of early Song Chan polemics, designed to cover up and lend legitimacy to the actual process through which the Chan school had recently (in the late tenth century) taken control of some leading public monasteries that had always been (and continued to be) regulated by the Vinaya.[48]

Following up on my lead, Yifa has recently demonstrated in much greater detail just how many aspects of monastic discipline treated in the *Chanyuan qinggui* derive directly from indigenous Chinese traditions of Vinaya exegesis and extra-Vinaya rule making.⁴⁹ She also breaks new ground by tracing many of the features of nominally Chan public monastic life in the Song back to traditional state controls on the sangha and the influences of Chinese culture in general.⁵⁰ The conclusion she reaches is that the *Chanyuan qinggui* may be located squarely in the tradition of Chinese Vinaya exegesis, state regulation of the Buddhist saṅgha, and indigenous innovation of monastic rules. Yifa's work proves beyond a doubt that the entire contents of the *Chanyuan qinggui* may be accounted for by historical precedents that have nothing to do with the figure of Baizhang. Nevertheless, in remarkable testimony to the enduring power and sanctity of the Baizhang legend, Yifa, speaking as a modern Chinese Buddhist nun, cannot bring herself to state this conclusion. The mere fact that Baizhang's "rules of purity" do not survive and are not attested in any contemporaneous (Tang dynasty) sources, she argues, does not mean that they did not exist.⁵¹ In the eyes of the Chan and Zen traditions today, Baizhang is still the "founding patriarch" of the Chan monastic rule.

Development of "Rules of Purity" in the Song and Yuan

The *Chanyuan qinggui* was reprinted in the first year of the Zhenghe era (1111), only eight years after its initial publication. A subsequent publication of the text, dating from the second year of Jiatai (1202), contains a prefatory note, which explains: "The previous printing of this collection flourished greatly in the world. Regrettably, the letters [of the carved woodblocks] have been rubbed away [by frequent printing]. We now reprint the text using larger letters carved in catalpa wood that it may be preserved and propagated."⁵² That Jiatai edition, too, was widely distributed and served as the basis for a number of subsequent reprintings. By the late twelfth century, when Japanese pilgrim monks such as Eisai began visiting the great public monasteries of Zhejiang Province in that central area at least,⁵³ the *Chanyuan qinggui* had gained a universal acceptance and authority equal to that of the Vinaya.

What accounts for the unprecedented success of the *Chanyuan qinggui* in this regard? It was certainly not due to the influence and authority of the compiler, Zongze himself. He was, as we have seen, a Dharma heir in the prestigious Chan lineage, the abbot of a public monastery, and a monk eminent enough to receive an honorific title from the court and have his biography and collected teachings published. Such distinctions were not so rare in the world of Song Buddhism, however. They indicate that Zongze had a successful career, but not that he was an exceptionally famous or influential monk in his own day. Nor was much glory ever reflected upon him for compiling the *Chanyuan qinggui.* None of his biographies even mention his production of that or any other set of monastic rules.[54]

Clearly, Zongze's compilation met a need that had not been satisfied by any other text of his day, but what was the nature of that need? The idea (conveyed by the *Chanmen guishi*) that Baizhang was the author of the first Chan monastic rule was widely repeated and accepted as historical fact from early in the Song. By the time the *Chanyuan qinggui* was compiled in 1103, Baizhang had plenty of prestige and authority as a monastic legislator but, ironically, he had no concrete set of regulations. That is to say, there was no single text, no collection of monastic rules, that bore Baizhang's name as author. Or, to state the case more precisely, when Zongze set out to collect as many Chan monastic rules and consult with as many knowledgeable senior monks as he could, that effort yielded the *Chanmen guishi* description of Baizhang's rules but no actual rule book attributed to Baizhang. It is unthinkable that Zongze, had he found such a text, would have failed to mention it or include it in his compilation of the *Chanyuan qinggui*. As noted above, he did everything in his power to legitimize the *Chanyuan qinggui* by minimizing his own input and associating the compilation with Baizhang.

Zongze's strategy met with complete success. The text that came to fill the gap left by Baizhang's famous but vaguely delineated rules was none other than the *Chanyuan qinggui* itself. In Chan literature dating from the thirteenth century, such expressions as "standards (*kaimo*) produced by Baizhang," "rules (*guisheng*) of the high patriarch Baizhang," "rules for major monasteries (*conglin guifan*) detailed by Chan Master Baizhang," and "Baizhang's rules of purity (*qinggui*)" sometimes referred in a general way to all the multifarious regulations and procedures that were use in the Chan monasteries of the day. In many cases, however, the aforementioned terms were also used to refer specifically to the most complete and best known collection of "Baizhang's rules," namely, the *Chanyuan qinggui*.[55] According to the *Fozu tongji* (Comprehensive record of buddhas and patriarchs), a chronology and encyclopedia of Buddhism compiled in 1271, "Chan Master Baizhang [Huai] hai was the first to establish a Chan monastery. . . . In later times [his rules were] spread throughout the world and called *Chanyuan qinggui*."[56]

Following the compilation of the *Chanyuan qinggui*, there appeared in Song-and Yuan-dynasty China various other collections of monastic regulations that used the words "rules of purity" (*qinggui*) in their titles, invoked the authority of Baizhang, and claimed to perpetuate his legacy. Many of those works refer explicitly to the *Chanyuan qinggui* in their prefaces or colophons, and/or incorporate parts of that text. It is clear that the *Chanyuan qinggui* was an important resource for the compilers of those later "rules of purity," not only in the sense of providing precedents that were already sanctified as "Baizhang's rules," but as a model for how to organize a large and complex set of monastic regulations.

The second oldest surviving "rules of purity" is the *Ruzhong Riyong qinggui* (Rules of purity for daily life in the assembly), written in 1209 by Wuliang Zongshou.[57] The text is also called *Wuliang shou chanshi riyong xiaoqinggui* (Chan Master Wuliang Shou's small rules of purity for daily life), or simply *Riyong qinggui* (Rules of purity for daily life).[58] At the time when Wuliang compiled this work, he held the monastic office of head seat (*shouzuo*), which meant that he was in charge of leading the so-called "great assembly" (*dazhong*) of ordinary monks who had no administrative duties, and thus were free to concentrate on a daily routine of meditation, study, and devotions. The rules found in the *Riyong qinggui* pertain almost exclusively to the facilities where the monks of the great assembly of a public monastery spent the majority of their time. The most important building for them was the saṅgha hall (*sengtang*), where each monk had an individual place (*tan*) on the platforms. There the monks sat together in meditation, took their morning and midday meals as a group, and slept at night. Nearby was a building called the common quarters (*zhongliao*), where they could study sutras, write, drink tea, and take an evening meal that was euphemistically referred to as "medicine" (because the Vinaya forbade eating after midday). Other facilities that served the daily needs of the assembly were the washstands that were located behind the saṅgha hall, the toilet, bathhouse, laundry place, and hearth.

As he stated in his colophon, Wuliang wrote the *Riyong qinggui* for the benefit of monks who were new to communal training in the great assembly, not for old hands or officers. He limited the scope of the work, moreover, to the routine daily activities of those monks, stating that:

> convocations in the Dharma hall (*shengtang*), entering the abbot's room (*rushi*), small assemblies in the abbot's quarters (*xiaocan*), sutra chanting services (*fengjing*), recitation of buddha names (*niansong*), inspection of the common quarters by the abbot (*xunliao*), the closing and opening of retreats (*xiejie*), [winter solstice and new year] salutations (*renshi*), packing personal effects (*zhuanbao*) and donning the bamboo hat [for pilgrimage] (*dingli*), and sending off deceased monks (*songwang*) and auctioning their belongings (*changyi*), are already included in detail in the regulations of the *Rules of Purity* (*qinggui*). Venerable [abbots] each have [their own] special admonitions [for their monasteries], so I will not make any further statement.[59]

In other words, because the rites and observances Wuliang listed here were already dealt with in the *Chanyuan qinggui*, he deemed it unnecessary to reiterate them.[60] Actually, two of the activities that Wuliang did see fit include in his *Riyong qinggui*—the procedures for taking meals and for going to the toilet—had been dealt with in great detail in the *Chanyuan qinggui*.

Wuliang's treatment of the mealtime ritual differed, however, in two significant ways: it omitted many instructions, such as those directed to monastic officers and lay servants, that were not directly relevant to the ordinary monks of the assembly, and it included the actual texts of the mealtime chants that those monks needed to know. Unlike the *Chanyuan qinggui*, the *Riyong qinggui* incorporated other liturgical material as well: verses to be chanted upon rising, donning robes, and hearing the evening bell. Wuliang's presentation of procedures for the toilet was basically the same in contents as the corresponding section of the *Chanyuan qinggui*, but the wording is sufficiently different for us to be sure that it was not based on that text. Because the section called "Using the Toilet" (*daxiao bianli*) appears at a rather odd place in the *Chanyuan qinggui*, alone in fascicle 7 rather than together with similar materials in fascicle 1, it may be a later addition not found in the version of the text that Wuliang was familiar with. In any case, Wuliang would have included procedures for the toilet in his work simply because they were among the routine daily activities of monks in the assembly.

In his preface to the *Riyong qinggui*, Wuliang explained his aim in writing the text as follows:

> If one has not yet memorized the regulations with regard to conduct, then one's actions will not be in accord with the ritual restraints. If even one's good friends and benevolent advisors do not have the heart to severely reprimand and harshly criticize, and if one continues on with one's bad habits, then reform is extremely difficult. In the end this [behavior] will bring desolation upon the monasteries, and induce negligence in peoples' minds. Because I frequently see such transgressions and evils, which are commonplace before my very eyes, I have collected the regulations produced by Baizhang and have studied them thoroughly from beginning to end. From morning to night, to avoid every particular offense, one must straightaway obey every single provision.[61]

Here we see that Wuliang too, like Zongze before him, claimed to have collected and consulted various earlier monastic rules, the authority of which ultimately derived from Baizhang. One difference, of course, was that for Wuliang the *Chanyuan qinggui* itself was a prime source for the "regulations produced by Baizhang." Wuliang also echoed the concern, evinced so clearly in that earlier work, that adherence to the rules was essential if the public monasteries were to stand up to the close and often unsympathetic scrutiny of the civil authorities.

The way in which Wuliang organized the *Riyong qinggui*, basically, was to take the reader step by step through the activities of a typical day in the life of the great assembly: rising, going to the washstands and toilet, donning robes, sitting in meditation, making prostrations, taking meals, bathing, warming up by the hearth, and going to sleep. For each of the activities in question, a number of dos and don'ts are stated in simple, declarative language. Upon arising, for example, "Gently push the screen aside with your hand, and exit to the washstand; do not drag your footwear, and do not make a noise by coughing."⁶² Rules such as these are addressed directly to the individual, as matters of personal etiquette that should be observed.

The *Riyong qinggui* also contains thirteen short passages, apparently quoted verbatim from a source (or sources) that Wuliang had in hand, that begin with the words, "The old [rules] say. . . ." Thus, for example, the passage concerning exiting to the washstand quoted above is followed immediately by this: "The old [rules] say: 'When pushing aside the curtain, one's rear hand should hang at one's side; when exiting the hall, it is strictly forbidden to drag one's footwear.' "⁶³ This citation and the others like it were devices that Wuliang used to lend authority to, and in a few cases to elaborate on, specific points that he had already made in the text. He did not say what source(s) he was citing, but a comparative check of the *Chanyuan qinggui* shows that none of the quotations derive directly from that text. The reader is given the impression, nevertheless, that the quotations came from some earlier edition of "Baizhang's rules." The only other instances in which Wuliang deviates from the use of the imperative voice are a few passages in which he gives the reasons for a particular admonition. After stating flatly, "Do not wash the head" (at the washstand), for example, he explains: "There are four reasons why this is harmful to self and others. First, it dirties the basin, and second, it dirties the [public] hand cloth: these are the things harmful to others. Third, it dries out the hair, and fourth, it injures the eyes: these are the things harmful to self."⁶⁴ For the most part, however, the only reason given for the rules is the implicit one; Baizhang established them.

Another Chinese text that is not called "rules of purity," but is nevertheless quite similar in contents to others that are, is a work entitled *Ruzhong xuzhi* (Necessary information for entering the assembly).⁶⁵ Although it lacks any preface or colophon that might tell us about its authorship or publication data, it is believed on the basis of internal evidence to have been written around 1263. The *Ruzhong xuzhi* opens with a section entitled "Procedures for Entering the Assembly" (*ruzhong zhi fa*) that is similar in many respects to the rules outlined in Wuliang's *Riyong qinggui* for waking, going to the washstand, donning robes, and taking meals. The *Ruzhong xuzhi* is much longer than the *Riyong qinggui*, however. In addition to the rules for individual monks in the assembly, it treats almost all of the major rituals and observances found in the *Chanyuan qinggui*, also providing liturgical materials (the verses to be chanted) for a number of them. In short, the *Ruzhong xuzhi* seems to have combined the contents and the main features of both the *Chanyuan qinggui* and the *Riyong qinggui*, with the exception that it did not treat the names and basic duties of the various monastic offices. Instead, it simply took for granted the bureaucratic structure established by the *Chanyuan qinggui*. Because it also lacks a calendar of events, the *Ruzhong xuzhi* could not have stood alone as complete set of rules for a monastery, although it is closer to serving that function than either of its two predecessors. My guess is it was compiled as a handy reference work for use by the monks in a single institution.

Chronologically, the next of the surviving Chinese texts to be styled "rules of purity" is the *Conglin Jiaoding qinggui zongyao* (Essentials of the revised rules of purity for major monasteries), or *Jiaoding qinggui* (Revised rules of purity) for short, compiled in 1274 by Jinhua Weimian.[66] In his preface to the work, Wemian stated that although Baizhang's rules (*guifan*) were already detailed, much time had passed since they were written. Later people, he said, had come up with various rules that were more up-to-date, but those were not always in agreement. Just as the Confucians had their *Book of Rites*, so, too, the Buddhists needed a standard ritual manual. Hence, Weimian concluded, he had compiled the *Jiaoding qinggui* in two fascicles, based on Baizhang and what he had learned in consultation with virtuous senior monks.[67] The rules of Baizhang that Weimian referred to were, in all likelihood, nothing other than the *Chanyuan qinggui*, which had been in circulation for some 170 years. His stated aim, then, was to update, augment, and standardize the ritual procedures found in that earlier text.

The *Jiaoding qinggui* differs from any previous extant monastic rules in that it opens with a number of charts that detail the seating and standing positions that the officers and other participants were to take in incense-offering rites and tea services held in various monastery buildings. Those are followed in the first fascicle with samples of what to write on the formal invitations and signboards that were used to announce feasts, tea services, and the like. The text then gives detailed procedural guidelines for the invitation and installation of new abbots, the appointment and retirement of officers, and numerous tea services. If the first fascicle focuses on what may be termed social rituals and bureaucratic procedures, the second fascicle is given over to rites of a more religious, didactic, and mortuary nature, including sermons by the abbot, entering the abbot's room, sitting in meditation, recitation, funerals for abbots and other monks, and memorial services.

The *Jiaoding qinggui* was clearly intended to standardize procedures for the aforementioned rituals and observances across the entire range of public monasteries. The text did include a copy of Wuliang's *Riyong qinggui*, appended to the second fascicle, but it was not really aimed at ordinary monks of the great assembly. It was, in essence, an updated ritual manual for monastic officers, and one that took for granted the basic organization and operation of the public monasteries. Lacking a calendar of events and any liturgical materials, it is inconceivable that the *Jiaoding qinggui* ever stood alone as a set of rules used to regulate a single monastery.

The next text to consider is the *Chanlin beiyong qunggui* (Auxiliary rules of purity for Chan monasteries), or *Beiyong qinggui* (Auxiliary rules of purity) for short, completed in 1286 by an abbot named Zeshan Yixian and published in 1311.[68] This lengthy work included virtually all of the religious rites, bureaucratic procedures, and guidelines for monastic officers found in the *Chanyuan qinggui* and *Jiaoding qinggui*. It also incorporated Zongze's "Ode to Baizhang's Standards" (*Baizhang guisheng song*),[69] as well as the text of Wuliang's *Riyong qinggui*.[70] In addition, the *Beiyong qinggui* established procedures for a number of rites that were not treated in any of the aforementioned "rules of purity," such as sutra-chanting services (*fengjing*) and prayer services (*zhusheng*) for the emperor; celebrations of the Buddha's birthday (*xiangdan*), enlightenment (*chengdao*), and nirvana (*niepan*); and memorial services (*ji*) for Bodhidharma, Baizhang, the founding abbot (*kaishan*), and various patriarchs (*zhuzu*). The *Beiyong qinggui* is also noteworthy as the oldest of the extant "rules of purity" texts to include a schedule of events, albeit a sketchy one, under the heading of "monthly items" (*yuefen biaoti*).[71] Despite the heading, this is basically an annual calendar of major rites and observances listed by the month (and often the day) of their occurrence.

The *Huanzhu an qinggui* (Rules of purity for the Huanzhu hermitage), written in 1317 by the eminent Chan master Zhongfen Mingben (1263–1323), is different in many respects from any of the earlier Chinese "rules of purity" discussed above.[72] In the first place, the text was evidently intended to regulate only one rather small monastic community, the hermitage where Mingben resided in his later years. It includes guidelines for just a handful of key monastic offices—the hermitage chief (*anzhu*) or abbot, head seat (*shouzu*), assistant abbot (*fuan*), stores manager (*zhiku*), and head of meals (*fantou*)—far fewer than was the norm at the great public monasteries of the day. It also establishes procedural guidelines for just a few basic bureaucratic functions, such as taking up residence (*guada*) in the monastery, alms gathering (*fenwei*), and "all invited" (*puqing*), which is to say, "mandatory attendance" at communal labor, funerals, and other events. The bulk of the *Huanzhu an qinggui* is given over to an enumeration of daily (*rizi*), monthly (*yuejin*), and annual (*niangui*) observances and rituals that the monks of the hermitage were to engage in, and the verses (mostly dedications of merit) that they were to chant on those various occasions. The text thus had the basic functions of a calendar and liturgical manual, as well as laying out a few rules and ritual procedures for monastic officers.

The *Huanzhu an qinggui* is especially valuable as a historical document because it provides an example, albeit a relatively late one in the history of Buddhist institutions in the Song and Yuan, of a type of material that must surely have been in use at all times in all monasteries, from the largest public ones down to the smallest disciple cloisters and merit cloisters. Any community of monks, even if it relied on one or more of the major "rules of purity" that were printed and in circulation, would also have needed its own daily, monthly, and annual schedule of rituals, as well as a set of liturgical texts that the monks in residence could use to familiarize themselves with the verses and *dharanis* that were chanted in connection with those.

The culmination of all the preceding developments came with the publication of the *Chixiu baizhang qingqui* (Imperial edition of Baizhang's rules of purity), which was produced by decree of the Yuan emperor Shun and compiled by the monk Dongyang Dehui between the years 1335 and 1338.[73] This was a massive work that collated and incorporated all the various elements of previous "rules of purity," including precepts and general behavioral guidelines for individual monks; procedures for routine activities in the daily life of monks, such as meals, bathing, meditation, and worship; descriptions of the duties and ideal spiritual attitudes of officers in the monastic bureaucracy; daily, monthly, and annual schedules of rituals; and liturgical texts, mainly prayers and verses for the dedication of merit. In his preface, Dehui states that he drew on the *Chanyuan qinggui, Jiaoding qinggui,* and *Beiyong qinggui* for source materials, and that he had been commissioned by the emperor to compile a single, comprehensive, authoritative set of rules for the entire Buddhist saṅgha.

The ostensible reason for the use of the name Baizhang in the title was that Dehui was abbot of the Dazhi Shousheng Chan Monastery (*Dazhi shousheng chansi*) on Baizhang Mountain (*Baizhangshan*) in Jiangxi Province. That is the same mountain where, according to Chan lore, the patriarch Baizhang is supposed to have founded the first Chan monastery.[74] Although Dehui made no claim his work was written by Baizhang, the use of the Baizhang name in the title clearly signaled the legitimacy and orthodoxy of the rules, despite their Chinese origins. As Yifa notes, in later centuries the *Chixiu Baizhang qinggui* was indeed mistakenly ascribed to Baizhang himself, but is well to remember that in the Chan tradition "Baizhang" was not simply a historical figure. He was a vital spirit to be worshiped, and a symbol of the indigenous monastic institution; in that sense the ascription is true.[75] In any case, the *Chixiu Baizhang qinggui* was so complete in its contents and so authoritative, having been endorsed by both the emperor and the spirit of Baizhang, that it effectively supplanted all previous "rules of purity," including the *Chanyuan qinggui.* It became the standard reference work for large Buddhist monasteries in China (with the exception of the Tibetan institutions that were patronized by the court during the Qing dynasty) into the twentieth century.[76]

The story of Baizhang's rules was closely associated with the Chan school, which certainly reaped the most prestige from it in the Song and Yuan, but as I have argued, the figure of Baizhang appealed to all Chinese Buddhists as a kind of cultural icon and national hero. That was only possible because there was a tacit understanding among them that the "rules of purity" were the common heritage of the entire Chinese saṅgha, not the exclusive invention or property of the Chan school. Although it dominated the public monastery system in the Song, the Chan school did not monopolize it. As we have seen, the Tiantai school too held rights to the abbacies of a number of public monasteries throughout the Song, as did a revived Nanshan Vinaya school from around the early thirteenth century.

It is clear from the *Gozan jissatsu zu* and other records of Japanese pilgrims that regardless of whether they had Chan, Teachings, or Vinaya lineage abbacies, all the public monasteries in Zhejiang Province in the early thirteenth century had virtually the same arrangements of buildings and ritual accoutrements. Chan monasteries, of course, had mortuary images of Bodhidharma and Baizhang in their patriarch's halls (*zutang*), and all of the former abbots enshrined there belonged to the Chan lineage. The patriarch's halls at Teachings monasteries were identical in basic layout and function, but they naturally featured Tiantai lineage patriarchs and former abbots. By the same token, the Dharma halls at Chan and Teachings monasteries were identical, but Chan abbots who took the high seat there engaged their audiences in "questions and answers" (*wenda*) about old cases (kōans), whereas Tiantai abbots and other senior officers lectured on the classics of their exegetical tradition. The saṅgha halls in both Chan and Teachings monasteries had the same arrangement of platforms for meals, sleep, and meditation, but Teachings monasteries also had specialized facilities for the more complex routines of meditation and repentance (the so-called "four samādhis") associated with the Tiantai tradition.[77]

The *Jiaoyuan qinggui* (Rules of purity for Teachings monasteries), compiled in 1347 by Yunwai Ziqing, was the Tiantai school's counterpart to the *Chixiu Baizhang qinggui*.[78] It too was clearly based on many earlier materials, and it held a great many elements in common with the Chan rules of its day. The features that best distinguish it from its Chan counterparts are procedures for Tiantai-style retreat halls, and the stipulation that the abbot and other senior monks lecture on Tiantai texts. The basic monastery layout, bureaucratic structure, and ritual calendar that it describes are essentially the same as those found in Chan "rules of purity."

Although they are very similar in contents, there is no question of the *Jiaoyuan qinggui* being simply a copy of the *Chixiu Baizhang qinggui* or other Chan "rules of purity," as some modern Zen scholars would have it. For one thing, the preface explains that Ziqing based his compilation on an earlier Tiantai manuscript that had been lost in a fire. That might sound like an excuse designed to cover up reliance on the *Chixiu Baizhang qinggui*, but the fact is that the Tiantai school had its own tradition of compiling monastic rules that went at least as far back as the eleventh century. The eminent monk Zunshi (963–1032), a champion of the Shanjia branch of the Tientai tradition that reconstituted itself in the early Song, was a monastic legislator whose rules predate the compilation of the *Chanyuan qinggui* (the oldest extant Chan code) by seventy years.

Zunshi rebuilt the abandoned Tianzhu Monastery (Tianzhusi) around 1015 and had it recognized by the court as a public monastery with a Teachings (Tiantai lineage) abbacy. In a document entitled *Tianzhusi shifang zhuchi yi* (Principles for the ten directions abbacy of Tianzhu Monastery), dated 1030, he established a set of ten principles that all future abbots should honor.[79] Zunshi's *Beili zhongzhi* (Additional rules for the assembly),[80] published in the same collection,[81] makes it clear that the monks of Tianzhu Monastery trained in a saṅgha hall (*sengtang*) with platforms for sleep, meals, and seated meditation. Zunshi's monastery also had a Dharma hall (*fatang*) where large convocations were held,[82] and an abbot's quarters (*fangzhang*) where monks would "enter the room" (*rushi*) for instruction.[83] All of those facilties and activities are described as basic features of Baizhang's monastery in the *Chanmen guishi*, but they were evidently common to many public monasteries in the eleventh century, not just those with Chan abbacies. Zunshi's rules for the bath and toilet, found in the same collection of materials from Tianzhu Monastery, are similar to those included later in the *Chanyuan qinggui*.[84] Approximately three centuries elapsed between Zunshi's formulation of his rules and Ziqing's compilation of the *Jiaoyuan qinggui*, and no intermediary "rules of purity for Teachings monasteries" survive. Nevertheless, it is clear that both the Chan and the Tiantai schools shared in the ongoing institutional development of the public monasteries over that period, and that the monastic rules they used were nearly identical at both the early and the late phases of that development.

The Nanshan Vinaya school also produced its own version of a "rules of purity" in the Yuan. The *Luyuan shigui* (Rules for Vinaya monasteries), compiled in 1324 by Xingwu Xinzong, is very similar in contents to the *Beiyong qinggui*, published in 1311.[85] In his preface, Xingwu stated that "Baizhang Dazhi adapted the Vinaya system (*luzhi*) as rules of purity for Chan monasteries (*chanlin qinggui*) and presented it to the world where it flourished and spread, but the Vinaya practitioners (*luxuezhe*) of our house [the Nanshan school] never achieved anything like that."[86] In compiling the *Luyuan shigui*, clearly Xingwu hoped to rectify that deficiency and reclaim for his Vinaya school the credit it deserved for the major role it had played historically in the development of Chinese monastic rules. The Nanshan Vinaya school was a relative latecomer to the competition for the abbacies of public monasteries in the Song; it was the product of a revival in the thirteenth century, not the ancient unbroken lineage (*zong*) that Xingwu strove to depict in his guidelines for images in Vinaya monastery patriarch halls. Xingwu tacitly admitted that fact in his preface, conceding that in compiling the *Luyuan shigui* he had consulted Chan monastery rules (*chanlin guishi*). Nevertheless, his work also stressed the features of public monastery life that were historically most closely associated with the Nanshan school of Vinaya exegesis, especially the rite of receiving the 250 precepts of a fully ordained monk on an ordination platform.

Conclusion

Modern scholars have treated the *Chanyuan qinggui* as the oldest extant example of a genre of indigenous Chinese monastic regulations styled "rules of purity." The genre is said to have been invented by the Chan patriarch Baizhang, and even those scholars who view him more as a symbol than a historical figure are inclined to agree that the "rules of purity" literature in general is a product of the Chan tradition. The evidence adduced in this chapter suggests otherwise. The monastic regulations contained in the *Chanyuan qinggui* and later "rules of purity" were neither the invention of Baizhang nor the exclusive property of the Chan school. They were, in fact, the common heritage of the Chinese Buddhist tradition during Song and Yuan. Nevertheless, by promoting the figure of Baizhang, the Chan school was able to take credit for the entire tradition of indigenous monastic rulemaking, and it succeeded in providing the Chinese Buddhist saṅgha at large with a native son whose prestige and authority as a monastic legislator rivaled that of the Indian Buddha. The *Chanmen guishi* set the stage for that remarkable coup with its claims about Baizhang, but it was the *Chanyuan qinggui* that gave substance to the Baizhang story and brought the Chan "rules of purity" into existence.

NOTES

1. The difference between "public" and "private" monasteries is explained below.

2. Two of Daoxuan's most influential commentaries on the Vinaya were the *Sifenlu xingshi chao* (Guide to the Practice of the four-part Vinaya, T 40.1–156) and the *Jiaojie xinxue biqui xinghu luyi* (Instructions on the ritual restraints to be observed by new monks in training, T 45.869a–874a).

3. Among the earliest recorded instances of this are the "Regulations for Monks and Nuns" (*sengni yaoshi*) written during the time of emperor Xiaowu of the Southern dynasty (r. 454–464) by a monk official who was designated by the court as "controller of the saṅgha" (*sengzheng yuezhong*) in the capital (T 50.401b; cited in Satō, *Chūgoku bukkyō ni okeru kairitsu no kenkyū*, 55). Another early example is the "Sangha Regulations in Forty-seven Clauses" (*sengshi sishiqi tiao*) composed in 493 at the behest of the emperor Xiaowen of the Northern Wei dynasty (T 50.464b, cited in *Chūgoku bukkyō ni okeru kairitsu no kenkyū*, 59). In 637 the Tang emperor Taizong had a new legal code written that contained a section called "Regulations Regarding the Taoist and Buddhist Clergies" (*daoseng ge*). As Stanley Weinstein notes, this text was nominally based on the Vinaya, but it "covered a wider range of clerical activity than did the Vinaya and invariably prescribed harsher penalties," in *Buddhism under the T'ang* (Cambridge: Cambridge University Press, 1987), p. 19; also see Michihata Ryōshū, *Tōdai bukkyō shi no kenkyū* (Kyoto: Hōzōkan, 1957), pp. 115–135.

4. For example, the "Standards for Monks and Nuns" (*sengni guifan*) improvised by Daoan when he was unable to obtain a complete Vinaya-*pitaka* (T 50.353b–c; T 54.241a.); and the "Rules in Ten Clauses" (*lizhifa shitiao*) formulated by Zhiyi in 595

for his monastery on Tiantai Mountain and recorded in the *Guoqing bailu* (One hundred records of Guoqing Monastery), compiled by his disciple Guanding (T 46.793b–794a).

5. For a useful overview and a number of detailed studies of Chinese Buddhism in this period, see Peter N. Gregory and Daniel Getz, eds., *Buddhism in the Sung* (Honolulu: University of Hawai'i Press, 1999).

6. T. Griffith Foulk, "Myth, Ritual, and Monastic Practice in Sung Ch'an Buddhism," in Patricia Buckley Ebrey and Peter N. Gregory, eds., *Religion and Society in T'ang and Sung China* (Honolulu: University of Hawai'i Press, 1993), pp. 167–191.

7. Ibid., pp. 163–164.

8. For a detailed account of the ideological dimensions of that competition, see T. Griffith Foulk, "Sung Controversies Concerning the 'Separate Transmission' of Ch'an," in Gregory and Getz, eds., *Buddhism in the Sung*, pp. 220–294.

9. Takao Giken, *Sōdai bukkyō shi no kenkyū* (Kyoto: Hyakkaen, 1975), p. 62.

10. Statistics indicating the preponderance of the "Chan" designation in the early Song are found in the *Baojing siming zhi* (Annals of Siming in the Baojing era), edited in 1227; cited in Takao Giken, *Sōdai bukkyō shi no kenkyū*, p. 67.

11. The *Gozan jissatsu zu*, compiled by a Japanese pilgrim monk and preserved at Daijōji in Japan, is a collection of drawings and diagrams that represent the ground plans, furnishings, and other physical features of major Chinese monasteries in the early thirteenth century; *Zengaku daijiten* (Tokyo: Taishūkan, 1978), 3.10–32.

12. *Zengaku daijiten*, 3.10–32.

13. When this process was multiplied over hundreds of years by thousands of heirs to the "buddha-mind lineage" (*foxinzong*), the school that claimed "not setting up scriptures" (*buli wenzi*) as one of its principles ending up producing a collection of discourse records (*yulu*) and "records of the transmission of the flame" (*chuandenglu*) vast enough to rival the Indian sutra and commentarial literature in sheer volume.

14. T 50.770c–771a. For an English translation and brief overview of the text, see T. Griffith Foulk, "The Legend of Baizhang, 'Founder' of Chan Monastic Discipline," in Wm. Theodore de Bary and Irene Bloom, eds., *Sources of Chinese Tradition*, 2nd ed., vol. 1 (New York: Columbia University Press, 1999), pp. 517–522.

15. For a full account of the various recensions, quotations, and pericopes of the *Chanmen guishi* (Regulations of the Chan school), see T. Griffith Foulk, "The 'Ch'an School' and Its Place in the Buddhist Monastic Tradition" (Ph.D. Dissertation, University of Michigan, 1987), pp. 328–345.

16. T 51.250c–251b.

17. T 51.250c–251a.

18. T 51.251b. The text of the *Chanmen guishi* as it appears in the *Jingde chuandeng lu* has interlinear commentary that was written by at least one other person.

19. For a detailed account of this process, complete with references to historical evidence, see T. Griffith Foulk and Robert H. Sharf, "On the Ritual Use of Ch'an Portraiture in Medieval China," in *Cahiers d'Extrême-Asie* 7 (1993–1994): 177–186.

20. HTC 120.209b2–12. Unfortunately, only the preface survives, not the main body of the text.

21. HTC 148.299a. A nearly identical passage is also attributed to Shouduan in

the Fozu tongji along with Huihong's judgment that this arrangement should be the norm throughout the empire (T 2035: 49.422a9–12; cf. T 2035: 49.464b19–21).

22. Zongze's preface is translated in full below.

23. My discussion of Zongze's biography in this section is heavily indebted to research done by Yifa, *The Origins of Buddhist Monastic Codes in China: An Annotated Translation and Study of the Chanyuan Qinggui*, Kuroda Institute, Classics in East Asian Buddhism (Honolulu: University of Hawai'i Press, 2002), pp. 101–107.

24. ZZ 2B, 9, 2.

25. This is typical of the "records of the transmission of the flame" (*chuandeng lu*) genre, to which the *Jianzhong jingguo xudeng lu* belongs.

26. *Lebang wenlei* 3 (T 47.192c).

27. Yifa, *The Origins of Buddhist Monastic Codes in China*, p. 101.

28. Ibid., pp. 101–102. The account found in the traditional hagiographies is not only sketchy, it is also cliched, for exactly the same type of information is given for every heir to the Chan lineage in the *Jianzhong jingguo xudeng lu*.

29. Ibid., pp. 102–103.

30. It is not clear whether Zongze is referring to an increase in the number of monasteries in China, an increase in the size of existing monasteries, or an increase of complexity in the organization and operation of monasteries. The verbal binome he uses to describe the increase literally means "to creep and spread" (*manyan*) in the manner of overgrown, tangled vines. Certainly Zongze used this verb in a pejorative sense, for he tells us that he finds the phenomenon unbearable to watch. It is difficult to imagine that a Buddhist abbot would be so offended by an increase in the mere number of Buddhist monasteries in the land. I surmise, therefore, that he was railing against a profusion of complicated and inconsistent written rules and ritual procedures.

32. For Chinese original see Kagamishima Genryū, Satō Tatsugen, and Kosaka Kiyū, eds. and trans., *Yakuchū zen'en shingi* (Tokyo: Sōtōshū Shūmuchō, 1972), p. 3.

33. Or, if the criticism is to be taken as real, perhaps Zongze meant that because the "Buddha-mind" (*foxin*) is formless and signless, to make a show of "transmitting" it is to commit the error of imputing form and signifying something, which is like a self-inflicted wound.

34. Zongze accurately describes that process as it is portrayed in the Vinaya. Modern scholars, of course, believe that the ramification of basic Vinaya rules as violations were adjudicated and the addition of new ones as the need arose was an evolutionary process that went on for centuries.

35. There are two major recensions and a handful of variant editions of the text. For details, see Yifa, *The Origins of Buddhist Monastic Codes in China*, pp. 108–110. That account is based on Kagamishima et al., eds., *Yakuchū zen'en shingi*, pp. 5–11. The text I describe here is the modern edition contained in the latter work.

36. Zongze's *Principles of Seated Meditation* also circulated as an independent text, apart from the *Chanyuan qinggui*. For a translation of the text and comparative study of the genre it belongs to, see Carl Bielefeldt, *Dōgen's Manual of Zen Meditation* (Berkeley and Los Angeles: University of California Press, 1988). Bielefeldt's translation and brief introduction may also be found in de Bary and Bloom, eds., *Sources of Chinese Tradition*, 2nd ed., vol. 1, pp. 522–524.

37. Kagamishima et al., eds., *Yakuchū zen'en shingi*, p. 13.

38. Ibid., pp. 20, 2, 28, 38, 39, 41.

39. Ibid., p. 257.

40. For a translation of the "One Hundred and Twenty Questions," see Chun-fang Yü, "The Chanyuan Monastic Code," in de Bary and Bloom, eds., *Sources of Chinese Tradition*, 2nd ed., vol. 1, pp. 525–529.

41. See T. Griffith Foulk, "The Form and Function of Kung-an Literature: A Historical Overview," in Steven Heine and Dale S. Wright, eds., *The Kōan: Text and Context in Zen Buddhism* (New York: Oxford University Press, 2000), pp. 18–20, 26–28.

42. For a summary of modern scholarly views on this subject see Foulk, "The 'Ch'an School' and Its Place in the Buddhist Monastic Tradition," pp. 299–300; also Yifa, *The Origins of Buddhist Monastic Codes in China*, pp. 9–35.

43. Foulk, "Myth, Ritual, and Monastic Practice in Sung Ch'an Buddhism," pp. 156–159.

44. See the following works of Kagamishima Genryū, "Dōgen zenji to hyakujō shingi," in *Dōgen zenji to sono in'yō kyōten, goroku no kenkyū*, (Tokyo: Mokujisha, 1974) pp. 181–192; "Hyakujō ko shingi henka katei no ichi kōsatsu," *Komazawa daigaku bukkyūgakubu kenkyū kiyō* 25 (1967): 1–13; and, "Kaisetsu," in Kagamishima, et al., eds., *Yakuchū zen'en shingi*, pp. 1–25, "Hyakujō shingi no seiritsu to sono igi," *Aichi gakuin daigaku zen kenkyūjo kiyō* 6 and 7 (1967): 117–134, and *Dōgen zenji to sono monryū*, pp. 47–48. See also Kondō Ryōichi's two articles, "Hyakujō shingi to zennen shingi," *Indobukkyōgaku kenkyū* 17/no. 2 (March 1969): 773–775, and "Hyakujō shingi no seiritsu to sono genkei," *Hokkaidō komazawa daigaku kenkyū kiyō* 3 (1968): 31–39; as well as Harada Kōdō, "Hyakujō shingi to Zennen shingi," *Sōtōshū kenkyūin kenkyū-sei kenkyū kiyō* 1 (1969): 5–14, and Kosaka Kiyū, "Shingi hensen no teiryū," in *Shūgaku kenkyū* 5 (1963): 126–128.

45. Martin Collcutt, *Five Mountains: The Rinzai Zen Monastic Institution in Medieval Japan* (Cambridge: Harvard University Press, 1981), p. 194. See also Kagamishima, *Dōgen Zenji to sono monryū*, pp. 47–48; and Kondō, "Hyakujō shingi no seiritsu to sono genkei," p. 41.

46. For details, see Foulk, "The 'Ch'an School' and Its Place in the Buddhist Monastic Tradition," pp. 366–379; also Foulk, "Myth, Ritual, and Monastic Practice in Sung Ch'an Buddhism," pp. 167–194.

47. Foulk, "The 'Ch'an School' and Its Place in the Buddhist Monastic Tradition," pp. 366–379.

48. Foulk, "Myth, Ritual, and Monastic Practice in Sung Ch'an Buddhism," pp. 191–194.

49. Yifa, *The Origins of Buddhist Monastic Codes in China*, pp. 53–74.

50. Ibid., pp. 74–96.

51. Ibid., p. 32.

52. For the Chinese original, see Kagamishima, et al., eds., *Yakuchū zen'en shingi*, p. 3.

53. For example: Wannian Monastery (Wanniansi) on Tiantai Mountain (Tiantaishan) in Taizhou; Jingde Chan Monastery (Jingde chansi) on Tiantong Mountain (Tiantongshan) in Mingzhou; Guangli Chan Monastery (Guangli chansi) on Aśoka

Mountain (Ayuwangshan) in Mingzhou; and Xingsheng Wanshou Chan Monstery (Xingsheng wanshou chansi) on Jing Mountain (Jingshan) near Hangzhou.

54. Yifa, *The Origins of Buddhist Monastic Codes in China*, p. 32.

55. Specific examples are given below.

56. T 49.466d.

57. ZZ 2, 16, 5. For an English translation and analysis, see T. Griffith Foulk, "Daily Life in the Assembly," in Donald S. Lopez, Jr., ed., *Buddhism in Practice* (Princeton: Princeton University Press, 1995), pp. 455–472.

58. This is the title as cited in the *Jiaoding qinggui* (ZZ 2, 17, 1).

59. ZZ 2,16, 5, 474b.

60. One of the rites listed in Wuliang's preface, sūtra-chanting services, does not actually appear as a section heading in any recension of the *Chanyuan qinggui* known today, although as I argued in the previous section, Zongze's text presupposes their performance.

61. ZZ 2, 16, 5, 472a.

62. ZZ 2, 16, 5, 472b.

63. Ibid.

64. Ibid.

65. ZZ 2, 16, 5, 474c–486b.

66. ZZ 2, 17, 1, 1a–28.

67. ZZ 2, 17, 1, 1a.

68. ZZ 2, 17, 1, 28–74.

69. ZZ 2, 17, 1, 57c–58a.

70. ZZ 2, 17, 1, 68b–70d.

71. ZZ 2, 17, 1, 71d–72b.

72. ZZ 2, 16, 5, 486–506.

73. T 48.1, 109c–1, 160b.

74. Like other famous Chan masters, it seems that Baizhang took his name from the mountain name (*shanhao*) of the monastery where he served as abbot. However, the original mountain name, and the mountain name still of the Dazhi Shousheng Chan Monastery, is Daxiong Mountain (Daxiongshan). It seems that the Baizhang is just a nickname for the mountain, one that may have stuck because of the famous patriarch who is celebrated as the founding abbot.

75. Yifa, *The Origins of Buddhist Monastic Codes in China*, p. 48. Holmes Welch repeats this mistake, presumably following his Chinese informants, in *The Chinese Practice of Buddhism* (Cambridge: Harvard University Press, 1967), pp. 105–108.

76. Welch, *The Chinese Practice of Buddhism*, p. 106. A commentary on the *Chixiu baizhang qingqui* entitled *Chixiu baizhang qingqui zhengyiji* was published in 1823 (ZZ 2.16–4,5).

77. For details, see Daniel B. Stevenson, "The Four Kinds of Samadhi in Early T'ien-t'ai Buddhism," in Peter N. Gregory, ed., *Traditions of Meditation in Chinese Buddhism*, Kuroda Institute Studies in East Asian Buddhism 4 (Honolulu: University of Hawai'i Press, 1986), pp. 45–97.

78. ZZ 2, 6, 4.

79. ZZ 2, 6, 1, 153d–155a. For a summary of those ten rules, see Yifa, *The Origins of Buddhist Monastic Codes in China*, pp. 35–36.

80. ZZ 2, 6, 1, 155a–d.

81. *Tianzhu beiji* (Additional Collection from Tianzhu Monastery), ZZ 2, 1, 155a–156d.

82. *Siming zunzhe jiaoxinglu;* T 46.925c–d.

83. *Siming zunzhe jiaoxinglu;* T 46.863a, 916a, 926c.

84. ZZ 2, 6, 1, 155d–156a; ZZ 2, 6, 1, 156a–d.

85. ZZ 2, 11, 1, 1a–53b.

86. ZZ 2, 11, 1, 1b.

Index